The Narrow Gate

BY BERTA HEES

Gig Productions, Inc.
Santa Fe, NM • Santa Cruz, CA
2006

Author: Berta Hees
Editing: Mary Lauren Karlton and Peter Sterbach, Gig Productions, Inc.
Front cover concept, photography, and design: Peter Sterbach, Gig Productions, Inc.
Interior book layout and design: Dustin Macdonald, Macdonald Design, Inc.
Back cover photograph: Arianna Nolan

*This book is dedicated to the late
Sister Mary Wilfrid Yore,
Society of the Holy Child Jesus,
and to her friend, my high school teacher,
Sister Mary Eulalia,
Immaculate Heart of Mary.*

This is a true story.
The names of certain individuals, places, and organizations
have been changed to protect their confidentiality.

Acknowledgments

I would like to thank the many friends, family members, and professionals who helped make this book a reality:

To Sister Mary Wilfrid Yore, S.H.C.J., who taught me how to love unconditionally, and who was the catalyst for this book.

To my mother, whose writing skills taught me discipline.

To Sarah Haskell, who put the early chapters into my word processor before I left Pasadena.

To my friends in my writing class at Pasadena City College, for telling me to put away my easel and write.

To my childhood friend, Brenda Koplin, who edited or, as she prefers to say, "corrected" some of my early chapters.

To Aunt Alice, who read what I wrote and then inquired, "How do you do that?" Her amazement spurred me on.

To my friend, Helene Van Oosteen, who deserves credit for her uplifting visits to my home in Aptos. After reading some of my work, she ran into my bedroom one morning, crying, "Berta, you are a writer! It must be painful to write about such events in your life, but keep going."

To my caregivers. Of course, little could have been accomplished without them—in particular, Irma Alvarez, Nubia Wolfson, Vilma Reintería, and Lily Rose. They made it possible for me to stay in my home here in Aptos as well as the one in Pasadena.

There are so many others. Arianna Nolan, Jehan McCloskey, and Erica Pagels are among the long list of people who deserve credit and admiration. While they took care of me and life around me, I was able to work undisturbed on my project.

To Claire Chappatte, my dear friend and housekeeper, whom I met in a Bible study class at St. Joseph's in Capitola, became a loving friend who gave me endless emotional support.

To Bill, my older son, who was courageous enough to read about the events that shook all our lives before the manuscript went to the printer.

To Michelle Taché and Ida Tarantino for allowing photographs to be taken of their gate for the front cover.

To my editors and publishers, Mary Lauren Karlton and Peter Sterbach—of Gig Productions—and to my neighbor, Donna Van Dijk, who introduced me to them. Working assiduously and with great tact and charm, Mary and Peter brought this book to life. Peter, with his clear understanding of the English language, was instrumental in keeping the project moving along smoothly to the end. They also saved me a great deal of time and many headaches by overseeing the entire project from start to finish and tending to all the details—everything from commas to copyright to cover design.

Finally, I thank Our Lord for keeping me alive and well so I could enjoy the sense of accomplishment I now feel from reaching my goal to help others.

Preface

Go in through the narrow gate; because broad and spacious is the road leading off into destruction, and many are the ones going in through it; whereas narrow is the gate and cramped the road leading off into life, and few are the ones finding it.

— Matthew 7:13-14

In this memoir, Berta Hees writes about an eight-year period of her life marked by a series of unexpected events that lead to her spiritual transformation. Influenced by her Victorian upbringing and by the culture of Southern California, she lives contentedly as a devoted wife, mother, and artist.

Berta invites us to share Easter, Thanksgiving, and Christmas in her Southern California beach home with her loving husband, three daughters, and two sons. We begin to feel we are part of the family, living life as it should be.

But then, with the sudden death of her husband Bill, Berta's life takes an abrupt turn from the comfort, security, and predictability she once knew. The new challenges confronting her are magnified when life deals her another unexpected tragedy—paralysis. Faced with the impairment of normal bodily functions, her daughter's divorce, and the loss of her dreams, she slips into a deep depression that carries her to the brink of suicide.

We feel her anguish as she struggles to find a reason to carry on. And, like her dedicated caregivers, we want to help her to stand up and walk again.

But, it is not by walking that Berta Hees will transcend the hardships of this life. Little does she know when she travels to Italy that she will be taken on another journey—a journey of spiritual awakening and understanding. An epiphany she experiences there provides the key that she needs to pass through the narrow gate to a new beginning that has no end.

— Peter Sterbach
Gig Productions, Inc.

Chapter 1

Death of the Seventh

For in the wreckage of my April
Christ lies slain
Christ weeps in the ruins of my spring.

—Thomas Merton,
"For my brother reported missing in action"

Chapter 1

It was Sunday, March 23, 1980. Just an ordinary day.

The entire weekend had been sunny, spring-like. Our sons, Bill and Morgan, were tossing a Frisbee in front of our home as Sunday afternoon drew to a close. Sam, our golden retriever, was running and jumping, trying to catch the disc in midair. Soon, two of our daughters, Dana and ten-year-old Jennie, had joined the game. My husband, Bill, was taking pictures of our children.

I was sitting on the patio enjoying the shouts and laughter of the children as they played. There was a salty nip in the air. The gentle sea breeze and the heat of the sun were making me drowsy. I hadn't slept at all the night before. After wandering around restlessly for hours in my bedroom, I sat on the balcony for a while, looking out at a sleeping St. Lo (the California beach community we called home). Then, I tried to get some rest on the sofa. Finally, as the dawn arrived, I got dressed and slipped out of the house to attend Mass.

I was feeling annoyed at my husband Bill and with myself. At a gathering we had attended Saturday evening, Bill circulated among the guests while I chatted with my friend Jane. As usual, he was unable to connect with anyone and soon returned to my side.

"Hello," he said to Jane.

Jane tried to engage him with a friendly "Hi Bill, how are you?"

"Fine, thanks," he replied.

And that was it. After Jane looked at me and then at Bill, the conversation died.

"I'll catch up with you later," she said and then walked away.

While at Mass, I knelt down and prayed for patience and for help in cultivating tolerance. I asked God to take away the annoyance I felt toward my husband.

Bill could not leave my side at parties. I am sure he was unaware of how smothered I felt as a result. I never once discussed it with him during our twenty-five-year marriage. Lately, however, it was beginning to get on my nerves. He was a dear, sweet man. But, he didn't feel particularly at home at social events. He was not interested in small talk. I must admit that it was not something I came by naturally either. Still, over the years I made an effort to hold up my end of the conversation.

When I returned home from Mass, I prepared our customary Sunday brunch: roast-beef hash with a poached egg on top, juice, coffee, and a Danish. After brunch, some members of the family went to the beach, some played tennis, while others talked with friends who were visiting. Eventually, the entire family showed up at the beach to catch a swim before sundown.

Now, Sunday afternoon was coming to a close. The children were showering and preparing to leave. From the kitchen, where I was trying to figure out what I could whip up for dinner, I could see my sleepy husband stretched out on a chaise on the terrace. Dana stepped into the kitchen to announce her departure.

"I'm leaving now, Mom. Should I go down to the terrace and kiss him goodbye? No, I guess not. He's fallen asleep, and he looks so peaceful," she said, answering her own question.

"I'll give him a hug for you," I assured her as I washed the salad greens.

"Tell him I didn't want to disturb him," she said on her way out.

Soon after Dana left, Bill IV, my older son, came to say goodbye. But he didn't want to disturb his father either.

"I'll tell him you said goodbye," I told him.

Jennie, freshly showered and snuggled up in her quilted robe, was quietly drawing at the breakfast bar in the kitchen. Morgan was sprawled out on the living-room couch, watching sports on television.

After setting the dining-room table, I went upstairs, showered, put on a robe, and lay down to take a catnap before dinner. Then, Bill, after awakening from his nap on the terrace, walked into the bedroom and prepared to go jogging. As he was about to leave the room, he paused to put his hands on the edge of the dresser, leaned forward, pushed himself away with a sort of "let's-get-this-over-with" gesture, and then walked out the door.

As I watched, I thought, *How handsome he looks!* I loved his wavy brown hair, that patrician profile, and those ruddy cheeks glowing through his tan.

About an hour later, the bedroom door opened. It was Jennie. With one hand on the door handle, she just stood there and stared. Time seemed to stand still for what felt like an eternity. Then she said softly, "I think you'd better come, Mommy. Daddy's fallen down, and I think there is something wrong with him."

Jumping up from the bed, I tightened the sash on my white bathrobe and bolted toward the door. Jennie let go of the handle and took a step back as I tore past her and down the stairs.

I found Bill lying on his back on the kitchen floor with his eyes wide open. One hand was extended out to a pile of trash that had spilled out from a wastebasket that must have overturned when he fell to the floor.

Morgan was giving his father CPR while whispering in his ear, "I love you, Dad." Jennie approached slowly, not comprehending what had happened. She stood silently watching.

Stunned, I stared at the figure on the floor. His cheeks were pale. His eyes glazed over. His mouth discolored. Still struggling to accept the reality of what had just happened, I knelt down to hold him in my arms.

"Oh Billy, darling, please don't leave me, please don't leave me," I pleaded. Suddenly, I felt numb—oddly disconnected from myself. The voice I heard, the body I moved around in were mine, but I felt removed from both. It was as if I were outside of myself, watching and listening from a distance.

All was silent.

Then a voice spoke gently. "C'mon, Mom." It was my son, Morgan. "I've phoned the paramedics. They're on the way," he continued. Then he reached out and slowly helped me to my feet. As I struggled to stand up, my eyes remained fixed on my husband. Bill's head dropped gently toward his right shoulder. His eyes rolled back. Then a sigh escaped from his mouth followed by a rush of air. In that moment, I sensed his spirit slipping away from his body.

There was a look of disbelief on Morgan's face as he stared down at his father. It was the sort of look one has when something special has been lost forever.

Bill had given each of his children his patience, energy, time and money. But, most of all, he gave his love—unconditional love.

"I understand how you feel, Morgan," I said.

I looked at my youngest daughter. "Jennie, go down the hill and get Dr. Madison. Hurry!"

She took off immediately. I watched her from the dining room window. The image of that brave little girl flying like the wind, her bathrobe billowing out behind her like angel's wings, touched my heart.

Within minutes, a siren screaming in the distance announced that the paramedics were on their way. Moments later, the paramedics were in the house, on the floor, doing everything they could to save my husband. He did not respond.

I felt a strong urge to kiss him. But, afraid this would waste precious time, I just stood there as they carried him out. I watched quietly as they carried his body across the patio and through the gates of the home he had so lovingly built for his family.

"The doctor said we can meet him at the hospital now," Jennie said when she returned. I went upstairs and threw on some clothes.

It was early evening when we arrived at the hospital. Outside, it was cold. The sky had become overcast and gray. Inside, the hospital seemed unusually quiet. Not a person in sight. The walls were stark white, so sterile and bare. I felt irritated by the fluorescent light that was flickering over the magazine tray. An old edition of *People Magazine* had fallen to the floor. As I went to pick it up, I noticed an ad on the back page. In large letters were the words: "Father's Day is a day to remember someone special."

"Mrs. Hees?"

Somewhat startled, I shuddered and dropped the magazine. Taking a slow, deep breath, I turned around to face the young nurse and replied, "Yes, I'm Mrs. Hees."

"I thought you'd be comfortable here," the nurse said, as she ushered us into a chapel-like room.

Another woman, one of the staff personnel, directed me to sit at a small table. She put some papers in front of me.

"Your husband's birthdate?" the woman asked. I pushed the papers aside and collapsed on the table. Pleadingly, I looked over at Morgan. He and Jennie were sitting on a sofa next to Mike, a friend of the family who had driven us to the hospital. Morgan proceeded to answer the questions for me. My mind was a complete blank.

When the doctor came in, I got up and walked over to him. I looked in his eyes and knew what he was about to say. Still, it came as a shock when I actually heard the words.

"I'm sorry, he's gone." Unable to hold back his emotions, the doctor left the room.

It pained me to see the look on Jennie's face. In an effort to comfort her, I went over and sat by her side. As I put my arms around her, she was unable to contain her emotions any longer and burst forth, "Daddy, my daddy, I want my daddy!"

She immediately broke away from my embrace. Still screaming, she began twisting from side to side and thrashing around with her arms in utter frenzy. I was tempted to grab her arms. Instead, I leaned out of the way.

There was no comfort to be found. There was nowhere to run to. No daddy to help her. Not now, not ever again. I let her express her pain as I slumped down into the couch.

Since Bill had died at home, the doctor advised that an autopsy be performed. At the suggestion of the doctor, Morgan and I refrained from seeing Bill again.

Jennie took my hand and then her brother's as we walked out of the hospital and followed Mike back to the car. I didn't remember the ride home.

That evening, friends came over to offer their condolences and to help in any way they could. As they quietly came and went over the days that followed, the word spread throughout St. Lo that a respected member of the community had died.

The living room was barely lit. As the darkness of night descended upon us, the mood became increasingly somber.

Sarah, a friend of my daughter Dana, came over to greet me, pulling me away from my thoughts. "Hello, Mrs. Hees. I am here to do whatever I can for you and Jennie."

I looked over at my little daughter curled up at the end of the sofa. "Jennie needs some help right now," I replied.

Sarah sat down next to her. "Jennie, would you like to sit on my lap?" she asked. Jennie climbed up onto Sarah's lap like an injured kitty looking for warmth and comfort. Now and then during the course of the evening, I could hear Sarah whispering consoling words in her little friend's ear.

"Every time God closes a door, He opens a window," I heard Sarah say.

Jennie came back in a cheerful voice, "That's from *The Sound of Music*." Her darling response was a comfort to me and an indication that she was in good hands.

Every so often, I went over to the fireplace and stirred the embers. It was March, and, although the days were warm, the temperature would drop quickly at night. I couldn't seem to stop shivering.

Everyone appeared to be moving in slow motion as they passed in and out of my vision like shadows moving across a wall as the light of day changes. I heard muted voices floating through the air with remarks like "I'm so sorry," or "I can't believe it. How could such a thing happen to your family?"

"I'm very tired," I told Morgan. "Did you phone your brothers and sisters?" I asked.

"Yes. Don't you remember? When we came home I asked you if you wanted me to call."

"Ah yes, I do. Thank you, darling." I was finding it increasingly difficult to remember details.

"Oh Jennie, dear, a nice neighbor brought us some dinner. Could you warm it up for all of us? I think the three of us should eat something before we go to bed."

We picked at our food in silence. As I thought about how maturely those two had conducted themselves, I reached over, took them by the hand, and said, "I love you both very much. God bless you."

"God bless you too, Mom," they replied in unison.

"I'll close up the house," said Morgan.

My legs felt like iron stumps as Jennie and I climbed the stairs that led from the patio to my bedroom. Jennie decided to bring the cat with her. Thomas—or "Tom Cat," as we liked to call him—provided us much comfort, something we all needed at this time. My husband had loved our family pets. Tom would always climb onto his lap whenever Bill would sit down to watch television.

That evening, the two of us—and Tom—snuggled up together in my bed. I slept soundly all night.

In the morning, I was awakened by the sound of voices downstairs. Then I noticed that Jennie had left. I got dressed and hurried down to the kitchen, where I was greeted by my son Bill and my daughter Dana. Bill had driven all the way to Santa Cruz (where he was attending the University of California) and turned right around the minute he heard the news. I put my arms around him and gave him a warm hug.

"Oh, thank God you're here."

Then I turned to Dana and thanked her for coming. "Are you all right?" I asked her. I thought back to the other day when she had asked me to give her father a goodbye kiss.

"I should have kissed him," she said regretfully as tears welled up in her eyes.

Then, Jennie began to explain to her siblings: "I was sitting at the counter drawing a picture when Daddy came into the house. He leaned up against the sink. Then, I held up my drawing to show him. He turned to look and said, 'That's very nice.' As I went to put the drawing down on the table to work on it some more"—pausing, her eyes filling with tears—"I heard the wastebasket fall over. Morgan was in the living room. I called him but he didn't come." Her head dropped down to her chest.

"I didn't react right away," Morgan interjected. "Jennie kept calling. Suddenly, I understood the seriousness of the situation. As I ran to the kitchen, I knew what I would find. As I gave Dad CPR, I kept whispering in his ear, telling him that I love him."

"Did he hear you?" I asked.

"Yes, I think so," Morgan replied. "Then, I quickly phoned the paramedics."

My daughter Leslie flew in from Sun Valley, Idaho, along with her daughter, Riley. (She had left California after her divorce from Paul.) We embraced, cried, and embraced again with a special warmth.

Lesile told me, "When Morgan phoned with the news, I cried so much. Riley said to me, 'Mommy, when are you going to stop crying?'"

Later that day, Leslie and I walked around the streets of St. Lo. We talked about her divorce. The divorce had left us alienated for some time.

"Dad came over to see me in Pasadena when he was in town. He wanted to help. I felt so grateful to him for trying." Leslie began to cry before continuing. "I wish it were possible to have seen him one more time." She paused, looked around the living room until her eyes met mine, and then she smiled and said, "Oh, Mom, It's so good to see you."

~ ~ ~

On the third day after Bill's death, we began a little ritual. As letters of condolence arrived in the mail, we would all go out and sit on the patio and read them aloud to each other. During one of our readings, I looked over at Leslie, who was sitting on the edge of a chaise in the morning sun. As she listened to me reading one of the letters, her head dropped, and her face took on an anguished expression. I then noticed that the faces of all my children were marked with grief. Their glazed eyes, staring out at nothing, spoke volumes to me. In an effort to change the topic, I set the letters aside and proclaimed, "I can't seem to sleep past two in the morning these days."

"Really, Mom? Neither can I," said Leslie. "It's like all of a sudden I hear an alarm clock go off in my head."

The days just seemed to drag on and to be lacking in purpose. Bedtime was a time I came to welcome more and more. My granddaughter Riley nestled in bed between Jennie and me, displacing the cat, who was accustomed to curling up at my feet to keep me company through the night.

One night, Jennie suggested we say the Our Father and then sing *You Are My Sunshine*, something that her father did with her every night before going to bed.

"I think that's a good idea," I agreed.

We all joined hands and began reciting in unison: "Our Father who art in Heaven, hallowed be thy name . . ." This was followed by a rousing rendition of *You Are My Sunshine.*

My quiet prayer to God was a thank-you for all the sympathy cards and condolence notes, which had shown me that my husband's humility, generosity of spirit, and kindness had not been overlooked. I had concerns that people in the community might not recognize him for the man he was, as his reclusive nature made him appear distant at times.

~ ~ ~

The autopsy was performed in San Diego. And, it was there that Bill's body was cremated, as instructed in his will. We were all feeling reluctant about going to pick up Bill's ashes. Then, Leslie came up with a fine idea. "Since we'll be in the area, let's all go to the San Diego Zoo," she suggested. "Jennie and Riley will love it there. Besides, it'll help us take our mind off things."

The zoo served as a comforting reminder of spring and renewal. Newborn animals were everywhere to be seen. The elephants attracted us immediately. Bill had recently spoken about going to Africa. Once in a while, we'd see a protective patriarch watching over his brood, reminding us that the man who had looked after our family was gone.

"My legs feel so heavy, and I'm exhausted," I complained as I bent over to rub my calf muscles.

"I'm tired too," Leslie added. "Let's go home."

We passed by the crematorium on the way. Bill's ashes had been placed in an urn wrapped with plain brown paper. As I walked back to the car, I began to grasp the reality that this was my husband in the container I was guarding. I gently cradled the urn in my arms. Then, I looked over at my children. Suddenly, I felt especially close to each one of them in that moment.

We sat quietly in the car for a few moments. No one spoke. The only sound was that of sniffles and the wiping of tears.

We started down the road. The car radio played softly, and the lyrics of a song spoke to each of us in different ways:

We made our mistakes along the way.
But, somehow, deep in my heart,
I needed you and you needed me,
Still.

When we arrived back home, we all gathered around the dining room table to begin planning the memorial service.

"Who ever thought we'd be doing this!" commented Bill.

We began to reminisce about the many celebrations we had enjoyed around this table over the years: Thanksgiving, Christmas, Easter brunch, birthdays, and especially the candlelit dinners with the whole family present. Then there were the years when it was just the three of us: Bill, Jennie, and me.

As the chatter of those I loved filled the room, I diverted my attention toward the window to gaze at the magnificent view. The California coastline, with its unique beauty and serenity, had always held a special, warm place in my heart. There was something so soothing about looking out over the ocean all the way to the horizon. Perhaps it was the purity and the vastness of it all. Or maybe, it was the one thing that remained a constant in my life over all those years.

"Remember the wind-driven rain at Thanksgiving?" My attention was pulled back to the dining room.

"Yes, and the fog banks that rolled in so swiftly over the bluffs."

"That's right! I swear I can still smell the salt air and seaweed. The wind was so blustery that afternoon, but then it calmed down right about sunset when more than half the sky was covered with orange feather clouds. And then all those pelicans passed by our dinning room window at eye level. What an amazing sight that was! I'll never forget it."

~ ~ ~

Early Saturday morning, the children and I gathered on the terrace. God provided an especially beautiful spring day, which was a welcome change from the overcast skies of the week before.

The first thing we saw below our house on the hill was the flag flying at half-mast. We were overcome by the sight. In spite of our pain, we were overflowing with gratitude.

"Oh look!" exclaimed Leslie, pointing toward the beach.

The people of St. Lo were clearing the beach of the seaweed, drift-wood, and rocks left behind by the winter storms. The children wept in grief and gratitude as they watched the neighbors doing their part to help the community and our family.

In the late afternoon, we left the house and walked down the hill. Soon after, other family members and close friends came to join us. I couldn't help but notice how lovely Leslie and Dana looked in their breezy, white summer dresses cradling bunches of roses and daisies in their arms. The boys wore loose-fitting shirts and slacks. As they approached the sea, a slight breeze turned up the tips of their shirt collars. Jennie and I wore our Austrian peasant outfits that Bill had always been so fond of. The puffed white sleeves of the blouses peeked out from buttoned bodices that were attached to flowered skirts. The colorful aprons tied around our waists made us appear quite attractive. I carried Bill's ashes in a blue and white French apothecary jar, which had the name "Violetta" glazed on the front. At one time, that jar decorated the top of his dresser.

Moving silently toward the beach, I caught a glimpse of the chalk-board nailed to the cabana:

> *Notice: Services for Bill Hees*
> *Day: Saturday, March 29, 1980*
> *Time: 4:30 P.M.*
> *Place: Cabana area.*

In the past, I had written so many messages on that board for festive events that took place during the summers that now were part of the life I once knew.

I looked down at my bare feet as we walked up the weathered wooden stairs leading to the cabana. All the children were barefoot as well. At some point, without a word, we had shed our sandals all at once.

I smiled at everyone as I sat down on the low brick wall that encircled the cabana area. With my sons on either side of me, I watched with delight as my daughters began handing out the roses and daisies to all of our friends.

"I'll take care of that, Mom," young Bill whispered as he took the jar of ashes from me.

I spent a few moments taking in my surroundings. There was an unusual, gentle sweetness and serenity to the day. The sea was calm. My skin was caressed by the warm, soft breezes coming off the ocean. A subtle scent of salt and seaweed filled the air. The sky was clear and a light powder blue, accented by the white wings of seagulls effortlessly riding the air currents along the water's edge. Suddenly, I began to feel myself gliding along with them. My spirit began to merge with the spirit of the sea. Soon to be the new custodian of my husband's memory, the ocean shared with me a message of eternal essence. I heard it say:

Twilight and evening bell,
And after that, the dark!
And may there be no sadness of farewell,
When I embark.

For tho' from out our bourne of Time and Place
The flood may bear me far,
I hope to see my Pilot face to face
When I have crost the bar.

It was the steady and clear voice of Kevin, my daughter Dana's love, reciting the final verse of Tennyson's "Crossing the Bar." The words floated over the sand. The children and I followed them to the water's edge. As I cast a handful of Bill's precious ashes to the sea, the wind blew them back at us. It felt as if Bill's spirit were reluctant to leave. My son Bill once again took the jar from my hands, bent down on his knees, and gently poured the rest of the ashes onto the water. We then tossed our flowers into the ocean. With our arms around one another, we said our goodbyes in silence, spoken only from our hearts.

One by one, friends and family made their way over the beach pebbles to cast their floral tributes. As everyone gathered once again on the sand, I thanked each one for coming.

I asked our former Pasadena neighbor and fellow St. Lo resident, Dick, to hold my hand while I read aloud a personal tribute to my husband. The last lines were:

> *God has taken him during this Lenten season just before we celebrate the event that took place on Earth so long ago, only to change our lives forever.*

The service completed, everyone walked quietly back up the hill. There, to my surprise, a buffet was set out on the dining-room table. Two friends stood ready to serve behind a bar arranged on the picnic table on the front patio. There were so many guests that they overflowed from the front patio, down the steps into the living room, and through the French doors onto the terrace.

Soon, everyone was conversing. I could hear the laughter of someone who was catching up with an old friend from town. As I moved through the crowd of familiar faces, I would smile and say "Thank you for coming." In return, I was warmed by their kisses and hugs.

The hugs and smiling faces of the children—as the guests said their goodbyes—were obvious indications of how much they had enjoyed the day. But, somehow, I could not share in their delight. I was engulfed by a terrible loneliness. The void that accompanies the loss of a spouse is not easily filled.

I was also starting to feel quite anxious about the task ahead of me: a meeting with the lawyer to discuss my financial future, which was fraught with uncertainty. As a way to keep myself busy, I decided to clean the house. While tidying Leslie's room, I found this unfinished poem tucked in the back of her bathroom drawer:

> *You've only left us for a time*
> *To watch us from another space.*
> *And, we the ones you left behind*
> *Have only dreams left in your place.*
> *The days keep moving slowly on.*
> *The empty nights are slower still . . .*

– Leslie Hees De Groot
Unfinished, March, 1980

A few years later, a very young Jennie wrote her own expression of this period of time in a poem she called *Death of the 7th*:

Confusion, frustration, anger, sadness,
Shock, bewilderment.
6 different emotions shared by 6
different beings who remained after
the 7th one left.
6 approached the ocean that
awaited him; it shared their emotions.
The tide ebbed and flowed,
the gray-blue of the waters stirred,
white caps formed, and crashing breakers echoed;
they appeared to express an emotion
concerning the death of the 7th.
6 returned to scatter the last part
of him that they would see other
than in memory. A father and a
husband to them was he.
Death of the 7th.

Jennie Jane Hees
Age 14
1984

Sometimes, it takes a long time to say goodbye.

Chapter 2

IN THE BEGINNING

We get to think of life as an inexhaustible well.
Yet how many more times will you
Watch the full moon rise.
Perhaps twenty. And yet it all seems limitless . . .

—Paul Bowles, *The Sheltering Sky*

Chapter 2

Four-and-a-half-years before Bill's death, at his request, we sold our home in Pasadena and moved to our summer residence at St. Lo. Bill now had to commute to work. He would leave the beach early Monday morning and return Wednesday evening. Jennie, in those days a six-year-old blonde little sprite, had just entered first grade in a new school in a new town. The older children came and went as they pleased—work, marriage, and school schedules permitting.

It wasn't so easy for me, however. Making such a big change posed a few questions that needed to be answered. As I had never been separated from my husband during our twenty-five-year marriage, I was now concerned about the impact this move would have on our relationship. Would Jennie turn inward now that she was far away from her childhood companions? I worried about how she would adjust to making new friends in school. I know I would miss all the good neighbors and friends we were leaving behind. Would the beach be too lonely during the winter months? I was acquainted with the few full-time residents of St. Lo, but many of them were considerably older.

I would also dearly miss seeing Leslie now that our visits together were reduced to the occasional weekend. I enjoyed the kind of adult relationship we shared. Her family life added a lot to my life. It would fill me with joy just to watch her daughter Riley playing with Riley's Aunt Jennie. A big part of the life I cared so much about was now gone. St. Lo, guarded and gated, made me feel like Peter Pumpkin Eater's wife: locked up and kept very well. At forty-five, I felt too young to retire.

Bill, on the other hand, would probably adjust easily to the change, I thought. Ever since he built the beach house in the '60s, he had a strong desire to live there. But he never once asked me how I would feel about leaving one life behind to start another. And, as I was never one to speak up for myself, he never knew how uneasy I was about the change.

Like many women of my generation, I did as I was told. It never occurred to me to consider my own feelings. I had played the game of "everything's all right" for so long that I came to believe it was. What sustained me along the way were my creative nature, my spirituality, and my ability to make the best of any situation.

Having to sell our furnishings brought up a lot of feelings for me. There's personal history associated with furniture and artifacts collected over the years. Family memories hold much more value than the few dollars being exchanged for the objects.

One day, in the midst of our big move, Bill asked about bringing some ladies over from the office who were interested in buying some of our things. The day the ladies arrived, I saw a side of my husband I had never seen before. He strutted around like a peacock does when looking for a mate. When one of the women showed interest in a particular item, I jumped in with something like "I'm sorry, that one's going to the beach."

After a few such comments, Bill interjected, "Oh she never wants to sell anything."

I thought: *Who is this person?* Bill, who had always been such a gentleman, in that moment became someone I no longer recognized. Ignoring my husband's poor manners, I went on with the job: "I'm sorry, this piece of furniture isn't tagged." It felt as though my married life was disintegrating before my eyes.

My first garage sale was so exhausting that I decided to hire professionals to do the rest. The move added to the stress of the preceding years, which included the birth of my fifth child, Leslie's wedding, and breast cancer. Jennie was born ten days before my fortieth birthday. A large wedding for Leslie was held at Mission San Luis Rey. The reception took place in St. Lo. Two years after the wedding, I was diagnosed with cancer, which resulted in my having to get a mastectomy. Because of the operation, I started to have doubts about my womanhood. And I was experiencing debilitating respiratory problems. But what disturbed me the most was the thought that I might never get to see Jennie grow to adulthood.

By the end of June, 1976, we were settled in at St. Lo. Aggravated by the move, my old back problems returned. My back brace provided some relief from the pain.

As stressed and irritable as I felt, I chose to bite my tongue. I managed to distract myself from my feelings by meditating and reading. To appear more relaxed around those I loved and to ease my physical discomfort, I performed fewer tasks and rested as much as possible. Still, my resentment concerning the move continued to build. At times, I would overreact to some trivial incident when I was no longer able to contain my repressed anger.

Outside, the weather was fair. The sea and sand were shimmering in the sun. I wore a T-shirt that was imprinted with "*Je suis fatigué.*" When I went out for a stroll, I could alert friends that I was in need of some quiet time. However, as one acquaintance passed by, she said, "You are not!" But inside my body was a raging storm. It felt as though there were a vise bearing down on my throbbing head. My left leg was hot, then cold. And my asthma made breathing difficult. Tired and ill, I went to the hospital.

Once there, my right leg lost some of its mobility. Brain scans, blood tests, electrodes attached to my head yielded insufficient data for diagnosis. My own diagnosis? Exhaustion, fear of the unknown, and anxiety over what life had in store for me.

After returning home, I spent most of July in bed. Little by little, my body came back into balance, and my leg regained its strength. By August, my aches and pains subsided.

I started getting out to swim and to enjoy the beach with family and friends. I organized the "Wednesday Night Wiener Wroasts" as a way to bring the neighborhood children together. Jennie contributed by helping with the shopping. Every week we loaded up two shopping carts with hot dogs, popcorn, potato chips, cookies, and all those indigestibles so loved by young tummies. Then we'd haul them over to the cabana in time for the gathering.

There was always a good turnout: children of all ages, their parents, a few pets, and friends visiting for the summer. As the children played in the sand and enjoyed their snacks, the adults entertained themselves by sharing stories, telling jokes, and gazing over the ocean. Quite often we would see a pod of dolphins putting on a spectacular display as they jumped over whitecaps sparkling in the early evening sun.

After several successful summers, Jennie's interest waned, and I grew tired of putting out all that effort. So, we found someone else to take over.

The season changed, and I changed with it. The streets and the beaches were quiet now. The light was different too. It was softer, kinder than the hot summer sun. The low tides revealed little treasures left in the wet gray sand by the higher tides of summer. Jennie and I spent many an afternoon collecting shells, sand dollars, and bits of colored glass. Then, accompanied by our dogs—Sam and Spot—we would take a leisurely swim before dinner. Our cat, Thomas, loved to watch us from the shore but always kept enough distance from the water's edge so as not to get wet, just as any self-respecting cat would do.

Now, with Jennie in school and Bill in town for three days, I found I had a lot of time to myself. Feeling the need for a creative outlet, I began to paint. Fortunately, the workspace I needed was not hard to come by. Across the street from our home was a beach house—seldom occupied in the winter—that belonged to my husband's Aunt Alice. Off to one side, nestled in a cluster of overgrown oleander, was a charming little building that we referred to as the "playhouse"—so named because that was where Alice's children and teenage friends would meet to play the upright piano, spin records to dance by, read books by the fireplace, do jigsaw puzzles, or play board games such as checkers. They would spend many a pleasant afternoon drinking Coke and sharing conversation. This building became my art studio. It was away from the main house, so I was quite alone there, alone to bring life to empty canvases, singing as I worked in celebration of the gift that God had given me. Each day blended into the next as I felt myself slip into the eternal present.

As Bill, Jennie, and I moved through the autumn months, our anticipation to reconnect at the end of the day grew. When Bill would return from work on Wednesday evening, he could expect four outstretched arms and lots of kisses. I made a silent prayer of thanks for his safe return. Bill would often come bearing gifts: candy and toys for Jennie, and usually art books for me.

I can recall one day, warmed by the winter sun, when Bill and I were out on the patio sipping wine and enjoying a Greek salad. Noticing in that moment how very beautiful, sensual, and special our new life was becoming, I looked across the table at Bill and said, "Is this the way it is always going to be?"

"I hope so," Bill said, smiling. It was a broad smile that exposed his well-formed gleaming white teeth, reminding me of photos I had seen of Ernest Hemingway, one of my favorite writers.

Leaving behind my old life and reveling in the new, I could feel my heart pumping my lifeblood throughout my body as I took in the sublime surroundings of sun and sea. I found myself slipping effortlessly into a contemplative, prayerful state.

The holiday season brought many joyful moments. Regardless of all the work it would entail, I so looked forward to the weekends when those I loved—family and friends—would come to visit. During those times, life was bursting with laughter and with the greetings of our children's friends, who wandered in and out of the house while the adults sat sunning themselves out on the terrace with drink in hand and many a story to share.

Thanksgiving Day brought wind, rain, and an invigorating coolness. The beach was empty as the dark sea pounded the shore. The smoke from nearby chimneys suggested that we were not alone in celebrating our gratitude on this day. Knowing this made our turkey dinner that much more enjoyable. We took turns in sharing our thanks for the many blessings in our lives: good food, friends, family, freedom, and health.

Leaving the dishes for later, we decided to all go out for a walk together in the brisk November night. Donning boots and raincoats and bringing the dogs with us, we toured around the wet streets engaged in spirited banter. And we bumped into friends doing much the same. Children were jumping with total abandon into the puddles. Dogs ran up to pull at their pant legs. There were dogs of every variety: big, small, longhaired, short-haired, black, white, brown. But they all had one thing in common: they were excited at seeing their buddies again and intent on having fun. No doubt they were joining in on the celebration, canine style, as they wagged their tails, sniffed each other, chased each other down the street, and ran up to their masters, barking for attention. Needless to say, by the end of the evening, we were tired, yet fulfilled, and ready for bed.

There would be many such playful moments and heartwarming gatherings during the Christmas and Easter holidays that followed. It seemed that a day wouldn't go by without someone dropping by to engage us in a round of tennis or calling to invite us over for a drink. Sometimes we stayed for dinner, enjoying conversation and laughter. These were rewarding times that would etch their way into our memories forever.

In the summertime, families returned, embraced each other, and then moved into their small cliques. As a rule, the renters were snubbed by the community unless they were acquaintances of the homeowners.

New Year's Eve was rather quiet that year. The homeowners came to escape the crowds brought into Pasadena by the Rose Bowl parade. There were fewer celebrations at the beach. With a few exceptions, everyone was in bed and asleep when the clock struck midnight. They were saving their energy for New Year's Day. Some spent their time relaxing in front of the television watching the parade or the Rose Bowl game, while others hit the tennis courts, played volleyball on the beach, or took to the beach to unwind and read a book. This was a time to kick back and forget the stresses of life, a time to connect with family and enjoy the beauty that St. Lo had to offer.

Friendly, safe, and architecturally appealing, the private haven of St. Lo—for the few who lived there year-round—was a world unto itself. For someone with a nature as romantic as mine, St. Lo satisfied the sensual and spiritual sides of my being, providing the kind of environment where I was free to express myself through painting, writing, and conversing with God.

As January, 1977 drew to a close, a gentle quietude settled on the now deserted beach. Whenever I was inclined to find some comfort, I had to go no further than the windows of my home. Some days, the sky was as crystal clear as the glass I was peering through. The vast seascape, cloaked in the somber serenity of winter, was a feast for the eyes and food for the soul. As I stood there listening to the seconds ticking away on the grandfather clock in the kitchen, I would marvel at the magnificent beauty before me. This environment spoke to me of God's grace and of the eternal nature of life and served as inspiration for the voracious artist in me.

Oh, how wonderful to be forty-six years young! Elated and radiating joy, I felt as though I were flying through life with my little Jennie on one side and Bill on the other. Life was good.

There were those special days when it feels as if everything were perfect—couldn't be better—like the days I sat on the patio entertained by shadows dancing on my arms and legs as sunbeams filtered through the purple leaves of bougainvillea stirred by the gentle afternoon breezes. Or the time Bill, Jennie, and I sailed paper boats on the slough as the seagulls hovered above in the crimson sky of sunset, getting ready for their next dive.

Sometimes, what makes life so special is its simplicity, with moments no more complicated than that of our dog Sam tearing down the beach for the mischievous thrill he got out of causing gulls to take flight. Or how he pranced with pride towards us to drop beach rocks at our feet.

As March approached, Bill increasingly broadened his exercise program. He and his friend, Brad, started playing tennis together on a regular basis. Brad had a little girl who soon became Jennie's friend. A swimmer throughout the year, even in the winter, Bill now began jogging every day. He would temper his workouts by taking time out to tune out the world around him, sometimes remaining on the beach to read a book long after the light had faded. At times, I would have to step out on the terrace to ring the ship's bell hanging by the door to remind him that dinner was almost ready.

The sweet days continued. Each morning I would sit by the bay window of the dining room and look out at the ducks on the lagoon and at the gulls circling at eye level beyond the shingled rooftops and brick chimneys of the timbered houses below.

There seems to be something about sorrow's ability to intrude in the best of times. There was a death in Bill's family. Bill's cousin, Rathbun—who was in his sixties—had died of cancer. Bill and Rathbun were extremely fond of one another, though they only got together occasionally. The loss was hard on Bill. And it caused me to reflect on my father, who died when I was only fourteen. His loss left an invisible but indelible scar on me.

Fortunately for me, by marrying Bill, I not only gained a husband and companion but also a father figure, someone to shelter and protect me from the dangers and hardships of life.

Bill was deeply committed to his children. He and Jennie had an especially close relationship. When he was home, he would take her to school in the morning and pick her up in the afternoon. It became their quality time together. As a special treat, they would always stop at the Yogurt Hut on the way home. Each time, they would sample different flavors of yogurt until they decided on their favorite.

With the Easter holidays approaching, there was a great deal for which to be thankful.

Beauty graced the patio when Jennie came home wearing a bunny hat that she had made in school. As she pointed to her pink and white ears and shyly tugged at the ribbons tied under her chin, I thought to myself, *I couldn't ask for a lovelier rabbit.*

Then Leslie arrived with her husband, Paul, and their daughter Riley. My mother followed, bearing a pink azalea that she placed by the front door.

Now the family was gathered together at the start of Holy Week. I acknowledged each day with a simple prayer that I recited silently while I stood looking at the ocean from my bedroom window. As I watched the ebb and flow of the waves and the foam spraying from the backs of the breakers, I celebrated all things eternal along with the beauty of this life.

On Holy Thursday, I was able to connect more fully with Jennie. We went to Mass where I watched the priest wash the feet of twelve children, who represented the twelve apostles. It did not appear at all odd to me that both boys and girls participated in the ceremony. In fact, I found it inclusive.

I went to church alone on Good Friday. The statues covered in rich purple drapes reminded me of the solemnity of that day. The recitation from the Bible concerning Christ's crucifixion made me even more aware of being alone. On Holy Saturday, I waited quietly for the resurrection.

The entire family went to Mass on Easter Sunday. Unfortunately, the experience turned out to be less than inspiring. The Mission was overcrowded and noisy, the sermon much too long, and the choir—who had sung exquisitely at Leslie's wedding—delivered a rather shoddy performance. I felt much more spiritually nourished when we returned home and we stood quietly on the terrace taking in the beauty of the breathtaking sky above and the powerful sea below. There was prayer in the movement of the sailboats on the slough, of people strolling on the roads, and of children hunting for Easter eggs in the garden or on the patio.

For Easter vacation week, Bill and I took Jennie on a trip to the Grand Canyon. Before our departure from the Pasadena train station, Leslie and her daughter came to bring flowers, hugs and kisses, and to say their goodbyes. "I feel like you are going away to Europe," said Leslie rather wistfully, tears welling up in her eyes. But when she was standing there waving as the train pulled out from the station, her expression changed to one of youthful abandon. I then remembered having seen that same expression years ago when she ran into the house and cried, "He kissed me! He kissed me! He finally kissed me!" after a date with Paul, the man who would become her husband. Later, at her wedding reception, I saw that expression once again when she scooped up little Jennie to dance with her.

Our second summer at the beach home brought with it even more activity than the year before. We attended to a copious influx of guests that year. The doors of our house were always open as children and their friends drifted in and out. Youthful laughter, music, and the chitchat of adults and teenagers excited to see each other filled the air.

Friday nights would be reserved for the family. The air was charged with excitement as we gathered around the dinner table. Our words gushed forth in a frantic race to be heard. The conversations served as a barometer of change. Occasionally, the children disagreed with one another. I saw this as a search for individual identity.

The only downside to summer was the seemingly endless trips to the market, wet towels everywhere, and a kitchen that resisted any semblance of order. The house, so orderly the rest of the year, was now in disarray. Whenever I wanted to sit in my favorite spot on the sofa, I found it occupied. If I went to the kitchen to pour myself a drink, locating a clean cup or glass was not easy.

The boys worked as lifeguards, carpenters, and painters that summer. On their days off, they were often doing laundry or tuning their own cars. So, instead of geraniums, petunias, and lobelia decorating the front entrance of our home, there were rags, oilcans, and discarded tools.

The summer of '77 was just like all summers of the past with one exception: St. Lo was undergoing a change. Many of the original residents had died or were moving away, and a new wave of homeowners joined the community.

"I feel saddened by the loss of the Forbes family," Bill remarked. "They were such good friends of my mother. Their daughters are still my good friends, but I suppose the house is too much to deal with now that Mrs. Forbes is a widow."

Bill's feelings were reinforced when a longtime resident said to me, "I'll give St. Lo four more years."

The older generation was giving way to the new—strangers who had no family connection to St. Lo. The children of the original families had moved away for various reasons. For some, economic circumstance forced them to sell their inherited homes in St. Lo and set down roots elsewhere.

When it came time to exchange farewells with the older children, young Bill showed no reservations about kissing me on the lips. It came quite naturally to him. The mother in me was flattered and grateful to know that her son was unlike many a growing boy who feels self-conscious about expressing his affection for his mother. *How very sweet*, I thought as Morgan left with tears in his eyes.

Towards the end of summer, I searched for an hour, a minute, a second alone. My body told me that I needed to slow down, and my mind longed for tranquil moments to clear out thoughts, to fantasize, to reflect on spiritual matters. Sensing my need for a rest, Bill announced his plans to take me on a trip to Spain. Naturally, I was taken by surprise: though he so enjoyed traveling, he rarely initiated the idea.

I immediately phoned the children to tell them about our plans. They heartily agreed to look after Jennie in our absence. But, just as we were getting ready to leave, we were informed of a dreadful air disaster on Tenerife. The news spawned my worst fears about Jennie being left behind if something were ever to happen to Bill and me. The newspapers reported that most of the victims were old, over fifty. Then it occurred to me. Bill was fifty. Was he *old?* Until that moment, I never had given much attention to the fact that we were aging. Before every flight we ever took, Bill would always try to reassure me with a statement like "Sure enough, someday I am going to die, Berta, but I just know it won't be in a plane crash. When I go, I would like it to be swift, for your sake. I never wish to be a burden on you." Reminding myself that God would ultimately decide when it was time for us to depart this world, I settled into the idea that there was no use worrying about it.

The journey to Spain brought us closer to each other. We felt light-hearted, even giddy at times, and less serious about life in general.

On one of our outings, Bill found a chestnut on the ground, picked it up and handed it to me. "When I was a child, we used to play a game called 'Conkers' with these." He was referring to an activity he had learned during the wretched years he spent at an English boarding school. Bill rarely spoke about this time in his life. Tossing the chestnut onto the ground in a way that indicated to me that he had come to terms with that part of his life, he put his arm around my waist, and I put my head on his shoulder.

After returning to California, we were less assiduous about the household chores and familial concerns. It was a refreshing change from the usual.

With Christmas on the way, I started to have mixed feelings about my life. There was the good news about Dana having graduated with honors from university, which had me feeling very proud. And there was the good news regarding my cancer, which left me feeling relieved. That beautiful, rainy Christmas Day—following the doctor's clean bill of health report—was truly a day worth celebrating.

I was changing into a new person. It was becoming more difficult to slip back into my motherly role when the older children came to visit. The days I spent on my own were producing another person. That someone was becoming independent. I learned that it was all right to say no, to politely disagree. I began to question my relationships. My faults became annoyingly visible. Instant results were my goal, and, since this was not always possible, I became easily frustrated. But painting began to teach me patience. The positive changes included the recognition of my ability to help others. In time, I would give that attribute more than a passing glance. The reawakening was gradual. It happened as the children grew up, left home, and left me with more time to get to know that stranger in the mirror.

My husband was changing. Shyly, he began to reach out to people. Like a turtle, he'd pop his head out to look around a little longer, but, when someone came too close, he'd retreat back into his shell again. He also informed me that our physical relationship was something less than he desired.

"Well, we were very young when we got married," was his explanation.

I wasn't sure what that meant, and I wasn't about to ask; I don't think I really wanted to know.

Understandably, my husband had trouble dealing with my emotional highs and lows, which stemmed from my restless, creative nature. As for me, I had always found it difficult to live with his stubbornness and with our problems communicating.

We began working to improve the relationship. Thanks to our continued efforts, over time we managed to come to a new level of understanding. Satisfied with the progress we had made and in celebration of our newfound respect for one another, we decided to start dating each other. There were times when, allowing ourselves to be spontaneous, we would take off down the coast without any plan in mind. We felt energized, exploring previously uncharted territory. If we came upon a new and attractive restaurant along the way, Bill would pull over, come around to open the car door for me, and escort me, arm in arm, to the bar, where we became like two infatuated teenagers giggling, and prattling, and tipping wine glasses in a toast to good fortune.

In January of '78, the heavens opened up, unleashing a wave of torrential rainfalls with winds gusting up to eighty miles per hour for days and nights on end. The howling wind and the clack and clatter of tree branches got so intense on some nights that I found it difficult to get to sleep. The slough rose until it overflowed its banks onto the old road that connected our town to the one just south of us. Between downpours, I took walks around St. Lo. There was so much water everywhere that I actually saw ducks swimming on the tennis courts. Everything was sopping wet: the fire-red eucalyptus leaves, the long blades of emerald green grass by the railroad tracks, the mustard-colored cobblestones, and even the lot below our house was waist-deep in water. Pearls of water were dripping from telephone wires, eaves troughs, and the end of my nose.

During one of my walks, I came upon two adjacent houses that we had rented for a while when the children were small. The first house took me back to an evening when a very young, very nervous hostess was single-handedly attending to a large number of guests out on the patio and was feeling annoyed that she had to wait so long for her husband, who was not to arrive until the party was almost over in spite of her every effort to remind him of how important it was to her that he come home from work on time that evening.

Returning from my reverie, I smiled when I realized that the woman I now had grown into would not be so tolerant of that sort of treatment.

As I peeked through the windows of the downstairs bedroom of the second house, I watched myself—a mother of two preteen daughters—picking up clothes and folding them into the drawers of a maple dresser while the girls were at the beach. Then I smoothed out the chenille bedspreads on the hastily made beds. Oh, how I always loathed that green linoleum floor. And I could have done without those scatter rugs too! They had been washed so often that it was difficult to tell what color they had been.

As the drizzling rain tapered off, so did my daydreaming. I decided to turn back home. There was no need to reminisce about the past, because the life path I now was on was straight, wide, secure, and bright.

My life was rich and full. It had achieved a balance. There was a particular sweetness about it. Jennie made her First Communion, and the presence of Jennie and Bill reminded me that I was needed. Still, I found time to nurture my talents, time to grow, time to change.

I moved my studio from the "playhouse" to Dana's upstairs bedroom. This new location was private and had better lighting. And, with the occasional activity on the street below, I felt there was a little more life around me as I worked. It felt more light and airy too, especially when I opened the windows to let in the sea breeze.

With regards to household chores, I decided to be less the perfectionist, less finicky. Of course, I continued to keep the house clean and tidy, it's just that I had better things to do with my time than to waste it on every little detail.

The month of September '78 turned out to be blazingly hot—well into the 100s. In the mornings, which were considerably cooler than the afternoons, Jennie and I loved to stop at the local café on her way to school. Often amusing and informative, the friendly chitchat among the regular customers taught me a lot about the issues and changes going on in their lives and in our local government.

Little did I know that on one of those mornings I was to get more than I had bargained for. There, sitting on the stool next to me, was a young man, perhaps in his early thirties. His long, wiry hair was disheveled and smelled of cigarette smoke. By the look of the V-neck T-shirt he was wearing, it was obvious that he hadn't changed his clothes for a few days. Hunched over a cold cup of coffee, he started fiddling nervously with the teaspoon and mumbling to himself. At first, I wasn't sure if he was actually saying something or just grunting.

I turned toward Jennie, who was sitting on my other side, and whispered, "We'd better go. You'll be late for school."

"No, Mommy, we have plenty of time."

At that moment, without intending to startle me, the man gently placed his hand on my forearm and pleaded, "No, please wait."

With a compassionate ear, I patiently sat there and listened as the young man shared his story of a life addicted to drugs and of his long struggle to eventually kick the habit. He concluded his lengthy monologue with "I can tolerate daybreak now. I just know I'll make it through another day."

He then dropped his head in silence and scratched his chin with his wrist. Without the need for a response, he turned back to his cup of coffee and gave it a stir.

He can face many a daybreak now, I thought, as I turned once more to look at the young man still sitting at the counter. *Love has found him.*

I counted my blessings when I said my prayers that night. I felt especially grateful for my family and that none of my children had a tragic story to tell.

With winter and my forty-eighth birthday came the realization that Bill and I were both changing. Were we facing a midlife crisis perhaps? I did not know for certain, nor did I think about it much at the time.

My marriage appeared to be going through a change for the better. Admittedly, there were many attractive men around me in my life, but I valued my marriage and family. Anything that might damage the trust of marriage was out of the question. When it came to marriage, family, and friends, I took a straightforward, virtuous approach to life. If I worked hard, walked with integrity, and prayed a lot, I believed I would be rewarded, not only in this life but also in the next.

Now, there were stories circulating about Leslie's marriage being in trouble. I decided to dismiss them as rumors. When she and I would talk on the phone, there was never a mention of a conflict existing between her and her husband. Besides, if there were any problems, I believed her Catholic faith would provide her the strength to deal with them.

I set aside all thoughts of divorce and midlife crises, and my eyes held fast to the beauty around me. How little prepared was I when they came to rest upon a young man named Damian.

Chapter 3

THE CATALYSTS

To fall in love is to create a religion
that has a fallible god.

—Jose Luis Borges, "The Other Death"

Chapter 3

Damian, a contemporary of my oldest daughter Leslie, was an accomplished painter who lived nearby. Up until now, my association with him had not extended beyond the occasional interaction on the beach that our families shared over the summers. Little did I know how that would change.

Damian was tall, slender and nicely muscular. He bodysurfed and ran a lot to keep in shape. His eyes were blue, smiling, direct, and his lips were full and well defined. His slightly hunched shoulders revealed a hint of shyness.

During the fall of '78, we spent a few informal moments together—typically nothing more than exchanging greetings or sharing brief conversations while swimming or while exercising our dogs on the beach. One day, I asked him if he might consider a painting class for me and two or three other women. "We would pay you, of course," I added. He said he would think it over.

Some weeks later, Damian approached me on the beach to say he would teach me. "But I don't want all those other middle-aged ladies around, just you," he stipulated. Then he added, "While you sketch, I'll sketch you, and that will serve as your payment."

After I returned home, I looked in the mirror, wondering if I looked like one of those "middle-aged ladies." No, my face and my figure were still youthful (a fortunate genetic gift from my mother's side of the family).

In the meantime, I continued painting on my own while awaiting his call. After a few weeks had passed, Damian called and asked me if I would like to start my lessons "today." Within a half hour, I made my way down the hill to his house, a sketchpad and some drawings in hand.

My mornings with Damian usually started around 10:30. By that time, I had taken Jennie to school, tidied up the house, and sipped my cup of tea. When I arrived at Damian's home, he would hang up my coat for me. On cold days, he would slip his jacket around my shoulders. I felt that the gesture was rather intimate and wondered if I should have asked for my own coat. No, I reasoned, that would seem silly and would give his casual gesture more importance than it merited. He also opened doors for me and brought me apples and cups of hot tea, and I felt that these courtesies were just good manners, a reflection of his upbringing. My husband had the same way about him.

Typically, we would spend the late morning and early afternoon working outside on the patio. I remember one time—when all my attention was focused on a painting I was working on—Damian suddenly popped his head through the living room door and asked, "Which way do you like my hair?" He had brushed his blond curls so that they formed a beautiful halo. Then he dashed out for a moment, and, when he returned with his hair all slicked back, he said, "Or this?" I knew he wasn't really asking for my opinion. Regardless of my preference, his hair would remain an unruly blonde halo framing his handsome face. He looked like a mischievous angel.

Our laughter melted away any nervousness and tension I might have had. As light-hearted as he was, Damian still made it very clear to me that he was the teacher and that I was the pupil. He would not hesitate to correct my work when he felt I was going in the wrong direction. "Draw the figure standing on the table in front of us," he once said, pointing at a small porcelain statue of an Asian woman. I began to draw the outline in one continuous line. "No!" he pointed out. "Everyone makes that mistake." He would usually end the lessons when he grew tired or had other obligations to attend to and told me that he would phone to let me know when he was free again.

Such was the pattern of our sessions together, except for the times when we met on the beach to paint pastel sunsets. We adjourned for weekends, holidays, my Spanish class, and personal commitments.

Painting had brought a deep sense of personal fulfillment to my life. I had a strong urge to create and was serious about improving. After all the years as wife and mother, I now had a private sanctuary in my being where I could go any time, a room that I allowed myself to enter as often as possible. When I woke up in the morning, I couldn't wait to start the day.

When the cold rains of November came, Damian and I worked by the warmth of the fireplace. There was always music playing. Damian's favorite was musical comedy, because it was happy and lighthearted. From time to time, we would have the pleasure of being serenaded by Damian's good friend, Greg, who was a very fine guitarist. He played and sang Spanish songs that both of us enjoyed. I often requested *Solamente Una Vez*, as this song was one of my husband's favorites. I knew the melody well, but needed a few more Spanish lessons before I could understand the lyrics.

Between rainstorms, Damien and I would often go out and walk on the beach to stretch our legs and get some fresh air. On sunny days, we would set up our easels on the patio to take advantage of the winter light. Sometimes we chatted, but quite often we worked in silence. The only sounds as we worked in the garage studio were those of the heater clicking on and off or the rumblings in our tummies as midday approached. We would satisfy our hunger pangs with apples and tea and then work for another couple of hours.

On the days when Bill was still in town, I would leave to run errands and pick Jennie up from school. But, on the days when Bill was not at work and could take care of Jennie, I would quite often continue working late into the afternoon.

Under Damian's patient direction, I gained confidence and skill. I often copied his pastels to better understand that medium. We looked through books of paintings, and I listened carefully as he explained to me about value. "Painting is light," he said. To get a better grasp of the concept of value, I did some casual sketches and studies, drawing free-form shapes to understand the relationship of objects and negative space. Incorporating such principles and techniques into my work helped to bring my paintings to life.

Damian also taught me how to draw the human figure. What I had learned from Damian proved to be very helpful when I studied life drawing at a nearby college many months later. Figure drawing and painting became my favorite subjects.

Unbeknownst to him, Damian was instrumental in helping me recognize my personal strengths as well. One time, during a discussion of our various talents—from ballet for me to acting for him—he told me, "You can be anything you want to be, Berta." With that simple remark, my self-imposed boundaries began to disappear. Suddenly, I felt like I could fly to the moon. No one had ever said those words to me before, ever. Certainly not my Victorian mother! And my darling husband would never have challenged the status quo with such an utterance. He was by nature and education an engineer and not all that adventuresome.

As a way of reinforcing the changes I was experiencing in myself, I wrote to Leslie:

> My life is at a high point. I am happy that my children—all but one—are grown and on their own. Each one of you should live life as best you can. As for me, I am going to live my life to the fullest. It has been too long since I have had so much time to myself, and it's wonderful!

Laughter. With Damian, there was always laughter! Often, he would look at me out of the corner of his eye and, with a slow grin, begin to tell a story or make some humorous comment.

One evening during the Thanksgiving holidays, as Leslie and I were sipping wine and catching up on each other's lives, I told her how excited I was about working with Damian.

"Uh-oh, Mom, you'd better be careful," she laughed.

"Oh now, don't be silly," I quickly replied, "I'm twenty years his elder, and very married."

I told Leslie about how Damian had admired her beauty and about how he had commented, " . . . but that fellow was always hanging around." He was referring to her boyfriend and future husband.

"Oh God, Mom," she sighed. "Don't tell me any more!"

My conversation with Leslie made me more aware of Damian's affect on my life. I became a little wary about our seemingly innocent relationship. For instance, on a day he left for town, he dropped by at my house to return a record I had lent him. Did he hesitate before he left, or was it my imagination? He stood in front of me for a moment as if he were waiting for me to do or say something. It was only for a second or two, but his gaze was unwavering. I nervously said goodbye and fled to the terrace to resume my reading.

I started feeling as if I were moving in and out of two very different worlds. On some days, I would be creating art and sharing laughter with Damian, and, on other days, I lived out my familiar roles of wife and mother. Living two lives carried with it a certain excitement, but also a certain risk. I prayed that my guardian angel would keep an eye on me. When I found out that Damian was attracted to my daughter Dana, I felt more comfortable with our relationship again.

~ ~ ~

Jennie's ninth birthday brought life into focus. After Bill and I watched her open her presents in front of the fireplace, we went down to the cabana and waited for the guests to arrive. As two clowns were putting on a show for Jennie, Damian showed up bearing gifts for the birthday girl. Among these were a seahorse, a chambered nautilus, and a tender note about growing older.

I would always have fond memories of this time of my life. I had spent many peaceful mornings in the L-shaped living-dining room of Damian's house. Propped up by some books on the rattan table in the dining room was my drawing board. Damian's easel was nearby. His palette and brushes lay on a small table that separated his work area from mine. Behind my work area was the kitchen. Damian and I would often take a break and chat there as we waited for the kettle to boil.

Damian had an extensive record collection that he kept in an armoire by the front door. He always made sure we had beautiful music playing as we worked. Opposite the armoire and under a hanging lamp was a game table with four chairs. Over by the bookshelves was the sofa bed, where Damian's father liked to nap. As I warmed my back by the living-room fireplace, I would often gaze out the windows of the French doors. There, out on the brick patio, Damian's dog, Chrissie—a large, white German shepherd—would stretch out on her rug warming herself in the winter sun. Free from any traffic noise, the living room was a warmer, more peaceful place to work than the garage. The only sounds were those of the surf, music, the crackling fire, the scratching of pencils, and our laughter.

I vividly remember one morning when I was sitting on the beach and happened to look up from the book I was reading. From where I sat, I could see Damian running with his friend Christopher, a former class-mate and fellow artist. I was captivated by the sight of the two young men flying down the beach like horses at a gallop. I was struck by the beauty and coordination of the human form as those two thundered along the sand into the wind. Side by side, with legs lifting high and resolutely, these two epitomized youth at its peak—full of life and bursting with energy.

The sounds, the colors, the smells, the conversations, how it felt—all of it—I was determined to remember every detail. *Someday*, I thought to myself, *I will slip this memory on like an old coat and draw it close around me.*

Later that very same day, while I sat enjoying myself with some friends in front of their beach house, I was struck by an image that contrasted sharply with that beautiful memory. I saw my husband jogging down the beach and felt a sense of uneasiness with regard to his physical condition.

My host, Ron, said, "Who is that man staggering around clutching his chest? Could that be Mr. Hees working out and trying to get in shape? Mr. Hees, it seems, has been reborn," he laughed. "All this jogging and swimming; we've been admiring Bill's new shape," he concluded.

My friend spoke in jest, and I joined in the laughter. However, the words stirred up a slight anxiety inside of me. "I am on the beach in case he needs mouth-to-mouth resuscitation," I said not quite jokingly.

~ ~ ~

Bill's cousin, Charles, came to visit, accompanied by his friend Laura from Amsterdam, a stunningly beautiful woman in her mid-fifties, tall, and rather stately. A woman of courage, she suffered many losses during World War II because she was Jewish. It turned out that we had much in common. She was also very interested in art. I enjoyed her stories about some of the contemporary artists she associated with in Amsterdam during the '70s. She revealed to me that she had survived a bout with skin cancer. I told her about my mastectomy.

Laura and I quickly developed a friendship during her brief visit. We would sit on the beach together and talk about life.

One afternoon, we were joined by Damian, who was accompanied by a beautiful girl. He introduced us to Beth.

"Beth lives nearby," Damian explained. "We met at the Bellas Artes in San Miguel de Allende." Damian talked with Laura about art trends and such until Beth, bored with the talk of art, began stroking his chest. At that moment, we chose to excuse ourselves.

As we walked up the hill, Laura cautioned me, "You'd better be careful. He is extremely handsome and definitely attracted to you."

I shrugged off the remark. "He's seeing my daughter Dana, and other girlfriends show up from time to time. It is quiet here in the fall and winter, so Damian and I often spend time sharing our differing views about life. Our age difference makes for some very interesting conversation."

Later, I told Damian that I liked the adorable girl he was with on the beach. He said, "She has a quietness about her that I appreciate. She has a certain innocence about her like Dana and you."

As the months went by, Damian and I began sharing our innermost feelings. "You know me better than anyone," he once told me.

Laura's story about her fight with cancer gave me the courage to tell Damian about my mastectomy. He said he had heard about my surgery, but, when I explained that I only had one breast, he laughed and said, "Oh, that's good news. I thought you didn't have any!" This made me laugh along with him. Then I realized that something important came out of that moment. As this was the first time I had verbally come to terms with my disfigurement, I suddenly felt more accepting of it. I would always love him for that.

~ ~ ~

My work with Damian continued as he helped me with a drawing I would give Bill for Christmas. During that time, I had the opportunity to watch him at work. When he made a decisive stroke on his canvas, it was usually accompanied by an audible grunt—a sort of vocal exclamation mark. As he attempted to capture some elusive detail, his lips moved as if engaged in speech. He would drum his fingers on the table while he stepped back to view his work. At such moments, he might turn to me with a grin on his face and commence telling a story about some of his crazy exploits, complete with gestures and in whatever dialect was called for to enhance the anecdote.

He recounted a tale about "drowning" in the Hawaiian surf. As a friend of his watched from the bushes nearby, people gathered at the edge of the surf and pointed at a body floating in the water. The lifeguards flew to the "rescue," only to find Damian had suddenly "revived" as they were about to administer artificial respiration. He sprang up and, together with his friends from the bushes, dashed down the beach, shrieking with laughter. This episode, like many others he described, took place when he was fairly young. Though he kept the little boy in him as he grew older, it was now balanced with the caring and sensitivity of an adult man who was always ready to help.

I finished my drawings a few days before Christmas. After a morning of hard work, I rested on the sofa bed, nibbled on apples and cheese, and studied my picture. I asked Damian if he thought it needed any changes. Pulling himself away from his own work-in-progress, he stood up, looked over the drawing, and then flopped down beside me, saying, "No, it's finished." Suddenly, I was afraid to look at him for fear that the intimacy I was feeling would overwhelm me. Perhaps he picked up on what I was feeling, as he repositioned himself over by the fireplace. I sprang up and gathered my things. After taking my cup and plate to the kitchen, I turned to say goodbye, and Damian was right there in front of me. My arms were cradling my artwork. I leaned over and gave him a quick kiss. Then, just before I opened the kitchen door to leave, I wished him a Merry Christmas.

"I'll see you again," he cried out to me as I walked down the driveway. I raised one arm and waved back at him in acknowledgement.

Feeling confused as I walked up the hill to my home, I reflected on Laura's remarks about Damian's attraction for me. *But he's going out with my daughter, so I'm sure Laura must be mistaken!*

~ ~ ~

Our attraction to one another took a backseat when we stepped back into our own lives. On his way out of town to spend Christmas with his family, Damian passed by the house to give Jennie a few presents and a kiss. Over a pot of tea, Bill and Damian discussed the portrait of Jennie that Damian was working on.

Christmas drew me back into my family life, where I was most comfortable and content. Once or twice, Damian phoned, but our conversations were awkward and brief. We had little to say to each other, and he usually called me "Mrs. Hees." I wondered why he was phoning at all, in fact.

Setting aside my drawing pad and art box, I immersed myself in Christmas preparations: wrapping presents, shopping for Christmas dinner, taking the drawing I had made for Bill to the frame shop, and, with Jennie's help, decorating the tree.

The following day, it was clear that Dana had met the man she would marry—Kevin. Dana invited Kevin to share Christmas dinner with the family. My daughter couldn't take her eyes off him the entire dinner. A woman in love has a certain radiance about her, a certain magnetism. Bill and I knew immediately that this man was "the one."

My husband and Kevin took an instant liking to each other. Bill, who was generally not much at ease with people, apparently saw in Kevin a man very much like himself. Kevin was intelligent, quiet, and thoughtful, but not necessarily intent on setting the world on fire, at least in my opinion. Seeing how comfortable the two of them were in the living room conversing after dinner, I said to the children, "It looks like Dad has found a friend."

Sadly, Bill would not live long enough to get to know the lovely grandchildren that the union between Kevin and Dana would produce. At times, during the difficult years after his death, I would seek solace in my imagination. I would close my eyes and imagine sweet Bill combing the seashore for shells and bits of glass with the grandchildren whom, in reality, he would never have the pleasure of knowing. The image kept me sane.

Along with the promise of Dana's new romance, there was some sad news that Christmas. When young Bill and Dana came to celebrate the holidays, they informed me that, during a visit with Leslie before they left for St. Lo, Leslie wept because she was unable to be with her family. Also, I now seriously suspected—though Bill and Dana never said so—that Leslie and her husband, Paul, were experiencing marital difficulties, and she was considering divorce, but hadn't made the final decision. Deeply touched by Leslie's sadness over her failing marriage, I decided to visit the mission where she had been married. I lit a votive candle and prayed for my daughter. I gathered all the strength I could muster to hide my tears by the time I returned home.

~ ~ ~

On New Year's Day, we decided to go to town for the parade. Early that morning, we gathered at Leslie's home for cocoa and donuts. She was striking in her banded felt hat and brown camel-hair coat tied at the waist. She looked tense, waiting for late arrivals and trying to control the kitchen crowd. Then, when we walked up the hill to watch the floats, she seemed fine. I enjoyed being with my daughter.

During the Tournament of Roses parade, Bill and I stood on the boulevard with our entire family, including Leslie, Paul, little Riley, and some of Paul's relatives. As the floats went by, everyone laughed and joked. Friends joined our group, and we offered them some milk punch, which was a family tradition on New Year's Day. I was glad to see no sign of tears in Leslie's eyes. She was smiling, obviously enjoying herself. When the parade was over, we walked across the boulevard to the club where we drank gin fizzes and ate brunch. Everyone reconnected with old friends, talking animatedly about their lives and wishing each other a Happy New Year.

On that fine January day, I saw no sign of discord between Leslie and Paul. What I did notice was the continuation into her marriage of the family rituals from her childhood. I was both happy and relieved.

Bill, Jennie, and I spent the first night of 1979 at our apartment in town. The next morning, I heard Bill merrily whistling while he dressed and prepared to go to his office. Jennie and I packed our suitcases and headed back to St. Lo. We were tired, but happy. After a light supper, we retired early, falling asleep to the soothing sounds of the ocean waves.

~ ~ ~

After the holiday festivities, St. Lo was virtually deserted, save for the few residents who stayed on to savor the quietude of the bleak winter months. I spent those early days taking Jennie to school, battling the flu, catching up with deskwork and housework, searching the local libraries for books on art, and studying Spanish.

Bill came home on Wednesday evening looking very tired.

"Were the children too much for you?" I asked after he settled in.

"No, I enjoyed being with the family," he said, adding, "I'm glad to be home, though."

"Did you see Leslie before you left town? Was she all right?"

He said he did see her, but offered little more information, just shaking his head and throwing up his arms. I knew he was working hard to try to save our daughter's marriage. I decided to leave him alone. If there were any problems, he did not wish to discuss them because he knew that it might upset me. Bill was very considerate that way.

"Well," I smiled, "Jennie and I are happy to have you back. It's been rather bleak here without you."

~ ~ ~

Leslie and I stayed in touch by phone. After one particular conversation, I hung up feeling disconcerted, not because of anything that Leslie had said, but because of her change in attitude. She was very defensive. I could hear anger in her voice, and she talked only about herself. There was nothing I could say without interrupting the monologue about how messed up her life had become. She claimed it all started in her childhood. "I am trying to find out who I am, Mother," she said indignantly.

Later, I phoned my sister Jeannette in Virginia. "We weren't close when our children were growing up, but I thought I would ask you for an objective opinion. It's about the changes in Leslie's attitude," I said to my sister, and then repeated Leslie's remarks about finding herself.

"Well, I've only raised boys. I don't know very much about raising daughters. It's possible you have just had your first encounter with the 'me generation,'" offered my sister. "I'm more outspoken than you are, so I probably would have said to her: 'Please, dear, just shut up. I did the best I could.' I know you'll never say that, so the best thing is to just listen to her. It's hard to love your children sometimes."

I thanked Jeannette for the advice and continued, "I wish we hadn't lived on opposite sides of the country all these years. We could have helped each other. I love you."

Leslie and I began to drift apart. Even later, when certain events would call upon her to take on a stronger role in the family, we still remained estranged.

~ ~ ~

I returned to my painting. It filled me with self-confidence, and I realized that I could work on my own.

"Damian's looking forward to working with you again, Mom," said Dana when she phoned one day. Dana and Damian were still seeing one another, even though Kevin seemed to be "the one."

"I don't know, Dana dear. I'm doing just fine on my own," I replied. But, after I hung up, I thought to myself, *I'll have to give that some serious consideration.*

Bill's cousin, Charles, came for a visit from the East Coast. He was staying just across the road in his mother's home.

During the course of my marriage, Charles and I became quite close. He was open to everyone. A great conversationalist, he talked with profound insight and irreverent humor about the vicissitudes of the human condition. I really enjoyed our talks, and we had in common a love for music and the arts. Charles was gay and an alcoholic. He was once handsome and youthful, but the ravages of drinking had taken their toll over time.

I adored him, and he adored me, Bill, and our children. "I'm glad you had so many," he once commented. "It makes up for me."

One afternoon, during his stay at St. Lo, Charles and I walked to the beach and sat on the steps that led to the sea. We talked as we enjoyed the view.

"I met this young Japanese boy on the New York subway and fell in love with him. Now, it's all over," he said, weeping. It was obvious he was heartbroken. I reached out and took his hand.

"What about Carroll?" I asked Charles, expressing concern for how Carroll—his lifetime partner—might have felt about the indiscretion.

"He understands. As you know, we've never been faithful to each other. The problem is I've never fallen in love with anyone else before," he explained when, suddenly, Damian came into view behind us.

"I'm back," Damian declared with a grin on his face. He spoke to Charles for a while and then said, "Well, back to work," as he headed for his studio.

"God, Damian is so handsome. And you are a very sexy lady," declared Charles, apparently noticing that there was something between us.

"Are you trying to promote something too?" I sighed in resignation. "Laura said that she thought he was attracted to me."

"No, I'm not, but one can't help thinking of the possibilities. And he's straight too!" replied Charles. I hugged him for being so forthright.

"Charles, the idea is preposterous. Damian is seeing Dana, and I'm twenty years his senior. There are elements in our working relationship that echo my relationship with you: the shared laughter, the love of music, and the easy manner in which we converse. When I started working with him, I thought he might be gay. That made it fine; it made me feel safe. During the hours we spent together, I even asked him if he was gay. He laughed and said, 'My parents thought the same thing. But no, I'm not. I fantasize only about women.'"

"Anything else I should know about," asked Charles.

"Well, there have been moments when Damian has looked at me in a way that made me feel uncomfortable, you know, in a sexual way. Only he can say if that is his intention. Maybe I'm imagining something that isn't so. Why would he be dating my daughter if he feels something for me? If that were true—" I stopped for a moment, "he would be a cad! Charles, does anyone say the word 'cad' anymore?"

"Probably not, Berta, but that's what makes you so unique. Your untainted, innocent view of life is so refreshing and appealing," Charles replied.

"I love you, Charles. You're my very, very best friend. Please, please take better care of yourself," I pleaded. "I need you."

We sat for a while longer watching the tide come in and listening to the sea crashing on the rocks.

"Charles, do you think I should continue to work with Damian?" I asked.

"Well, of course. I'm happy you found something for yourself. You moved here at Bill's behest. Yes, it's beautiful, but he must have understood what a big change he was making in your life with his decision," Charles answered. "You're doing fine."

So, occasionally, I would paint with Damian again. We slipped back into our teacher-student relationship, and I was comfortable with that arrangement. When Dana came for a visit, she went whale watching with Damian, Bill, Jennie, and Sophie, one of Jennie's friends. Everyone seemed content, except for my husband. He was irritable and tired when he came back from the adventure.

Bill's irritability showed itself when we went for a weekend picnic and hike with Jennie and our dog Sam. Bill kept yanking at Sam's choke chain. The more he yanked, the more the dog resisted.

"Bill, Bill, please stop yanking on Sam's leash! He doesn't like it!" I cried and grabbed the leash from his hand. "What's wrong? Why are you so irritable?" I asked him.

"I'm not irritable!" he exclaimed.

In fact, he was *very easily* irritated lately. Perhaps, part of the answer came when Leslie phoned me on a Monday morning after Bill had left for work.

"I'm going to divorce Paul," she said. When I tried to speak to her, she interrupted me. "I'm very strong. I'm very strong." She repeated this several times and then hung up.

I sat with the receiver in my hand, numb and unable to move. I was completely shattered.

Chapter 4

AFTERMATH

*Sometimes we suffer because God loves us
enough to give us some freedom to make mistakes.*

—John R. Wimmer

Chapter 4

Alone, I wandered through the house looking at Leslie's wedding pictures. I studied them and wondered what to do with them. Suddenly, my mind went blank and my body shook. So I bolted from the house and ran down the road to the cabana. There, I came upon two friends of mine. As I blurted out "Paul and Leslie are getting divorced," they looked at me in embarrassment. People of their generation—they were in their seventies—did not air the family laundry.

Then one of them put her arms around me, saying, "I'm shocked. Of all the families for this to happen to, I would have picked yours as the last."

Me too, I thought as I watched with envy this sweet couple—married for so many years—walk up the hill.

Feeling numb, I sat down on the white wooden bench in the cabana and stared at the ocean without really seeing it. My mind went over and over Leslie's message until Damian appeared in the cabana from his house across the road. I stood up as he approached.

"I know," he said. "Leslie and Paul are getting a divorce."

"How do you know that? Leslie just phoned to tell *me.* Did Dana say something to you?" I asked and then burst into tears. I quickly covered my face with my hands and turned away from Damian. If he answered me, I certainly did not hear him.

"Would you like to take a walk?" he asked.

"Yes," I sniffled in reply. "I just can't face that empty house right at the moment. Maybe a walk will clear my head."

As we walked up the hill away from the beach, I poured my soul out to Damian.

"I can't believe it. I thought they were only going through a difficult time. I prayed for them. I was positive that things would work out," I continued, wiping away tears every so often.

We came to a gate at the end of the road, opened it, and walked down a slope toward the railroad tracks. Before crossing the trestle, we had to scurry down the embankment to avoid an oncoming train. I slipped on the gravel and fell. Damian helped me up, brushed the last tear from my cheek, and asked me if I was all right. Leaving behind the subject of Leslie's divorce, we began to talk about our feelings for each other. There it was: Damian's first acknowledgement that something special had grown out of the mornings we had spent together.

"I've written a poem about the two of us, but, in the poem, Mr. Hees cries," Damian told me with a grin on his face. I smiled at his confession. The words told me that his attraction to me wasn't going anywhere.

"That is very sweet. I have grown very fond of our moments together as well," I told him, and, by uttering those words, I experienced a great sense of relief. Then, silence fell around us. I had nothing more to say, nor did he.

As we walked through the fields on the other side of the lagoon, I felt a terrible emptiness inside, a sense of great loss and anger. My new life, which I was beginning to truly enjoy, was being rudely disrupted by divorce. In an effort to ease my feeling of aloneness, I asked Damian to hold my hand.

"No, someone might see us," he replied, aware of the fact we were in direct line of the windows of St. Lo across the slough. Then he quickly reconsidered: "Well, maybe for a moment," he said as he reached for my hand.

We held hands all the way to the next town and beyond sight of St. Lo. I began to cry again. Damian strolled ahead of me to a nearby construction site so that I could weep in private, and without inhibition. He returned after I regained my composure.

When he returned, he gave me a kiss on the cheek. Then he said, "No, no, I can't kiss you. I like Dana, too!"

"Well, Leslie will soon be a free woman, so you can have her as well," I snapped, not able to contain my anger.

There was a moment of silence and uneasiness.

"I'm sorry, that was rude of me," I said as a way of apology.

We walked toward the highway and then headed home.

~ ~ ~

Holding a small bouquet of flowers that Damian had picked for me during our walk, I entered my home alone. I walked down a few steps to the living room and headed for the sofa, where I sat for some time, staring at the cold fireplace. Tears rolled down my cheeks, clung for a moment to my chin, and dropped into the flowers that were resting on my lap.

My thoughts were full of memories of Leslie and Paul. It was a sweet romance that had begun right here at St. Lo. And then, there was Damian and his poem, in which "Mr. Hees cried"! *He is dating my daughter, Dana! Why did he have to tell me about his attraction to me, which probably means that we won't be painting together again!*

Confused, angry, and bewildered, I threw the bouquet of flowers on the floor, slumped over, and wailed disconsolately, "My God! My God!"

Not long after, at Damian's request, Mary came over to comfort me. She was a neighbor who lived just down the road from us. She began by sharing the problems she was having with her children, and then she began to cry.

"I'm afraid I'm not going to be of much help here," she said as she headed out the door.

I phoned my mother to tell her the news, hoping that, for once, she might help me. Mother, who generally was not one to demonstrate her caring, surprised me with a sympathetic response. Naturally, however, since the news was unsettling to her, she became very upset by the time our conversation ended. I found myself having to phone her a number of times just to see if she was all right.

Then, Leslie's mother-in-law called to ask, "Berta, what happened?"

"I don't know, Susan. I'm as much in the dark as you are," I answered. She agreed that Leslie sounded programmed. She had also heard the same words: "I'm strong. I'm very strong."

I waited for my husband to call. Undoubtedly, he must have known that Leslie had phoned me. Days passed, and still not a word from Bill. After taking Jennie to school each day, I would return home to sit on the sofa—numb and paralyzed. The silence felt isolating.

At times, I would occupy my time reading Psalms from a Bible that Damian had loaned me. Tucked inside the book was a poem Damian had written some years ago. "His armor is dross" is the only line I can recall. This referred to the Devil, meaning that he could be conquered.

No one phoned. The waiting and wondering about Leslie's well-being became intolerable. I felt abandoned.

I told Jennie about Leslie's situation. Since she was only nine years old, it was difficult to explain divorce to her. I thought there was something wrong with people who divorced, and I was unable to tell her why I felt that way. Deciding that simplicity was the best approach, I told her, "Your sister is leaving Paul because she is not happy in her marriage. In time, everything will be all right." The look on her face during the days that followed was one I hoped never to see again.

Later, I told Leslie that I had spoken to Jennie about the divorce.

"Boy, I would like to have heard that one," was her comment. The antagonistic tone of Leslie's remark caught me by surprise. I said nothing in response to her comment.

The beach was empty. The house was quiet. I was feeling lonely, so I decided to phone Damian to see if I could come to his studio. "I'll just sit quietly in a chair and watch you work," I assured him.

"Fine, come on over. I'm working on Jennie's portrait," was his response.

The rain began to fall as I arrived at his studio. Damian was busy working on some preliminary sketches for Jennie's portrait. As I warmed up by the heater, he came over and handed me some art books to look at, and then he quietly returned to his sketches.

The heater clicked on, then off again. The wind outside signaled that a storm was on the way. I found a chair to sit on and put the books down on a nearby table. As I became engrossed in the books and appreciating the absolutely stunning illustrations, Damian rolled his chair away from his easel and placed himself next to me. He picked up my hand, kissed my fingers, and placed them on his cheek.

"What happened, Damian?" I asked, not expecting an answer.

"You are having a bad time right now, because your husband isn't here," Damian offered.

"Of course, you are right. I have no one to talk to," I said. "Thanks for letting me come over while you are working." I embraced Damian, and he returned my embrace. We stood together in silence for a moment.

"Oh Berta, Berta, Berta," Damian said passionately. He wanted to help me, to comfort me, to make me feel better. I broke away from the embrace before my sadness could completely engulf me. I felt that I would break down again. Picking up my woolen scarf and throwing it around my neck, I left his house and walked up the hill to my home.

When I got home, I picked up the phone and called Leslie. Oh, it was a wonderful talk! Her happy mood blew away my sense of isolation.

"Just a minute! Dad's here," she said. In the midst of our phone conversation, Bill showed up at her home. I wondered for only a second if he was there to try and patch up the marriage.

"I'd like to talk with him," I said.

"I'll tell him about our conversation. He's talking to Paul right now," Leslie explained. I could hear Bill and Paul laughing in the background.

Why is everyone so happy? Why am I the only one still confused and crying?

"Leslie, I feel upset and lonely because I'm so far away. What happened to your marriage?" I asked.

"Well, for starters, I was too young. Mom, I can't explain everything with Dad and Paul here." And then Leslie seemed to have turned away from the phone to join in the laughter. When she came back, she said, "I feel relieved now that the decision has been made on the divorce."

"You sound better. There is much less tension in your voice," I remarked. "Now I'll say goodbye, dear. I feel better too. I love you. Oh, is Riley nearby? I'd like to say hello."

"Yes. Goodbye, Mom. I love you too. Here's Riley."

"Riley, it's Gaga," I began, as soon as I heard my granddaughter's little voice. "How are you, dear?"

"I'm fine," she replied happily.

"I love you, dear," was all I could muster.

"I love you too, Gaga," Riley replied, using the name that my husband had called his grandmother. Somehow, it got passed on to me. I liked it.

Peace is difficult to maintain when there is a divorce in the family. It's like throwing a stone into still water. The ripples flow out and affect everyone who is dear to you.

That day, after I spoke with Leslie, her sister Dana phoned.

"I'm so relieved it's all out in the open. I'm tired of crying into my pillow every night," Dana said.

The phone now rang nonstop. "What happened, Berta? Why are Leslie and Paul divorcing?" was the question on the minds of family and friends. I truly didn't have the answer.

"I don't know," I would reply, leaving the caller up in the air. Sometimes, the caller would burst into tears!

One of my former Pasadena neighbors called to say, "I saw it coming, Berta.

Occasionally, Leslie and Paul were at the club when I happened to be there. At other times, I only saw Leslie with her friends. It broke my heart to see their marriage in trouble. I don't think the company she was keeping was of any help to her."

"What is happening to our children?" inquired another caller.

"I don't know," I replied, noticing that my voice was edgy.

Hoping to find an answer as to why the marriage failed, I phoned Leslie for more information. She was not receptive to the question of why she made a decision to divorce Paul. Unlike our recent conversation, her voice sounded mechanical. I listened to a list of her personality problems. According to her, I was to blame for some of these. Guilt-ridden, I sat down and played the piano for hours. Afterwards, worn out from the intensity of playing, I walked down to the sea. The sea was wild! As I rounded a bend, a rainbow appeared!

~ ~ ~

Finally, Bill came home. When I put my arms around him, instead of a warm embrace, I received a perfunctory hug. He seemed preoccupied but unruffled. He wasted no time in going out to jog. When he returned, he was absolutely wrung out.

For three days I had waited for him to come home. I needed to talk to him, to hug him, to cry on his shoulder, but apparently he had nothing left for me. He was worn out from talking to Leslie. Now that it was over, he just wanted to put it behind him, to lose himself into the sea and sand. As both of us were hurt, edgy, tired, and angry, we found it difficult to be there for each other.

The following day, Bill started talking about his visit with Leslie. "I said to her, 'If you can't manage your marriage, how are you going to manage a divorce?'"

I was surprised Bill had asked such a question. It was not like him to be confrontational. Anyway, Leslie had not responded. "She tuned me out," he said.

As we spoke, it became apparent no one had informed young Bill about his sister's plans. So, after dinner, we gave him a call. At the end of our conversation, he said, "I love you, Mom. I love you, Dad."

After hanging up, Bill and I put our arms around each other. I thanked him for his efforts, and we started to cry. Then I said in a serious tone, "Do you think we should ask for our money back?"

"What money?" inquired Bill.

"Why, the money for the wedding, of course." We laughed, which helped to lighten the mood for the moment.

It was not easy for us to move forward. The memory of Leslie's failed marriage was to stay with us for a long time.

~ ~ ~

A card came in the mail from the parents of our son-in-law Paul. They wished Bill and me a "Happy New Year." The greeting seemed ironic, considering the circumstances. With the card came their new address. They were moving north. Now that their beach house in St. Lo belonged to their children, it meant we would be seeing a great deal of my son-in-law. Regrettably, Leslie would no longer be with him.

One night, as I was setting the table for dinner, I came across the artichoke plates that Paul had given to us as a present. At the time, he had asked shyly if they were "all right." *They would always be "all right," and more,* I thought to myself as I placed them on the table.

I began removing all the pictures of my daughter's wedding and married life from the walls and the tables. As I was putting them into a box for storage in the attic, the phone rang. It was Leslie's mother-in-law, Susan. She was doing the same thing. I told her my throat was constantly raw from crying so much, and she replied, "Me too." We both started crying.

Instead of feeling better as the days progressed, I sank into depression. At three o'clock one morning, unable to sleep, I went downstairs, sat at the dining room table, and wrote a letter to Leslie. Later, to make sure there was nothing in that letter that might offend her, I read the letter to Bill.

"It's a beautiful letter," he assured me, "but don't mail it. She does not want to hear any of that right now."

Feeling frustrated and angry again, I tore the letter to pieces.

Bill cried out, "No, no, don't do that. Someday, when all this turmoil has passed, she will want to hear what you had to say."

But, believing Bill was wrong about this, I threw the letter out. As a Catholic, I believed that marriage meant sacrifice and compromise. Clearly, I was out of step with the changing morality of the secular world of the '70s.

I found some solace at weekday Mass from a responsorial psalm that read:

Praise the Lord, who heals the broken hearted.

Following Mass, I approached the priest and asked him to help me. He agreed to come by the house for a visit.

When I got home, I told Bill that the priest was coming to see me. His joy could not have been greater. He was so relieved I went to seek help that he made what was for him a heroic gesture. Although he was not Catholic and had no real interest in religion, I felt he truly supported me in my spiritual life. He asked if he could sit in on the conversation.

Father Mark was a soft-spoken man about forty years of age. As we talked, he did not stress the Church's position on divorce. He did say that the Church was having to adjust to the ever-increasing rate of divorce.

"The Church can no longer afford to disown those who find it necessary to dissolve their marriages," he said. "You must not consider your daughter a bad person because she is divorced." He then explained that Leslie's decision could not have come easily, and that I must respect the fact that the divorce was *her* decision and try to be more understanding. He told me I should phone her and make myself available to listen.

"You will have to bite your tongue," he said, pointing out that she was quite young when married and was now struggling to be her own person. Then Father Mark said something that would become an oft-repeated phrase in the years to come: "The mother is always the rejected parent. It is a classic pattern. You see, your ideas no longer work for her, and she wants to be free of you. In time, she will be your good friend again, so you must not close the door on your friendship with her." He then added, "I must say that this particular situation is a tragedy."

After the meeting, I wished my daughter a silent "good luck" from my heart, and I thanked God for setting me on a steadier course. The divorce, however, was only a dress rehearsal for the events to come, events that would change me mentally and physically.

Easter of '79 was complicated by the impending divorce. Bill, Jennie, and I were invited to Paul's beach house because Riley would be there with Paul's family. I thought that if Leslie were staying at our house and Paul and Riley were at her father's house, it might create confusion for our granddaughter.

For me, one of the most troubling ramifications of the divorce was in trying to figure out what to do with the love I felt for Paul and his family. Riley would innocently point the way. She came to spend the night with us. After tucking her into bed, we said our prayers.

"Don't forget my mom and dad," little Riley had requested. In that moment, the child let me know where all the lingering love should go. Divorce doesn't cut that affection out of your heart.

Early one morning, Jennie, Riley, and I went down the hill to visit our neighbor Margaret, who invited us to soak in the hot tub. We splashed around in the bubbles and watched Jennie's friend Irwin, a duck from the slough, come plodding towards us with a friendly "quack, quack."

The early morning mist rising off the lagoon was a sight to behold. The slough had a mystical feeling as the morning mist settled on the water like a soft white blanket. One could imagine an arm, with sword in hand, rising up from the mist, like something from the legend of King Arthur.

Suddenly, the two girls dunked their heads into the warm water of the spa and came up laughing, water sputtering out of their mouths. Afterward, the three of us jogged up the hill together to keep warm. We showered, dressed, and then I drove Jennie to school.

Upon returning home, Riley and I walked down to the beach hoping to find other children her own age. As I watched her play on the beach, I started to feel comfortable with life again. My youngest was in second grade, and, with Riley following close behind, there would be no empty nest.

The sun peeked through the gray clouds every so often on that fine spring morning. Damian came by to join us, and, after some hesitation, he sat down beside me. Since I had my sketchbook with me, I asked him to draw an Easter rabbit for Riley. Somehow, the rabbit didn't look very friendly. It was the eyes. They were full of mischief. So I added a few eggs and flowers to soften the picture. Then I ran up the hill to take a phone call, leaving Damian to keep an eye on Riley.

When I picked up the phone, I heard my sister Jeannette's voice.

"Hello, little Berts!" said my not-too-much-older sister. "I'm calling to see if you are all right. Mother phoned to tell me about Leslie's divorce. Well, you never know how one's children are going to turn out. The first thing you need to do is to take care of yourself. Paul and Leslie's wedding was beautiful, though!"

After thanking Jeannette for calling, after telling each other that we loved one another, we said goodbye. I walked back to the beach feeling strengthened by my sister's call.

When I returned to the beach, Damian and Riley were no longer in sight, so I walked across the road to Damian's studio to see if they might be there.

"Well, here you are, Riley!" I said as I walked in. "I see Damian is teaching you how to draw."

"See," said Riley, holding up her drawing.

"Ah yes," I began, "The rabbit looks much better. Such beautiful round blue eyes and lots more eggs too. It's lovely."

Soon after, Damian's mother, Jane, came to visit. After I introduced her to my granddaughter, she asked Riley, "So, are you having a good time with your grandmother?"

"That's right, you're a grandmother," said Damian as if he had just discovered the fact. Well, whether he had forgotten or not, I was not the least bit annoyed—in fact, I was grateful—that his mother had reminded us that there was an age difference of twenty years between us.

Damian's parents became my friends. Whenever we greeted each other, Damian's father, Bruce, always kissed me on the cheek. And his mother would read to Jennie as Damian worked on her portrait. They came to comfort me after Bill's death and later, when I became ill. Without a doubt, their support was admirable. When Damian's father was very ill, Jennie and I sent him some violets. After he died, Damian's mother phoned to tell me that the flowers were still blooming next to his bed.

~ ~ ~

We enjoyed some wonderful moments that spring. Bill and I accepted an offer from friends to make use of their condominium on Maui. With our daughters, Dana and Jennie, we ended up having the best vacation ever. Jennie and Bill went snorkeling while I sat on the beach and sketched. We went swimming together every morning. We loved diving under the water to listen to the sounds of the whales communicating to each other. We had picnics, read, played tennis, and took long walks along the beach in search of pretty shells. I had never seen Bill looking happier, not even at St. Lo. Everyone had such a good time that we all promised to return.

~ ~ ~

The final week of June, 1979, Bill and I celebrated twenty-nine years of marriage. He gave me some silver bracelets, which I wore constantly, that is, until my wrists swelled up in size from all the years of physical therapy that were to follow.

I gave him a drawing and a poem that spoke of our life together—a life that would continue to be buffeted by change, but was spiritually unbreakable. The last few lines of my poem expressed the essence of our married life—one that was marked by change, but was built on a strong foundation:

> . . . *the steel has been forged*
> *each by the other*
> *over the years,*
> *so take my hand,*
> *and we'll see life through.*

I knelt at Mass that day and thanked God for our beautiful life together and asked Him to bless the year to come. Kneeling before the towering altar at Mission San Luis Rey, I looked up at the carved wooden statue of the Virgin Mary standing in her niche to the right of the altar. A painted blue mantel covered her head and shoulders. She looked benignly at her worshippers below. For a moment, I imagined Leslie leaning over to place her wedding bouquet at the feet of Our Lady. Then, I studied the large crucifix that hung in the center of the altar. The arms of Jesus were spread out. His head, wearing the crown of thorns, tilted down at an angle as if he were sadly regarding centuries of broken promises lying scattered at his feet. *Leslie's divorce would soon be among them,* I thought.

I was feeling a growing need to connect with Leslie, so, when I got back home, I decided to give her a call. I thanked her for the flowers she had sent us. Then I asked if she'd like to come down for a visit. She accepted the invitation with undisguised pleasure. Leslie was excited that I had reached out to her and had invited her to the beach. I felt the call had been prompted by some signal act of grace received that day at Mass.

"Smooth move, Mom!" approved Morgan—using the vernacular of the day—when I told him about Leslie coming home.

"I am very happy for both of you," said my husband Bill, his eyes filling with tears.

My spirits were high throughout the week before Leslie's visit. I was anxious to tell her that I loved her. The shock of her divorce was wearing off. Excitedly, I prepared for her visit: planning menus, tidying the house, and putting flowers in her room.

My inner strength was growing. Life had been remarkably easy since my marriage in the '50s, until Leslie's divorce came into the picture. Now, I was reading my poetry to Bill before we went to sleep. I was no longer afraid of being unappreciated.

"It's beautiful! Keep writing," he said encouragingly as he moved closer to me in bed.

"Thank you," I said, pleased that he encouraged me in my creative pursuits. After setting the poetry aside and turning off the light, I snuggled contentedly down next to him.

Feeling energized, I set off to do some sketching the following morning. The old town of San Luis Rey was one of my favorite places. The main street, barely more than one block long, consisted of a dusty two-way road lined with pepper trees. There was one gas station with grimy pumps. The automotive repair shop, which was adjacent to the gas station, was littered with rusty parts. A good Mexican restaurant—I had tried it one time—graced one corner. And, set back from the road near the restaurant, was a cantina called "The Riverbottom."

I parked my boxy, blue and white Scout across the street from the cantina in front of an old one-storey house with a picket fence. After climbing up onto the hood of my car, I picked up my sketchpad and opened up a box of pastels I had brought with me. I worked on a sketch of an old shingled church with a steeple bell and a graveyard beside it dotted with white wooden crosses all tilted at odd angles. Then, I turned to sketch the cantina. Occasionally, I would stop to look toward the distant hills where cattle grazed in the warm summer sun. The tolling of the mission bells gave the surroundings an air of timeless serenity.

The serenity was broken when several inebriated men with beer cans in their hands emerged from the house near where I had parked. They headed in my direction, so I folded up my sketchpad, snapped shut my box of pastels, hopped down from the hood of my car, and drove away.

Driving down a highway lined with mini-malls, fast-food restaurants, motels, and gas stations, I saw a sign that read: "Benedictine Priory." Following the arrow on the sign, I found myself driving up a number of steep hills. When I reached the top, I saw a single-storey building reminiscent of 1950s suburbia. There was no sign of life, so I stayed in my car.

I had hoped to see a more monastic setting. In my imagination, I had envisioned a bell hanging next to the entrance with a rope that I could pull to announce my arrival. I saw gray arches graced by olive groves with monks silently praying their rosaries as they walked along the tidily raked gravel paths that separated the rows of trees.

Disappointed, I looked through the windshield at the valley below. I tried to imagine what it must have been like before the highway was built. In my mind's eye, I saw rolling green hills and pastures where cows and horses grazed. The green pastures were dotted with yellow bales of hay. A river snaked its way through the landscape and then disappeared into the sea. *This is what it must have been like when the Indians lived here,* I thought. The image of the Indian grinding bowl I had found on the beach one winter came to mind. I sat for a moment enjoying the view and then turned on the ignition. Leaving my pastoral world behind, I headed home.

When I got home, I changed into my swimsuit to swim with Bill, Morgan, and Jennie as the setting sun disappeared with a flash into the sea. The sky was streaked with red, yellow, orange, and purple.

I gathered my sketchpad and pastels and headed to my studio, where I worked on the sketch I had started of The Riverbottom cantina, which I planned to transfer to canvas later. My work was interrupted by Jennie, who came in with her hamster. Following close behind were Morgan and Damian. After each one of us kissed Jennie and her hamster goodnight, we got into a conversation about marriage, divorce, and life in general.

"I do feel a great deal of pain concerning Leslie's divorce. My belief in the sanctity of marriage explains why she never talked to me while she was making her decision. Living here at St. Lo has been an enormous adjustment for me. I was so far away when Leslie's problems surfaced. I felt left out," I said. "I need time to accept the changes."

"I hope I don't do something that is terribly wrong; I wouldn't want to be shut out of the family," Morgan commented.

The remark cut me like broken glass, although I knew that Morgan did not mean for it to have such an effect on me.

Then Damian piped up and said, "You have to let go of it," meaning the divorce. I changed the subject and started talking about my recent wedding anniversary.

"It has been twenty-nine years, and it all goes by like drifting smoke," I said. I had embraced married life completely and the security and comfort it provided me all those years. When I now tried to recall that life, it was all just a big blur.

~ ~ ~

During an early morning swim, the fish jumped out of the sea in front of me. Suddenly, I caught a glimpse of something that looked like a large black stick, poking straight up from the sea. *Jaws*?! I was back on the shore in a hurry. Damian was standing on the beach. I told him about the fish as I wrapped a towel around myself.

"They were probably leaping up just to look at you," he said, his face unsmiling.

"Thank you," I said. "That is very sweet, Damian."

Damian was preparing to leave St. Lo. Leslie was right when she remarked during a phone conversation that I would miss him when he was gone.

Walking home, I felt a sense of loneliness as I imagined the future without Damian. When I got home, I related the story about the fish to Morgan. His answer brought me back to the present: "Sometimes," he instructed, "fish jump out of the water when they are trying to get away from their predators."

I smiled at his very pragmatic explanation of the phenomenon.

~ ~ ~

The morning of Leslie's return, I was nervous, unsure of myself, afraid that I would become too critical, too pontifical, and would lack the forgiveness necessary to heal the wounds. I was hosing down the patio so that everything would look fresh when my daughter walked through the gate. The phone rang. I dropped the hose and went into the kitchen to pick up the phone.

"Hees," I announced, trying to hold on to the receiver with my wet hand.

It was Damian.

"Could you come down and say goodbye? My van is packed, jammed to the ceiling. If I have to make a sudden stop, I'm dead!" he said.

"Yes, I'll be down shortly," I replied. Returning to the patio, I finished watering, rolled up the hose, and went upstairs to put on some shoes.

Upstairs, I looked out the window and saw that Jane, Damian's mother, was still at his house. *Thank God*, I thought to myself. I pulled on my boots and left for Damian's house. When I got to his place, I noticed that Jane's car was no longer there.

"Where's your mother?" I asked Damian as I entered his home.

"Oh, she left," he replied, throwing his arms up in the air. He had a mischievous grin on his face.

I moved toward him slowly, saying, "Then I can say goodbye and thank you properly." My only intention was to embrace him, kiss him, and express in words my thanks for the painting lessons and for the sense of self-worth he helped me regain. But, he held my hand and didn't let go. Then he spun me around, and my inhibitions fell away. I claimed for myself the joy and the awe I felt in his presence.

He kissed me passionately and tenderly, and then he led me to his bedroom. There, he lifted me onto his bed and looked at me like a little boy. I reached out for him, and he came closer.

Our clothes came off piece by piece, but, to this day, I'm not sure how that happened. There we were: naked, with nothing to separate us. I think we were surprised by the wonder of it all, and yes, how peaceful and inevitable the moment seemed.

~ ~ ~

When Leslie arrived, we spent the weekend totally at ease, and at peace with each other. After my daughter left, life went on as usual, the sun rose and set, the tides were high, or low, and lightning did not strike me dead.

I expected to face guilt, shame, and remorse, but felt none of those emotions. I did ask for forgiveness, but in my prayer I said, "Thank you for the gift of Damian." After all, He could read my heart.

My momentary fall from grace did not change the love I had and would always feel for my husband. Before my involvement with Damian, it was very clear to me how deeply Bill loved me.

On the day we argued about the letter I had written to Leslie (the one I ended up tearing up and throwing away in anger), Bill said to me, "Why don't you have an affair with Damian? It would be good for you."

Both puzzled and hurt by his suggestion, I slapped him.

"Please don't, Berta," he responded, grabbing me by the arms. "You're breaking my heart."

"Do you dislike me that much?" I asked.

"No, I *love* you that much! I want you to be happy again. The changes in our lives have left you confused and depressed," he replied.

So, when the time was right, Bill's remarks helped me to remove the final barriers of my reserve. Did he think I was already involved with Damian? I didn't ask. Neither did I tell him later that I had been unfaithful. It did occur to me, however, that I never did anything without someone's permission.

Good can come from our mistakes, I discovered. Before Leslie's divorce, I thought there was something wrong with divorced persons. Father Mark had corrected me when he said, "You mustn't think of your daughter as a bad person."

Forgiveness was the lesson I learned from Leslie's divorce, which shattered my Victorian view of life. From my interlude with Damian, I came a step closer to understanding with compassion the complexities of human relationships.

~ ~ ~

Leslie gave her father and me a rare weekend alone. She took Jennie to town to celebrate Riley's fifth birthday. That July weekend, Bill and I shared the familiar summer rituals. On the beach, there was always a game of volleyball going on until sundown. Kites flew above the cabana. The tennis and paddle courts were always in use. Bill painted the wooden gates leading into the central patio while I painted on canvas up in my studio. Those two days were leisurely and easy. Bill and I were tender and affectionate with one another.

In late July, we celebrated Bill's fifty-third birthday. He was in great shape: slim, handsome, and nicely bronzed from spending time outdoors. We were all optimistic and high on life as we honored what would be his final birthday. The children and I decided to give him a special gift in keeping with his more relaxed approach to life: a bright red moped, which he secretly adored. Bill usually never bought anything for himself, so it was always a pleasure for us to give him a gift.

At first he thought the gift was extravagant, but the moped actually turned out to be a very practical means of transportation for getting around the streets of St. Lo. Instead of using his car, he would use the moped to run errands or for quick runs to the tennis courts for a game. Sometimes, with Jennie sitting behind him, he explored the back roads around town with his shiny new wheels.

At the end of the month, Leslie returned to the beach after a visit with my mother (her grandmother), Jean. During their visit, Leslie explained to Mimi (the name all my children called their grandmother) the reasons for her divorce. The conversation had gone well. What a relief for Leslie, as their relationship had never been especially nurturing.

Leslie's relationship with my mother mirrored my own. Mother cared, but she was critical to the extreme. My sister and I never quite measured up to her standards of behavior. Differences of opinion were unwelcome.

"Just get on with it" or "That's not up to snuff" were phrases that my sister and I would often hear. Her admonishment to "sit up straight, dear" was responsible for my excellent posture—while my more rebellious sister slumped in her chair on purpose. My mother started to make my sister Jeannette wear shoulder braces. Mother, born and raised during the reign of Queen Victoria in England, was only passing on what she had learned from her harsh upbringing. Queen Victoria didn't die; she was alive and well in our house.

The remaining days of July were marked by minor revelations. For example, one day, while my son Morgan was sitting on the beach and looking up at the house, he thought, *How beautiful*, as if seeing it for the first time.

"Interesting that you should say that," I said to him. "Not too long ago, I found myself wandering around all the rooms of the house and feeling a similar connection to our home."

Were we looking at our lovely home for the last time? I wondered. *Had God opened our eyes for just a moment to imprint in our hearts and minds the image of the place we loved so much, the place that was the setting for the joy we experienced as a family for so many years?*

Leslie's divorce continued to be a topic of discussion among our friends and neighbors in St. Lo. Divorce, drugs, and casual sex were all the major topics of everyday conversation. Some residents saw these themes as a product of the revolutionary '60s. Real tragedy had already struck those families who had lost a child to drugs. At the same time, there were parents who questioned their own lives. Had they missed out on the freedom their children now claimed as their right?

~ ~ ~

My son-in-law Paul came to see me, and the visits brought up painful topics of conversation. Nonetheless, it was important for us to clarify to each other that there was no one to blame. The divorce never changed my feelings for this sweet and gentle man.

"What happened to your marriage, Paul?" I asked him during his first visit.

"Leslie wasn't happy, and I want her to be happy," he said.

"Do you love her, Paul," I asked.

"Yes, and that is why we decided to get divorced. I just want her to be happy," he repeated.

I was upset to discover that he still loved Leslie. We were sitting on the sofa in the living room as we talked, and his presence in my home felt natural and comforting.

"I'm extremely sorry, Paul. I can see that you are depressed. Please come to see me whenever you're in St. Lo," I suggested. I didn't want to lose touch with him.

The divorce never changed my love for Paul one bit. He had played a significant role in the life of my daughter and was the father of my first grandchild. You can't simply erase such people from your heart.

~ ~ ~

That summer, hurricane Dolores raged through St. Lo. I was swimming, totally unaware that a hurricane was about to hit. Enormous waves pounded the shore, ripping up rocks and sand, throwing everything, including me, into collision with the waves. I thrashed around trying to free my feet, which were tangled up in seaweed. I got pulled down by the undertow as well. Eventually, a huge wave lifted me up and threw me face down onto the beach. I got up and ran to safety. The hurricane foreshadowed the turmoil I was to experience in my life for a very long time to come. Every time I came up for air, I would be sucked down again by the magnitude of the events that were yet to unfold.

~ ~ ~

Just as Bill and I were beginning to calmly resign ourselves to Leslie's divorce, she jarred us with her announcement in early August that she planned to move away from California to Sun Valley, Idaho. Riley would be going with her. Bill and I expressed to one another how deeply disappointed we were by her decision.

"It's too jet-setty for Leslie," explained her father.

"I'll miss Riley," I said.

We fell into silent resignation. We both slept fitfully and became irritable with one another. I stayed in the house, retreating to my hammock for hours. Up there on my balcony, wrapped in my cocoon, I wrote and listened to the voices of the passersby rising from the streets below. I felt I was *in* the world, but not *of* it.

Voices rose up from the tennis courts, bringing me out of my reverie. The comments made me laugh.

"Sorry I missed that," someone shouted to his opponent. "I'm having trouble with my forehand."

Whoosh, plop–silence–and then, "Golly, I'm having trouble with my backhand, too!"

Leslie and I continued to communicate by phone. She spoke honestly and movingly about a recent encounter with her ex-husband. Naturally, he was upset, knowing that his daughter would now be living far away.

"I put my arms around him," she said. "That'll be the last time I'll have to play mother." Leslie had resented having to play the role of mother to her husband during their marriage. She did reassure him that he could have Riley whenever she was not in school, all summer long, and at Christmas, if he liked. She also told him that she never regretted marrying him.

Speaking with me about her decision to leave the state was another matter.

"Sometimes I am filled with nausea and fear. It is such a big move," she explained. "I'm not ashamed of my divorce, Mother, but I am through playing the game of the gay divorcee. No more frizzy hair or false nails!"

About a week after our telephone talks, Leslie showed up unannounced to say her goodbyes. Together, we tucked Jennie into bed. And then, after dinner on the terrace, we sat in the living room and talked. A white, diffused light filled the room. It was very calming.

Before Leslie spoke, she gave me two gifts: the beautiful old painting of the Virgin and the porcelain statue of the Christ Child. Both had been expensive gifts from her non-Catholic mother-in-law, who, at the time, must have chosen them as an expression of her love for Leslie. I accepted the gifts knowing that it was a heartfelt gesture from my daughter.

Leslie showed me pictures of her new home and shared her apprehension about embarking on a new life. She had obvious concerns for her daughter's welfare. When she told me how her pediatrician had assured her that little Riley would be all right emotionally, I saw the tension disappear from her face. She looked beautiful, serene.

The following morning, after a leisurely swim together, Leslie and I hugged each other and returned to our lives. I would not see her again until after Bill's death.

Chapter 5

ON MY OWN

The room is as you left it; your last touch—
A thoughtless pressure, knowing not itself
As saintly—hallows now each simple thing;
Hallows and glorifies, and glows between
The dust's grey fingers like a shielded light.

—Edna St. Vincent Millay, "Interim"

Chapter 5

The skies turned gray, rain drenched the landscape, and the sea was full of big globs of black tar. The street dance, which was held on the road below our home, signaled the end of the season, the end of eight difficult months for Bill and me. We joined the other residents of St. Lo to dance with one another, with our children, and with our friends. However, the festivities did not cheer me up, and Bill retreated to our home as quickly as possible. After he left the dance, I looked up at the house and was surprised to see how dark and unfriendly it seemed. Bill had turned off all of the exterior lights and closed the doors leading from the terrace to the living room. He had drawn the curtains as well. Typically, our house was illuminated during a party, with doors and drapes left open to welcome family and friends. Feeling put off by his behavior, I wondered, *What is the matter with Bill?* On the following day, I spoke to Charles about the incident. Charles reassured me when he said, "He wasn't shutting you out, he was shutting himself in."

With my husband's permission, and giving myself permission as well, I took the train north for a weekend alone. I needed some time away to lick my emotional wounds. Before I left, friends offered some unsolicited comments and advice. "You won't like being alone," one forthright friend told me.

I did feel rather lonesome when I first stepped off the train, but, after renting a car and checking into the hotel, the loneliness disappeared. As suggested by friends, I phoned restaurants ahead of time to ask for a corner table. That way I avoided the discomfort of being seen dining alone in the middle of the room. Another friend had advised me to go shopping to allay my "inevitable boredom." But I found a better solution: I spent the weekend sketching the coast. Then I visited the natural history museum and zoo and browsed through the local art museum, where I signed up for a tour of private collections. The tour included an introduction to a professor from the art department of the local university. When the tour group arrived at her home, she showed us her studio, explained her work, and, with good humor, spoke about her recently failed marriage.

"He was like the Armenian," she began. "When asked why he kept his lamp under his bed, he replied, 'It's my lamp, and I can do what I want with it.' Unfortunately, this was the attitude he had towards me."

During the train ride home, I chuckled to myself when I remembered her remark. The woman across the aisle tapped me on the shoulder and asked me what I was reading. She saw the book in my lap.

"Oh," I said, somewhat startled because I thought she may have caught me laughing to myself. "I'm reading Virginia Woolf's *A Room of One's Own*."

"I read it long ago," she remarked. "Perhaps I should read it again. It applies to today's woman, don't you think?"

I opened the book and began to read until the blue-eyed young woman with dark curly hair who was sitting next to me picked up the conversation again.

"I'm running away from my foster home," she said, fixing her blue eyes on me. "My father's a Hell's Angel. He's in his forties, so I think he's probably settling down by now. I'm going to try and find him. Do you like my necklace, by the way?" She fingered the copper chain with a copper horse-head pendant that she wore around her graceful neck.

"Yes. Do you like horses?" I asked her.

"Oh, very much," she answered. "I used to ride them when I was little. My mother taught me until I was taken away from her. My mom has a drug habit. She has three other children by three different men. I don't know where the other kids are."

"How old are you?" I asked.

"Sixteen," she replied. "I'm going to live with my aunt in Hollywood. I think I'll be a model. Is there really a Hollywood sign?"

"Yes. But you should finish school first before starting a career."

"Oh, I will. I'm a good student. Math is my favorite subject," she concluded, and then turned to look out the window for a while.

I was reminded of the addict in the coffee shop at St. Lo. It left me wondering for a moment why perfect strangers struck up conversations with me, why they found me so accessible.

~ ~ ~

Bill met me at the train station near our seaside home.

"Your train is late!" he snapped when I stepped down from the train car.

I was about to apologize until I realized that it wasn't necessary. Obviously, it wasn't my fault that the train was late. Inwardly, I smiled at my growing strength.

Venturing out alone for the first time in my life, I had managed just fine on my own and enjoyed the trip. Years later, I would see that small journey as a preparation for the longer journey yet to come.

Fall arrived, and the crisp air and clear skies reminded me of the mornings when I began to work with Damian. A year had passed, and I missed our quiet conversations and the laughter. I felt wistful.

Damian returned to the beach from time to time, and I worked with him occasionally. One day, he said, "I miss you." His brush never stopped moving across the canvas. There was no need for a reply. The silence that enveloped us spoke of our deep feelings for each other. Some time later, I reminisced about that moment by writing a poem I called "Farewell."

> *Last year I was merry,*
> *This year I am mellow*
> *Has youth finally flown,*
> *Or was it that fellow?*
> *Was it that fellow*
> *Now packed up and gone . . .*

~ ~ ~

On Christmas morning, Morgan observed: "There is no Christmas spirit around here." It was a sign that the family had changed.

Bill, Jennie, and I went to Mexico for New Year's. We rented a house in Baja. While there, we witnessed spectacular sunsets from the roof. In the morning, lying in bed, Bill and I enjoyed watching the gold-red rays of sunrise as they crept across the carpet of our bedroom overlooking the sea. During the day, Bill and Jennie explored the tide pools for hours while I sketched. We took delight in the charm and simplicity of our environment. I remember how twelve to fifteen cats would battle for position as Jennie set out a saucer of milk on the front porch every morning.

On New Year's Eve, I prepared a special dinner, Bill made a fire, and Jennie decorated the living room with red, yellow, and blue streamers. By the light of the fire, candles, and stars, we enjoyed a quiet celebration that included a toast to what we hoped would be a better year for our family.

The next day as we packed our bags, I felt eager to go home. We had experienced some pleasant moments during our short vacation, but a gentle languor had begun to set in.

When we returned home, I found newspapers piled up at the gate, a cold house in disarray, unwashed dishes in the sink, and Jennie's pet bird dead in its cage.

My mother and uncle had planned to stay at the house in our absence, and I had arranged for a housekeeper to help them with the upkeep. I discovered, to my dismay, that my mother had sent the housekeeper away, locked up the house, and left. This was so typical of my mother's angry behavior. I surmised that she was probably furious at being left behind. I bit my tongue and cleaned up the house, internalizing my anger about the dead bird. It was not an auspicious beginning for the New Year.

I resumed my art classes and then decided to take a week off for prayer and meditation. As a result of my spiritual retreat, I felt prompted to sit down with Bill and talk about our relationship. When I asked him if he was happy in our marriage, he replied, "I haven't always been happy, but I've been content." I thought that was a very good answer. He told me that he believed he had been a better father than a husband because he felt "more comfortable with the children." Then he added, "Sometimes you annoy the hell out of me," and I replied that I felt the same about him. However, we agreed that we always loved each other and that the best of times were when the children were born and were growing up. We affirmed the positive role that each of us had played as parents and agreed to view as a normal part of life any future challenges that would present themselves within the family. Now, it was time to build something new for ourselves. It was time to fall in love again as mature adults.

Then the autumn rains came. The lagoon overflowed, flooding houses, streets, and tennis courts. Damian had returned to finish Jennie's portrait and to work in privacy for a short time. A friend telephoned to tell me that Damian's studio got flooded. "He wants you to come," he said.

I went to help Damian rescue his work. I took his ruined pastels to the sink, watching as the colors ran down the drain along with hours, days, even months of hard work. My heart ached at the thought of all of those wasted hours. But Damian just stood there laughing. Soon I was laughing with him as we jokingly made plans to create an underwater exhibit.

A few weeks later, I watched the furniture being removed from Damian's house—his mother was redecorating after the rains. I watched the rooms where I had spent so many happy hours become totally transformed. This coincided with my internal "redecorating." By pursuing projects outside the structure of family life, I acquired new strengths.

When the rains subsided, I emerged from the post-holiday blues. I slowly came back to life again, as I put behind me the events of the previous year and turned my attention to painting, writing, and spiritual studies. As a way of including Bill in my creative pursuits, I would ask him to comment on my work from time to time. Still, he needed his own creative outlet.

Bill enjoyed spending time in his workshop. When I heard about the wood carving class, I suggested that he enroll along with another member of our community.

"I'll think about it," he said.

To encourage him, I bought him a wood carving set and a small volume of instructions. They remained untouched on his workbench for several weeks, and then he slowly began to experiment with the tools.

As for me, I no longer worked with Damian and now filled the time with life-drawing classes at a nearby college.

Bill and I slowly settled into a life changed by the move to the beach and by Leslie's divorce. We were moving into our middle years like two horses getting used to a harness, so it was really all right that we weren't always in step.

I expected the middle years to be pleasant and comfortable, but we don't always get what we expect. One sunny day in March, Bill slipped away from me forever. With a final sigh, he vanished from my life. Without a goodbye, without a kiss, a touch, a whispered warning, sweet William had completed his journey in life at the age of fifty-three.

"It's very nice," were his last words. Life with Bill had been far beyond just nice. I had been blessed with a husband who was kind, intelligent, humble, and loving. He was my rock. Now I was left to drift like a boat without an anchor.

It is in the small tasks, the small changes that I really understood that I was a widow, that I was alone. Breakfast at 7:00 A.M., dinner at 8:00 P.M. had no meaning anymore. Bill's shirts in the laundry hamper would never make it to the laundry; the second set of towels in the bathroom had touched his skin for the last time; the pajamas hanging on the closet door had spent their last night in our bed. When a widow goes to sleep at night, she finds her bed too big for her. Once performed with joy and love, the daily chores now felt like a weighty cross that burdened the body and numbed the soul. There is another death, of sorts, that accompanies the loss of someone dear—your own.

~ ~ ~

After the funeral, the older children stayed on to help me put my affairs in order. We addressed the problem of my finances, as I now found myself without an income. This came as no surprise. I was aware that the money we had lived on had come from several trusts set up by Bill's parents and grandparents. Our children were the beneficiaries of the trusts. Consequently, I would have to sell the house in order to survive.

A few months before Bill's death, I pointed out to my children that, if anything happened to Bill, it would be necessary to sell the home we loved so much. Indeed, as we later discovered, he did not put his affairs in order before he died, so keeping the house was not an option. I remembered he once said to me in a weary voice, "You can do what you want with it after I'm gone. I've done the best I can." His words puzzled me. His statement implied I had a choice. Still, I could not believe that our home—the bastion of our lives where my children came to refresh their souls and where three generations of my husband's family had spent their summers—was now about to vanish from our lives.

Any decisions regarding the sale of the house would have to be postponed until the property was appraised. So, relieved for the time being, I stopped deliberating over the idea of leaving behind the home I loved so much.

In order to meet current expenses, I closed my savings account, applied for my widow's benefits, and invested the money collected from his life insurance, which would later be consumed by inheritance, death, and property taxes.

After a day battling deep depression, I awoke at three o'clock in the morning and had an apparition: I saw Bill standing at my bedside. He extended his hand. I sat up and reached out to take his hand in mine. So real! I felt flesh on flesh. The familiar warmth of his body, the smell of his hair left no doubt in my mind that he was really present. He smiled, but said nothing. Had he returned to bid me farewell?

Later that morning, I described the incident to my daughters. I told them that their father looked very happy. My daughters respectfully listened but made no comment.

~ ~ ~

Outside of settling my personal affairs, Jennie was my first concern. She was so stressed by the situation that her hair started to fall out, and she began demanding more of my attention. I tried to keep our lives as normal as possible by maintaining our routine. Still, if I went just a few houses away for dinner, she would phone and ask me to come home, crying, "It's too lonely here."

One time, while we were having breakfast in one of the small cafés we frequented, she pointed to a girl wearing a T-shirt with the number fifty-three printed on the front. "That's how old my daddy was when he died," she said as her brown eyes released a torrent of tears.

Picking Jennie up after school was now *my* job; those special afternoons she once shared with her father were gone forever. With downcast eyes, her lunch box banging against her knees, she would walk across the playing field to my waiting car. Then we would visit the yogurt parlor, just like she and her father used to do.

At night, I invited her to sleep in my bed. We comforted each other. Scattered across my pillows each night were math problems for me to solve, as well as poems and words of love that Jennie had written on scraps of paper. For a while, we continued our usual ritual of eating dinner by candlelight. But, as the weeks wore on, we found ourselves eating off trays in front of the television in our bathrobes.

After piecing together many clues, the children and I decided Bill had been aware that death was closing in on him. First, I found two sheets of yellow legal paper neatly tucked under the blotter on his desk. One sheet had a list of all the people I should contact in case of his death. The other had a list of personal items that he wanted to bequest to each child. In the pockets of his jogging suits were scraps of paper asking that I be notified "in case of an accident."

Because he died at home, an autopsy was performed. The coroner determined the cause of death to be advanced arteriosclerosis. I now understood why Bill had augmented his exercise program: he was attempting to free his clogged arteries. I remembered the time Bill collapsed in his office. (He recovered by the time I came to take him home.) He refused to see a doctor. The incident took place fifteen years before his death.

Bill's genetic inheritance made him susceptible to heart problems. Migraine headaches and high blood pressure plagued him throughout his life. During our last year together, I noticed several indications pointing to the fact that he knew his death was approaching. For example, one time at the dinner table, I had watched his eyes become teary whenever he looked at Jennie. When I bought him a new jacket, he commented that he would not live long enough to wear it out. He broke his front tooth and said, "I don't think it's worth getting fixed." Sometimes I greeted his remarks with amusement, thinking he was joking. He was not joking. He knew.

As he was without health insurance, Bill didn't want to put our finances at risk by having heart surgery. The cost of surgery would have necessitated a loan against the property. The property was to be my inheritance, and he wanted the property to be free and clear of debt. "I'll never be a burden on you" was his constant refrain throughout our marriage. But, such an operation could have saved his life.

Emotionally, Bill was guarded, immature and old-fashioned. He did not wish to burden me with the ordinary cares of life; I was the protected wife. After his death, my life became a personal and financial disaster. I would have to give up my home in order not to be financially dependent on my children.

The first week of May, Jennie and I were alone for the first time since Bill's death. Leslie moved away from California, Dana returned to her job in town, and the boys headed north to pursue their studies. I was invited to a wedding, and, though I was comforted by the presence of good friends, the fact that all of our friends were couples sharpened my sense of loss.

One evening, after going out to dinner together, Damian asked, "Are you all right?"

"People say I'm all right, so I guess I am," I replied. It was at that moment, however, that I realized how deeply exhausted I was from it all.

On Mother's Day, I was in town, so I decided to visit my mother. Inexplicably, she was so cold, so distant. I guess she was still punishing me for some imagined slight. When I couldn't take it anymore, I drove straight home, too tired to deal with my mother's inability to explain the cause of her anger.

When I came back home, the flowers and phone messages from my children brightened my heart. Little Jennie brought me lunch on a tray, a present too. (She was doing what her father would have done.) At bedtime, she fell apart. She cried out over and over again for her daddy. I sat on the bed and put my arms around her shoulders to comfort her. I realized that I was clutching a pair of theater tickets that Bill had purchased for us. It was too late to give them away, and I guess I probably never intended to because I was in denial, stubbornly refusing to accept the fact that we would never use them.

~ ~ ~

An event took place that would have a significant influence on my future. I missed an engagement with Sister Mary Wilfrid—the kind woman who had been responsible for helping establish the school my children attended through their formative years and who would become my spiritual director and loving friend during the unimaginably difficult years to come.

On that June day long ago, I left her stranded. We had made plans to share a meal at a friend's house. My forgetfulness upset and embarrassed me, but she forgave me.

Later, we had coffee together, and Sister spoke about Bill. "He had a sweet reserve," she said, referring to Bill. With those few words, she caught the essence of the man.

The following day, when Sister and I stood on the terrace together, I felt like a giant at five feet, eight-and-a-half inches next to Sister's four-foot-eleven-inch frame.

"It's very contemplative here," she smiled, enjoying the beauty of the terrace.

"I know, I know," I replied. "My soul expands every time I step out here to take in the view." Continuing, I said, "I found notes in the pockets of Bill's jackets that said, 'Please notify Mrs. William R. Hees III in case of accident,' followed by our addresses here and in town. He used to jog in town and here at the beach. Do you think he knew he was going to die soon?" I inquired.

"He was love," she said, almost as if she were describing God.

"Why didn't he tell me?" I asked.

"He had the gift of true love," she said.

Yes, it was as simple as that. My husband bore his cross in silence in order to spare his family any unnecessary grief and expense. Sister Wilfrid's remark eased my sorrow and assuaged my anger. In the years to come, when I spoke with Sister about my husband, her words were always the same: "He was love."

~ ~ ~

I left the beach to spend a night with Bill's stepmother, Jo. She was much loved by my children, my husband, and me. She had brought a sense of stability to the family and had kept a steady hand on Bill's troubled father.

For my children, she was the grandmother who took them to two matinees in one afternoon, who always sent the "perfect" presents, taught them to ski, and loved them unconditionally.

I shared with Jo details about how my marriage had undergone many changes over the past several years.

"It was Bill's decision to move to the beach. I was happy in Pasadena, but his mind was made up. He became short-tempered, and at times he was impatient. And, he was overly attentive to his physical appearance. When I cleaned out the apartment in town, I discovered that he was also unfaithful. In fact, before his death, I confronted Bill about the newspapers I found in his apartment—the kind you can pick up at a checkout stand that carries ads offering sex for sale. A number of ads were circled in ink. He dismissed the whole thing by saying that it was just a curiosity for him. But his lovemaking became lustful. It wasn't tender and sweet anymore. Well, I guess he was a man facing death and grasping at life. I talked to our son Morgan about my suspicions."

"What did Morgan say," inquired Jo.

"He said that it was true. He found some things around the apartment when he occasionally stayed there that indicated Bill was seeing other women. Morgan defended his father, saying, 'After all, he was in that awful apartment, working in town, and away from the place he loved. Mom, today's society has affected men my father's age. Sex is thrown at them from everywhere; magazines, movies, television ads all promote casual sex. After almost thirty years of marriage, he was probably wondering if he had missed something.' I was dumbfounded by Morgan's explanation. His compassion for his father was a marvel," I concluded.

"So, Morgan didn't ask how you felt about his father's infidelity?" asked Jo.

"No. There was some indication of Bill's deteriorating heart. I saw the signs, and, at the same time, I guess I didn't see them. I usually gave him a book as a present because he enjoyed reading so much. At one point, he said to me, 'Don't give me any more books. I'll never get through them.' Usually he finished an entire book in one sitting, sometimes staying up till 3:00 or 4:00 A.M. But Bill refused to discuss any problems, even if I brought them to his attention," I explained.

"He was always that way, Berta," she answered. "It was impossible to find out what was going on in that sweet head. As for the physical problems, he was a sick man." Jo, a registered nurse, told me how similar Bill's condition was to that of his father in his final years. "Don't blame yourself for things you had no control over. Let it rest. Bill loved you, and you returned that love. He was content. He said so," Jo reassured me. Just the same, I didn't sleep well that night.

The following evening, I kissed Jo goodbye and drove to an art gallery where Damian's work was on exhibit. Damian was standing with his girl-friend at the entrance. I glanced at him and said hello, and then I slipped away to speak with my mother, who was beckoning me to come to her.

"There's a picture of you hanging here. Have you bought it?" a friend asked.

I turned toward the picture and saw the red sticker, indicating that the painting had been sold. The likeness was not a good one, but the picture had been intended only as a composition, not as a portrait. Damian had titled the work *The Sunbather*. Right next to it hung *The Lifeguard*, which was a portrait of my son Morgan. Jennie's two portraits were also on display. I recognized a small oil painting on which I had done the underpainting.

As I prepared to leave, Damian took my hand and led me back into the gallery to meet his teacher. Damian had spoken about his teacher so frequently during the time Damien and I had worked together that I felt I knew him. This man had influenced Damian's life as well as his work, so much so that his influence extended beyond Damian all the way to me. As the three of us conversed, Damian held my hand. I found it comforting.

When I went home, I sifted through mementos of my marriage. My thirtieth wedding anniversary went by without celebration. Father's Day followed, and it was marked by overwhelming sadness. On the radio that day, I heard the strains of *Daybreak*, and in my head I could hear Bill singing along as clearly as if he were in the room. Dana and Kevin were with me, but the fact that they were together as a couple emphasized my sense of loneliness. Leslie phoned, weeping over the loss of her father. To make matters worse, the geographical distance that separated us accentuated our grief.

Just before Dana left, I cried on her shoulder and thanked her for her support, her solace. The parting was extremely difficult. (She would soon be leaving California to live with Kevin in Santa Fe.) I remember how Dana broke down and wept uncontrollably as she waved goodbye, her anguished sweet face streaked with tears.

Morgan came home from university before Kevin and Dana left.

"I'll stay here this summer to be with Mom and Jennie," he said to Dana as he hugged her goodbye. His decision brought comfort to Jennie and me.

It was July, the anniversary of what would have been Bill's fifty-fourth birthday. I woke up in the early hours of the morning. A gray mist hung over St. Lo as I walked to the beach and placed daisies and roses on the water. Watching them drift away, I thought about how Bill and I had drifted apart, so far from all the beauty, goodness, and principles that were such a part of our life together.

Chapter 6

INTERMISSION

My life closed twice before its close;
It yet remains to see
If Immortality unveil
A third event for me

—Emily Dickenson

Chapter 6

My first year of widowhood was an emotional rollercoaster. Along with the profound grief I felt at the loss of my husband, at times I was overtaken by fear, rage, and insecurity. Often I would slip into a state of numbness, which deadened the pain and contributed to making me feel empty and disconnected from the outside world. But there were some bright times too. My sense of humor, my love of life began to bubble up to the surface.

Leslie came for a visit with her friend Vanessa. The two young women were in perpetual motion from the moment they arrived. They cooked, they cleaned, they did the grocery shopping, and they took me to the movies.

Before their visit, I enrolled in an intensive summer art course. I usually left the house early before anyone was up and returned exhausted in the evening. Vanessa and Leslie amused themselves in my absence. I regretted that Leslie and I had little time to talk privately.

Leslie's visit ended on a sour note when I overheard her talking to a friend on the phone. Her conversation was punctuated by profanity. The expressions—at that time, so widely accepted by her generation—shocked me, and I pointedly let her know that her language was offensive to me. I overreacted.

"How could you, Leslie?" I yelled in indignation. "I can't believe what I'm hearing!" But there was another reason for my strong reaction. Leslie was speaking to a married man with whom she had been involved, and I simply did not think it was proper for a woman to talk to a man that way. And it was even more disturbing to me that she involved herself with a married man. He wasn't much younger than her father. Furthermore, he and his wife and children were acquaintances of mine. I first met them in the '50s. However, I could not cast the first stone, considering my involvement with Damian.

"Welcome to the '80s, Mom," was my daughter's only comment.

When Leslie returned to her home, she phoned me. I could tell she had been crying. "I don't think I can come home again if that is the way it is going to be," she protested.

I thought back to the nineteen-year-old Leslie who had left my home to marry, to live happily ever after. I had a hard time adjusting to the new Leslie. Now, reshaping herself after the divorce, she decided to "let it all hang out."

~ ~ ~

I bumped into Damian early one morning as I was walking Sam, our dog. He looked puffy-eyed, disheveled, and was eating from a box of Doo-Dads.

"Like some?" he asked, thrusting the open carton in my direction.

"Not for breakfast," I replied. "Why are you eating that stuff now?"

"Because they were there," he replied in his nonchalant voice, the voice he used when you've asked a silly question. His directness always amused me. It was a quality I loved about him.

Damian showed up later that afternoon with Jennie's portraits, the ones that had been on display. At his request, I joined him for coffee in the garage. I sat in one of his mother's old chairs while he painted, and we caught up. Our conversation was like a stroll into the past, easy and comfortable like the chair I sat in.

The night before Damian left the beach, he came to my studio. I asked him to embrace me. I felt safe for the first time since Bill's death.

"I'm too old for you," I said with sadness, with regret.

"In years, perhaps, but not in spirit," he replied.

~ ~ ~

In the middle of a very warm August, my spirits sagged. Pierce, my lawyer, came to the house to discuss my financial future with my children. I stood on the same spot in the kitchen where Bill had died, and I prayed while Pierce and the children gathered on the terrace for their meeting.

After the meeting was over, Pierce said to me, "Dana began her comments by stating what her father wanted, which was to take care of you. I was deeply touched by Dana's remarks."

Pierce set up a trust to which the children would contribute on a monthly basis. In return, they would each receive an interest in the lot I owned, which was located below the hill where our house stood.

For a time, my circumstances appeared to be more secure. However, I made a promise to God, as people often do in similar situations: *If I sell my home, I vow to loosen my ties to all material things and to devote myself to my spiritual life.*

Shortly after the August meeting between the lawyer and my children, Jennie and I left for our first vacation alone. Martha—a strong, organized, and caring friend from Pasadena—had invited us to her lakeside home in Nevada. Unaccustomed to traveling without my husband, I felt insecure and apprehensive about the trip.

Upon landing in Reno, there was no sign of Martha. "I'll be there in my gray and white Bronco, Berta," she had said on the phone on the day before we left California.

I watched with increasing anxiety as all the other passengers from the plane left the air terminal. Jennie and I sat alone in the baking sun, waiting. I phoned Martha's home, but there was no answer. The bus for the lake was about to leave, so we climbed aboard. I wanted to be closer to our destination before nightfall. I told the bus driver at least three times where we were going. Sensing my uncertainty, he smiled and said, "I'll let you off at the lodge. It is not a scheduled stop, but you'll be closer to where you're headed."

The bus had only four other passengers, so Jennie chose a seat next to a window. After I sat down beside her, she plucked the straw hat from my head and placed it on her own. Then she peered up at me from beneath the brim, smiled, and settled back to watch the scenery. The gesture was so playful, I wanted to hug her. Instead, I leaned over and whispered in her ear, "This is the first of many adventures we'll have together." The words were as much for my own benefit as for hers. They gave me courage.

When we got to the lodge, I headed for the nearest phone. There was still no answer at Martha's house. It was 7 P.M., and Jennie was curled up on our luggage looking weary. She was one very tired little traveler.

"Do you have rooms available?" I asked the desk clerk.

"No, I'm afraid not," he replied.

"Do you know where this street is?" I inquired, showing him a slip of paper with Martha's address on it. He said he did not.

I walked over to Jennie and explained our situation: "We'll have to find a motel or take a cab to Martha's and hope someone will be there. What shall we do?"

The cab arrived, but the driver said he couldn't find the street on the map. "The dispatcher is looking," he said. I told him to head back toward an area we had passed when we were on the bus. Coincidentally, at the same time the dispatcher found the location, we pulled up in front of Martha's house.

A young woman was walking by with her children. I rolled down the window and asked her, "Do you know Martha?"

"Are you Berta?" she asked, and then, "Martha's in the hospital. Her husband is on the way up from L.A. He'll explain the circumstances. If the house is open, go inside and make yourselves comfortable. I'm just across the road if you need any help."

I ran to the front door and found it open. After dismissing the taxi driver, Jennie and I settled in, ate scrambled eggs, and then greeted Joe, Martha's husband, when he arrived. Before talking to Joe, I tucked tired Jennie into bed. Joe explained that Martha had fallen in the driveway while picking flowers for my room, had struck her head, and was in the hospital for observation. Joe and I sat in the living room discussing the situation. He said, "Martha and I want you and Jennie to stay. I'll leave with Martha and take her to L.A. when she is well enough to travel."

Jennie, Joe, and I went out for dinner the following night. I met Joe's parents and his sister before he left. His parents had a cabana on the shores of Lake Tahoe, and they invited Jennie and me to visit.

Though we missed Martha's presence, her vitality, Jennie and I stayed for a week. In the mornings, we walked to the lake through a meadow where horses grazed, where wildflowers grew, where squirrels and chipmunks played. We swam, picnicked, sunbathed, and were entertained by friends also on vacation in the area. In the evenings, we strolled along the streets, and I noticed the lighted interiors of neighboring homes as families gathered for dinner. On Friday night, the fathers came back from the city—much like it was at St. Lo—and I felt a deep, deep longing for the way things used to be, for the family life I used to know.

One night we drove Martha's jeep to the town where she had made a reservation for a dinner show. She had told me all about the dinner show during one of our visits to the hospital. When we got to our destination, the lights in the casino dazzled Jennie's eyes. Her excitement was palpable, even contagious! The evening became even more enjoyable when we were seated at a table with a group of teachers attending a convention. They showed immediate interest in Jennie's academic endeavors by asking her about her studies.

After dinner, when the star of the show sang *You and Me Against the World*, my daughter and I held hands. Then, Jennie turned to me and said, "I love you, Mommy," repeating the last line of the song.

There was a small graveyard surrounded by a white picket fence that Jennie and I passed on the way to the lake each day. One morning, we walked into the cemetery to read the headstones. On one of them were carved the lines of a poem. I read them aloud:

> *One by one earth's ties are broken*
> *As we see our love decay;*
> *And the hopes so fondly cherished*
> *Brighten but to pass away.*
> *One by one our hopes grow brighter,*
> *As we near the shining shore;*
> *For we know across the river,*
> *Wait the loved ones gone before.*
> *E.R.*
> *Died August 29, 1890*
> *Age: 63 years.*

Bill was only fifty-three, I thought. *Why did he have to die so young? We didn't get to finish our journey together.*

When we returned to St. Lo, it was September—time for Jennie to go back to school. I decided to go on a trip to the Southwest with a married couple who were neighbors and friends of the family. This journey, like all the journeys I would make in 1980, was freeing, frightening, exciting, lonely, adventurous, and one more step toward personal independence. Also, it gave me the opportunity to visit Dana in her new home and to talk and laugh as we hiked along golden paths covered with the leaves of quaking aspen trees.

In October, the cracks in the family trust began to appear. Some of the children were faithful about honoring the agreement, others were not. At times, I had to remind some of my children to send me my monthly check. This was so upsetting. As a result, my thoughts began to gravitate towards a vague plan, a plan that included selling the house.

Would it not be better to move further south, where Jennie could go to school, and I could pursue my art more seriously at a university? I thought. *Perhaps an apartment or condominium would be better. A smaller living space would require less upkeep, so we'd be free to pursue other interests.* I prayed for guidance.

Charles came for a visit, which helped to distract me. He kindly offered his assistance in ways large and small. He drove Jennie to her soccer games, and, together, we cleaned out Bill's closet and his dresser. I gave Charles the clothes he wanted, including the tweed jacket that Bill said he would never wear out. I found solace in that. After he left, Jennie and I got busy making plans to go to Northern California for Thanksgiving.

When we arrived in San Francisco, we were warmly greeted by my friends, Paul and Mary Louise. Staying with a family brought us in touch with the familiar, comforting sounds of a home that was full of life and functioning well. After giving me a sweet hug, my host went to watch "Little Lord Fauntleroy" on the television with Jennie. My hostess showed me upstairs to my room and left me to rest while she prepared dinner. I stretched out on the bed and listened to the sounds of their young son practicing for his next piano lesson. A foghorn sounded in the distance, and it made me feel as if I were a little boat safe and snug in a harbor.

I slept soundly that night.

When I woke up in the morning, my eyes scanned the room. The room had belonged to Helen and Anne, my friends' daughters. A toy lamb, worn from much hugging, slept soundly on a shelf, a tired leg dangling over the edge. A green frog, his pink tongue visible, stared at me with bulging eyes. There was a megaphone on a shelf with the word "Navajos" printed on the surface. I recognized it as a memento from the same school where my daughter Dana had been a "Cherokee." Schoolbooks, paper flowers, a photograph of my hosts' children running down the beach made everything seem as if time had come to a halt in that room. It also added to my increasing awareness of how swiftly life had changed. The girls, who had lived in this room years ago, were now grown up, living and working thousands of miles away.

Morgan and Katy, his sweetheart, were both attending university in the Bay Area. They came by in the late afternoon to pick up Jennie and me. Waving goodbye to our friends, we drove to Bill's home near Santa Cruz to celebrate Thanksgiving.

Bill's house overlooked Scotts Valley. The area was quiet and peaceful, far from the din of city life. Jennie and I spent our nights there sleeping on a waterbed, an experience that produced a great deal of laughter but little sleep. During that first year of widowhood, I slept in many a strange bed while visiting my children and friends. It left me feeling rootless and alienated.

Thanksgiving morning, we all gathered in the kitchen to prepare dinner. Bill had done all of the shopping and proudly pointed out that the turkey was fresh. The shy remark echoed his father's natural humility. It also tugged at my heart.

We left the turkey to roast in the oven and then drove to Big Basin, where we hiked through the redwoods, enjoying the towering trees, filtered light, and birdsong. It was like being in a grand cathedral.

By the time we returned home, we were ready for a feast—the exercise had whetted our appetites. We arranged ourselves on the floor of the den, dinner plates in hand, and watched an old movie depicting Hollywood's version of how the Pilgrims landed in America. Engrossed in the movie, we didn't notice Bill's absence as much as we would have if were sitting around a table to have a formal meal where there would have been an unoccupied chair at the head of the table.

While Morgan drove us back to San Francisco, my mind was a jumble of thoughts. I thought about the phone call from Leslie and Dana, which had made the holiday complete. I also thought about Bill's response when I suggested that I might sell the house. ("Go for it, Mom!" he had said supportively.) And then I shut my eyes and replayed the past few days: images of the boys playing catch with Jennie on the lawn, of Katy bent over her homework, and of me walking through the morning mist and getting lost. I remembered how, during this walk, I had stopped in the middle of the road and burst into tears, wondering where my old life had gone and what was to become of me in the future.

Early in December, when I happened to be in town, I decided to attend another exhibit of Damian's work. Only a few blocks from the gallery in Westwood, Bill and I had made our wedding vows in a small, intimate, mission-style church more than thirty years earlier. The sweet little church was gone, replaced by an enormous, cold, charmless edifice. Sitting in those strange surroundings, listening to the Mass in another church, made me feel as if part of my past had vanished and that my future was uncertain.

~ ~ ~

On December 21, Morgan, Jennie, and I went to a small airport in L.A. It was five o'clock in the morning as we prepared to board a plane that would fly us to Leslie's home in Idaho for a Christmas reunion with the entire family. It was dark and drizzling out, and the runway lights looked blue, blurred, and jewel-like.

Cody, the pilot, greeted us with a warm smile as we boarded the blue, white, and silver jet. "You're eager to go," he said as we strapped ourselves in. After reaching cruising altitude, the co-pilot served us hot chocolate and donuts. I was settling down to read the paper when the co-pilot appeared and asked me if I would like to go up front. Thrilled at the invitation, I made my way quickly to the cockpit.

The pilot motioned toward the co-pilot's seat, and I sat down to watch the sunrise. The colors on my palette at home paled in comparison to what

I saw before me. Oranges, reds, yellows, transparent yet luminous whites emerged from an inky, indigo blue sky.

"Yes!" I exclaimed when the pilot asked me if I would like to fly the plane, my sight still blinded by the morning sun. After a few careful instructions, I flew the plane on its wobbly course. Then, I lowered the nose and pulled it up again at the pilot's request.

Re-entering the cabin after my solo flight, I said to my children, "I was flying the plane!"

"We could tell, Mom," laughed Morgan as he looked at me and then at Jennie. They rolled their eyes at each other.

My heart almost stopped as we prepared for landing at the airport near Sun Valley, Idaho, which was surrounded by tall mountain peaks. We dove nose down into the valley, and then, at the last minute, pulled up the nose of the plane and touched down. The plane screeched to an abrupt stop. I was so excited as we disembarked the plane and stepped into the cold and snowy landscape that was now Leslie's new home.

Leslie greeted us, smiling her brightest smile and holding a bouquet of wildflowers. She was accompanied by my granddaughter Riley, Dana, and Leslie's boss, Dee.

"I hope you had a nice trip," said Dee.

"It was great fun. Thank you for sending the plane to bring us out here," I replied.

We jammed ourselves into a waiting car and then "pop!" the cork flew out of a champagne bottle, which was then passed around to everyone. Though it was very festive, we didn't need champagne to make us happy; it was enough to be reunited as a family again.

As we crossed the bridge into town, Leslie commented, "The mother of several small children was killed here last Christmas. She hit a patch of black ice."

"Oh, what a tragedy," I said.

The house I stayed in belonged to a boyfriend of Leslie's. I was to meet him later: a tall, blonde, handsome, sweet man who loved my daughter and little Riley. Initially, I had mixed feelings about staying in a house that belonged to Leslie's boyfriend, though the house was certainly very comfortable and the rent was acceptable, considering my finances.

The arrangement was that Jennie and Riley would stay with me. Leslie's condo was already overflowing with guests: Dana, Kevin, Morgan, and Bill. At my place, we would have a comfortable area in which to gather and celebrate the holidays.

In the living room, stood a tall fir tree waiting to be decorated, the refrigerator was stocked with food, and I found a pewter vase in which to put my wildflowers. I placed the vase of flowers on the mantle where they were illuminated by the winter light pouring in from a large picture window. They looked good enough to paint. I did end up painting them in pastels.

In spite of the beauty around me, in spite of everyone's efforts, including my own, the holidays were painful. Grieving is a process. Each stage of shock, anger, and depression will eventually bring acceptance. However, the road to acceptance is a very bumpy one. My behavior was normal and crazy all at the same time. Instead of feeling closer to my children, I felt isolated and disconnected, removed from their youthful concerns.

Leslie was busy working much of the time, but, as Christmas approached, she took some time to invite me into her new life. I visited her at work, met her friends, and saw her new home for the first time. In her home, she displayed photographs of me everywhere, along with all of the gifts I had made for her over the years, which made me aware of how deeply she cared for me.

How sad, how painful it must have been for her after the divorce, and now her father's death, I thought. The visual reminders of how much she loved me made me feel unworthy, humble. I had been too slow to understand the motivations for her divorce and too slow to forgive her for it. Bill's death should have brought us closer together, and I came to the realization that there was much we could and should have shared.

It was snowing on Christmas Eve. Jennie and Riley sat quietly beside me at Mass. The church was intimate, lovely with its Gothic-style stained-glass windows, open-beamed ceilings, and dark wood. Red poinsettias were arranged in a cluster around the altar, and candlelight alone lit the interior of the church.

The priest walked past the congregation toward the altar. He was surrounded by children dressed as angels and shepherds singing *Silent Night*.

I watched the snow falling silently outside the stained-glass windows and looked around for my older children. Although we had not discussed it, I assumed they would attend Mass on this first Christmas since their father's death. When it was evident that they weren't coming, I started to cry, deeply disappointed that they couldn't or wouldn't share the moment with me.

Riley, Jennie, and I walked home through the falling snow. We stopped in front of a store window and looked at the toys left behind for next Christmas. They looked so forlorn, except for the ballerina doll dressed in a silver and white tutu that stood on one toe as she went round and round on a turntable. She looked alive and expectant, like the three of us.

When we got home, we knocked on the door. Riley, Jennie, and I prepared a surprise for anyone who happened to open the door that evening, which, in this case, turned out to be Morgan. As the snow fell, we held hands, and sang *Silent Night* to Morgan. Tears ran down his cheeks, and he hugged each of us in turn. At least, it was some sort of acknowledgement that the pain of this first Christmas without Bill was very deep for me. Why weren't the children more solicitous and understanding?

On Christmas morning, after opening our presents, the family drove into the countryside for some cross-country skiing. Being a novice, I ventured out on my own, following tracks laid down by other skiers. There were only two sounds to break the stillness: first, the occasional plop of snow as the heavy laden, dark green branches gave up their burdens; and then, a skier gliding past me in the opposite direction, who nodded his head, smiled, and cried out, "Merry Christmas!"

That evening, I was tired from my physical exertion, menopausal, and angry because I felt so alone and left out. Small things upset me. There was a chorus of "nos" when I wanted to hang up Bill's Christmas stocking on Christmas Eve. I didn't understand why not one of my children, except for Jennie, had attended Mass with me. At dinner, I became sullen and silent. In the morning, I flew into a tirade. "Can't someone put their arms around me and tell me that it's okay?!" I yelled.

Tired of my mood swings, Leslie left the house, taking Jennie and Riley with her. All alone, I again pleaded for someone, anyone, to put his or her arms around me, to love me, to tell me everything would be all right. My outburst helped to relieve my mounting tension, and I suddenly felt much better.

With the passing of Christmas, some of the tensions disappeared. We went to a lovely restaurant for dinner. My children's faces were radiant, and it was a joy to watch them laughing and enjoying themselves. To add to our joy, a friend of Leslie's poked his head around the corner of our booth to offer a cheery greeting: "Hi! I just wanted to see all of you having a good time."

Leslie had introduced me to the dark, handsome flirtatious young man when he came to visit at the house I was staying in. "So, this is Mom," he had said when Leslie introduced us.

The following day, he picked me up for breakfast. We drove in his pickup truck to a local café. The café was a warm and cozy refuge from the snow and cold. After we ordered our bacon and eggs, it was confession time again as I listened to his story.

"I'm looking for a more spiritual life," he began. "Leslie said that you are a Catholic."

The waitress served our food, and, as we ate, he explained his search for God. Recently, the search had taken him to a Norwegian hilltop with his girlfriend. He had left her there, without a goodbye. I smiled in amusement as I imagined some lovely creature sitting in the ice and snow, still waiting for a word from our Creator about when her boyfriend might be back to retrieve her.

After that breakfast, the passing of the holiday, and the joyful dinner with my children, I began to feel stronger and more at home. So, I decided to take Jennie and Riley skiing on the snow bunny slopes. We laughed and fell down a lot!

Feeling adventurous, I took the little girls to the lodge at the bottom of the slopes and enrolled them in a beginner's ski class. I signed up for some private lessons.

"You'll love Jean-Pierre. We all love him," said the girl behind the desk at the lodge as she handed me my lift tickets.

"I hope so," I replied with a smile and then walked to the slopes to meet my instructor.

Jean-Pierre was fifty-seven, a charming French Canadian with a kind smile and gentle manners. It didn't take us long to discover that we had much in common. Both of us were recently widowed and grieving. He revealed to me that his wife was the woman who was killed on the bridge—the one who Leslie had mentioned while we were driving in from the airport. His wife had left him with three young boys.

I had a few lessons with Jean-Pierre and found that I really enjoyed his company. We had in common the recent loss of our spouses. I had just turned fifty, and Jean-Pierre was close to my age.

One afternoon, he asked me to meet him for a drink. Morgan drove me to my engagement. "I never thought I'd be driving my Mom to meet a date," he said with unconcealed amusement. I kissed him on the cheek, hopped out of the Jeep, and, after entering the Lodge, I got cold feet, but not from walking in the snow! The ladies room was a great place to hide while I sorted out what to talk about on a date. What does one talk about when one hasn't dated for thirty years? Eventually, I made it to the Duchin room, or the "Doo-dah" lounge, as the locals called it.

Jean-Pierre was waiting for me in the lounge, sitting with a friend, a rancher who had four nearly grown daughters. I joined the two of them, and, at one point, the conversation turned to child rearing. That was a subject I could sink my teeth into. I began to relax.

"My parents were tolerant of me, so I am tolerant of my little girls," said Jean-Pierre's friend. "It helps to have a sense of humor when it comes to raising your children," he laughed.

It was sound advice but, regrettably, not the approach I took with my children. "I just wish I hadn't taken parenting so seriously," I said to Jean-Pierre. "When a major problem arose with one of my children, I usually overreacted."

My date with Jean-Pierre was very pleasant. He talked about his three young children, their mother, whom he dearly loved, and how difficult it was to support them, to give them the time and the love they needed.

Leaving the lodge in his pickup truck, we drove to a nearby ice rink to pick up one of his sons from hockey practice. I waited in the truck while Jean-Pierre went inside to find his son.

I greeted the boy as he climbed in the truck and sat beside me. He was about nine or ten and totally adorable. His pale skin was dotted with freckles. Dark lashes framed his blue eyes.

Jean-Pierre dropped me off at home.

"I'll see you on the slopes tomorrow," I said.

While the children went cross-country skiing, I continued my downhill ski lessons with Jean-Pierre. Each day, I improved, but not without incident.

After coming off the ski lift one morning, I stayed in a crouched position, with ski poles tucked under my arms, and skied straight down the slopes. As I picked up speed, Jean-Pierre came to me and pulled my body up, adjusting my form.

"That position is for downhill racers only," he laughed.

Another time, I hit a patch of ice and fell down on my tailbone with such a thud that my teeth clenched. *Oh, my spine!* I thought to myself, but I continued skiing downhill anyway.

Calmly and gently, Jean-Pierre taught me how to ski.

"We're taking the lift to the very top this morning," Jean-Pierre informed me one day.

It was my luck that the lift broke down as we were a quarter of the way up Dollar Mountain.

"Have you ever gotten off one of these things by sliding down a rope?" he asked.

"No," I replied, as I looked down at the snow far, far below.

"You'll be fine," he said, and smiled his gracious smile. I smiled back. It was nice to have someone taking care of me.

The ski lift suddenly jerked back to life, and took us to the top of the mountain. The view from up there was spectacular. The mountain ranges stretched across the entire horizon. As I started to ski downhill, I immediately fell two or three times.

"It's okay. We'll just get all that stuff out of the way," Jean-Pierre said patiently with an understanding smile on his face.

Then I got into the rhythm of skiing.

"You ski just like my wife," he told me one day as I gracefully made my way down the mountain.

After a few lessons, we started feeling very comfortable with each other.

"Would you like to have a drink with me this evening?" he proposed. "I'll pick you up at your house."

"Yes, that would be lovely." I accepted the invitation and went home to prepare for my second date with Jean-Pierre.

We went to a quiet Western-style bar where everyone knew Jean-Pierre. We shared stimulating conversation over a few drinks, and he ended up asking me to come home with him.

"I don't know, Jean-Pierre. You might like me better with my clothes on. I've had a mastectomy," I said.

"As a matter of fact, dear one, I am not a breast man. I prefer the derriere," he assured me, in his soft French accent.

At his home, I met the woman who was taking care of his children. They spoke in French for a while, and then she looked at me and said, "Très jolie." I was too embarrassed to even say "Merci."

The children said "Goodnight, Papa" to their father, and retired to their rooms.

"You must be hungry," said Jean-Pierre. While I sat at the dining-room table, he scrambled some eggs, fried bacon, and made some toast. It was delicious, and I loved the feeling of being in a home again.

I stayed until early morning, having slept with my ski instructor.

"Oh my God, Mom, not your ski instructor!" was Leslie's remark concerning my little adventure. I suppose it seemed like such a cliché to her.

My son Bill, on the other hand, was supportive. He even drove me to Jean-Pierre's place for our New Year's Eve rendezvous, and, as I left the car, Bill said, "Have a wonderful evening, Mom."

I turned to wave at him as I walked through the snow toward the house. He was smiling an encouraging smile.

That night, after Jean-Pierre and I made love, he whispered, "I'll take you home now or in the morning. I have to work tomorrow, so I need my sleep."

At first, I felt that I wanted to stay with him, but then I had a change of heart. I wanted to wake up in my own bed, in my own surroundings.

I looked toward the dresser at the foot of the bed. Lovingly arranged on top of the dresser were pictures of his wife and their adorable children. Rosaries hung on the framed mirror.

"I want to go home now," I told him. I think the rosaries over the mirror had something to do with my decision. I felt I had strayed.

Before the memory of that moment slipped away, I came to think of our interlude as just two people caught in inexpressible sorrow who had come together to comfort each other.

Jean-Pierre's last words to me were: "Here is my phone number. I know you probably won't phone me when you get home, but, if you need to talk to someone, I'll be glad to listen."

~ ~ ~

The holidays behind us, Jennie and Morgan flew home with me. I was a woman on the verge of making a major life change. I now seriously considered selling the lower lot, renting out the house for a year, and living in a room or a small apartment further south. This would give me time to see how I felt about selling the house. The family trust needed time to go into effect as well. I was still calling to remind some of the children to deposit their checks.

The winter months were almost over. The early morning sun filled the room as I awoke each day. A small statue of the Virgin Mary on the dresser cast a shadow that moved across the room and eventually faded. That was the earthly explanation concerning the shadow, but, for me, the shadow was a comforting sign from God as Lent and the first anniversary of Bill's death approached.

Prior to the first anniversary of Bill's death, Leslie came home to tell me that she was leaving Idaho to live in California again, and Damian told me he was leaving to paint in India and, with luck, to travel to other parts of the world.

When Jennie was out of school, we left for town to stay with my mother for a while.

One evening, while Jennie played cards with my uncle, I sat by the fire with my mother and told her about all my feelings and about all my experiences since Bill's death. She was very receptive, comforting, and very kind. In the morning, she brought tea and toast to my bedroom. I think she liked being a mother again, and I liked being someone's child, at least for the time being.

Soon after the visit with my mother, I had to face the burden of some large and unexpected expenses. I found out that I owed an additional year's taxes on the house. Moreover, the offices of J.P. Morgan in New York called to tell me that more taxes were due on the trusts.

I turned to the children for help, explaining that the taxes owing on the trust were their responsibility since they were the benefactors. The situation was disagreeable for everyone, including me, and it heightened my anxiety.

One day, as I searched for an equitable solution, I walked by the refrigerator and yanked the Lenten calendar off the door. I looked at the picture of Jesus and told Him in no uncertain terms what I thought of Him. It was an amazing relief! Feeling better, I retrieved my Lenten reading, C.S. Lewis's *A Grief Observed*, from the living room, returned to the kitchen, and sat in my rocking chair. As I rocked furiously, I prayed with fervor until I was jerked back to reality when the phone rang. It was my lawyer.

"I have good news," he told me.

The government owed me money on estate taxes already paid. The refund was not taxable and had accumulated interest. Also, the court had made me Jennie's conservator, and those funds were now released to me so that I could cover her expenses.

Another stroke of good fortune came my way. I received a phone call informing me that my house was rented for August and that the tenant was given the option of leasing it for a year.

I was on a lucky streak! A good friend, Victoria—never to be forgotten by me or God—came by and handed me a check for $35,000, to be repaid without interest whenever possible. I couldn't believe Jesus had answered my angry prayers so swiftly, and, of course, I remembered to thank Him for his generous support.

~ ~ ~

It rained almost constantly that March, but, on March 23 (the anniversary of Bill's death), the rains stopped.

I was feeling more optimistic about life.

Jennie, dressed in green overalls and a yellow shirt, accompanied me as I walked to the beach, carrying daisies and roses in hand. We made our way across the gray rocks just as we had done a year ago, and then threw the flowers, one by one, into the sea. Finally, at peace with death, we stood at the edge of the water in silent remembrance of dear Bill.

At Easter, I decided to visit Aunt Alice in town while Jennie visited Dana in Santa Fe, New Mexico. I was looking forward to my trip to Europe with my friend Esther, who was recently widowed. She had invited me to accompany her and other members of her family. I accepted. Dana had already sent me a few small going-away gifts. "Bon voyage and love," she wrote in the note that accompanied them.

After a week apart, Jennie and I hooked up in Pasadena after a party for the trip home. On the way, the car had a flat tire, which turned out to be an omen: I would soon find out that my next journey would be a very different kind of journey—paralysis.

Chapter 7

PARALYSIS

It is not the beginning of the end;
it is not the end of the beginning,
but it is the beginning of a new beginning.

—Sir Winston Churchill

Chapter 7

The week after I returned home from my visit with Aunt Alice in Pasadena, I was so absorbed in thoughts about the future and about my normal routine that I ignored the buzzing of numbness in my right leg. On Sunday, I played tennis, occasionally stopping to rub my leg in an effort to minimize those annoying sensations. By Sunday evening, my body from the waist down felt as if it were encased in stone. Uncomfortable, but not alarmed, I walked down the hill to have dinner with friends. Just as dinner was ending, Jennie phoned and asked me to come home, so I thanked my hosts and walked up the hill to my house in the company of two elderly friends. One of them was unsteady on his feet from a combination of age and wine. I braced his back with both my hands. We laughed as we made our way up the hill. (When paralysis first rendered me helpless, we reminisced about that evening. "*I* should have been pushing *you*," he later remarked.)

Monday morning, my body felt more flexible, but, as I was driving Jennie to school, I couldn't feel the gas pedal, and that really frightened me. Tuesday morning, I drove Jennie to school again.

After returning home and showering, I went to the kitchen to prepare a cup of tea. As I stood at the stove, my right leg shuddered. About to lose my balance, I grabbed the edge of the kitchen counter. I didn't know what to do! Clinging to the counter, I made several attempts to stand on my right leg, but it would not support me. Leaning against the counter, with only my left leg supporting me, I managed to turn off the burner. I held on to the counter with both hands and hopped a few feet on my left leg until I reached the two steps leading down to the dining room. After bracing myself in the doorway, I then hopped down the two steps to the dining room. Hopping across the floor, I grabbed the banister next to the three steps leading to the living room. I then made my way to the sofa, where I collapsed. I picked up the phone from the coffee table and called my friends and neighbors, Don and Mary. They rushed over within minutes, and, after assessing my situation, Don said, "Berta, you belong in the hospital."

I stubbornly refused to leave the house until Bill arrived.

"I can't leave until Bill is here to stay with Jennie," I replied firmly. In response to my own words, I picked up the phone and called my son Bill.

"I'm on my way," was Bill's immediate response to my cry for help.

Having to come all the way from Northern California, he would be very late in arriving. In the meantime, I phoned the doctor, who rushed to my side and urged me to check into the hospital immediately.

"Oh dear!" I cried when now even my left leg shuddered and became immobile. Almost immediately after that, I felt warm urine streaming down between my legs.

"You definitely belong in the hospital," the doctor kept repeating.

"If you could carry me up to my room, I'd be more comfortable," I pleaded.

The doctor carried me up the stairs to my bedroom and placed me on my bed. After making me as comfortable as possible, he said, shaking his head, "I'm not happy leaving you here like this."

My choice to refuse hospitalization meant that I would have to make it through Tuesday night all on my own. Incontinence had become a serious problem as I waited for Bill to arrive. Unable to walk to the bathroom on my own, I phoned Larry, the guard on duty at the gate of the compound.

"Larry," I said, "I'm sick. Could you come over? I need help getting to the bathroom. Please don't be embarrassed by what you see here, just come."

He responded instantly to my phone call, carried me to the bathroom and then back to my bed. I thanked him and said, "Bill should be here soon."

As he left the room, that short, stocky, dark-haired ex-Marine turned toward me and said solemnly, "I want to help you and Jennie in any way I can."

I knew Larry meant what he said. He and two other guards, Larry and Mal, had watched Jennie grow up. When Jennie was very young, she would call out, "Hi, Mr. Guard," whenever she passed them on the road.

Soon, Bill arrived. His presence gave me some peace of mind and was a great comfort to Jennie. After greeting one another warmly—neither of us understanding what was happening—I asked him to run my bath.

"Perhaps warm water will help," I said as he gently put me into the tub. However, I was unable to brace myself with my legs, and I kept slipping under the water. After a few minutes, Bill lifted me out of the bath and set me on a small bench. The trunk of my body teetered unfamiliarly back and forth, so I gripped the edges of the bench with both my hands. I could not feel the bench beneath me.

"Bill, Bill," I called out to my son, who was waiting for me in the bedroom. "Would you please put me back to bed? I'm losing my balance!"

I was confused and, for the first time, genuinely frightened. I had no understanding of the seriousness of my situation. Bill managed to get me back to bed.

"I've removed the sheets, Mom, and placed a layer of beach towels on the mattress," Bill said.

"I'll wrap them around my hips until morning. Th-thanks," I stammered.

I have no memory of seeing Jennie at that time. Bill took her to school in the morning after calling the doctor.

The doctor came by that morning. He stood at the foot of my bed looking sad and puzzled. "What is going on here? Your reflexes were fine when you came to my office a month or so ago complaining of some numbness in your right leg," he said.

The doctor phoned the paramedics. When they arrived, they stood at my bedroom doorway for a while, trying to figure out how they would get me down the stairs to the patio. They gave up on the idea of using a stretcher and carried me down the steep and curving stairs in a blanket. In my blanket-hammock, I swayed to and fro across the brick patio. I thought, *I'm leaving my home in the same way my husband did.* The image of his body being carried out on the swaying stretcher came to mind.

On the way to the hospital, I laughed and joked with the paramedics. I had no idea how serious my condition was at the time. At the hospital,

I calmly filled out the admittance forms and, smiling, handed them to a staff member.

"We're going to X-ray your spine," said a male technician who was standing nearby. He wheeled me down a corridor and into a room where I was lifted onto an X-ray table. As the tilt of the table was changed during the procedure, my legs spasmed and flopped from one side to the other.

I was shocked to find that I needed assistance to turn my body from side to side. The technician also had to line up my hips with my upper torso. When my body lay flat on the table, the technician tilted the table until I could see my legs. All sensory feeling in my legs had vanished.

My eyes widened in terror at the sight of my legs splayed out in odd positions like a rag doll. Urine was running down the table and soaking my white robe. I wasn't smiling anymore.

After I was X-rayed, I was taken to a room with two beds and hooked up to an intravenous unit that dripped steroids into my veins. My abdomen became enormously swollen with bodily fluids, and the pain was comparable to a continuous shock treatment that rose from my feet to my diaphragm. Due to risk of infection, the doctor didn't catheterize me. To make things worse, I had to endure the entire day without painkillers. Meanwhile, the paralysis crept toward my chest.

When my mother and my uncle, Phil, came to the hospital, she went into her familiar routine of telling anyone who would listen—particularly the doctor and nurses—that she was a doctor's widow and knew more than they did about my care. Whenever I was hospitalized, she presented herself in this way, creating bad feelings among the staff and unnecessary anxiety for me. My apologizing for her behavior sapped what little energy I had.

I sent my uncle out into the hall to pry my mother away from one of the nurses. Then I told her, "Please, Mother, mind your own business." She sat down next to my bed. She was tight-lipped and angry, so I reached for her hand, and, after I let her know that I wanted the comfort of her presence, she visibly softened.

However, in a pitiful plea for attention, she started talking about the cataracts on her eyes. Then, when a new nurse came on duty and remarked, after looking at my chart, "You look about thirty-eight years old!"

My mother, hoping to elicit a similar compliment about her age, sat erect in her chair, her eyes sparkling, and announced, "I'm eighty-four years old." The nurse looked at me and winked. I then asked my mother to leave.

That evening, the doctor told me, "Your paralysis could be permanent." I didn't cry out. All I felt was confusion and disbelief. He looked at the nurse standing by my bed, and, as he patted my arm, he said to the nurse, "Take care of this very nice lady." He left the room without telling me what was wrong. The diagnosis would eventually be multiple sclerosis. That diagnosis didn't stick, however, as the doctors became increasingly baffled over the next six years about the reason for my paralysis.

Helen, the nurse who remained by my bed, asked me about my last name. "Hees, that's a Dutch name, isn't it?" she said. "I'm from Holland," she explained as she bent over my bed, her round face shining, and took my hands in hers. Then, I broke down completely. Helen listened to me patiently as I spilled out the litany of recent events in my life.

I spoke of my husband's recent death. I spoke of my children, especially Jennie. Then, the nurse asked me if I had any faith. "Yes, I am a Catholic," I replied.

"So am I," she said. "I also know what it is like to lose a loving husband." She spoke of her children living in various parts of the world, but, "still close in spirit, as yours will be once they move away from home." She kissed my hand and left the room.

I drew back the curtain surrounding my bed and looked at Georgiana, the woman sharing the room with me. During the late morning and afternoon hours, we exchanged brief stories about our lives. She was young, chronically ill, and her entire life had been spent in and out of hospitals. I soon found out we were neighbors; from her apartment directly across the lagoon, she could see my house.

Georgiana's loving nature came from her parents. Each day, they came to the hospital to cheer up their only child. Georgiana's parents extended their love to me. Her mother plumped up my pillows, filled my water glass, brushed my hair, and cut up my meat at dinnertime. She performed gestures of kindness my own mother was incapable of.

"You might want to think about calling your son," said Georgiana.

"Should I tell him what the doctor said, or do you think that would be too hard for him to take?" I asked.

"No, you tell him the truth. It's time for someone to share your burden," she replied. Good advice from one so young at such a time.

When I phoned my son Bill and told him I was paralyzed, he came back with "I know," which indicated to me that the doctor must have informed him earlier. I asked to speak to Jennie, and, oh, when I heard her voice, my heart melted. I wished I could have reached through the phone to hug her.

A friend, who had been with my son that day, later told me that Bill, after our brief conversation together, had left the house to visit with his friend, John, probably because he missed his father and needed someone to talk to.

During the night, I was transferred to intensive care. As an orderly wheeled my bed down the hall, the Dutch nurse ran alongside, holding my hand and praying with me. We began in unison, "Hail Mary, full of grace . . ."

And then, this loud cry broke the quiet of the hospital corridor. "Oh, no, please, please no!" It was my own voice, but it seemed to originate from some distant source.

I was taken to a dark, somber room. My bed faced an alcove several feet from the foot of my bed. I could see the night nurse working at her desk. Her lamp was the only light, except for the green blips on a machine that was monitoring my vital signs and the red lights that flashed signals from other wires attached to my body.

The pain was so severe I couldn't sleep. After moaning for hours and repeatedly asking for help, the doctor finally came and administered a small dose of Demerol. As I fixed my gaze on the green blips, the tension in my body went away along with the pain, and I drifted off to sleep.

When Bill came to visit the next morning, I grabbed the bar that hung above my bed, pulled myself up and greeted him with a cheery "Hello," as if it were just any other ordinary day. Then, the paramedics came by and hoisted me into another van for another ride to another hospital, to another room.

That room was directly across form the nurses' station. It had a glass wall through which they could watch me and my blips. When the doctor decided my condition had stabilized, they moved me to a regular hospital room.

This time I was alone. If I turned my head to the left, I could see the skyline over the coast. It was a beautiful spring day. The clear blue sky was dotted with white puffy clouds. If I were home, would I be walking the dog on the beach, tending the spring flowers on the terrace, or just daydreaming? Turning my eyes away from the view, I realized that I might never do those things again. An ache tore through my chest and settled in my heart. The unceasing physical pain now had a constant companion: the emotional pain of fear, depression and despair. My new journey had begun.

It was May, the month dedicated to the Virgin Mary, and I felt my faith strengthen. All of a sudden, I recognized this new crucible in my life as a spiritual journey; there was no other explanation for it in my mind. *He has captured me for Himself,* I thought. The Christ I believed in had not caused my affliction, but allowed it to happen to me for a reason. Therefore, He would lead me through these circumstances without my falling far from his sight and grace. Oh, I might lose sight of Him from time to time, but He never abandoned *me*. With the eventual loss of my home, the mortification of the flesh, I was free to follow Christ.

"Come, follow me," I heard again and again in my head.

"But what about Jennie? You can't take her mother away too?" I murmured, fearing the possibility of death. I began to sob.

To believe in a spiritual journey is one thing, to live it is quite another. I would lose sight of my path many, many, many times under the yoke of helplessness, loneliness, fear, anger, and pain. I would not understand the depth of my sorrow for a very long time.

Because I was unable to fully grasp the severity of my affliction, my spirits remained high during the first weeks of my illness. I firmly believed that my condition was temporary and that my paralysis would leave just as swiftly as it came. I reasoned that I had already suffered enough from the loss of my husband, my daughter's divorce, and my bout with cancer.

Over and over I would say aloud, "He can't take so much away without giving something back."

I made friends with several of the nurses, but I grew especially fond of Charlene. She was a young black woman married to a Marine Corps medic. Because she worked the nightshift, we had time to get acquainted after her other patients settled in for the night. She shared pictures of her family members—who were from Alabama—with me. I was moved by the love and the joy I saw captured in their faces. I envied Charlene because she had such a close-knit family. After my father died at the age of seventy-five—I was fourteen—my family consisted of only my mother, my sister, my Uncle Phil, and Aunt Peggy. Phil and Peggy had no children, so I didn't have any cousins. After marrying Bill, I suspect I created the family that I longed for by giving birth to five children. Charlene talked me through many difficult moments.

One night, after I went through an especially challenging day, she drew the curtains around my bed and encouraged me to "let it all out." I grieved for myself, for my family, for the wreckage of my life. Afterward, Charlene bathed me, changed the sheets, replaced the catheter, and promised to care for Jennie on her day off if needed. Then she put her arms around me, put her cheek against my cheek, and said, "I love you." Her compassion was healing. I fell asleep cradled in the arms of a beautiful angel.

That night, as Charlene cleaned me up, I looked closely at my body, which now seemed so unfamiliar to me. "That good, strong, body," as a friend had once described it. Yes, that body that now was covered with flesh that had turned a waxy yellow; that body that now felt nothing to the touch yet internally was wracked with pain; that body that was incapable of movement, except for the involuntary spasms. I felt betrayed. Only a short time ago, that good, strong body had been walking briskly, confidently through life.

After a few weeks, I was able to sit up in a chair with help from the staff—it was supposed to be good for the circulatory system even though the blood pooled in my feet. This small accomplishment gave me a false sense of progress.

One day, as I was sitting in a chair, my blood pressure dropped. Nauseated, clammy, and sweaty, I reached out my hand in an effort to greet a visitor, and I suddenly fainted. My upper body slumped forward and down to my knees. After an orderly laid me back down on the bed, I became conscious again. Then, the nurse brought me a glass of orange juice to boost my blood sugar level. The visitor fled, never to return—a reaction I would have to adjust to over the years. A serious illness reminds people of their own mortality.

Every day, friends came to visit and express their love and compassion. The visits from my children and my husband's relatives brought me the most joy.

Leslie—now home from Idaho—along with Dana and Jo Hees, came to visit me. They brought me flowers, cheese sandwiches, and fruit. They washed and brushed my waist-long hair.

I laughed for the first time since my hospitalization when Aunt Alice brought me a bed jacket. "Practically new," she declared as she slipped it around my shoulders. "I've never worn it." Alice was both thoughtful and prudent where money was concerned.

Together we discussed the tragedies that had befallen Bill's family. A few days after her visit, she phoned to say, "I'm praying for you." Alice was not at all religious, so I found the remark rather unexpected. But I appreciated the sentiment all the same.

Jennie made her first visit to the hospital accompanied by her brother Bill. I noticed how pale she looked as she hugged me. They both informed me they were managing just fine at home. Bill told me he was enjoying making repairs around the house, and Jennie said she was looking forward to summer vacation.

Dr. Katz, the psychiatrist from rehab, showed up during their visit. He asked me many questions about my house and suggested how it might be made more functional to accommodate my condition. All my answers were negative. Living in that house, with all of its stairways, would be unmanageable for me now. I began to cry.

Bill, seeing my depression, commented, "I'm a carpenter. I can fix anything she needs."

The changes to the house would be costly, and I had no idea how I would come up with the money to cover the construction expenses. I already had plenty to worry about: my medical bills! (I was uninsured at the time, waiting for a new policy to be approved.)

"You're covered, Berta," Dennis, my insurance broker, assured me. "You had cancer eight years ago, so that shouldn't be an issue." That was such good news! However, before I signed the papers, I became paralyzed. The following day my policy was cancelled.

I shared my worries about my financial situation with Dana. A day or so later, Dana came to see me at the hospital, accompanied by my neighbor, Don. Together, they worked out a plan to sell my lot if and when that became necessary.

My spiritual life continued to be nourished by a lay minister who came to the hospital each day. He brought me Communion.

The Sacrament of the Sick is a blessing for possible healing. As was requested by Mary Jane, a friend from Pasadena who was ill with cancer, the sacrament was administered by a local diocesan priest.

Monsignor Brady, the head of my parish and Jennie's school, brought me letters written by the children in her class. Some of their parents came in person to say, "Not to worry, just get well. We are all praying for you." I would close my eyes to visualize an ascending cloud of prayers rising toward Heaven. Determined to recover, I hung onto every spiritual act. When I learned about the assassination attempt on the Pope, it felt to me that we had been shot down together, in a sense.

"All right, God, the Pope and I can both get well together," I said out loud. Determined to recover, it seemed like a reasonable demand.

Physical therapy began with range-of-motion exercises—that meant bending and stretching each leg at the knee, then pulling the entire leg out to the side and back in line with the body. Occasionally, I sat on the edge of the bed trying to stabilize myself, but I had no balance and would fall over backwards.

My state of mind was directly affected by my physical condition. I would sink into depression if I was not well rested or if I was suffering from bladder infections or bedsores. The only way I could deal with this was by writing in my journal. As soon as the pen hit the paper, the anxiety melted away. On the days I was free from such afflictions, I felt at peace, eager to get myself back on my feet.

I was sitting in a chair trying to eat my dinner when Dr. Katz came to talk to me about my move to Duane Rehab Center. The subject of being institutionalized made me ill. I wanted to go home. I was returned to my bed feeling sick, angry, anxious, and I wanted to cry. I waited for the night to fall.

The dark and quiet night became my friend. When the other patients on my floor were settled into bed, the lights were extinguished, with the exception of a light at the nurses' station. I put on the earphones of the Walkman that Leslie had given me, and I listened to the tapes that had accompanied the gift. I particularly enjoyed Barry Manilow. The darkness and the music were my only refuge from the agonies of the day. I didn't even feel bothered when the orderlies came every four hours to turn my body over in order to prevent bedsores. As I fell asleep, I was only dimly aware of their flashlights, their whispering voices in that dark, safe place.

Just before I was moved to rehab, my mother began to interfere again by prevailing upon another doctor to move me down the coast to Memorial Hospital. The next day, I received a call from that same doctor, who told me, "I would be happy to see you, but you are already in good hands where you are, and I think moving you to a new hospital and then again to rehab would only add to your distress." I agreed with him that it would be too much for me. "Yes," he said, "I tried to explain that to your mother."

Before hanging up, I spoke to the doctor's nurse, Valerie. She said, "Your mother means well, but she is rather difficult."

The next day, Valerie phoned to tell me that my mother had accepted my decision. There was a pause, and then Valerie said, "Mrs. Hees, your mother sent me the biggest bouquet of flowers I have ever seen."

"Valerie, it's my mother's way of apologizing for being so difficult," I explained.

On a Thursday morning, I was transferred by ambulance to Duane Rehab. The ambulance took me past the places that were a beautiful part of my life for a brief period of time. From the rear windows of the ambulance, I could see my home. It looked lonely standing there on the hill. The joy of family life no longer filled its rooms. Where was our dog, Sam? Where was Thomas, the cat? Were they wondering where everyone had gone?

I saw the road I had walked with Damian the dreadful morning Leslie phoned me to say she was divorcing Paul. The road was empty. Did Damian know about what had happened to me? No, he was far away in some distant land.

Wiping the tears from my eyes, I looked out the window to my right. There, above the freeway, stood St. Patrick's School, the school that Jennie was attending. Was she sitting in her classroom at that moment unaware that her mother was going by? I waved at her.

Still crying, I saw, through the blur of tears, the lagoon where the family went water-skiing together. I recalled that I had sketched out there not so long ago.

All gone, all gone, I whispered to myself. Those precious moments had slipped away as quickly as the views from the ambulance. Yes, it was sad, but the saddest sight of all was that of my daughter Dana who was driving my blue and white Scout behind the ambulance. Because she was alone in the car, I waved and smiled at her to give her courage. Every now and then, Dana had trouble keeping up with the ambulance. When she caught up and came into view again, I noticed that her lovely face looked tense and vulnerable. At the age of twenty-six, her fine-boned face made her look almost like a very young girl. What was she thinking? Like me, she was probably wondering if this was really happening. I never loved her more than at that moment.

The attendant sitting next to me in the ambulance took my pulse. "Are you going to be all right?" he asked. "What happened?" After I explained about the onslaught of paralysis, he said, "I hope it isn't permanent. With your permission, I would like to pray for you."

I began to cry. The sun dried the tears on my face as the paramedics lifted me from the ambulance and onto the stretcher on the sidewalk in front of the rehab center. It was very, very hot.

As soon as I was settled in my room, I was besieged by one hospital staff person after another. The lady with the menus arrived first. *How could anyone think of food at a time like this?* I thought. I handed the menus back to her, assuring her I would eat whatever she chose for me. Various nurses checked my pulse, my blood pressure, took a urine sample, and manually emptied my bowels.

"Oh, you poor thing," said the nurse after the process was over. "You'll feel much better now."

Dr. Katz came to my room to see how I had survived the trip. Yes, I survived the trip, but I wasn't sure I was going to survive the arrival. It was bewildering; it was exhausting.

Evening had fallen by the time Dana had completed the task of filling out forms and settling my belongings. She bent over to kiss me goodbye, and I noticed how tired her delicate face looked.

After she left, I was filled with sorrow for Dana and her siblings. Guilt swept over me—an unreasonable guilt. I felt that I had brought misfortune to the family. Knowing that it wasn't really my fault didn't help me at all. I felt frightened, too keyed up to sleep. I called out for my husband throughout the night.

When morning came, the nurses tried to get me up by using a transfer board. My useless trunk muscles were unable to be of any assistance. The nurses lifted me into the wheelchair and steered me to the physical therapist's office.

I had an attack of vertigo before the interview with Dr. Sharp and the physical therapist. Once there, I was shown how to angle my wheelchair for transfer, how to move the footrest, how to remove the arm from the chair: all in preparation for the simple acts of standing up and sitting or lying down someplace else, acts I normally used to perform every day without thinking. Dizzy and tired, I fell out of my chair and onto a raised mat, at least halfway onto the mat. The physical therapist had to pick up my legs and swing them, along with my torso, into some sort of normal position on the mat. While on my back, the physical therapist asked me questions about function.

Function? What function? I began counting the losses of bodily functions that now plagued me as I was put through a series of tests. That morning I would discover that I could not raise my head while on my stomach; I could not sit up from a prone position; I could not roll from side to side, or turn over from my back to my stomach or vice versa; I could not manage a strong cough, because my diaphragm was weak.

"I can't do this," I raged, as they wheeled me back to my bed.

Hell on earth had begun.

Chapter 8

REHAB

*I have learned to love despair
and the futility of human
arrangements*

—Lord Byron

Chapter 8

On my second day back at rehab, Dana, Jennie, and Morgan (who was home from U.C. Berkeley) came over to share dinner with me. When they arrived, I was crying because they had lost so much—their father, their home, and a once active and highly involved mother.

Members of the staff had strapped me around my waist after putting me into my wheelchair and pushed me to the dining room. At the table, I looked at my children with bewilderment, as if to say, "What has happened to me?" Then I looked at the dinner on my plate—a gelatinous gray mass of chicken. And then, in spite of my restraints, my muscles failed me, and I fell facedown into my dinner. I began to sob.

The following day, Morgan returned to visit me in another room where I would remain until I was released. I took comfort in looking at the dear objects he brought and lovingly arranged on my bookcase. Morgan had brought me a beautiful yellow rose in a bud vase that he placed on the bookcase shelf next to my books on Degas and Seurat and some family pictures. On my nightstand, he had placed new tapes, a letter, a chocolate bar, and a cheese sandwich. Certainly, cheese sandwiches were not good for my digestion. Still, I recall that one of the better moments I had in rehab was when, in the quiet of the night, I enjoyed a cheese sandwich and a small carton of orange juice that the nurse had brought at bedtime. From the ceiling, Morgan had hung a cloud mobile one of the nurses had stitched for me at the hospital. Later that night, I watched it twisting and turning as I listened to Barry Manilow on the Walkman while enjoying my forbidden treat—my delicious cheese sandwich—in privacy.

In the drawer of the nightstand, I kept my correspondence, my rosary, a book entitled *Woman Before God*, a Walkman with tapes, and, on a shelf below, my journal.

The other patients emerging from the bathrooms brought home to me the realization that this simple, daily task would never again be quite so simple for me anymore. I was wearing an indwelling catheter, and the bag hanging by my bed was emptied when necessary. My bowels never moved even though I took laxatives, drank lots of water, and ate a balanced diet. (Too many cheese sandwiches perhaps?) It became impossible to manage eating three meals a day. Without the message from my brain getting through to my intestines, elimination was drastically hampered. Consequently, my abdomen became bloated. The staff tried to get me to use a bedpan, but, without the use of my upper body muscles, it was very difficult to balance in a sitting position. The effort used up what little energy I had available to me, so the nurse had to manually empty my bowels, and, like the catheter, it was an even more invasive procedure. Then there were the times I was lifted onto a portable toilet chair next to my bed. I suppose they were hoping gravity would serve me, but it didn't.

I had no trouble falling asleep, as it was a welcome escape. It was as comforting as when the orderlies at the hospital came to turn me every four hours. (I would easily fall back to sleep the moment they left.) These visitors in the night seemed like guardian angels rustling their wings.

Miz' Linn was the name of the woman in the bed nearest mine. She kept my spirits up during those first few days by sharing stories about her life, which took a difficult turn when she left home at sixteen.

"I was married seven times. I had a problem with my husbands always wanting me to mother them, and I wanted children, and they didn't," she explained. "I finally had two daughters with my seventh husband.

"I learned how to love, thanks to my mother," she continued. "She died when I was nine. I was her baby. And she was so good, so loving, so caring; I have passed that on to others."

Miz' Linn told me that she had always supported herself. "I have to laugh every time I read my horoscope," she said. "It always says, 'work hard.'" And how she laughed! Her cheeks were like ripe apples kissed by the sun, and her vibrant energy belied her seventy-plus years. She used every swear word known to man—and then some—but only in frustration at the crippling arthritis that had left an otherwise strong woman incapacitated.

When I was admitted to rehab, my lower back was covered with bedsores. The nurses kept yelling at me to stay off my bedsores. As yet, no one had explained the dangers of bedsores (which result from the loss of circulation caused by pressure). My fears, my tension, my anxiety were heightened each time I was told, "If you don't stay off the bedsores, they will be down to the bone!" The nurses' attitude seemed harsh. After all, what did I know about paralysis and the many other problems associated with that state? I felt like a child again, being punished by my mother for some inadvertent transgression of mine.

Each patient had an occupational therapist and a physical therapist (otherwise known as the O.T. and the P.T.) with whom they met twice a day. Our schedules were posted on a blackboard across from the reception desk. We were expected to show up on time and without assistance at meals and at our various therapy sessions.

I found it impossible to use the sliding board to get out of my bed, so the staff assisted me for a while until I learned to do it myself. I was a determined patient, so I learned rather quickly. My weakened upper body muscles made everything—sliding, pushing my chair, sitting up—extremely challenging, and the horrendous pain that coursed through my body from my diaphragm to my toes never left me—ever. (To this day, pain is my constant companion.)

A team of medical practitioners reevaluated my progress. The team was made up of an M.D., a psychiatrist, the O.T., the P.T., a social worker, and a nutritionist. I detested those meetings. Like my physical care, they were invasive, and I reacted to everyone's questions in a defensive manner. "Are you depressed," they would ask. "Oh, no, not me," was my usual answer to that question. At one of the meetings, I asked the psychiatrist if I could be excused from occupational therapy. Though he was concerned about my depression, he granted me permission to stay in bed and write instead of attending classes in arts and crafts.

Writing became my best medicine. Somehow, putting pen to paper helped minimize the emotional anguish, helped me forget the physical pain, and provided an outlet that would help me gain understanding about the unexpected turn my life had taken. I wrote about each new procedure I had to face.

~ ~ ~

I began to learn how to catheterize myself. Writing about the process somehow lessened the humiliation I experienced during that procedure.

"I have to catheterize myself every four hours to avoid urine accidents," I wrote in my journal. Because of the loss of sensation, it was not painful. My nervous system objected when I inserted the rubber tubing into the urethra. The preparation for catheterization was the most difficult part. My upper torso had to be supported by pillows, which I could not easily arrange behind my back on my own. My spastic legs refused to stay separated, and my knees would not stay bent. As I inserted the catheter, my legs would snap shut like a clam. If I was lucky enough to collect urine in a container, my efforts were often in vain, because the sudden jerking of my legs sent urine and Betadine—a dark brown antiseptic—flying everywhere.

I was told to keep trying to train my bladder. Pat, the night nurse, a good and patient teacher, showed me how to be as independent in my care as possible. "Yes," she said, "it is possible to control your bowels." Together, we looked at "how to" slides, and like a baby, I began to learn all over again the process of retraining this basic bodily function.

The spiritual side of my being was well looked after. A priest brought me Communion on Sundays. A friend attended daily Mass for two weeks, offering them up for my recovery. Many people sent me letters of intent—cards that inform you about who is saying prayers for you—to tell me novenas and rosaries were being said and Masses were being held for me around the clock. Those prayers succeeded in lifting me out of despair and provided a life preserver when I felt I was drowning. Years later, that safety net of prayers, rosaries, Masses, and the Holy Eucharist I received continued to support me.

During my time in rehab, there were lots of "firsts": the first time I slid down the board by myself from bed to wheelchair; the first time I slammed into the bar release of a heavy door in order to open it; the first time I learned to make a bed and set a table using mechanical devices for assistance; the first time I drove a car with hand controls and pulled my folded chair into the car to rest behind my driver's seat. I found all this maneuvering distasteful, demeaning, exhausting, and extremely painful.

The determination these maneuvers demanded of me was beyond the level to which I was accustomed.

The misfortunes in my life were piled so high I could no longer see over them. Mornings used to be my favorite time of day. Energized by a good night's sleep, I had once greeted each day as though something beautiful and new would happen. These days, in the mornings, my mind sustained a gallop but my body remained at the starting gate. The conflict brought frustration, tears, anger, and depression. Without the ability to balance myself, it was an ordeal to move my legs across the bed with my hands, to sit up, to slide into my chair, to brush my teeth, wash my face, brush my hair, and then wheel myself to P.T., where the ordeal of transferring began. Then I had to wheel myself down to another P.T. session and had to endure the whole process again. Then I performed more exercises to strengthen my upper body by tugging on various pulleys and squeezing them together across my chest.

The tall and graceful person I had been was gone. Oddly, the person I had become conflicted with the old images of myself that were still locked in my brain.

Who was I now? My spinal chord stretched like an archer's bow, pulling me to the right. My feet would fall off the footrests, and, since I lacked sensory perception, I would unwittingly run over them with the wheelchair. Intense spasms tore down my back, throwing me over like a Raggedy Ann doll. As I sat perfectly still in my wheelchair, my feet would beat a drum-like rhythm on the footrest. It felt like an elephant was bearing down on my back. The nerve pain from my lower diaphragm down to my toes was unceasing.

One day, confronting the seriousness of my illness for the first time, I asked the doctor, "Will I ever be well again?"

"Oh no, not at your age," Dr. Katz replied. I was fifty years old. His remark caused a determination, like that of my mother's, to well up inside of me.

I prayed to God for wrinkles and gray hair. *Please, Lord, let me skip the middle years. How about an easy death?* I pleaded. I wanted to disappear.

The weekends brought some peace. Free from therapy and with only half the staff on duty, I could visit uninterrupted with family and friends, read, write, ask the nurses to shampoo my hair, or simply stay in bed. Quite often, guests came over during lunch. On the one hand, I appreciated visitors, but, on the other hand, I was so self-conscious about the new me that I felt uncomfortable in front of people, especially my own children. When friends talked about their everyday cares, I felt disconnected from all of that. At best, I was a polite listener with a hollow laugh.

When my children came to see me, they tried to keep up a brave front. The sadness, the hopelessness, and the bewilderment they felt were obvious in their sighs. "Oh, Mom"—said in a despairing, sympathetic, not-knowing-what-to-do tone of voice—was an oft-heard utterance at the end of our visits. Emotionally and physically, I couldn't handle small talk.

Little by little, I felt more at ease in the rehab center as I adjusted to institutional life. The sights and sounds became a little less annoying, except when a semi-ambulatory patient rose from his or her chair to perform the everyday activity of going to the bathroom, something that I was no longer capable of. At mealtime, the older patients, afflicted with strokes, diabetes, or arthritis, were kind and encouraging. They passed me food, as my muscles no longer allowed me to reach. They cut up my food when necessary. Two hands are required to perform this task, and I needed one of mine to hold onto the arm of my chair for balance. At times, I tried to hide that handicap—mostly from myself—by not eating what I couldn't manage with a fork or spoon. Everyone smiled in spite of his or her various afflictions; everyone wept because of them. The young patients were no different in this regard, except that their conditions were generally not the result of illness or old age but incurred by motorcycle or automobile accidents.

There was a young quadriplegic—the victim of a motorcycle accident—staying across the hall from my room. In the two years since he had been in rehab, every square inch on the walls surrounding his bed had become papered with pictures of rock stars, and he had an extensive record collection that I usually enjoyed listening to except on those occasions when the volume was cranked up on his stereo.

On the evening of his twenty-first birthday party, the nurses closed the doors to our rooms. I could hear the laughter and the clinking of glasses. I could also detect a faint sweet smell wafting into my room.

"What is that?" I asked my roommate. She informed me that it was probably marijuana. My heart smiled, and I silently praised the staff for their compassion and courage. They could all have been dismissed if the administrator of the hospital had found out that they had permitted this.

I wanted to get well so I could be a proper parent to my children again. It pained me to think that my sensitive and compassionate children, born into a loving home, had such a burden put on them as a result of my illness. Most of them were still in school, and they had their whole lives ahead of them.

One evening, Leslie phoned from her home in Sun Valley, Idaho to say, "I am slipping into depression. So, I'm seeing a psychologist." Not two years since her divorce and only fifteen months since her father's death, the family structure no longer was the support system she once knew. However, youth being as resilient as it is, after many tears, she announced she had fallen in love with a man named Michael.

"Why are you so depressed then," I inquired.

"Because he is going through a divorce, and, until the divorce is final and a financial settlement is reached, we cannot be seen together," explained Leslie.

Dana and Kevin visited from their new home in Santa Fe, New Mexico. They had already been together for a few years and still were not married. I was never comfortable with the idea of my children choosing to live with their partners out of wedlock. But, at a time when Dana had a lot of responsibilities—still coming to California to care for Jennie and dealing with my finances and my home—I was glad she had Kevin for support.

She complained that her sister Leslie was not doing her fair share. I listened to her complaints, and then Kevin and Dana told me about two lectures they had attended put on by the Leakey Foundation, an organization my daughter had worked for after graduating with a degree in anthropology from university.

"The speakers kept scratching themselves and moving their arms about just like the primates they are studying!" said Dana. She parodied the gestures, and it made me laugh. With tongue in cheek, Dana, Kevin, and I concluded that another study should be funded to study the humans studying their subjects.

Before Dana and Kevin left that day, I added a photograph to my growing collection. It was a picture of an altar in a small adobe church where they had attended Mass on Easter Sunday.

Dana came back the next day with Jennie. I listened as Jennie read aloud some of the letters her classmates had written telling her to keep her spirits up. Dana took some photos of me on my bed. While the camera clicked away, I had an acute attack of "mental loneliness" (a phrase my friend Laura had used in her recent letter from Amsterdam to describe the sense of emotional isolation from family and friends). After hugging the girls goodbye, I saw them wave one more goodbye outside the window as they were leaving.

The last goodbye—for a while—was when Dana and Kevin showed up a few hours later. They were returning to New Mexico. I hugged my daughter many, many times before she stood in the doorway, waved, and was gone.

Then, soon after Dana left for New Mexico, Mother and Uncle Phil started dropping by to show their caring. Again, my mother sorrowfully tried to elicit sympathy for herself by drawing attention to her current ailment: a sprained ligament. I listened as she told me how hard it was for her to walk.

"Mother," I sighed, "I am paralyzed; I *know* what it's like not to be able to move."

Then, Charles arrived from New York to tell me his Dutch cousin, Pave, was coming from Amsterdam for a visit and that he was planning to take Pave to the Mission where Leslie had her wedding and where Charles had accompanied me to Mass on several occasions. His cousin was a Catholic who practiced his religion—unlike Charles, who had been baptized in the church but didn't care to go to Mass. The news that Charles would be attending Mass brought me joy. I thought perhaps my illness might bring those around me closer to God, especially troubled Charles, who was battling alcoholism. There was purpose here and hope in this moment.

Sister Wilfrid seated herself on a chair next to my bed wearing her dark blue veil, a few gray curls framing her face. Her tiny, aging, and ailing body was clad in a sensible dark-blue cardigan sweater and skirt. Her feet dangled above the floor. It appeared the two-hour ride from my old home town had not tired her in the least. She looked directly into my eyes with her steel-blue eyes and graced me with her usual large welcoming grin. Then she became serious. She reflected the trust that comes from living one's life close to God in the way she carried herself—her posture erect and strong, her demeanor calm and confident.

"I have lighted four blue vigil candles for you, and they will burn twenty-four hours a day," she said.

"Thank you, Sister," I replied.

This tiny woman, still sitting tall in her chair, addressed me directly with words I would hear over and over again, year after year: "I would take it all away if I could." In a way, the burden was slightly lifted because she carried the cross with me for the next eleven years until she died. And, even after her death, I knew I could ask for her intercession with Our Lord.

Sister Christina, Jennie's teacher, visited me the following day. She spoke not of Jennie, but about her own personal crisis. Sister was being transferred to Florida, and she did not want to go. "I love my students, and I love California, especially the coast." For a little over an hour, she shared her fears, her shifting moods, and her anxieties about the unknown in a life that was about to change for her.

The conversation was a precursor of things to come. For many years, I believed people came only to console me and to help me, and, although that was certainly true, I came to realize that they were also interested in sharing their own stories, which, once told to someone who was also suffering, became less heavy to bear.

The month of June brought with it doubts about my recovery. To seek comfort and understanding, I read my little book *Women Before God*. Opening it for the first time since entering rehab, I turned to a passage about having patience during illness—patience, a simple notion but not one I was well practiced in up to that moment. I ate life in big bites, as I might eat a chocolate chip cookie that I swallowed hurriedly while reaching for the next one.

To calm my fears, I slept with my rosary wrapped around my hand. Still, the thought of going home terrified me. Bill was dead, and my children were off living their own lives in various locales, except for ten-year-old Jennie. And I was supposed to look after her? I couldn't even look after myself. For many, many, nights, I asked God if, perhaps, He had made a horrible mistake.

For the patients in rehab, the fear of going back home was common. Some patients would return after a few weeks crying and depressed. My roommate Dorothy was among the returnees. She had sufficiently recovered from Guillain-Barre syndrome.

"When I first came to this place, the only way I could call the nurse was by pressing the button with my nose," she told me. After a year of rehabilitation, she had recovered from her paralysis enough to be able to move about with the aid of a walker. Watching her improve gave me renewed hope.

One day, shortly before she was discharged, I was very depressed, so she sat by my bed and said, "You have your arms and your mind. You can hear, see, touch, and smell. Each one of our senses makes life worth-while."

Dorothy, almost recovered, went home to share the rest of her life with a retired schoolteacher, who was her best friend and loving caregiver. However, a few weeks later, Dorothy returned, unable to cope with the pressures of everyday life. Apparently, the advice regarding our senses had not worked for her. I grew concerned for myself.

The bed I was transferred to was situated next to a large picture window that overlooked a rose garden. After Miz' Linn left, after much discussion among the staff, after much paperwork—which the staff detested—I was moved to the bed that had a view of blue sky, clouds, and roses.

A beautiful, dark-haired eighteen-year-old girl now occupied my old space. She was a paraplegic as the result of an automobile accident. She too was a returnee, because she could not take one more day at home watching TV, seeing her older sister go out on dates, having her friends drift away. The poor girl often cried even though the young male orderlies came to flirt with her or to take her out for dinner with a group of other young patients.

We sat and watched her TV together. She introduced me to *Magnum P.I.*, which became a great escape for me. She often spoke of opening a boutique "when I am older and stronger."

Every evening, her parents came to visit, and, one evening, her father walked over to my bed, dropped his head, and wept as he said, "I wish it had been me." Both she and her parents were deeply distraught when I left rehab. I don't know what became of her.

A handsome middle-aged woman, who, like me, had recently lost her husband and was now a double amputee because of diabetes, was brought in to share my room. She had returned to rehab because she felt unable to deal with life in the outside world. All her children were grown up and had moved out. Her large home presented too many obstacles—stairways, for example. The physical care was extremely difficult, and help was not easy to find. Day after day, she sobbed over her eroded life.

I thought of my home with its many stairways. What about help? Would my children help me, or would I have to live with someone I didn't know? Fear gripped me as I contemplated these issues.

Of course, you would not be able to stay in rehab forever. At some point, you would be sent home for good or ill. There was one exception, that of a woman by the name of Carla. Carla was a short, stocky, gray-haired Italian woman in her late sixties who, like Miz' Linn, had worked all her life standing on her feet. Half of her right leg had been amputated. But she had not lost her feisty spirit. The day they strapped on her prosthesis, she slid down her sliding board into her wheelchair, pushed herself to the washbasin, hopped up, and brushed her teeth.

"Ah, now I can go home to my family," she said. Her family, an enormous clan, couldn't wait to take "Grandma" home.

I envied Carla because there were so many people doting on her. My mother and uncle were too old to help me. My children were either in school or had left California. Carla's family visited her constantly while we were recuperating. She was never depressed, never angry, and looked forward to going home to sit in front of the TV for "as long as I like."

I was taken out for several Saturday daytrips, then an overnight trip, a weekend—all in preparation for my return home. If all went well, I would be sent home for good.

My visits home did not turn out to be all that successful. I had so much bottled up anger, and I took it out on the children. On my first trip home, while sharing what was meant to be a special dinner with my family, I looked at my daughter Dana, and said, "You did this to me."

She did not react right away, saving her anger for a later date.

On the patio—where happy, smiling faces had gathered in the past—in the glow of candlelight, with fresh flowers on the table, I wanted to pretend just like the children that nothing had changed. Instead, fear, anger, and frustration took the place of reason. I wanted my children to know what I was feeling, but I felt incapable of expressing my feelings in a reasonable manner. Dependent on my children financially, physically, and emotionally, I felt like a guest in my own home. I was brokenhearted to be without my husband for support; brokenhearted because the medications made the food and wine tasteless; brokenhearted because my bladder and bowels could betray me, releasing their contents at any moment; brokenhearted because the nerve pain, exacerbated by stress, electrocuted my body; brokenhearted because the wheelchair was too high for the table, where I once had the luxury of sitting comfortably in a chair; brokenhearted because the food on my fork fell down the front of my dress, as I had a hard time controlling my muscle function; brokenhearted because my once erect body now listed toward my right and went into spasm uncontrollably.

"You did this to me," is what I said, but what I meant was, "You are living with a man you are not married to." The blame had to be placed somewhere, so, on that occasion, I chose my daughter as the one to vent my repressed anger on.

Everything was dark that night, especially the shadows spreading over the brick courtyard into the corners where I wanted to hide. The candlelight reflected off the puzzled eyes of my children while I sat bewildered and frightened in sorrow's shadow, unable to cry, unable to break through my stoic demeanor, and unable to shake my pride.

The nurse was still blow-drying my hair when Morgan arrived at rehab to pick me up for my first weekend at home. Leslie and Jennie would be waiting for me when I got home. The morning ritual, which usually left me tired, became even more complicated with the nurse's announcement; "You are having your period." I stared at the dark-brown blood staining the sheet, and so I went home with the additional annoyance of my first menstrual period since paralysis—an added hormonal stress on my already fragile emotions.

Then, to make things worse, my mother, angry at not being invited to my brief homecoming, showed up unannounced. She greeted Leslie with one of her steely looks, which managed to upset my daughter. I shared Leslie's displeasure, especially since we had planned to postpone Mother's visit until later when I would feel more settled.

So there I sat on the patio for one full hour—choked with tension, my body rigid and going into spasm, nerve endings firing full blast—trying to talk to my mother, her face frozen in Victorian self-righteousness. I tried to smile, but she remained aloof. I tried to be loving, but she did not respond. Grateful, for once, that I had to do my catheter, I excused myself and rolled away to my room, where Leslie helped me into my bed.

Unwilling to let my family know how helpless I was, I stuffed pillows behind my back for balance and forced my legs apart with more pillows so they would not snap back together and send flying the light, the mirror, the container full of Betadine, the catheter full of urine, and the urinal. The task of catheterization completed, I handed the urinal to Leslie when she returned to the room. She emptied the container and sat down at my bedside.

"What else, Mom?" she asked.

"Put the other items on my nightstand, dear. Can you help me onto my side? I need to get off a bedsore."

"Sure," she replied. Then she rolled me over onto my left side.

"Stuff the pillows along my spine so I won't roll back."

"Done."

"I'm going to rest now, dear heart. Thank you."

An hour later, Mother came to my room and broke down. She told me how sad, worried, and helpless she felt. Before she returned to town, she went to the market and bought me a filet mignon for my supper. The gesture said "I love you." It was easier for her to express her caring through actions like this. She found it difficult to say the words aloud.

The following day, my friends from the beach, Esther and Helen, brought me lunch. Our children had attended Catholic school together. I shook my head and wept as I said, "It is so hard. Pray for me."

We shared the salad, fruit, and toasted bread that had been lovingly provided by my guests. They had brought roses from their gardens, which Leslie artfully arranged as a centerpiece for dinner that evening—our final dinner on the patio together. Dinner was brought to me on a tray from then on.

Alone again, after my luncheon guests departed, I slumped in a chair like a tired child and stared at the walls encircling the courtyard. My eyes followed up the stairs to Jennie's room with its canopied beds and window seat flanked by shelves filled with books and toys. They traveled across the bridge that connected the two wings of a U-shaped house and into my studio, where my easel stood close to a window seat. Sketchpads and drawings covered the twin beds; I had taped some drawings to the walls. My eyes meandered up the stairs that led to my bedroom, where I viewed the vaulted beam ceiling painted with a blue wash and the wrought-iron chandelier that held pastel-colored globes, giving the room a muted rainbow-hued, foggy atmosphere on dark winter nights. I looked at the bank of French windows and doors that opened onto the balcony, which ran the full length of the room and from which you could see the ocean and the coastline stretching south. I looked at the bed to my left with its blue and white woven spread and deep fringe that settled randomly on the white carpet. Then my eyes moved to the right and across the carpet to the sofa and chairs that flanked the raised brick hearth of the fireplace. At the far end, I saw the two steps that led to the bath. I closed my eyes and spoke out loud the following words: "This is the room where I meditated, sat by winter fires to read, write, and sketch; the room where Jennie lay in her infant crib; where I had intimate conversations with my daughter Dana when she came home from school; and where I occasionally kicked off my sandals and shed my clothes to dance in response to the music that sang in my heart; the room where my husband and I made love; and where he prepared himself to go jogging just before he died."

My former neighbors from town, Dick and Elizabeth, came to spend a weekend at their beach house. They generously offered to help rearrange my living area. We shared a lot of years watching our children grow. Elizabeth was an interior designer and had helped me redo the beach house when Bill and I moved there to stay. Now, she, her husband, and their eldest son, Patrick, began to maneuver Bill's desk and filing cabinet into Morgan's room. Up steep stairways through narrow doors, they moved beds, easels, lamps, and rugs. Before she left, Elizabeth said, "I'll do the pretty stuff later. But, for now, it's more important that you feel comfortable that things are where you can get at them." I did feel a little better as I rested in my new room later that afternoon.

After a three-hour struggle to get up the next morning—and feeling tired physically and emotionally from the activities of the day before—I cried, "I wish I were dead. I can't live like this!" I took my arm and brushed everything off the top of Bill's desk, put my head on my arms and wept.

Leslie and Morgan reacted angrily at the outburst. "Oh, c'mon, Mom, stop behaving like this!"

Then, without warning, I had a bowel accident. After Morgan sat me on the bedpan without further results, I struggled from the bed to the wheelchair and made my way over to the bathroom. After wheeling my chair toward the toilet, he locked it in place. Then he pried my legs apart. I had to be positioned in reverse on the toilet, facing the wall. I learned this technique in rehab. It was standard procedure for paralyzed individuals using the toilet so as not to fall off the seat. Because my legs were spastic, my knees locked themselves on either side of the plastic seat screwed onto the top of the toilet bowl. The seat gave me the extra height needed to transfer from my wheelchair. The seat was in the shape of a horse collar with the opening toward my rear.

"I'll lean forward, Morgan, and grasp the bar," I told him. The bars were screwed to the walls on either side of the toilet. "I'll press down on them to elevate my hips. You can then shove my rear onto the seat."

Done! However, my legs lagged behind, so Morgan lifted my knees one at a time and aligned each foot with my hips. I collapsed onto the seat and burst into tears.

Wiping at my tears, I saw Jennie out of the corner of my eye staring at her broken mother, limp and askew like one of her rag dolls. As the tears ran down my cheeks, I thought of the times after an afternoon swim when Jennie and I, covered with sticky sea water and sand, used to enjoy taking a bath together in the sunken tub behind me, splashing and laughing the hour away. I could also hear laughter through the open bathroom window and the chatter of people I knew, as they headed down the brick steps that led to the tennis courts. It tore at my soul to think about it.

When I got back to bed, Leslie gave me a sponge bath. The whole weekend, she was a splendid nurse and housekeeper, taking charge like a pro—cooking, shopping, and bathing and dressing me. One night, we even made a small attempt to discuss our relationship since her divorce and what was happening to our family.

On Sunday, before leaving for Berkeley, Morgan threw himself down beside me on the bed, put his arms around me, and sobbed his goodbye. Touching his curly head, I was reminded of his father.

I asked him if Katy, his girlfriend, would join us. Soon after, when she came to the room, I said, "Please take care of Morgan."

Only two years before, Katy had come to say goodbye after an exhilarating Labor Day weekend visit. "I don't want to go," she had said, her eyes brimming with tears of joy, a smile on her face. I longed to see those tears of joy, not the sad tears I was witnessing now.

A little ritual began that would comfort me like a warm blanket until I left the beach. Aunt Alice, who was in residence with Charles across the street, would walk quietly into my room, sit by my bed, and hold my hand. We never spoke, since she wisely understood that just the touch of another human being was enough.

One time, after Alice had left, I spent a peaceful Sunday afternoon on my bed and ate a very good supper on a tray. Then, Charles, holding my hand all the way, drove Leslie, Jennie, and me back to the rehab center.

My depression returned, and my therapy sessions did not go well. My experience at home only deepened my dread of beginning a new life that seemed so unreal to me. I did not know how to begin. I didn't want to stay in rehab; I didn't want to go home. I begged Dr. Katz to tell me that I would recover, but he said, "I have never seen M.S. strike the spinal cord with such rapid devastation. The spinal cord does not regenerate."

I never gave much thought to aging or illness. Both my parents remained healthy and attractive well into old age, and, before paralysis, I still looked and felt quite youthful as the mother of a young child, and I was enthusiastic about my future. But now, I realized that, if there were a future for me, I would spend it confined to a wheelchair and alone. Remarriage was not an option. In my mind, my life seemed like one of those European cities bombed out in World War II.

A few days after my return to rehab, Leslie and Jennie stopped by with lunch to tell me about their trip to Disneyland the night before. "It was wonderful, Mom, we had a great time," said Leslie after I asked her how it went. Jennie's eyes smiled under her new hat, which had her name spelled out on the brim. I took pleasure in seeing that my girls had had a pleasant time.

Leslie was becoming a mom again, but this time to her little sister. She was very capable in a crisis, remaining strong and active. Once the crisis had passed, however, she would fall apart. But then, she would take some time alone and suddenly reemerge with new plans. After seven years of marriage and bringing up one child, now being divorced forced her to learn how to live life on her own, and, although somewhat scarred, she was wiser. When I expressed my trepidation about returning home, she told me not to try to solve the problems of the future, but to think only of today—exactly the same advice my psychologist had given me that morning.

The morning of my thirty-first wedding anniversary, I felt profoundly alone. In an effort to make some sense of my dreadful circumstances, I read the Bible and said my rosary to find comfort, yet found solace in neither. Numbness informed my whole being that day; nothing anyone said or did gave me relief from my feeling of alienation.

Friends phoned with words of support, usually ending the conversations with statements like, "I don't understand why so much has happened to you."

"We spent a lot of time looking for something you would like," said Leslie and Jennie when they came to visit one afternoon. They handed me two posters, one of which read, "Don't quit," and the other, "You can if you think you can."

I quit and *I can't* were my unspoken answers. Enough was enough. I refused to just smile politely as a way of accepting each new setback. Even a visit with Aunt Alice and Charles did not cheer me up, as constant bowel and bladder accidents interrupted our moments together. For one who loved beauty, I was surrounded by shit! "Happy anniversary," I once yelled out in despondence to no one in particular.

In the late afternoon, a young nurse took me outside and wheeled me across the graveled surface that surrounded the rose garden, the same garden I could see from my window. The heat had brought the roses into full bloom, and the warm air was filled with an intense fragrance. From time to time, the nurse stopped to pick some blooms to place on my bedside table or to weave the flowers into the braid that hung down my back. Nevertheless, sadness would not leave me.

The excursion through the rose garden was done as an effort to help a depressed patient. They monitored all patients for signs of depression. The staff tried to be casual by saying in an overly cheerful voice, "Are you all right, Mrs. Hees?"

One day I answered back, sarcastically, "Look at me! Does this look like *all right* to you?!"

They also observed our food intake. "You're not hungry today?" they would ask in the same cheerful voice if we left our food half eaten. Their questions seemed annoying, unnecessary, and patronizing to me, especially when they already knew the answers.

Over and over again, I said to myself, *I want to die.*

"I'll never be well again," I told my mother as we spoke on the phone during this time. Her receiver went down so quietly, so slowly, I barely heard her goodbye. My mother did not want to hear that I was giving up. She was overcome with emotion.

With the onset of summer, Jennie came to rehab to say goodbye. She was leaving for Nantucket to spend a month with two of her childhood friends and their hospitable parents. I would miss having her around for the summer. I would also miss the many summers we had shared at St. Lo and all the rituals that came with them.

The nurse, who was losing her only child, sensed my loss. She lifted Jennie onto my bed and drew the curtain around us. I hugged Jennie, and I cried as I told her how much she meant to her father and me.

"You are such a comfort to me now," I told her. Then, I kissed every inch of Jennie's sweet face, and, after she hopped off the bed to leave, she ran back to hug and kiss me all over again.

Immediately after Jennie left, I thanked the nurse for giving us our privacy.

"I understand," she said, "as I have a young daughter, and she is leaving me for good. She has cancer. She is my only child, and I cannot have any more children."

I reached out and held her hand for a very long time.

After Jennie left, I abandoned all hope of getting well. I slept without my rosary for the first time since entering rehab. My heart pounded, my throat constricted, due to the terror I felt. Had God abandoned me? I wanted to yell, "Where is everybody, anybody, somebody, my husband, God?" but I could not utter a sound.

In these dark nights of the soul, I felt I had no future, not even a limited one. I was in crisis, spiritually: I felt a separation from God and His Son. And, I anguished over practical matters too, like selling my home. But, where to go? Back to town, I suppose, where Jennie could attend the school her brothers and sisters attended. There she would have the support of family and friends, or so I reasoned over and over in my mind. Then I would abandon that solution and wondered if I should forsake earthly things altogether. Was there a religious order somewhere that would allow me to spend my life in prayer—as a paraplegic? Was that possible? Back and forth, back and forth my mind would go until I was so worked up I could not get out of bed to eat my dinner because of the increased spasms and pain caused by the stress I was creating. I became so upset that I could no longer concentrate when I tried to read. Speaking with my mother, to my roommate Dorothy, or to my psychologist brought me no relief.

I went home again expecting to spend a Saturday with Leslie, Bill, and Bill's friend, John. Before Bill came to pick me up, worry had grown into fear. Once a time of joy, summer at the beach now felt intimidating to me. I could no longer enjoy sitting on the beach or swimming in the ocean. All those people, all those familiar rituals. I felt I would be reduced to a mere spectator. In the past, my husband and I gladly welcomed our children's friends into that summer world of laze, ease, and casual grace.

When I was settled on my bed, and Leslie and I were alone in the room, she said, "I have someone I want you to meet as soon as you are rested and comfortable." As much as she had stirred my curiosity, I closed my eyes and let myself drift off to sleep.

Sometime in the early afternoon, as the sunshine flowed in through the open door and the heat rose from the bricks on the patio, I opened my eyes to the sweet sounds of a harmonica. From my bed, I saw a tall, slender, handsome man with one long leg hanging over the arm of the easy chair—the chair had been a wedding gift to my husband from his grandmother—his brown eyes smiling while he played the harmonica. It was easy to like him immediately because of the graceful musical introduction, and because his ruddy cheeks and patrician air reminded me of my husband. Calmness settled over me as his gentle manner, relaxed presence, and easy conversation tore away all the self-consciousness I felt about my paralyzed condition.

Although I did not know it at the time, Michael—my future son-in-law—with a strong, loving hand, would guide my children through the rough years to come. The foundering ship I was sailing on now had a new captain. I always remembered that moment, because it was filled with a special joy and light. It was not just the light of the summer sun spilling into the room and illuminating that kind, supportive man playing the harmonica so sweetly just a few feet away from my bed; it was as if God had lit a candle in the darkness of my life.

After I had a peaceful night's sleep, Leslie and Michael, both looking tired from the strain of the previous day, returned on Sunday to bring me home. Bill and his friend were already on their way north, so the house was rather quiet when I got there. In an effort to battle fatigue, depression, and tears, I decided to make an inspection of the kitchen, from where I could also survey the living room and dining room.

The house looked worn and disheveled, like me. I wondered what had happened to Ciela, who used to help me keep it in shape. Had the children let her go, or did she simply not return after I became ill? I noticed that the purse I had been using the day I became paralyzed was still hanging on the back of the chair where I had left it two months earlier, indicating to me that Ciela had probably not been around to put it back where it belonged. I neglected to get clarification from my children about this.

The kitchen surfaces were covered with salty, sticky grime, and all the floors were dusty. Lampshades were askew, dining-room chairs were standing at odd angles to each other, and pictures hung crookedly on the walls, as if someone had rushed hurriedly by them. It no longer felt like my home; the lack of caring told me so. I felt forlorn, and I was frustrated at my inability to straighten up my house and at my inability to summon up the energy to tell my children to do something about it. After returning to the patio to gaze again upon the stairways—of no use to a person in my condition—I thought how the Devil himself could not have contrived an uglier twist of fate.

The summer residents came to offer their love and support. During their visits, my body recoiled in the chair as I tried to disappear from view. *Please, please go away,* I thought to myself. *Come back tomorrow, and I will be well.*

When I visited a friend for tea, I realized how impossible it was for a cripple to get around in St. Lo. The quaint entrances with their shingled, sometimes gated doorways usually led to brick steps that ascended to inner courtyards. One exception was my late mother-in-law's former home. I went there after tea to have a drink with Joanne and Mike (the present owners) and their friends. My husband, in his youth, had been Joanne's very first date—her husband was a lawyer who would eventually assist me in the sale of my home. I heard little of the conversation among the people gathered there. Instead, I stared at the extra-wide chaise lounge where Bill and I had once made love in the sun on a pleasant fall afternoon in the early '60s. Overcome by emotion triggered by past memories, I was wheeled home for a visit with Sister Christina, who was waiting patiently.

"But who will be here to greet me? Who will stay with me at night?" I worried aloud to Sister Christina.

"He will. He will," said Sister with total faith and trust, the kind of faith and trust I did not possess at that time.

I knew her prayers were answered when Leslie phoned me after my return to rehab to say, "I have a surprise for you. I am going to stay on until you are settled, and Dana is going to cancel her trip East and join me."

My heart soared with joy, and I wrote in my journal that night: "The sacrifices my children are making will not go unnoticed by God."

And the answers to the prayers kept coming. Amy, Jennie's companion from the previous summer, phoned to say she would come. "I'll look after Jennie," she said, and then she offered to quit her job exercising horses at various racetracks around the country to work for us. "I can't imagine having your privacy invaded by some housekeeper," she said.

That evening, I dined with Betty, the only other M.S. patient in rehab. I told her about Sister's prayers, and we spoke at length about how close to God we felt. Because of the possibility of dying from M.S., life suddenly seemed more vivid. *Home*, I thought, *I am preparing to go home*, not entirely sure whether I was referring to my earthly home or to a heavenly one.

Chapter 9

THE WHEELCHAIR WALTZ

I thirst for the sands
Of a glorious white place,
With the end of gray
And the honey to taste.

—Elaine Branch, "The Need"

Chapter 9

A nd so it began—the next chapter of my life. My husband's death was only the prelude.

Leslie held my hand during the final conference with my medical team on Tuesday, June 30, 1981. The touch of her hand kept me from falling apart. The remarks of the medical team helped her to understand the life I would be facing at home. I was both relieved and afraid when we were told I would be released the following Friday. Having to manage at home was going to be difficult, but being able to go at my own pace might be a welcome relief from the regimentation of rehab.

"All your needs are met in rehab, so it may sound odd to say, but I am glad that you are out of the hospital routine and that you can do what you like at home and will have the children around you. You may cry a bit, but not too long . . ." Laura wrote later, reaffirming how I felt that day.

The wait that day seemed an eternity. Hair shampooed, body washed and diapered, bags packed, and release papers signed, I was ready to leave at noon. But, still I had to wait.

Occasionally a staff member would look in on me and say, "Oh, you're still here!" As the hours crept by, my anxiety grew, my nerve endings fired away, and my diaper grew more sodden. I could not feel my bladder release, but the wetness against my skin and the odor told me I was in need of a change. Soon, a staffer took pity on me, helped me on a bed, and changed my diaper.

Then Leslie finally showed up at 5 P.M., accompanied by Aunt Alice. As we headed home, Leslie explained how she had not wanted to come for me until she had put my room and bath in order. We spoke a little. Alice occasionally leaned forward from the back seat and patted my shoulder. The three of us were fatigued and feeling uneasy. I slipped into thoughts of my future as the scenery outside the car window brought back memories of the past.

As we drove through the St. Lo gate, I found it strange that I was coming home after two months in the hospital and rehab when I was still very ill. *Weren't you supposed to be well after a hospital stay,* I thought, *or at least on the way toward wellness?*

When we pulled up, I slid from the car into my wheelchair using the sliding board. Leslie lifted my feet out of the car and placed them on the footrests, as I was unable to do it for myself. As she opened the doors to the patio to wheel me through, she explained to me that our friends, Virginia and her mother Esther, had come by in the morning to move potted plants, tables, and chairs so that every area of the courtyard would be attractive and accessible. A terracotta pot, adorned with a lizard figurine, had been placed in the center of a wooden dining table.

"Oh, where did that come from?" I asked my daughter.

"That is a present from Phil," she replied. Phil, dear Phil, lived alone nearby, isolated long ago from his family, one that went back to the early days of Southern California. Although he drank excessively—to no one's harm but his own—he had a beautiful, shy soul.

Phil had purchased one of my paintings, a study of Whistler's *Arrangement in Black and Gray,* commonly known as *Whistler's Mother.* In 1979, I was asked by one of my art professors to paint my rendition of that particular masterpiece. In my version, Mom was sitting with her severed head in her lap, so I called the work *Rearrangement in Black and Gray.*

"She reminds me of how I feel most of the time," Phil had commented. I, too, felt rearranged, and, when I gazed upon the pot with the lizard, I felt I had joined Phil in his world of the lonely and the isolated.

When we approached the entrance to my son Bill's room, Leslie opened the door.

"Just a minute," I whispered. I paused for a moment before going in.

I glanced up at the blue Dutch door of my bedroom. I looked at the room that was going to be mine now, and said, "All right, Leslie, let's go in now."

The brass bed was covered with a blue spread—the color of the raiment worn by Our Lady in paintings of the Ascension. Comfortable, puffy pillows, in the same shade of blue, were propped against the headboard. A sign that proclaimed, "Love you"—Jennie's handiwork, complete with crayoned hearts—leaned up against the pillows. On the walls, hung a few of my favorite paintings. Family photos and a vase of fresh flowers sat on a long, low table underneath a window. For my convenience, a marble top sink had been installed at wheelchair height in one corner of the room.

However, the object that most caught my eye was a new book on the table nearest my bed. Leslie had carefully selected it, and the title spoke to me of how she felt. *Beauty and Sadness*, by Yasumari Kawabata, is the tale of a novelist and his former mistress, an artist living in Kyoto. I read the book during my final summer at the beach. The story evoked parallel images of my recent past and the tragedy of the present.

Moving through the connecting bathroom to Morgan's bedroom, I was delighted to discover that the room had been rearranged into a new studio for me. My work was leaning up against the walls, and the easel with the unfinished work I had begun before my illness was in the center of the room. The efforts of children and friends to make my homecoming as comfortable as possible made me shed tears of love and gratitude.

Leslie uncorked a bottle of champagne, and, while Alice, Leslie, and I were sipping and talking, the phone rang. "Hello dear. This is your sister calling from Virginia welcoming you home," said Jeannette. I began to cry again.

"Oh dearest sister, please—"Jeannette's voice cracked, and she began to cry as well. Although we had been physically separated for most of our lives, we shared the same opinion about our "common frustration about mother," as she put it when she had written to me in January of 1979. I loved her. I wanted to hug her. I knew she would accept me as I was, in spite of my affliction. With that phone call, a renewed and deeper relationship with my sister began. I needed her support.

A call from Morgan soon followed. Then, Dana came to join the celebration. Alice said, "Ta-da," returned to her home, leaving us alone to talk. Leslie uncorked another bottle of champagne.

The three of us—Leslie, Dana, and I—found it easy to live in the present moment for the next hour, putting aside all concerns about the future. We missed little Jennie, but realized that she must have been happy in Nantucket with her childhood friends—and former neighbors—Molly and Sarah.

"I completed all my driving lessons, but I don't plan to drive anymore," I told my daughters.

"Why?" they asked.

"My upper body strength and balance are very poor," I replied.

Then we discussed how soaking in a hot tub might be of benefit to me.

"Dr. Wolff said the heat would be good for me," I said. "I agreed with him, but not above a certain temperature or my skin would blister."

"Why, Mom?" asked Dana.

"Lack of circulation.

"Speaking of hot tubs," I continued, after taking another sip of champagne, "Jennie and I walked down the road to Norah's hot tub the day before I became ill. I was hoping that a soak would make my weak and tingly legs feel better." Silence fell over us for a moment until I reflected aloud: "What a lovely evening that was—golden in the last hours of the day."

The three of us were quiet again.

"I'm so sick of everyone poking, prodding, and questioning me. All I want is to be left alone," I said with a sigh of relief. Conversation came to a halt. We were struggling to think of something to say on what was meant to be a celebratory occasion.

"Well, uh," I began, "Charles was so sweet to come and pick up my bath chair yesterday. He also paid half my hospital bill," I said with a little smile.

"Oh," Leslie cried in surprise, "I'll remember to thank him. He's very concerned about you, Mom."

"I know, and I'm concerned about him. I told him so, pleaded, in fact, for him to stop drinking. 'I need you, Charles,' I said to him. 'I am frightened to death of the responsibilities facing me at home. Your mother is worried about you as well.' 'That's true,' he agreed."

Leslie and Dana nodded sympathetically.

"Home, home, home! It's good to be home," I blurted out in a forced tone of happiness, trying to cheer them up. "We'll pray for Charles. Now, let's finish the champagne!"

However, it was not the home I once knew. My movements were so restricted that the place seemed foreign to me. Why, I couldn't even butter a slice of bread because the kitchen counters were too high! Our home would have to be sold. Leslie, Dana, Bill, Morgan, and Jennie would leave, taking with them the spirit of the house, the memories of a charmed family life. Bill's essence—as husband and father—would forever remain inside those walls. The ocean claimed his mortal remains; his spirit dwells in the home he built. The house is his tomb.

~ ~ ~

The first five days at home, visiting nurses came and went. I was unable to settle down, so one of the nurses brought me some marijuana to ease the nerve pain. I puffed away, but to no avail, so I gave it up after two or three efforts. *The Psalms!* I thought, remembering one nurse's suggestion. I found some solace in Psalm 42, verse 10 and 8:

> *Deep calls unto deep*
> *in the roar of your cataracts;*
> *All your breakers and your*
> *billows pass over me.*

And:

> *I sing to God, my rock:*
> *Why do you forget me?*
> *Why must I go about in mourning,*
> *with the enemy oppressing me?*

Sleep was my only relief. The darkness of the night, the quiet of the house, the classical music on the radio, the anti-depressant I was taking: all helped me to fall asleep. Unfortunately, mornings were always the same, colored a deep indigo blue. The light never streamed through the windows. Night and day blended into one another. Everything was black. I woke up depressed by the onerous routine before me of having to take care of my body.

What kept me going? Occasionally, I had a day free of bowel and bladder accidents along with a lessening of nerve pain. On one of those days, as I made an effort to get out of my hospital gown and into my jeans, the zipper would not zip over the abdomen, which had lost all muscle tone. Those old jeans symbolized a life of informality when I painted, drove my Scout, and walked the dogs on the beach. I discarded the jeans, shedding my old life like a snake sheds its skin.

Courage, courage, courage—I heard the word over and over again. I was sick of family and friends repeating that word. One day, I threw the subject of courage out at Marge, an acquaintance of mine in her seventies, who agreed with me that the situation was unbearable.

"I've thought of you all night," she once said over the phone. "I can't get you out of my mind. If I were you, I'd just swallow a pill. People are always trying to give advice and be positive, but I'm looking at the situation realistically." I agreed with her. What a relief it was to hear someone speak the truth. But, where would I find the pill?

For me, the most effective words were those that came in the mail one day. A note from Nancy Dunn—a woman who had suffered many trials and who had demonstrated considerable strength in spite of them—declared, "What a wonderful example of courage you can be for your children." That was all. It was so positive, so to the point.

A note from Amsterdam read:

> Lieve, dappere, Berta, do not compare yourself to those who are not handicapped, or to those who are blind or have heart disease, if only for the reason that you are uniquely you, in spite of the fact that you are not the Berta you used to be. For you are still that same person of wonderful strength and courage, always ready to help others, someone who is so wonderful to talk with about all the things that bother us in this big world.

Maintaining courage for the sake of others was what those letters were talking about. I had five children who needed me. Clearly, one of my children still needed me very much—Jennie.

~ ~ ~

During the summer months, I was caught unawares that I was headed for an emotional breakdown. The frequent visits of children, friends, and nurses kept me afloat. Some friends who lived nearby thoughtfully installed an electric lift so that I could enjoy the living-room terrace "just like Charles Laughton did in the movies," as Laura had suggested in a letter. Esther brought me flowers everyday, and her houseguest from England became my hairdresser. In the late mornings, Morrie came to wash and blow-dry my very long hair. Virginia brought me half of her Communion host on Sundays. My neighbor, Ruth, had ramps placed in her home to make it easier for me to visit. Others brought me slippers—they fell off; books—couldn't concentrate; food—couldn't taste it; caftans to wear—I wore them.

I wheeled myself over to Esther's rosebush and fruit-tree garden to have lunch; to cocktails at my neighbor Ruth's home—where I found I couldn't put my glass on the table without losing my balance and falling forward; to tea with a nun whom Antonia—another St. Lo resident—had graciously invited to her home on my behalf. I was quickly brought home when I broke into uncontrollable sobbing.

Leslie got me ready for what turned out to be a monumental excursion to San Diego's Old Globe Theater to see Shakespeare's *Much Ado About Nothing*. She struggled, with heartfelt longing, to turn me back into the mother she once knew. She slipped one of my prettiest caftans over my head, knotted my hair into a chignon, and put flowers from the garden in amongst the strands. I felt overdressed when my friends came to visit in their simple slacks and shirts.

When we went to the theater, I was wheeled to the disabled area far from my friends. Throughout the performance, my wet diaper and pressure sores worried me constantly.

During intermission, my companions wheeled me into the ladies room, which was packed with women fixing their makeup and adjusting their hairdos. Apparently, my entrance was seen as such a great inconvenience to them that they all grabbed their purses and quickly headed for the door. It was as if the Red Sea had parted. Some of them even danced a little two-step in order to avoid me.

In the mirror, I saw a face puffy from steroids. I quickly looked away. *This is not the real me*, I thought.

As we were driving home after the performance, I stared out the window and withdrew into my shell, uninterested in the conversation of my friends. They spoke of fashion, home decorating, and gardening—matters that now seemed to me of little importance. They spoke to each other as if I were not present. I felt alienated from these friends and their interests. Would I ever again be a part of that sort of light-hearted conversation?

~ ~ ~

The next day, Norma came up the hill to see me. "This woman needs new clothes," she announced. Norma was speaking of Irma, my new caregiver/housekeeper. Norma's very strong British demeanor reminded me of my mother. Sometimes it put me off a bit. Nonetheless, her statement was valid. In the state I was in, I hadn't noticed that Irma wore the same dress day after day. It was the very dress she was wearing the first time I saw her when she showed up at the house with Leslie and Dana.

Leslie had found this precious woman after a lot of time spent sitting at the kitchen desk dialing, dialing, dialing the phone. Day after day after day, I could hear her working the phone trying to find help. Norma aided Leslie in the search, and together they found Irma. Irma had been working for a quadriplegic in Newport Beach. Irma's employer ran an employment agency. It was through the agency that Leslie and Norma found Irma.

Irma was cheerful, experienced, and spoke very little English—she was from Nicaragua—but was willing to learn the language. Her suitcase had been stolen on the way to the United States, so Norma took her shopping for clothes. Supplied with a new wardrobe and a Spanish-English cookbook, she went to work.

I used what Spanish I had retained from my classes to converse with Irma. Here was God at work again. What more important reason could there have been for learning Spanish?!

On a soft, warm, and dreamy kind of day, I said to Irma, "It's time to go down to the terrace. I want to try out the lift that has been installed."

Irma wheeled me into the lift from the patio level. I pushed a button and descended to the living room.

Very posh indeed, I whispered to myself, quoting a line from Laura's letter. Irma took over after I landed. She wheeled me out to the terrace; she transferred me to a contoured chair; she brought me a glass of water.

I sat on the terrace, shaded by an umbrella. The umbrella's scalloped edges danced in the warm, light breeze. This captured my attention until a turtledove landed on the low brick wall beside me. The turtledove quickly hopped up and perched himself on my head. He walked around in my hair. *Could it be one of the two birds I had left in Norah's care?* (Indeed, they had escaped from their cage while in her care.) I thought that surely the Holy Spirit had landed on my head! *A great sign,* I thought. *What could it mean? A sign of hope, perhaps?*

The following day, my friend Lorna came to visit. After seating herself beside my bed, she said, "When you are feeling better, I have something to talk to you about."

Lorna and her husband, Rob, owned a house on the beach. It was at their house one fine Sunday afternoon that we saw Bill jogging down the beach. Rob made the remark about "admiring Bill's new form."

"When you see the For Sale sign go up on #25, you'll know he's in intensive care. He doesn't believe in health insurance."

How prophetic those comments came to be when Lorna visited me again on one of my so-called "good" days.

"My husband and I want to buy your home," she informed me.

I was not surprised by this in the least. It troubled me though. Did Lorna and Rob have their eyes on the house, wondering when disaster might strike so that they could purchase it?

The conversation of long ago with Rob and Lorna, the Spanish lessons, the turtledove landing on my head: all of these things opened the narrow gate a tiny bit more. The threads of a new life were being woven together.

I agreed to go ahead with the sale of the house. A lawyer, who was a friend of Rob, Lorna, and me, would handle the transaction. His name was Mike. Mike had driven me to the hospital the day of Bill's death.

I rejected the first offer Mike brought me. Although Lorna and Rob were fortunate enough to own beachfront property, their house was old—built long ago as a summer house. It needed a lot of work. Besides, the beach was rapidly eroding. Whereas my home was built in the '60s and was meant for year-round living. The views were stunning.

After some minor haggling with Lorna and Rob, I accepted the offer at Mike's recommendation.

"You'll be out of here by winter; you don't want to be here in the winter," suggested Mike. He was right. It would be too depressing.

I wasn't greedy. "It's only bricks and mortar" was my comment to Lorna as I signed the papers.

For Lorna and Rob, the house was a trade-off: they sold their home for exactly the same amount they offered me for mine.

Why wasn't I heartbroken over the loss of my home? Sure, it was painful, but I still owned the lower lot. That property gave me the option of building something more suitable if I wished to do so.

Paul, my ex-son-in-law, came to see me after hearing about the sale of the house.

"I thought you might need cheering up. Would you like to go for a swim?" he asked.

"Sure," I grinned.

After some preparation on my part, Paul literally ran down the hill, pushing me in my wheelchair.

"Wow, that was an exhilarating ride, Paul," I gushed, as we reached the seashore.

"Wait until we get into the ocean," he excitedly remarked.

With me in his arms, he waded out to the breaking waves.

"Oh, my God, I've forgotten how invigorating this is!" I squealed, after going under the first breaker. Several more breakers washed over us.

"You must be getting tired, Paul," I inquired.

"No, the water keeps you buoyant," he shot back as another wave rolled over us.

It became evident that Paul was tired as he carried his sodden burden—me—back to the shore. I caught sight of Norma giving us the thumbs-up sign.

"Thank you, Paul," I said, and then I planted a big kiss on his cheek.

~ ~ ~

People around me expected that I would fully recover. It occurred to me that people connected my illness with the aftermath of Bill's death. It was a possibility, because I had not completed the grieving process. Perhaps, once I had time to get over the loss, I would be able to get up and walk again.

At my home, the visitor traffic was beginning to concern me, because it was interrupting my personal care and much needed rest. Leslie made a large sign on poster board that read: "Mom's resting" (on one side) and "Welcome" (on the other side). Around the messages, she painted pretty decorations of flowers, birds, and seashells. Then, she placed the board on an easel outside the doors to the patio. The traffic-control system worked well, allowing us all more time to ourselves.

Leslie left for Idaho. On her return, she was accompanied by Michael. They stayed in the bedroom that I had so loved sharing with her father. I felt a little uncomfortable about the idea of them now sharing that particular bed in my house—especially out of wedlock—but I was beginning to accept this new way of life that the social revolution of the '60s had produced. All the parents of my generation were confronted with the sexual freedom of their children—something virtually unheard of when we were their age. I didn't have to like it, and I left it to God's judgment.

One evening, Michael rolled up the rugs in the living room, put on some LPs, took my hand, and spun me gracefully around the floor in waltz time. I couldn't stop smiling as we sailed across the room doing the wheelchair waltz. I felt so alive! Round and round we went, Michael holding my hand and spinning me around as he pushed my chair across the floor. I felt as though I were flying. I grew dizzy, and Michael was out of breath. As we came to a halt, he bowed to me and kissed my hand. Michael, the man Leslie loved, totally accepted me as I was.

But it wasn't always waltzes, teas, and cocktail parties. There was one time in particular that stands out in my mind: the evening we headed over to a nearby restaurant that overlooked a lagoon. The stuffy humid air of that August evening, combined with the overpowering smell of Indian curry, made me feel quite ill. Halfway through the meal, Leslie and Michael took me home. Along the way, I moaned, "Oh, my God," and stuck my head out the window to take in the fresh air so as not to pass out or throw up. When the cold sweats hit me, we were turning the corner at Harrison's Pharmacy, a place all of St. Lo frequented for many years. It was the only landmark I remember on that ride home. Somehow, as I wiped my brow on my arm, the sight of it helped to bring me comfort.

The blood pooling in my feet was causing a quick drop in blood pressure. Once I got in bed and put my feet up and my head on the pillow, I started to feel better. This kind of nausea—brought on by low blood pressure—became quite common, but, with years and years of therapy, the bouts began to occur less frequently and eventually stopped.

Back on the summer party circuit, I joined a very large gathering of friends on Louise's patio. As I sat in my chair in the quietest corner I could find, the beautiful dark-haired twenty-something daughter of my neighbors on the hill approached. She started talking to me but then suddenly burst into tears. "Oh," she cried, upset with herself for the display of emotion after seeing me in a wheelchair for the first time, "I promised myself I wouldn't cry." And then, she knelt by my chair.

I put my hand on her arm and said, "Well, now that the body is gone, I'll have to work on the soul."

Soon after the encounter, I was joined by Betty, a summer visitor, who, along with her husband Ted, had wheeled me down the hill to the gathering. She now asked, "Would you like to go home?"

"Yes, I would, thank you," I replied. As she pushed me through the crowd of people, I honked the red bicycle horn attached to the arm of my chair.

"My God, Berta, that's just like you," someone said, laughing, as I made my way toward the exit. *Was* that just like me? Had I a natural ability to make fun of life when times were tough? And did others recognize that part of me? Maybe so. I guess I had a sense of the ridiculous but never thought anyone noticed, until now.

Another person also recognized my lightheartedness, as was confirmed in a letter that came from China days later:

Li River Hotel

Dear Berta,

I don't know the full extent of your illness, nor do I really know what to say. My father wrote me and informed me of your illness, of which he said he had mentioned in a previous letter—one I never received. From Hong Kong, I spoke to him by phone, and he told me more about your condition. My God, was I shocked. Of all people, Berta, it certainly doesn't seem fair that such a thing should happen to you.

Since that conversation, I've tried to think of something I could write you that might lift your spirits or console you. You're on my mind all the time. And I've prayed a lot for you. You have the kindest, gentlest spirit of anyone I've ever known, and, for that reason, I've always respected and loved you, and that spirit I'm sure will not change with time or with infirmity. That is what is essentially you.

Much love to you and the family,

Damian

Kweilin, China

Damian had sent me some postcards—always respectfully addressed to Berta and Jennie—before he found out about my illness. In them, he described his painting adventures in Thailand, China, and India—how he mixed vodka and gin with his acrylics so they wouldn't freeze when he trekked into the Himalayas. As I read about his adventures, I imagined traveling with him. Upon learning about Damian's trip to Kyoto, Japan, it seemed to me to be more than a coincidence when Leslie brought me a copy of *Beauty and Sadness*.

On Valentine's Day of the following year, when I read the poem Damian had sent, I discovered that he and I were thinking along the same lines:

> *While wandering through distant lands*
> *By Kweilin peaks and towers*
> *While trudging hard on desert sands*
> *Or by Kashmiri brooks and flowers,*
>
> *My mind would wander back to you,*
> *To your shy little smile*
> *And the way we would wile*
> *The hours in our painting repose.*

At present, the hours passed in despair, then hopefulness, and then raging anxiety about the future. Trying to help me in some way, my daughters told me about Irma's former employer.

"Mom, the woman's husband left her after she became a quadriplegic. Like you, she had to sell her home," Leslie began.

"That's true, Mom," Dana agreed. "She now lives in a pretty mobile home park in Newport Beach, where her neighbors keep an eye on her. She enjoys playing bridge and running an employment agency from her home."

"She is much worse off than you are, Mom," Leslie added. "She can't breathe on her own, and she has a basin under her bed. Her bodily functions are involuntary. Her son takes her sailing. He straps her to the deck of his sailboat—to the breathing apparatus too!"

"How does she run her business?" I asked. "She can't pick up the phone."

"There is a special communication device set up by her bed," Dana answered.

Would I ever be as accepting of my fate? My arms were strong, and, although my diaphragm was weak, I could still breathe on my own.

"I don't know how I'm going to do, my darlings," I commented. "I just don't know."

~ ~ ~

Sunny summer days of July made me yearn for the time when I was able to play with Jennie on the beach—sunbathing, swimming and picnicking—like I used to. On a good day, I settled for the present moment and finally being able to concentrate enough to read the newspaper. I read the paper for the first time since my homecoming. My ability to concentrate returned slowly.

I had another small awakening one day when Amy pushed me past the cabana. As I took in the scene on the beach—a group of young boys playing volleyball, and people lying on their towels watching the game—sadness gripped my heart. I would never be part of that scene in the same way again. *You need to let go, and begin to understand that for some very good reason your life has changed,* my inner voice advised.

Continuing to search for an explanation for why my body had failed me so suddenly, I went to visit a neurologist in Pasadena. The interview had me coming away feeling that my condition was hopeless. The neurologist pointed out the window at a man maneuvering himself from his wheelchair into the driver's seat of his car. "Wouldn't you like to be able to do that?" she asked.

"No," I replied, and then angrily left the office.

Esther, whose strong support at St. Lo was commendable, opened up her Pasadena home to me so that I could rest up before my long drive back to the beach. She picked me up after my appointment. The old familiar landmarks that we passed during the drive reminded me of a happier time.

Frannie, Esther's daughter, greeted us at Esther's home. Frannie, who was a medical student, helped me with my physical needs. In the morning, Frannie wheeled me onto the terrace for breakfast. It was a gorgeous sunny day—not a cloud in the sky. The birds were chirping, and, at the far end of the large green lawn, the flowers were in bloom.

"Hello, dear," said a familiar voice from behind my chair. Sister Wilfred, at Esther's request, had come to see me.

For the very first time during my illness, I surrendered completely. As I lay my head on her small shoulder, I felt all the pent-up tension in my body dissolve.

"Is there someplace I can go just to sit and say my rosary, perhaps a convent?" I pleaded.

"Maybe later, but not now. You have a little girl who needs you," replied Sister. I was disappointed; there was no escape. My tears turned into sobs. Sister continued, "You can only live moment to moment. Your mind is too fragmented by the sudden events in your life to be thinking about what lies ahead."

I felt a little better, but only a very little better.

Before I left Esther's, we watched the wedding of Prince Charles and Diana on television. We all drank champagne together, sharing in the ceremony. Even Sister had a sip—just a sip—from my glass.

~ ~ ~

On the way back to St. Lo, I found myself caught up in a whirl of emotions again—despair, fear, anger, with an occasional glimmer of hope.

When July came to an end and August began, I was filled with trepidation about my future. Where would I be in September when my children returned to school or to their homes?

I decided to phone Aunt Alice. She always was a great comfort to me, sitting at my bedside and holding my hand while giving me the space to let go and shed my tears.

One evening, as she was bringing me dinner, she tripped and fell on the bricks outside on the patio. When she entered my room, her face was scratched and bloody, but the food was still on the plates. "I scooped it up. I'm sure it's all right," she said.

"But Alice, your face!" I exclaimed.

"I'll take care of it later," she replied.

Alice poured two glasses of wine from a bottle she found in my refrigerator. *A bad idea*, I thought, as she had already reached her capacity by the time she had arrived at my gate. We ate spaghetti and sipped our wine in silence, smiling at each other every now and then.

The mail brought a letter from Charles. In it, he expressed concern about his mother:

> *To my knowledge, she has not gone to see her bone doctor about that shoulder which has been hurting her since she fell two weeks ago (when she got the bruise on her forehead). She is so damn stubborn and independent, which makes it difficult for those who love her, and it doesn't do her much good either. (It's so easy to criticize our mothers!)*

Oh yes, Charles, yes indeed, I thought, as I read those words.

My mother recently paid me a visit with her friend Maria. Irma, Maria, my mother, and I formed a circle and held hands.

"I see you walking again," said Maria. We prayed together, and then Maria laid her hands on my head. "I am a channel," she said. I didn't know quite what she meant, but I wanted to believe I would be walking again. We said the Our Father.

Mother's friend had brought me a ray of hope.

Jennie phoned from Nantucket. I pretended to be cheerful, but I was scared to death of her return. I worried about what kind of mother I would be when she came home. I felt panic at the thought of not being able to carry out my responsibilities as a mother and at my fear of letting her down. The day she came home to stay with me, I broke into tears as I saw her walking through the gate. David, the father of Molly and Sarah—the girls that Jennie spent the early summer with—looked puzzled. Surely, he must have thought that I would be overjoyed to see Jennie. I thanked him for having taken my young daughter to the East Coast. The prettily tanned and excited eleven-year-old stood before me.

"Give me a hug. I'm so sorry about the tears," I apologized. Now she was mine to care for, and I had no idea how I was going to go about it. I knew I would not be comfortable with anyone until I learned to be comfortable with myself.

I was so glad to have Amy with me; she made the situation a little easier. Each morning at 5:00 A.M., I was awakened by the sound of boots clomping around upstairs—Amy, preparing to leave for the racetrack at Del Mar, where she exercised horses for a living. It wasn't financially feasible for Amy to quit working entirely.

She would take Jennifer along, who was always delighted to go. While Amy exercised her mounts, Jennie drank hot chocolate and ate donuts while watching the grooms, stable boys, and jockeys go about their work. Jennie found it exhilarating to be there. She got especially excited when she was allowed to ride the lead pony—with the horses following behind—out onto the track.

Once, when she came home in the afternoon, I watched her walk down the stairs—dressed in her bathing suit, her beach towel on her shoulder—on her way to some empty spot on the beach. I envisioned waiting for her in the sand. Without the familiar umbrella in place, without any family nearby, I imagined she must have felt lonely. On the other hand, her friends were there on the beach. So, quite possibly, her feeling lonely was just an assumption on my part.

My son Morgan phoned with excellent news: in September, Jennie would be returning to Mayfield School—her old school in Pasadena. She had completed kindergarten at that school before we moved to the beach at St. Lo. Mrs. Thompson, her kindergarten teacher, had taught all of her brothers and sisters. The thought of her returning to the warm embrace of Mayfield School of the Holy Child Jesus gave me a greater peace of mind about the future. Jennie was going back to a school and reuniting with friends she had not wanted to leave. And, she was leaving behind unpleasant memories of a school where she had stayed without complaint since our move in 1973.

Sister Christina, one of the teachers Jennie had liked at her school, wrote to tell me that she had landed safely in Florida and was already teaching sixth grade. " . . . a good little group. I guess I'll survive the loss of California."

Well, I thought, *we would survive too.*

With the help of a real estate agent named Emily, Morgan had found two houses he thought would be suitable for a disabled person, and either one could be leased or bought.

The day Amy left with Jennie to take care of matters at Jennie's former school, the tears ran down my face as Jennie gently kissed me goodbye.

"I'll only be in town for two days, Mom," said Jennie sympathetically. I wept, because someone else was doing the job that I, as a mother, had always done. Alone in my contour chair, I wrote down these thoughts:

> *Something else has been taken away from me—the pleasure of driving my youngest child to school.*

While Jennie was away, I sorted through her clothes with the help of Esther and Joyce—the lively mother of Jennie's friend, Leigh. Joyce brought the clothes down the stairs to the patio; Esther and I sorted through them.

My former life was all too present in those clothes, so it was with great stoicism that I approached the job. Esther happily took out two T-shirts with the Trash Can Tennis Tournament logo printed on them that Jennie had outgrown. Her young grandson could wear them for a year or two before he would outgrow them. When her father was alive, we made it a habit to buy Jennie a T-shirt from the places we visited. The "I left my ♥ in San Francisco" shirt went into the pile of discards, as well as those with memories of the Grand Canyon, Vancouver, B.C., and Mexico.

On another day, my mother and two of her friends, Peggy and Gloria, helped me tackle the dining room, living room, and kitchen. They helped me down the stairs to the dining room. As I sat in my wheelchair, Peggy and Gloria presented me with books, bric-a-brac, and well-used items from the kitchen. In a short time, the dining room was filled with years of accumulated treasures and the not so treasured. I asked Peggy and Gloria if there was something they would like for themselves. It was my way of saying thank you. They selected a few items, and the rest I donated to the Pasadena Art Alliance to sell at their art auction. Only four years before, I merged the furnishings of two houses into one, discarding a great deal of my life in the process. Now, He was peeling away another layer.

Bruce, Damian's father, volunteered to help me sort through my personal belongings. He carried me up the stairs to my bedroom and settled me into my wheelchair. It was the first time I had seen my room since I was taken to the hospital. My once beautiful bedroom was now in total disarray. The bed sheets, pillows, and bedspread were all lying in crumpled heaps on the mattress. Cushions had been removed from the sofa and were on the floor near the fireplace. Newspapers were strewn all over the white carpet. Bureau drawers were half-open, and lampshades askew. The wastebaskets were full and on their side. The furniture was covered in dust, indicating that no one had cleaned the room after Leslie's and Michael's occasional visits or perhaps the whole time I had been in the hospital and rehab center. I felt violated and dishonored.

Bruce quickly sensed my dismay and suggested that we start cleaning out the bathroom. So he wheeled me across the carpet, pulled me up the two steps that led to my closet dressing-table area, and pushed me into the bathroom. Starting on Bill's sink first, I discarded everything except for his shaving brush. Then we moved on to my personal belongings.

Jane, Bruce's wife, brought us lunch on a tray. Jane, pushing aside crumpled blankets to make a space, placed the tray at the foot of my bed, then quietly left the room.

As we ate lunch and drank some wine, I wanted to know how Bruce felt about my brief relationship with his son, but I wasn't able to bring myself around to asking. I did tell him, "I received a letter from Damian explaining that you had told him about my illness."

"Yes, I thought it best for him to know what happened to you," he said, smiling sweetly.

Amy and Jennie returned from town. While they were away, we had sorted through clothes and all the things that the family had accumulated over the years. It seemed like, bit by bit, order was being restored again. I was beginning to feel better about my living situation.

During that time, a very disconcerting situation came to pass. Amy and Paul had begun a courtship. Amy expressed her concern about the discomfort it caused for me. Seeing Paul courting Amy was too reminiscent of Paul and Leslie's early romance.

"You don't really need that going on now," Margaret said to me about the relationship between Paul and Amy. She was right, but I said nothing. I was too tired. All of my precious energy was focused on moving. Anyway, the romance didn't last long.

I had some time to spend with friends now that many prayers had been answered and that a lot of bothersome tasks were behind me. I listened to others express their bitter disappointments with life. Their stories broke through my loneliness.

"Berta, do you know how loved you are?" said Carol. "It's like Bill's funeral; it has brought everyone together in a way we have not been before."

No, I wasn't aware of any love directed at me. I was aware only that there was an outpouring of love among the members of this small community for each other.

I was especially touched by the support I received from my children's contemporaries. It truly surprised me that they would take time to write and to actually come and help me. Two of them came to measure my room and to go shopping for a waterbed. They knew that bedsores were a problem for someone in my condition and reasoned that the waterbed would help me avoid getting them. We later decided that, since I was moving, maybe that idea had better wait.

Teresa was a young woman who would expend a great deal of her time and energy on me, both at St. Lo and in Pasadena. She came over one Monday morning to help ease my emotional pain. After placing a call to Michigan, she handed me the phone and said, "Talk to Patsy." Patsy graciously spoke to me about her life with multiple sclerosis. It was not an easy conversation for either of us, but it did help me to speak with someone who was going through the same hell.

My last lunch on the terrace occurred on a picture-perfect day. The view of sand, sea, cabana, tennis courts, quaint rooftops, and the coastline toward La Jolla provided a feast for the eyes. I'm sure I would miss it more than I could imagine. How fortunate we had been to have lived so happily for so long in such a place. I ate a delicious quiche, salad, papaya, and drank some wine, all provided by and shared with everyone who had been so supportive.

Sister Christine wrote to me about "being silent." In an effort to prepare me for my departure, she said, "Ask for nothing; just let Him look upon you with love. He sees and understands your suffering." I played a tape she sent me about a nun who was healed of arthritis by Jesus and then became a healer herself.

September finally arrived, and so did Damian. How I was cheered by his phone call! How wonderful to find myself speaking of things other than my troubles. He spoke about his journeys, his love for the Chinese people. Before we hung up, I told him I loved him and thought about him often.

"I think about you all the time," he said.

The afternoon Damian came by, I was talking to Leslie and Dana as I sat in my chair next to the stairway leading up to my former bedroom. As Damian walked through the gates and on to the patio, I noticed he had not totally left India behind. The vest he wore was covered with embroidery and tiny mirrors. A pair of khaki shorts and leather sandals completed the look of a traveler who had just returned from far-off, exotic lands. My daughters greeted our friend, spoke for a while, and then left us to be alone with each other.

"You look just the same to me," said Damian in his usual cheerful voice. He certainly was the same relaxed, blue-eyed, humorous person who had appeared so unexpectedly in my life. I reached for his hand, kissed it, and placed it on my cheek. The sun cast a spotlight that caught the two of us in a moment of quiet before he sat down on a nearby bench to tell me about his adventures. My body relaxed into the wheelchair. He was accepting of my condition as if nothing had changed. To Damian, I was a loving soul mate, a *compañera*.

A few days later, as I was resting on my bed, Damian came for another visit. He walked through the bamboo curtain that covered the open doorway and nestled in beside me. He was so casual about intimacy that embarrassment never came into the equation. He shared the pictures of his trip with me. Meanwhile, I prayed my body would not betray me with incontinence. I was feeling both happy and distracted.

After I reconnected with dear Damian, it was time for me to take a trip into town and look for a new place to live. Morgan, with the assistance of our realtor, Emily, found two houses for me to consider buying or leasing. With Morgan at the wheel of his father's car, I felt secure, much more secure than during other drives I had taken. I was my old self again.

I found that I could again enjoy the passing scenery, though I had seen it a hundred times, maybe more. The little excursion was downright therapeutic.

We never looked at house number two. I bought the first one I saw, a Santa Fe-style adobe. The house had been remodeled and on the market for some time. Although appealing to many prospective buyers, not one person knew what to do with it, owing to its unique characteristics. To me, its uniqueness was the very thing that attracted me most about it. I fell in love with it immediately. I felt that, with a few minor modifications, it would be perfect for my needs. For one thing, Jennie's school was nearby. And, as Morgan wheeled me around the nearest corner to check out the neighborhood, I admired the much larger classic older homes shaded by magnolias and adorned with the old-fashioned streetlamps so character-istic of the west side of this very Midwestern-looking town. As we moved along the sidewalk, Morgan said, "We can't put you just anywhere, Mom. You're a classy lady."

"Classy? I don't know, Morgan. I feel quite ordinary." I reached behind me and patted his hand. "Thank you, Morgan," I said.

Back at the beach, things were moving along rather quickly as Elizabeth took charge of moving my furniture just as she had done when we moved to the beach. She would be redecorating for me once again.

Theresa helped me sort through my clothes. It became a party of three as the wine flowed freely. With Damian next to me on my bed, Theresa would disappear into my closet and then reappear with some item of clothing held underneath her chin. "Yes or no?" she inquired.

"No," I would say, and Theresa would drop the discards onto the floor.

"No discussion," said Theresa, as a piece of clothing sailed through the closet opening to join the mounting pile.

"Definitely not!" cried Damian, waving his arm in the air.

In the end I was left with nothing more than a few caftans and some nightgowns. Goodbye to the bathing suits, the shorts, the T-shirts, the blouses, the skirts, the slacks, the jackets, and most of my shoes. I now wore high-tops to prevent foot-drop, a common occurrence among para-plegics. They were adorned with laces that Jennie bought for me. Some were decorated with whales or hearts. "If you have to look at your feet, Mom, they might as well look pretty," she had said. Theresa, Damian, and I were laughing heartily—we were more than a little tipsy from the wine—as we disposed of the old Berta.

When the day of departure was upon us, Joyce offered to drive Jennie, Irma, and me home to Pasadena. First, we had to figure out how to get Irma past the border patrol just north of St. Lo. We found out she had come from Newport Beach without her green card. With Joyce's wonderful can-do nature, we managed to solve the problem. She sent a scout ahead to see if the border check was open. We received the news via telephone that there were no guards on duty. We approached the border patrol with Irma sitting in the back seat, wearing a blonde wig to disguise her dark hair. Jennie was sitting next to her.

"All systems are go!" cried Joyce as we flew past the checkpoint. The dizzying wheelchair waltz from home to hospital, to rehab, and back home again was over in September.

Chapter 10

EXILE

I am wearied with sighing;
every night I flood my bed with weeping;
I drench my couch with tears.
My eyes are dimmed with sorrow;
they have aged because of all my foes.

—Psalm 6

Chapter 10

Lightning flashed across the sky, and rolling thunder roared on the first night in my new home. Earlier that day, there had not been any sign of an impending storm; not a drop of rain fell as I sat in the living room and celebrated yet another new beginning with Vicky, Anne, Pat, and Judy, my old friends from Pasadena. For a moment we sat quite still staring at each other in surprise when we heard the storm. All conversation ceased until I smiled and said, "It's God welcoming me home." My four dear friends—whom I knew since my marriage to Bill in 1950—then raised their glasses of champagne, turned their eyes upward, and toasted the Creator.

After spending two days at Esther's home and one remarkable night in my own, I was finally able to assess my new surroundings.

The Santa Fe-style adobe was built around a central courtyard with a fountain in the middle. The courtyard was brick with attractively land-scaped areas on the right and left. Two very tall palms rose toward the heavens, their slender, graceful trunks swaying with the wind. French doors from the patio led into the galleria, the kitchen, and my bedroom. There were no steps for me to overcome when entering the galleria with its deeply recessed windows facing the patio. To my right was the living room, which rose slightly above the brick floor of the hall. With a little effort, I could push myself into the living room. Like the rest of the interior, the walls of this room were white troweled stucco, giving the room a pleasing, vintage appearance. The old beamed ceiling was from the original late '20s or early '30s Spanish-style building. There was a fireplace with a rounded opening but no mantelpiece, and the floor was wooden.

Down a short hallway was the master bedroom, which had a fireplace like the one in the living room. On the right side of this fireplace was the door to the courtyard that opened onto a brick ramp for easy access, and on the left was a large window that opened into the room, so I could see and hear the rustling banana leaves. Two similar windows faced the street. This provided an excellent view of the busy neighborhood, where children might be walking to school and neighbors might be seen exercising their dogs. The closet was long and wide, with shelves for purses, sweaters, high and low bars for changing garments. My chair slipped through very easily. The bathroom was off the hallway leading to the bedroom, so I could roll into the shower after the lip was removed. The toilet was in a cubicle next to the shower wall, and on the opposite side of the bath was a commode that extended the width of the room with a mirrored wall above. An opening under the sink allowed me a comfortable place to sit between drawers and cupboards on either side. White tile covered the counter tops and the floor, and the entrance—widened to accommodate my chair—had a folding door and faced the window on the wall between the shower and the sink.

The dining room had brick floors and was the central room connecting the two wings of the house. The dining room fireplace faced the French doors that led to the deck. A pergola, covered by an old wisteria vine, rose above the deck. It created a summer breezeway—a beautiful shady spot to read or have tea. A ramp led through the second doorway from the galleria to the brick-floored kitchen. In the center of the spacious area was a large wood-topped island surrounded by counters containing the sink, built-in range, ovens, and a double-door pantry. A dining area opened to the patio and faced a pretty view. Wonder of wonders, there was a door from the kitchen into the garage, so I wouldn't get wet when it rained!

The house stood below sidewalk level. A green lawn, divided by a brick walkway, led to a door set in an adobe wall. Decorative rocks, cacti, and bougainvillea added charm to the garden. A divine fragrance wafted from the bed of roses and the gardenia bushes. The ornamental plant I loved the most was a dwarf lemon tree, which was always covered with yellow fruit. It squatted on the lawn outside my bedroom window. I called the house "El Monasterio." It would be my sanctuary for many anguished, occasionally happy, years—the years I would spend becoming "another Berta," in Laura's words.

I rested for two days after moving into my lovely new home. Rest, however, had taken on a new meaning. Every four hours, I had to endure the ritual of catheterization. After the morning catheterization, Irma helped transfer me to the toilet from my wheelchair. Back in the wheelchair,

I wheeled myself over to the shower, and, with Irma's assistance, I got up on the shower chair. The cleansing warm spray felt soothing and helped ease my pain. Again, with Irma's help, I dried myself off, got dressed, and combed my hair. My morning routine was a struggle. That's the best way I know how to describe it. It was exhausting, and I would often have a crying spell when I was done.

One day, as I sat astride the toilet, facing the blank white wall in front of me while waiting for my bowels to move—and not knowing if they did, for lack of any sensation in that area—an idea came to me.

I thought of all the pictures stacked against the wall in the living room. I would hang the nude line drawing Jirayar Zorthian had done of me at my husband's request. I ended up hanging it over the toilet to remind me of happier times. I occasionally laughed at the memory of Jirayar coaxing me out of my clothes.

Irma decided to try her hand at housekeeping with limited success. I remember how, on one attempt to do the laundry, she washed the white clothes with the colored ones. Irma brought piles of clean but strangely hued clothing from the laundry room. The unwashed clothes got mixed up with the washed. One day, she left the floor mop in the laundry tub next to the washing machine. The water flowed out from the hoses that hung over the rim of the laundry tub. Eventually, it became a pastel river that ran out into the hallway. Thank God for brick floors. The flamingo-pink mop head now matched my dressing gown.

~ ~ ~

In the midst of settling into my new home, I had an appointment with a neurologist, which was neither helpful nor hopeful. She suggested that multiple sclerosis was not the problem and told me that I had a virus of the mononucleosis strain. According to the neurologist, the cause of my sudden paralysis was a mystery, and I found that difficult to believe, because my family health history was excellent. Most of my family members had led healthy, productive lives and enjoyed an active and robust old age. I, on the other hand, was plagued by cancer and paralysis at middle age. My sister had her share of suffering too: a bout of polio in the 1930's with no lasting effects, and, following her graduation from high school at sixteen, she had to spend a year in bed after contracting tuberculosis. She had to be hospitalized due to a collapsed lung. After recovering, she went on to University to get her Bachelor of Arts degree. "I'm happy for the delay. I'm now the right age to go to college," she said to me at the time. In spite of her recovery, I wondered why so many of our generation were so afflicted.

Irma was determined to help me walk again when I told her the doctor had not made arrangements for my physical therapy. When she was young, she had experienced paralysis—the result of her falling from a tree. After the doctor said she would never walk again, her mother hired a healer. The healer exercised Irma's legs until she was back up on her feet and walking again. The injury left Irma with a sexy swing in her hips as she walked. I enjoyed watching her sashaying across the patio, and, for a time, we laughed together about the legacy of her paralysis. Because her own ordeal made her sympathetic toward my condition, she wouldn't give up on me. Day after day, week after week, she helped me exercise my legs. And, when she left me to rest on my bed, she would prop up my feet until they were flexed in a vertical angle so I wouldn't succumb to foot drop. I was grateful for her assistance and dedication, and I felt that Christ was present in His servant—Irma Alvarez.

~ ~ ~

September came with a phone call from St. Lo.

"It's lonely on the hill without you," Don declared.

After our pleasant conversation, I felt compelled to search for photographs taken in the fall of '79. As I looked at the photos of the interesting designs that the low tides left etched in the sand, I thought about the reason I had taken them. They were reference shots for some abstract art projects I had in mind. In one photograph, Jennie was down on her hands and knees looking for possible treasures exposed by the receding tide. I found a photo of Damian. He was standing at the surf line with a surfboard tucked under his arm. Chrissie—his dog—and Jennie were standing nearby. Here was a picture of my granddaughter Riley snuggled under one arm, Jennie under the other, all bundled up in parkas, wool caps, and scarves. And then, in early 1980, a picture of Jennie putting roses and daisies on the water to commemorate the first anniversary of her father's death. The honey-hued fall and winter light illuminated all those pictures. The contrast between those moments caught by the camera and my present state made me feel profoundly sad.

My son Bill came to visit from Northern California. He took an immediate interest in my new home by installing shelves in the garage, adding more bookcases, putting furniture in place. And then he left for St. Lo to pick up the rest of my belongings.

After he returned, he drove me to physical therapy. During this first visit to P.T., my status was reevaluated. The therapist seemed somewhat pleased that my abdominal muscles and right leg had regained an infinitesimal measure of strength.

When we came back home, Bill and I sat in the living room to talk. Bill sat in a wing chair. On the table beside him rested a cloth mermaid. She sat in an overstuffed armchair. Her long blond hair trailed down the back of the chair. Two small seashells covered her breasts. She had been a gift from my son Bill years before. The mermaid—once a whimsical decoration for our beach house—now occupied a prominent place in the house as a reminder to keep smiling.

"You ought to get a dog, a watchdog," Bill said.

I had just told him about the intruder that tried to break into the house after I moved in: "Two nights after moving into the house," was how I began, "I heard a noise coming from the living room, so I slid from my bed into the wheelchair, pushed myself into the living room, and turned on a table lamp. There was a man standing on the deck. Strange, I wasn't frightened, but I called the police right away. He had left, or so they thought after searching the outside of the house. 'Get a dog,' one of the policemen said. After they left, Irma helped me back to bed. I heard footsteps crunching on the gravel path outside my bedroom wall."

I looked at Sam, our family dog, sitting by my son. Sam, a golden retriever, was now living with Bill. He was such a good-natured animal that he would probably show an intruder the way to the family silver. "All right, we'll get a dog," I said, with not an ounce of conviction in my voice. Pets require a great deal of time and care. "Irma, would you object to caring for a dog?" I asked her.

"They have fleas!" she replied with disgust.

So, I decided to install an alarm system instead.

As a diversion, Bill made a suggestion: "Would you like to go to the club for lunch? It will get you out of the house." "I don't know. The thought of going there makes me nervous," I confessed. "Well, if you're with me, I'll go."

Returning to the club we belonged to in Pasadena was just fine as far as I was concerned. Friends and acquaintances were quick to greet me. Members of the staff expressed their concern and would call me at home occasionally with ideas about how to take care of myself. "Rest, eat well, and pray," was the advice the staff gave me. They were even kind enough to bring books to my home.

The following day, Jennie was ready to leave for Santa Fe, but, dear Lord, Bill left first! Youth does not linger when time tells it to move on. Bill had helped me settle in, spent time with his little sister, and, after a night out with a childhood friend, decided to return to his own life. I had hoped he would stay until after Jennie's departure. I needed the strength his presence gave me.

Jennie and I waved goodbye as we watched Bill—with Sam sitting beside him—turn and smile his father's smile through the window of his truck. Then Michael arrived from Santa Fe. I saw Jennie holding his hand, and then the two of them raised their arms up to form a bridge as they walked past the fountain and through the gate.

My heart went with Jennie and Bill. I felt totally empty. *Oh, Holy God,* I thought, *am I going to spend the rest of my life watching friends and family come and go?*

Alone in the living room, I turned to the sounds of Jean-Pierre Rampal for solace. Music had always given me solace, but the particular piece that was playing reminded me of Christmas Day in 1980: I was alone waiting for the children to pick me up. We were driving to Galina to go cross-country skiing. The gifts had been opened, and I played the very same musical selection while I picked up wrapping paper and ribbons. I remember how this simple task accentuated my loneliness.

Where are you, Bill? I said to myself. *We used to do this together.*
I wheeled myself to my desk, stared out the window at the arbor, and
began to write:

> *Left Out*
> *Waiting again, forever waiting*
> *Always being left behind,*
> *Smiling, waving, "have a good time"*
> *says a voice, is it mine?*

I put down my pen and thought of the weeks since my new beginning
in September. There was much to be thankful for: Rosemary, a Mayfield
mother, came to announce, "We've got you covered!" meaning that a
carpool had been arranged for Jennie. On another day, while Rosemary
and I were visiting on the patio, she took after a thief who had stolen
Jennie's bicycle from our driveway. She returned with the bicycle after
having curbed the thief with her car only a few blocks away. They let the
thief run away. Ginny and another friend phoned to ask what they could
do and later came over to fold piles of laundry and do some ironing as
well. Annette, the mother of Bill's friend John, came to help me put things
away, but we ended up with little accomplished, as the house lacked the
space to store everything. Tired of seeing photos and paintings stacked
against the wall, Annette returned one day armed with a hammer and
picture hooks. David, my godson, drove me to physical therapy; his sister,
Meg, drove me home. Their mother, Mary Jane, took Jennie shopping. On
the days that I couldn't stop crying, Mary Jane would drive me around
town. She was a cancer survivor like me. As we drove around, we talked
about the deep affect that the ordeal of cancer had on our lives. Esther
supported me during the many years I remained in Pasadena. She would
come for visits, or invite me to her house for lunch. Friends let me use their
swimming pools so that I could exercise my limbs. With Morgan's help,
I was able to get in and out of the water. Hot tubs made my skin blister, so
for the moment we avoided them.

With the absence of Jennie and Bill, I came to realize that being alone
was part of my healing. Happy with Irma, I came home to someone who
was anxious to hear the news about my physical therapy. After bringing

me tea, she would drop down by my chair and weep and pray. Then it was off to bed for a nap in a peaceful house.

~ ~ ~

One warm October day, Damian came by with some of the work he had done in India and Asia.

"I particularly like this work," I remarked, referring to a study of an Indian sitting on a ledge with soaring peaks in the distance behind him. "Would you like to see the house?" I asked, setting the picture aside. Damian wheeled me through the house.

"It's definitely you," he commented, smiling.

We ended up on the patio, where Irma brought us lunch. We ate and sipped some wine as we enjoyed the fine October day. Except for the space we took up in our little corner of the universe, nothing else existed. Damian talked about the difficulties of living life as an artist and about his new girlfriend.

"But, I don't want to marry," he admitted.

"I miss my husband, Damian. It isn't so much about the fact that sexual intimacy has been taken from me, it is the comfort, security, familiarity, and companionship of married life that I miss."

Damian gently touched my hand. He caught my gaze.

"It's the security of married life you miss. Sex is only a part of life; it's not everything," he pointed out.

The irrepressible romantic rose up in me. "We are like Heloise and Père Abelard, except I feel as if *I* am the one who is castrated!" Imagining those tragic lovers from the distant past lent our situation a certain poignancy. "Like Abelard, you were my teacher; Heloise was Abelard's pupil. However, you won't become a priest like Abelard. Heloise became a nun, and, at some point, like her, my life will be devoted to God too," I predicted. "We will never cease to care for each other. Our love will only deepen, just as theirs did."

When Damian kissed me goodbye on that warm October afternoon, the lines of a poem he had sent me came to mind:

When habitation has ceased to be
For ten thousand eons or more,
Who will stand alone with me
To sing of the beauties of yore?

For nothing will then matter
Of our twenty years that us scold,
For our eyes like babes will be opened
To pause and laugh at the old.

I ended up confused by love—the love of God, the security of marital love, the joyful surprise of unexpected love. To calm my mind, I flipped through an old sketchbook until I came upon a sketch I made of my own hands. Circling around the hands and through the fingers were the following words: "He has pierced my hands and feet. He has numbered all my bones." The old sketch reminded me of the final years of my marriage, which were painfully scarred.

Painting was no longer easy for me, as my body tensed up, brushes fell to the floor and rolled out of my reach, and, reaching for an easel that was all but beyond arm's length, I stretched my back muscles, causing severe nerve pain throughout my entire body.

When I couldn't stand it any longer, Irma would take me outside into the sun, hoping the warmth would bring me some relief, or she would put me on my bed. But I have a mind that never quits, so I was unable to relax very easily.

One day, I listened to our family cat, Thomas, howling to be let out. I was on my bed, and Irma had retired to her room. Old and lonely, Tom had probably wondered where he was, wondered where everyone had gone. One day, he went away to die. I thought about how graciously he accepted death. My wish was that humans could do the same. The ringing of the phone interrupted that reverie.

Jennie was calling from Santa Fe. "I love you," she said. I detected a tone of loneliness in her voice. Her sisters had gone out for dinner, so I sought to comfort her. Then, she asked me if she could stay two more days.

"No, you are missing too much school," I replied. Jennie was crying when we said our goodbyes. It occurred to me she was probably happier with her sisters.

I was happier alone, but afraid to admit it was so. Irma would bring me breakfast at 8:30 A.M. I would watch the morning news for a bit, and then she would return to collect my tray and help me with my range-of-motion exercises, my bath, and the slow process of dressing. Going to my phone to try and find a weekend replacement for Irma filled the remaining hours of the morning. Sometimes a friend would show up with lunch for the two of us, and afterwards I would return to my bed to be cleaned up, rest, or read a book. If I had any energy left, I would get up to work on a drawing. That activity was usually followed by a quick wash, a clean nightdress, supper in bed, some TV, and, finally, blessed sleep.

My routine varied with the weather. A cold house meant tea at 4:30 A.M. and a trip to the kitchen after struggling off the bed and into a warm robe. While there, I began to teach Irma how to cook and how to serve a meal. A willing student, she was so proud when the meal turned out exactly right.

One beautiful evening, Irma brought a lovely supper tray to the living room, where I was enjoying the music on the stereo and the fading light tinged with pink from the sunset. There was no one with whom to share the moment. I found reassurance in the fact that I was alone but not lonely. This unveiled a truth about me that had gone unrecognized by me in the past. As a married woman, I had sought to have time alone in order to retreat into the world of my imagination.

I found a caregiver to substitute for Irma. She seemed agreeable and willing to help. I instructed her about my care, but she spoke nonstop about her deceased husband and his final illness. I had to escape to my bed in order to avoid her as much as possible until Irma returned.

One morning, she woke me up from a dream in which a pale, ghostly Bill was walking me through our home in St. Lo. "You didn't have to do this," Bill was saying. Was he referring to the sale of the house? I didn't know. But, it was the caregiver's incessant talk about her dead husband that prompted the dream, and the question posed by Bill in the dream upset me.

~ ~ ~

Jennie came home from Santa Fe. A young friend brought delicious Chinese food to share with Damian and Christopher—the other artist I had known at St. Lo, who had visited often since my move to Pasadena to cheer me. As we ate, I delighted in watching the two men competing like little boys over the answers to Jennie's homework. It was a happy evening, a good start for Jennie.

There was a bout of rain for several days, and Jennie came down with a cold. I kept her home and, at the same time, worried about her missing more school. "Pobrecita," said Irma, who tucked her into bed, put flowers in her room, and gave her aspirin with hot water and lemon juice.

Since her return from Santa Fe, Jennie spent most of her nights sleeping on the sofa in my bedroom, although Leslie had told me on the phone, "She should be sleeping in her own bed."

I had answered, "She'll do that when she is ready."

We would fall asleep listening to music, especially to the film score from *On Golden Pond.* Jennie had no idea that the stage play of that name was the last theater performance her father and I had attended, and I never mentioned this fact to her.

I had recovered from the shock of so dramatically having to rearrange my life, but mentally and emotionally I was still in turmoil. The darkness of night became my friend. Nighttime was when I felt some sense of relief from the despair and hopelessness of the daylight hours.

A depressed person is often unaware that they are in a depressed state. It did not strike me as odd that I had joined the Hemlock Society or that I kept my husband's bone-handled knife within easy reach, just in case.

In my mind, my handicap separated me from Jennie, and I saw only three lonely people living in the house. Jennie slept not only in my room, she slept in Irma's as well, hugging a toy bear that Leslie had given Jennie when she was born. The bear only played a few notes of its wind-up tune, but it didn't matter to Jennie. She was so attached to that little creature.

"I've cried all over him. I've even wiped my nose on him too!" she told me. Jennie's skin was ashen beneath a veil of sadness that covered her young face.

Irma was feeling lonely too. Alone without her husband, son, and daughter, she was separated from mainstream life in Southern California by language, customs, and food. She returned early on her days off because she was afraid of the unfamiliar world outside my home. Mutual faith bound the three of us together as we prayed for my recovery: "We believe in the Holy Spirit, the Lord, the giver of life . . ."

My damaged emotional state was aggravated by the places I had to see or visit. The hospital where I had to go for therapy was the same hospital where I saw the birth of my last three children, where I was once a cheerful volunteer pushing others around in wheelchairs. At times, it was necessary to drive past my husband's former place of work, the super-market where I shopped for years, the pharmacy, the dry cleaners, restaurants where we had dined. Once a memory was reawakened, I would sob uncontrollably.

My paints lay idle, even though Damian had set up a sort of studio at one end of the living room. Whenever I saw him or spoke to him on the phone, my mind was tricked. Every time I heard the sound of his voice or saw his familiar gestures, everything seemed just like it used to be. However, it was all too much a part of the past I had to put away, that I had to forget.

My relationships with my older daughters continued to deteriorate. Because we were so happy in the early days as a family, I expected the children now would be living nearby and willing to help me. I was mistaken about that. The recent tragic events in our lives fragmented the family. The survivors were seeking to heal their wounds. Tragedy, like divorce, was damaging to our family.

"Where are your children?" was a question I was asked again and again. I had no answer.

Leslie suggested that I go into therapy. "It has helped me a lot," she explained.

I did turn to psychotherapy, but I was deeply suspicious of the process. I suspected that psychotherapy would lead me to blame my circumstances on some childhood trauma. *Isn't that what usually happens?* I thought.

Sigrid, my therapist, was a slight, attractive middle-aged woman, and her professional manner bordered on steely. After I described to her the sequence of events prior to and including paralysis, the comment she made about Damian is one I would always remember.

"It was something for yourself," she had said. So clearly stated, so clearly true, I repeated the phrase over and over so that it would be carved indelibly in my memory.

Aunt Alice and a nurse gave me support on my second visit to therapy. They sat in the waiting room while I talked to Sigrid about the death of my husband.

"You have returned to a place where you have spent most of your life," she said.

"First, your mother ran your married life without giving your own needs much thought. You have never been free to speak up for yourself."

Sigrid gestured at my legs, saying, " This new freedom for a woman who has never been free can be terrifying. We have a lot of work to do." Before I left, she cautiously suggested we try self-hypnosis.

When we returned from the session, Alice and I had lunch out on the patio. We ate what she referred to as her "special sandwiches." Typically, that meant cucumber and watercress on white bread, the crusts cut off, and then the sandwich sliced diagonally. It was teatime at high noon.

"Alice, Sigrid as much as said I did this to myself. She said that I had never been free, and, when I found myself without Bill, I put myself in this position."

Alice, ever thoughtful and blunt, said after what seemed like an eternity, "Nonsense. I'd ask for my money back and find another therapist."

When dear Alice left, the nurse put me to bed, but not before asking for a sample of my husband's handwriting.

At three in the afternoon, I awoke, and, as I sipped tea the nurse had brought me, I listened as she accurately described my husband after analyzing his handwriting. One of her remarks struck me with force: "You received a lot of the feelings he felt for his mother. Bill was antisocial, disliked parties, had no close male friends. He was a loner." That was not good news, as Bill had a lot of contained anger toward his mother, although he treated her with gracious civility. He was a baby when his parents divorced, and his mother retained custody. When she moved to London, England, Bill attended day school there. Ebba—his nanny—took care of him while his mother, still very young, was caught up in the Roaring Twenties. Eventually, he was sent away to boarding school. Summerfield was a school for English and foreign aristocrats. The only American boy, he was referred to as "that boy from the colonies." Boxing was a sport commonly taught in England's public schools, and Bill took it up to defend himself, winning two small silver cups in the process. When he got older, he would often return to New York City to spend the summers with his father. It was during one of those vacations that he refused to return to England. His alcoholic father became his role model. His mother remarried an English barrister who was eventually killed in World War II.

"Yes, I used to see him hiding his tears behind a newspaper when I put him on the train for boarding school," his mother explained to me one day. "But, Berta dear, all the little boys went to boarding school in those days." In the end, Bill was the injured child of alcoholics, divorce, and too many stepparents.

How did I feel about his parents? I found them highly attractive people defined by the era they lived in—the Roaring Twenties—a handsome, affluent couple who led a glamorous and carefree life that ended in sadness. I loved them, and I loved their son who had told me, "I would have never married if I hadn't met you."

Unable to deal with all of the emotions and unanswered questions brought up by my psychologist, I turned to Mary Jane for help. "I suggest you talk to Father Moretta," was her advice.

Father Moretta, a priest from the parish I preferred to attend whenever possible, came to see me. He was new to the parish, and I liked him immediately. Father Moretta came from the inner city of Los Angeles. He was young, ambitious, funny, tough, streetwise, and completely dedicated to the church. When we first met, he seemed surprised by my appearance.

"I thought you were much worse off from the way your friends described you," he commented. Once again, I recounted for him the painful events of the last few years. "You are a very strong lady. If you ever get up on your feet, you're going to be something else," commented Father Moretta. I wasn't sure what he was implying with that comment.

When I got to the part about Damian, I prefaced my explanation with a remark my husband tossed out while we were arguing about a letter I had written to Leslie: "I think you should have an affair with Damian, it would be good for you."

Father Moretta raised his eyebrows, smiled, and asked, "So you took him at his word?"

"Yes," I replied. "Once. No, twice."

"Are you sure twice is correct?" he grinned.

"Positive. The third time I was a widow," was my true and final answer.

"Have you been to confession and Communion lately? Oh well, you've already made your confession. I'll return and give you absolution and Communion."

On his return visit, he said to me, "What has happened to you is evil. You can choose to run away from God or become closer to Him. You are going to be a saint."

"But I don't want to be a saint!" I yelled in protest. Mary Jane, who was present, began to laugh.

For years, she would remind me of the incident. "I don't want to be a saint!" she would screech and then start to laugh. "I'll never forget that one!"

~ ~ ~

The holidays were approaching, and I was dreading them. Morgan had come home from Berkeley for Thanksgiving. But, sadly, Bill phoned to say he had no money, his car wasn't working, and he had a sore throat, so he was unable to come to Pasadena for the holidays. Jennie's eyes filled with tears when she heard the news. (I could not fill the empty spaces in her life. My sense of inadequacy haunted me.) Dana phoned, sounding very happy, and said, "Don't worry, the whole family can come here to Santa Fe for Thanksgiving dinner next year." She must have known how depressed

I was when I read her two poems by Edna Saint Vincent Millay, beginning with "Lament":

> *Listen children:*
> *Your father is dead . . .*
> *. . . Life must go on,*
> *And the dead be forgotten;*
> *Life must go on,*
> *Though good men die;*
> *Anne, eat your breakfast;*
> *Dan, take your medicine;*
> *Life must go on;*
> *I forget just why.*

And then, I recited "Exiled":

> *Searching my heart for its true sorrow,*
> *This is the thing I find to be;*
> *That I am weary of words and people,*
> *Sick of the city, wanting the sea . . .*

Thanksgiving concluded with dinner at the club with my mother, uncle, Aunt Alice, her grandson Richard, Morgan, Jennie. When we returned to my house, we all settled around the fire.

"Isn't this cozy?" beamed Jennie.

~ ~ ~

My fifty-first birthday was marked by a visit to the hospital for therapy. Strapped down to a slant board, I was tilted into an upright position. The reflection in the mirror was unrecognizable. I looked like a scarecrow with legs and torso akimbo. Seeing myself hanging on that "cross" made me think of the crucifixion. *I am like the Christ*, I told myself. "Happy Birthday," I said sarcastically to the image in the mirror.

I received phone calls from most of my children. Leslie sent flowers. Aunt Alice came over with a gift. She had even called Leslie in Idaho to find out what I might enjoy. It was a brand new Sony Walkman to replace the borrowed one I had in rehab. Alice's gifts were usually something of a personal nature, something she might like to buy for herself. I imagined her purchasing something new, in a store surrounded by electronic gadgets. The image of Alice surrounded by objects with which she was decidedly unfamiliar brought a smile to my face. I felt joy as we ate the lunch she had prepared. The effort on her part to obtain the gift bespoke such tenderness and love. The feelings it brought forth lifted me out of my depression momentarily.

I returned to my sessions with Sigrid, trying to get insight into the deteriorating relationships with my daughters. Leslie, it seemed, was still smarting from my reaction to her divorce. As I reviewed that situation, I expressed to Sigrid that, with her father's sudden death and my sudden paralysis, we had been robbed of the time to mend our relationship. Dana, who still could not forgive my accusation that her situation with Kevin caused my illness, took exception to "that whispery voice you use on the telephone," as she put it. She implied that I was looking for sympathy. I didn't bother explaining to her that my diaphragm—affected by my paralysis—simply did not allow my lungs to expand completely. The bodily changes were so new I did not understand them myself. Also, that voice was the voice of a depressed, suicidal person. My tone of voice was symptomatic of depression, though I did not know that at the time.

Accepting Sigrid's suggestion to try hypnosis as a way of relieving anxiety, my first attempt was successful in that I seemed to respond well in that altered state.

"What do you see?" was her question.

"The face of my mother," I replied. Yes, there she was; her face was larger than life, like an actress on a movie screen. No surprise there, as Sigrid and I both knew that my relationship with my mother needed attention.

On another visit, Sigrid and I delved into the practice of self-hypnosis.

"Imagine a warm white light seeping down your body and coming out different colors at your feet. Possibly you are lying in the sand. You can feel the sand in your hands. You hear the sound of voices drifting across the beach. Perhaps, the sun is obscured by a cloud, and it becomes chilly.

When the sun comes out again, you get up and walk down the terrace to the sea. The sea leaps up at your feet. You might even go for a swim. Afterwards, you probably walk up a hill."

"It's St. Lo you are describing," I cried. Tears streaming down my face, I told Sigrid about the walk I had taken hundreds of times up and down the hill in St. Lo.

The holidays drove me over the edge. Judith, Jennie's godmother, recognized that I could no longer cope when she heard me say to Jennie, "Say goodbye to your mother." What I really meant was that I was going to commit suicide. Somehow, Judy understood the hidden meaning in those words.

When I checked into Cedars-Sinai, I was greeted by Father Vincent Martin, O.S.B.—the Catholic chaplain who gave me Communion before I was taken to my room. With a great deal of noise and clanking of keys, a male nurse pushed aside the steel accordion door after undoing several locks. I was wheeled to what I thought were my permanent quarters. The room had the appearance of an upscale motel. Chocolates and hot cups of tea awaited me as soon as the staffers settled me on the bed.

Oh, how peaceful, I thought. *I'll be cared for without any responsibilities of home and hearth.*

After one night, I was transferred to a cell-like room with a bath. The bed was a built-in bunk, somewhat high off the floor and affixed to the walls. So narrow was the bed, I couldn't turn over on my side without the help of an orderly. Worried about bedsores, I couldn't relax. The tearful screams in the night of the other patients kept me on edge.

One time, a patient wandered into my room even though there were restrictions against the patients or family members entering our "cells." The young woman stood next to my bed and stared, her face expressionless. I offered a smile and a friendly "hello" to relieve my apprehension. As the minutes ticked by, she did not utter a word, her face remained blank, and I imagined she had mayhem in mind. Finally, she left the room just as soundlessly as she appeared.

On another day, the public address system announced, "There is a pair of scissors missing from the nurses' station, and we will be searching all the rooms."

Clank went my bedroom door. *Clank, clank, clank* went all the doors, as I suppose they were electronically locked. My room was thoroughly searched, as was my person. Everything went back to normal when the scissors were discovered at the nurses' station, where they had been all along.

I started to make the acquaintance of some of my fellow sufferers. A young woman with lupus had been a guest in my home at St. Lo one summer when we had rented it out for a month. "Oh, it was so beautiful," she said. "I'm very sorry you had to sell it."

There was a young police officer who, while making a drug arrest, had PCP thrown into his face. It seeped into his pores and completely altered his personality. As his personality shifted, he ended up losing his job and then his wife and kids. Return to normalcy was going to be a very, very slow process for this unfortunate man whose life had changed so drastically while answering the call of duty.

I enjoyed meeting Joan in a class where we shared writing poetry as a form of therapy. She had been abandoned by a young lover with whom she shared a longtime relationship and had suffered a nervous breakdown as a result. I introduced her to a poem I had written about Damian entitled "Question from an Older Woman":

> *When I am old,*
> *and you are still quite young,*
> *Will you steal a glance*
> *across my withered brow,*
> *And wonder how we came*
> *to sing our song not long ago?*
> *Or, will your heart be tender*
> *and remember*
> *The face that came to love you*
> *in its final burst of youth.*
> *Now*
> *tell*
> *the*
> *Truth!*

Joan asked me for a copy, and I happily gave it to her.

Occasionally, we would have group therapy, where everyone gathered around a gentleman who—it was whispered—was famous worldwide in psychiatric circles. Sitting in a chair—the rest of us arranged in a semi-circle like a group of admirers—he would throw out a question, then, pausing for a moment, he would lean forward in his chair, stretch out his arm, point a finger at someone, and bark, "Say what you're thinking." I suppose it was meant to catch us off guard as we each in turn attempted to respond to the command.

When my turn came, I would answer, "I'm just watching everyone's feet move and wishing they were mine." He finally stopped pointing at me.

I took advantage of the art classes that were available. I tried to draw a picture of Jennie, but the pencil no longer moved smoothly across the paper in definitive strokes. Lines jerked and wobbled, creating a sketch that looked like it might have been made by a kindergarten student.

The movie *One Flew Over the Cuckoo's Nest* came to mind as we lined up at the nurses' station to receive our medication from paper cups and which we swallowed on the spot with a glass of water.

There were diversions available for all those who were ambulatory, and that was everyone except me. Trips to the movies were on the sign-up sheet, but the bus or van necessary for transport was not wheelchair accessible. A group of women made a trip to Chippendale's to tuck money in the briefs of nearly naked men. Well, I suppose that was a sort of therapy for some. *Only in Beverly Hills,* was my immediate thought.

I enjoyed the peaceful ward when everyone was out on an excursion. I obtained permission from the neurologist to continue physical therapy, so it was my diversion to leave the locked gates behind and travel long corridors that were covered with art, and whose glass walls provided beautiful views.

At last, the sessions with Dr. Rosen, my appointed psychiatrist, began.

Dr. Rosen told me I was in bad shape.

"Oh yes," I replied with polite sarcasm, as momentarily my "ethereal veil"—as Sigrid had called the curtain that covered me—slipped open a crack. Smiling that polite smile of my past and present life, I found myself drifting away from Dr. Rosen to another state of consciousness where everything looked like a watercolor painting awash with dim and hazy pastel colors. My untrained soprano voice sang aloud the various melodies that appeared in my head until anger surged up in me when he asked me, "Why did you have five children?"

"I'm Catholic," I replied.

"Well, uh, yeah," he said, with a question in his voice. We were off to a bad start.

After several sessions with Dr. Rosen, he decided that it was time for me to meet with my daughters for therapy.

Dana phoned Damian after his visit with me to find out how I was doing. (Since non-family members were not allowed, my son Morgan suggested to Damian that he could just present himself as my son Bill. The ruse worked. No one even noticed him slipping into my room, where we talked before he slipped away as quietly as he had come.) Leslie phoned from Pasadena to say she had taken Jennie shopping in Beverly Hills. *Only a few blocks away*, I thought with great sadness. The girls had been talking to Dr. Rosen, but I had not visited with them face to face since my confinement.

Preparing me for our family visit, Dr. Rosen told me that my daughters were afraid of me. He told me that Jennie no longer wished to live with me and was afraid of me as well.

All right, I must think about that, I thought.

I listened as he said, "You appear unapproachable to your children." I remember the nurse's comment at the beach that I should appear "more vulnerable" to my children. I was my mother's daughter after all, at least in that respect. Victorians—and my mother was raised in England when Queen Victoria sat on the throne—saw any sort of weakness as a fault, illness included, so one kept soldiering on without complaint.

"Leslie," Dr. Rosen said, "has accused you of blaming her for her father's death." Startled by that comment, I sat in silence when he added that Dana had accused me of blaming her for my paralysis. Ah yes, the angry moment at the beach while we ate supper had raised its ugly head again! Selective finger pointing was at work. Someone had to be responsible for the destruction in our lives. Clearly, it was me, and Dr. Rosen was arming me for the worst possible confrontation with my daughters by breaking the rules of his profession: he had divulged what my daughters had told him.

Before returning to my room, I stopped at the nurses' station and asked them to call Father Vincent Martin's extension. He would come to see me in the early evening, but I needed some immediate comfort, so I picked up the eggshell-colored card with the brown crosses printed on the front that Father Vincent had given to me. Inside, it read:

> *May your stay at Cedars-Sinai bring you refreshment for the soul as well as health for the body and peace for the mind.*

I searched for Sister Vicky's letter, because her heart, like mine, had been broken.

Dear Berta,

I know you have been walking a very lonely road for some time now, but somehow I feel certain that that is how it has to be. It's a time when there are no yes and no answers, no black and white answers, a lot of questioning, even doubting. The old familiar landmarks are gone, and the resting places are no longer there to give you confidence and security. Like Elijah in the desert, you have called out, "Lord, I have had enough! Let me die, I am no better than the rest of men." But, Berta darling, we can only go "home" when God calls us, and it is clear from the story that He was very close to Elijah then and was leading him to greater things. It sure does require faith to walk this path, and yet it is the only path that will lead you to experience God on a deeper level. And, just as I was reminded, I am reminding you—we have to be careful of that self-pity, which is so soul destroying. But that is quite different from the compassion and caring that you should, that we should have for ourselves.

Live in the present. The past is gone, and we have no claim on the future. Pray to God to reveal his plan for our lives, and trust Him unconditionally. Remember what Jesus said in the Bible: "Can a woman forget the child of her womb, but even if she were to, see I will not." Remember Berta, you are unique, God's masterpiece. Human nature is the greatest of God's creations, and His love transforms all that is created. I think it was Pope Pius XII who said, "God with His love neither destroys nor changes nature but perfects it." Could he have put it more beautifully?

When Father Martin visited me in the evening, I revealed what Dr. Rosen had told me that morning. Together, we prayed for the understanding and forgiveness needed to restore the family that had once taken such delight in each other's company.

"Sister Wilfrid wrote to tell me how happy she was that you had greeted me on my admission to this hospital. She said she had contacted you to inform you of my arrival," I said.

That evening, Father Martin's powerful presence and the peace that surrounded him spoke to me on a deep level. He had been imprisoned too—not by paralysis, but by the Japanese. He sat in a prison cell waiting to be executed.

"I feel imprisoned, Father, and I will probably be my own executioner," I said.

He gave me Communion, we prayed the Our Father, and then he left me. Before going to sleep, I read Isaiah, chapter 40 to the end, recited Psalm 23—"The Lord is my Shepherd"—and remembered how, in the Gospels, Jesus himself tells us, "Do not be afraid. Fear not"; and then, Deuteronomy, chapter 31, verse 8: "The Lord himself will lead you and be with you. He will not fail you or abandon you, so do not lose courage or be afraid." I was brought up to do as I was told, so I decided to follow the advice Sister Vicky had offered in her letter.

The day finally came—Wednesday, January 13, 1982—when I met with my daughters, Leslie and Dana, in the company of Dr. Rosen. The girls were sitting as I wheeled into the small room where our therapy session was to take place. I was wearing my spiritual armor from the previous evening and was smiling and singing behind "the veil."

We discussed why my children did not come to my aid when I so needed them. They said that I store up my anger, and then, at inappropriate moments, I have outbursts, accusing them of outrageous things. Consequently, they were afraid of my explosive reactions when they confided in me, and so they kept their distance. I didn't remember the angry outbursts, except for the time when Dana phoned home from boarding school to say she was smoking marijuana. Her father took the phone away from me on that occasion.

"Dr. Rosen told me that you were upset about the Valentine I sent you on the first Valentine's Day after your father's death," I said to Leslie.

"Mom, it was a picture of a heart dripping blood!" she said.

"It was a simple pen and ink drawing of the Sacred Heart. Yes, it is broken in two, but that is how I was feeling at the time. You being a Catholic, I thought you'd understand the significance."

Leslie glared at Dr. Rosen. "How dare he tell you what we told him in confidence! That is not what a professional should do," she protested. ("I can't stand him," she told me later when Dr. Rosen was out of sight.)

I pled guilty to their charges that I indulged in sudden angry outbursts. I had conveniently wiped them from my memory and only thought of the idyllic side of our lives.

Jennie was our first concern. Leslie and Dana told me that they had spoken with Jennie's teacher.

"She is going to get an 'incomplete' for all her classes this quarter," Dana explained.

"It breaks my heart to hear that," I admitted.

"She looked so upset when we told her we were going home," Leslie revealed.

Then why are you leaving? I thought. (For some reason, I didn't pose the question to my daughters.)

~ ~ ~

"Why did you betray my daughters?" I asked Dr. Rosen at our next meeting.

"Because we have little time to try to correct this relationship," he replied.

It was the beginning of another long and painful journey to become "another Berta," as Laura had written. Well, I had to start somewhere. So, I admitted to myself that I wasn't the perfect daughter, wife, or mother. It was quite a relief to make that realization.

"But please, God," my prayer began, "make us a family again. Help us support each other; help us forgive one another; help us love one another unconditionally. Thank you for the gift of parenthood. It taught me to be of service to others even if I did it poorly at times."

I had been concerned about Jennie since last May. I had become an empty vessel with nothing to give her. Nevertheless, she was deeply loved for ten years by two parents and four siblings who adored her specialness. That was the well from which she could draw.

I had written a poem to release my feelings and to better understand how my daughters felt about me. Now, in a group therapy session with my fellow sufferers, I read the poem aloud for the same reasons:

> *"You have a viper's tongue," she said.*
> *"We are all afraid of you as well,*
> *except perhaps one son.*
> *You say one thing but do you mean it?"*
> *questioned my accusers.*
> *"You accused me of my father's death,"*
> *the brown-eyed girl continued.*
> *The gray-eyed daughter aimed her tongue*
> *at my paralyzed legs.*
> *"You said I did that to you.*
> *You throw our confidences in our faces,"*
> *continued my accusers,*
> *my children,*
> *my flesh.*

After everyone in the group had spoken, we were asked to make lists of truths and questions about ourselves. These are the lists I came up with:

Truths:

I don't know whether I can survive without my legs.

I do need some time alone without the responsibility of a child.

I don't know if I can deal with loneliness.

I do miss not having my children around me or at least close by—especially since Bill's death.

I do know that, after being here with Sue (a widow and a member of my group), all the feelings I've had since Bill's death are common to widows—including those feelings that come up with respect to children. It is a strain on the children now that their mother needs looking after and a strain on me because I was unable to maintain my independence.

I do not think the children can have any understanding of the anguish of last summer.

Jennie is not happy with me!

Questions:

Is God drawing me closer to Him? (See Job and Elijah for parallels.)

Does He want me to give up all and join Him on this earth for a little while—as a nun?

Would family counseling be good for Jennie and me?

Through the jumble of turmoil and guilt, I remembered Dana's feelings following her father's death and prior to the onset of my paralysis. She had hoped I was feeling better and getting things straightened out in my head. She found that his death caused her to reevaluate the priorities in her life. Family came out on the top of her list.

"I think I have inherited Dad's penchant for familial concerns," Dana revealed to me during that time. Her father would have agreed with her. "I've been a better father than a husband," he had told me before his death.

As for me, "The Madonna" was what some of my friends called me. I often heard the word "serene" in reference to myself. Was I too distant? Was it my "ethereal veil"? Was I independent by nature but had acquiesced to my upbringing and the mores of the times? I had thought myself a good mother. At one time, I played out that role with confidence, but now my effectiveness as a mother was in question. I felt that I had failed as a mother, and that, to me, was worse than being paralyzed. 🐢

Chapter 11

BABY STEPS

I am being driven forward
Into an unknown land.
The pass grows steeper,
The air colder and sharper,
The air from my unknown goal
Stirs the strings of expectation
A clear pure note
In the silence.

—Dag Hammarskjöld, *Markings*

Chapter 11

A t the end of January, I was released from Cedars-Sinai Hospital, which felt like being released from jail. My first week back at home was spent quietly and contentedly alone with Irma. Jennie was staying with Anne, whose parents were close friends of my mother-in-law and Aunt Alice. Together with her husband and two children, they graciously agreed to take care of Jennie until I could restore my emotional balance. Jennie and Kate, Anne's daughter, had been babies together, attended kindergarten together, and were now in the same class at Mayfield. I prayed that the separation from Jennie would not be permanent.

Just before I left Cedars-Sinai, one of the nurses had remarked to me, "I don't think you found what you were looking for in this place." No, what I was hoping to find was peace, a place to grieve over divorce, death, and illness. Alone with Irma, I could allow myself to be depressed without having it be a burden on Jennie. I spent my time resting, continuing therapy, and socializing a bit. On Irma's birthday, we ate at a Nicaraguan restaurant. On Super Bowl Sunday, I enjoyed watching the game on television at the home of friends. Both occasions lifted my spirits, but a phone call from Damian was the highlight.

"Now I'll be able to see you more often," Damian told me on the phone. His aunt, who had lived nearby, had died, and he was moving into her home.

Inspired by Damian's message, I began to sketch again. It was a struggle for me. Balancing therapy, dealing with unceasing nerve pain, and the routine of bodily care left me little energy to draw on. Emotionally, I walked a fine line.

Weekends were barren. The phone never rang, and no one came to see me.

In the past, I would await the weekends with great anticipation, as there was always something going on. But now, weekends were even bleaker and lonelier than the weekdays. Hardly anyone called anymore, nor did friends come by to visit, caught up as they were with family matters. How could I blame them for that? I recalled how I used to hustle through Fridays, putting things in order, preparing for gatherings, or planning meals with friends and family. But now, when the week came to a close, I felt forsaken. God was to be my only companion, but I had not yet learned to appreciate the solace and joy that could spring from that communion.

Eventually, I would overcome the loneliness that came as a result of Bill's death. Indeed, the thought of pursuing my own desires was exciting. Those desires were simple. Completing my university degree, educating Jennie, and travel made up the list. Almost thirty years married and content, I wanted to be alone, but not in my current state. This was not what I had in mind at all—this persistent loneliness, anger, and confusion.

I remember complaining to Sister Vicki when she stopped by on a particularly bad weekend, "Look at me. Here I am, sitting at home in my wheelchair while Irma is out taking her English class."

In an effort to lift my spirits, Sister said, "Don't allow yourself to get worked up over everything. If you see the good in things, you won't feel so angry about your situation. For example, Irma could not go to school if it were not for you," she reminded me.

I felt I needed time to internalize that message of selflessness, so I changed the subject. "A friend recently returned from St. Lo, where she attended a party in my former home," I said. "My friend then communicated, 'You are not there anymore. It seemed strange going to your home and not finding you there.' Also, she mentioned that Damian was at the beach with his girlfriend. It warmed my heart that she had missed my presence in my former home, but I must admit that I felt resentment toward the people who now owned it." I told Sister that my friend's mention of Damian brought to mind the day he showed up at my former home after Bill's death.

"His arms were full of pussy willow branches. When I told Sigrid, my shrink, about that, she asked, 'Why pussy willows?' I was puzzled by the question. I didn't know what she was getting at. 'Well, Damian said that they were the only things blooming in his garden,' I told her. I saw only beauty in his gentle offering. I still do."

"It was indeed an odd question, especially if she was searching for some sexual innuendo in her question. Let it go," advised Sister Vicki.

"Sister," I began again, "I am being assailed by memories that I thought I had neatly tucked away—for instance, the long morning walk I took with Damian after I learned of Leslie's plans for divorce. He paused to kiss me and pick flowers for me. I was very confused and upset that morning. Damian was seeing my daughter Dana at that time, so I wondered how he could be attracted to me? I had to take a good look at my feelings for him. Had they changed from affection to something deeper?"

"That wily old Devil is trying to win you over," she answered. "He is stirring up the past in order to pull you away from the God that loves you."

Apparently, my reminiscences were stirring up memories and pain for Sister Vicki. The priest she loved was on his way to the Philippines. "Do you think that's him in the plane flying overhead?" she said, at hearing the sound of a jet roaring over my home.

Sister was concerned that he might become involved with the Filipino girls. "Many priests have succumbed," she said. "The girls are lovely, and they go after the priests. Of course, he and I could not be sexually involved. But, knowing how he gets aroused whenever we're together, I'm afraid he might end up channeling his feelings for me by getting sexually involved with those girls."

I told Sister Vicki that the kind of relationship she had with her priest is the best kind of relationship two people can have. "Marriage or an affair is not the ideal. Marrying someone you love and raising a family is no guarantee against occasional tedium. And besides, you just end up being each other's best friend anyway. To live at a distance from each other is more difficult, but, in its own way, more exciting. Something blossoms between the two souls that is more intriguing than physical love. What I am trying to say, dear Sister, is that, when a relationship where true human love exists but cannot be consummated, the love two people feel for each other remains in a state of perfection—you know, like your love for Christ."

"I suppose you're right. Many priests and nuns have renounced their vows in order to pursue marriage, only to be eventually disillusioned by it," Sister replied, her eyes tearing up. "At twenty-three, my vow of celibacy seemed simple enough, as there was no one in my life at the time, someone who might give it new meaning. But, things were no longer so simple once I met him." She then described the brief moment when he had held her in his arms. It was the moment when they had declared their feelings for one another. With tears still in her eyes, a smile now lit up her face.

"Sister, your honesty and candor has helped me understand my relationship with Damian more clearly," I commented.

Still smiling, she said, "I find it easy to share my feelings with you."

Before leaving, Sister reminisced about her father, describing him as a tall, good-looking man who commanded a presence when he entered a room. He died suddenly when Sister was ten.

This made me think of Jennie, of how her father's death might affect her life.

"You have that same kind of presence, Berta. Our friend, Father Al, said that your presence is one that is immediately felt, that you are beautiful, and that, when you walk again, you will be even more magnetic."

She then looked at me intently as she sat beside me on my bed. "My yes, you *are* very beautiful, Berta," she declared, as if she had discovered it for the first time.

I replied to her comment saying that, aside from the physical attractiveness she spoke of, I found that people were now also drawn to me to share their stories with me and to discuss the difficulties in their lives. "Perhaps it's the wheelchair," I said in jest. "After all, I am quite the *captive* audience, don't you think?" We laughed.

Still, the truth of the matter was that I felt I had a new calling as a sort of counselor that could lend a compassionate ear to others.

~ ~ ~

When I resumed my visits to therapy, Sigrid said, "Before, you had a rather distant look and reserve about you. I found it was difficult to get through."

I related to her the dream I had about giving birth to two girls. Sigrid interpreted this as my rebirth.

When I returned home after this visit, Sister Vicki phoned to tell me I had made her laugh when she was so close to tears about her life.

I told her about the dream and Sigrid's interpretation. "I'm reborn, brand new. My second life as a new Berta is just beginning," I shouted into the phone. "It's very, very difficult," I reminded her.

Imagine that. I'm actually helping Sister Vicki, I thought, as I put down the phone and wiped away my tears. Seconds later, the phone rang again. This time it was a friend who called to tell me how much our recent conversation had helped her. God's message was beginning to become clear to me, still I began to cry again as I whispered to Him, "But why do I find it so hard to help *myself*?" I felt like a newborn baby—my nervous system was very sensitive and vulnerable, and I cried a lot.

My feeling of being reborn didn't last long.

A day or so later, I phoned Sigrid for help. We went through the reasons behind my depression: perhaps Jennie's absence that week, the poem from Damian that rekindled all those memories I had been trying to push away, or my nagging worries about my ability to run a home?

"Maybe it's the Devil testing me again. I wish the tug of war between good and evil would stop," I said to Sigrid.

Sigrid asked me to have a dialogue with my body and to write it down. Eventually, I did write the dialogue, and it went like this:

Berta: "How are you this evening?"

Body: "Uncomfortable, bloated, nerves are stinging. I feel like a pin cushion totally covered with pins."

Berta: "Probably because I have been emotionally upset today. What other parts bother you?"

Body: "My eyes are tired from crying. But the fear in my stomach has begun to subside. I wish you wouldn't think of Damian. The memory of that relationship leaves me feeling hurt and only reminds me that I am no longer able to make love. To perform sexually with this unfeeling, uncomfortable, no longer graceful torso, well, I rebel against it. I am only reminded of how tall and sensual I used to be. I hate what I have become. It is totally opposite to what I used to be."

Berta: "I loved that other body as well. Walking on the beach, along the sand, into the waves, dancing in the summer to the orchestra below my house, moving back from my easel to view the work in progress and dance a few steps to the music playing on the stereo, setting the table, stretching out on my bed, moving under the shower, running with Jennie, the dog, or by myself, sliding into a booth in a restaurant, standing when the Gospel is read at Mass. All are lost to me now. Where would you like to be tonight?"

Body: "Walking down the steps into the living room at the beach house. That large, but romantic room so softly lit and elegant, filled with treasures from a life shared with my husband. My legs would take me, as they did so often, to the sofa, where I would join him for an ordinary evening, but an evening I saw as extraordinary if only because I thought those moments together would never end. How could such a beautiful existence end so drastically, and in such a hideous manner? I think of that other body on the kitchen floor. That was the end of the most beautiful part of my life."

Sigrid pointed out that I was making progress. "You have bought a new car, and you are taking a writing course," she pointed out. Letting go of yesterday's joys, learning to not plan the future and to just let things happen, come what may, was an uphill path that had to be walked slowly and gradually. I felt unsteady in my new life—like a baby. I might or might not learn to walk. Inevitably, relapses would occur. I was depressed once again.

"You ought to talk to Father Moretta," suggested Mary Jane. Father Moretta came to see me the following evening. It was late, around 9:00 P.M. He gave me the Sacrament of the Sick and a rosary that had touched all the sacred places in Jerusalem.

"What's with this litany of self-pity? You're a strong, independent woman, Berta," Father said. He did not berate me for my suicidal thoughts. But, gently, he counseled me, "I know you have been given a lot to bear, but suicide leaves a permanent scar on the lives of those left behind. Jennie would always carry it with her. Get out of here," he suggested, referring to the house. "Stay in touch with the world. Fall in love," he advised me, pausing for a moment before continuing, "only not in the physical sense."

He then described a bride-to-be he had recently counseled. "She was not only physically beautiful, but she also had a very joyful nature." Indirectly, he was saying that, in contrast, I was a melancholy person.

Amen. He was right about the melancholy. It was a time when I had an absolute need to be by myself, to curl up in a world of my own creation. However, there was a lack of understanding by family, friends, and counselors about "staying in touch with the world." I certainly wasn't a young, excited bride-to-be venturing into matrimony. I was tired from hours of preparing myself for the day and from the pain I had to endure just performing ordinary tasks. What they saw was a normal person carrying on a normal conversation, perhaps comfortable in her bed, in her chair, eating at a table. In truth, what they were seeing was themselves in those situations, relaxed and pain free.

"On a scale of one to ten, how do you rate your pain?" the doctors, nurses, and therapists would ask me.

"Ten," I would insist over and over. "It feels as if the paralyzed part of my body has been doused with gasoline, and someone has thrown a match on it."

I prayed, *Please God, let me know, really know that I am strong. I don't understand why people perceive me as being strong. I've spent my entire life doing as I was told. Only through You will I begin to recognize the strength that others see.*

One day in writing class, I read to the class an essay I had written, entitled "Damian Again."

"You write as beautifully as you paint," said one of the students.

"Send it to the publishers right away," said another.

"Thank you, God," I said silently. I felt a slight stirring of strength. It came from the encouragement of my fellow classmates.

The second anniversary of Bill's death would have passed unnoticed if my daughter Leslie had not phoned from Idaho. Was I through grieving? If I was, Leslie was not. She was sad, and events in her own life were calling her back to that day two years ago. Michael's father had died, and Michael was away. She also wanted Michael's divorce to be over so they could get on with their lives.

"I don't like the position I'm in; it's not comfortable for me," she declared about the situation with Michael. She then spoke about her daughter, Riley. "When she returns from her summer stay with her father in California, it takes a long time until I feel she's mine again."

I was sad to hear her so depressed. At the same time, I also felt relieved to realize that my daughter was holding on to some traditional values. "I'm going to church to light a candle for my father," she said, before hanging up.

Our driver, Zylstra, took me to Aunt Alice's for lunch and then drove the two of us to the cemetery. At the cemetery, I was unable to get to Bill's bronze plaque in my wheelchair, so I watched from the car as Alice waved a camellia at me, indicating she was at my husband's marker. Then she went to place flowers she had picked from her garden on the graves of other family members.

On the following morning, I went to P.T., where the wife of a man in his fifties approached me. She informed me that he had been diagnosed with Guillain-Barré Syndrome. After a year of depression and a bout with pneumonia, he was learning to walk again.

"Don't give up," the wife said to me.

My therapist, who was standing nearby, remarked to me as the woman walked away, "That woman is a fighter. In fact, she fights *too* hard. One has to be realistic." Her remark gave me pause to reevaluate my own condition, as I believe she was talking to me. Does every victim of paralysis believe at first that the condition is only temporary?

At home, I wondered if I was trying too hard. Should I cut back on my therapy? Would it be best "to accept it for now," as other people suggested?

The phone rang. I was sitting at my desk, so I answered it immediately.

"Hi, Mom, it's Morgan." His voice sounded sad. "I couldn't sleep last night. A couple of days ago, it was the anniversary of Dad's death. I put some flowers on the waves at the Berkeley Marina in his memory. I love you, Mom, and I don't like what has happened to our family," he said, choking up.

Listening to Morgan express his terrible caring—at times, it overwhelmed me—made me determined to struggle on. I would try to remember how much the children were suffering too. The loving, close-knit family life we once knew was coming apart. The children's grief over Bill's death and my condition was splintering the family.

~ ~ ~

"I feel perhaps that things may be changing, Irma," I began when she came to my room to see if I needed anything. "I now understand how much the children have been hurt by what has happened."

"Your children haven't changed. It is you that has changed," Irma said when I told her that we were coming together as a family again. "Your children are very *sensitivos y humildes*. I saw this in Leslie and Dana right away. You have more of your mother's vanity, and now you are much more *humilde*." I would have preferred the word "reserve" instead of "vanity."

I made an effort to acknowledge my anger, to examine the reasons behind it, and then to change my attitude. *I'm out in the world, Father Moretta*, I thought when Jeannette came to pick me up and take me to the Pasadena Garden Club fundraiser. There were many table settings on display. Jeannette and two other ladies had chosen "Tea at the Vicar's" as their theme. The judges thought that one of those three exhibits was too cluttered. I disagreed, as I remembered my aunts, Jessie and Margaret—who were both Brits—and their opulent high teas. My sister and I were required to attend them every Sunday at their home in South Pasadena.

It was a pleasant afternoon. My absence from home allowed Irma time to go shopping. When we were home again, she told me how upset she had become watching other families shopping together. "I felt lonely," she remarked.

I said, "I understand how you feel. I feel lonely too when I see friends leading normal lives and then going home to family, not to an empty house like I do. I'm angry too, Irma, knowing I am not a part of their world anymore."

Then, having acknowledged out loud the reason for my anger, I measured my present life against my former life. A glimpse of a useful life—writing and ministering to those in need—came to mind.

This is my house, I thought as I looked around the room. *I chose it. And I can choose how to spend my time as well. Independence doesn't depend on one's legs; it is a state of mind.*

~ ~ ~

One morning, as I picked up the cross of my daily routine, I took a good look at those slow, monotonous moments. Why not enjoy the unhurried introduction to the next twenty-four hours, allowing myself to be lovingly cared for by Irma, enjoying every moment as she brings me breakfast in bed, cleans my body of my nightly accidents, tidies my bed and bath, showers and dresses me, thereby relieving me from all those tiresome tasks of my former life.

As the "ethereal veil"—to quote Sigrid—that covered my life and me began to lift, I saw myself as a perfectionist reinforced by moral and religious beliefs and by the values and conditioning of my mother. Hence, my inability to deal with Leslie's divorce. I was so proud when I saw Leslie walk down the aisle of the old mission and place her bouquet at the foot of the statue of Our Lady, demonstrating the true meaning of marriage to the guests that had assembled. The moment was underscored for me when the priest read the passage from the Bible regarding "the good wife." Now

I began to see that I was hanging on to an illusion. The attachment I had to keeping up appearances would later cause my depression when the marriage came to an end.

Then, when I looked at the last years of my own marriage, it was almost unbearable. With respect to my husband's impotency—caused by his then undiagnosed arteriosclerosis—I did try to talk to him, but his refusal to acknowledge the problem shut the door on that discussion. And when I confronted him with the evidence I found in the apartment in town that led me to suspect him of infidelity—a newspaper that ran ads for call girls, some of which were circled in ink—he dismissed my suspicions as silly. So, I dismissed my suspicions as silly too. It was difficult to imagine sweet, kindly, gentlemanly Bill as an unfaithful husband. It also destroyed the perfect image I had of him during our almost thirty-year marriage.

The other Berta, as I remembered her to be, was kind, inclusive, polite, and sensitive. It frightened me to let her go and to face the imperfect stranger who now inhabited my paralyzed body. Holy God, it saddened me to see the flaws of the present Berta. Who had I become? Was it the familiar Berta, or the flawed stranger? What about the less than idyllic ending of my marriage? Was human love imperfect? I felt like an actor on the stage after the curtain has closed. The person I had been up till now would have to be abandoned in order for me to return to my true self.

Those very nice women doing their volunteer work at the flower show were not going to be part of my future. Because of my growing awareness and ever-changing priorities, I now directed my sympathies toward a woman in an electric cart who sat next to me in a movie theater. She had M.S. and was raising two sons on her own. And there were the women in my writing class. I talked to Donna, who had rheumatoid arthritis, and to Molly, who quietly listened as I told her about how I had lost some of my friends.

"Well, you've got two new ones," declared Donna and Molly as they wheeled me out from the classroom.

"A whole new life is about to open up for you," said Molly.

Walking behind us, a woman remarked on how much she liked the story I had written that day: "She's good, isn't she?"

"Yes," said Molly, "and she knows it," giving me a giant push toward my waiting car. While being driven home in the pouring rain, I felt totally exhilarated.

I wanted to tell Sigrid about my small success in writing class.

"Wait," said Sigrid as I began to talk at our next session. "Your mother phoned me. I'm surprised a woman that narcissistic hasn't phoned before. She's got to feel threatened."

"She used to call me, Sigrid, and go on and on about how intelligent and talented my sister is. My sister is all of that. However, my sister had to hear all about *my* wonderful life when Mother talked to *her*. What do you make of that?"

"Divide and conquer is her method, Berta. You should have been in therapy years ago," was Sigrid's reply.

Mother's comment on her next visit was: "Your house will be lovely when you get it all fixed up."

Thinking about Sigrid's words, I replied in a conversational tone new to me, "It *is* lovely, Mother, just the way it is." Months ago, I would have said nothing at all.

I'll write an essay called "Damaged Goods," I thought to myself. The best things I inherited from Mother were her fighting spirit and her love of beauty in nature, music, and the arts.

~ ~ ~

The rain poured relentlessly as the first of April approached. The phone rang. I lifted the receiver and heard mother's voice on the other end. I had asked her to call me in the mornings because it comforted me to hear the voice of a family member. With the exception of my sister and my children, she was my only blood relative. But after talking to Sigrid, I wondered if confiding in my mother was a mistake now that my inner strength had begun to grow. Mother had obligingly phoned, and, no longer threatened by her, I had a few warm, even loving, conversations with her that brought a kind of peace to my new life.

On Holy Saturday, I was full of tears and was consciously trying not to think of Easters past. "But it is difficult," as my daughter Dana said on the phone the day before. When I awoke that day, I took the time to meditate. I wanted to be closer to Christ in that quiet place where He was laid to rest. My thoughts strayed constantly to Easter egg hunts from the past. Back and forth my mind went from the tomb to egg hunts. In reality, I was sitting in a wheelchair on a patio in Pasadena while the sun shone, enveloping me in its warmth.

Damn! Even the music playing on the radio was wrong. The song, *The Gentle Rain,* matched the weather outside and the not so gentle rain within me. I stared at the rain from my living room after Irma rescued me from the patio. I wished I had been staring at the rain falling outside the dining-room window at the beach. There, I would have heard the music on the intercom and been looking at the sea and the sky. Bill might be walking the dog or sitting in the living room or working in the garage. Perhaps the kitchen door would open and he would walk in wearing his Macintosh, bowing his head as he stopped to wipe his feet on the doormat. Memories!

Easter Sunday came. Riley and Jennie were with me. Although it rained all day, we had a very lovely Easter. I was snapped out of depression by the sounds of two little girls in the house trying to play the piano, coloring eggs in the kitchen, and running around laughing and giggling. We had brunch at the home of another family. My mother had been invited, but she declined "due to other plans."

I was on top of the world when I went to bed Easter Sunday night, but then Riley's departure for Sun Valley, Idaho saddened me so much that I burst into tears. Irma put her arms around me, and I wiped my tears away so Jennie wouldn't see them.

We spent the evening watching *The Waltons.* On the night table beside me was Jennie's Easter card, declaring, "I love you very much!" The gnawing tiredness left me empty, and, even with Jennie beside me, I felt desperately lonely by Easter Monday.

After Jennie's departure, I wrote Dana to tell her about Easter, 1982:

My dearest Dana,

The two little girls and I had a joyous Easter in spite of some rain. When Jennie stood in the doorway of my bedroom, looking so lovely in her navy robe, saying, "It was a wonderful Easter," my heart overflowed with happiness.

My strength and courage are taxed beyond belief these days and, I fear, for many days to come. The holidays bring a painful reminder of all the joyous years we've spent together as a family. Try as I may, for I truly want to let the past go, living in the present is so painful physically and emotionally. I still cling to happier times.

But Easter brought great joy, as it should, and we all had a happy day. Today, I am resting, as I do most every day. This seems to be the pattern of my present life. If I expend great amounts of energy one day, I am in bed the next day.

It is almost a year since paralysis struck. In spite of the doctor's diagnosis that I would never walk again, I try not to believe it and always hold on to hope. How else can I go on?

I still feel lost in this body. It is so unfamiliar, and, because of my age, I feel I will never adjust. I resent the loss of my freedom, which was snatched away so cruelly at a time when my mid-life seemed to be unfolding through art, and doing things with Jennie, and for her. I can't understand, I really can't, why God slammed the door and threw away the key. Oh, Dana, how I long to be running down the hill towards the sea!

If one has faith, it is said that all things work for our good. But, what is good about stumbling through the days with a broken heart? True, there are happy days and moments when, for a few hours, I fly free again. But it is so hard, so hard to endure the rest.

When little Riley left, I watched Jennie walk her to the car. The tears and the anguish welled up again. Irma wrapped her arms around

me, and I quickly wiped away my tears before Jennie reentered the
house. Now, Jennie is gone too—to join you in Santa Fe for the
remainder of her Easter vacation.

I never signed or sent the letter. I wrote it as a way to help alleviate the terrible state of depression I was experiencing after Easter, after the children left.

A secretary from my ex-son-in-law's office had come to collect my granddaughter. "My, she travels a lot for such a little girl, and such long distances for so short a time," she remarked. Little Riley would travel to Idaho to stay with a friend. There would be no family to greet her, as her mother had been first in Hawaii and was now in the Los Angeles area. I had not heard from Leslie, although I heard she was somewhere nearby.

Jennie was the next one to leave. She spent the rest of her spring vacation in Santa Fe with her sister Dana, would visit with me for a night and then return to her other home. The rain was gone, but the Santa Ana winds took its place, reminding me that the heat of summer was on its way—my first summer in town for many, many years. I never thought I would miss the parties at St. Lo with all their snubs and meaningless chit-chat. Now, I felt nostalgia for them.

Sigrid told me during this time of spring and new beginnings that I would never be free until I freed myself up inside.

"I do not blame anyone, even myself, for this state of dependency," I explained to Sigrid. "I was brought up during a time when, for the most part, girls remained close to home until they got married. And that is the path I followed. I was happy to fall in love and start a family. That experience turned out to be a lesson in selflessness that only brought joy to my life."

Now without a partner, I had to learn to speak up for myself. Two incidents occurred that added a few more bits of clay to the sculpture of the new Berta.

My mother called me asking for money. Since my mother had always responded to *my* requests for money over the years, I felt I owed her in return. I phoned my accountant instructing her to send my mother whatever I could afford.

After my father's death, Mother found herself in a difficult financial situation. To her great credit, she managed to educate my sister and me by selling her possessions as needed to do so. Eventually, she got a job at the Ambassador Hotel in Los Angeles, where, due to her social connections, she started the Office of Public Relations. There she entertained world leaders, diplomats, and practically everyone from the entertainment world. With her gracious manners, her gift as a hostess, her ability to write her own copy, her love for the press corps, she reigned supreme. Considering how adored she was by friends and those who worked under her, it was a mystery to my sister and me why she could not pour out her emotional largesse to her daughters.

In addition to settling the financial matter with Mother, I now had to address the current questions from my daughter Dana. Dana had sent a letter to Mike, my friend the lawyer who had sold my beach house. In the letter, Dana said that, now that I was better again, she wanted to be reimbursed for the money she had sent me before I sold the beach house. I was not about to pay Dana again. After all, *I* was the one who had to borrow $35,000 to pay the taxes on the children's inheritance. So I instructed my accountant to tell Dana that the money she was asking for should be paid by Bill and Morgan when they receive their final share of their father's estate.

Dana had also inquired about her interest in the Hees Family Trust. Her father Bill had asked Dana to make sure that she and her siblings would take care of my financial needs if anything should happen to him. My lawyer had advised me to set up the trust to repay the children the monies they were to send me to keep me afloat after Bill's death. I told my accountant, that, according to the trust, the payments to the children were to come from the sale of my lot if and when I sold it. I decided that the payments to the children from the sale of the lot should be equal to the amounts I received from those of my children who had honored their father's request to take care of their mother. Barely a few months into my wobbly emotional and financial recovery, the children's demands for money opened my eyes to the fact that it is not only love that counts in relationships, but also money. After shedding some tears, a surprising inner strength took hold. Physically, it felt as powerful and sudden as if I were rear ended on the L.A. freeway.

At the suggestion of my therapist, I began the search for a young woman who might be a good companion for Jennie for when she came back home to live with me again. Many interviews took place until I finally settled on Julie—twenty-something, single and sweet.

The physical therapist suggested I continue therapy at home. "I really can't tell you that you can expect continued improvement," he said, referring to some slight muscular changes in my legs, "nor can I guarantee that your condition will remain the same. You have a lot of synergy, and this could just be overflow."

"Should I continue to try to move my legs?" I asked him.

"Yes, certainly you must keep trying," he replied. But I knew the hospital therapists were through with me. I cried all the way home.

I retreated to the comfort and safety of my bed. Talking aloud to Bill's spirit, I recreated in my mind the first fall afternoon following our move to the beach. I recalled that Bill and I were eating salad and drinking some wine on the patio while the shadows of the leaves danced on the wall.

"Is this the way it is always going to be?" I asked Bill's spirit, just like I had said it back then.

I drifted back to that afternoon. I could see Sam, our dog, running back and forth across the balcony and scratching himself against the wood. Or was it old Spot? The children appeared, their faces tanned, cheeks sunburned. I remembered every· smell, every sound, every brick, shingle, grain of sand. Suddenly, I was pulled away from my reverie when Nadia came over for my flute lesson.

"Na-ajia está aquí!" Irma announced loudly from the front hall as she buzzed Nadia in.

The reason for my taking flute lessons was to help strengthen my diaphragm. The flute lessons were my idea. All my life I've had a great love of music. As a child, I studied piano and ballet. My favorite radio broadcast as a teenager was *The Gas Company's Evening Concert*. I would imagine falling in love to the strains of Borodin, Rachmaninoff, and Chopin. I still attempted to play the piano on occasion, but not without some difficulty:

my feet were useless when it came to using the pedals, and I had trouble supporting myself on the bench because of my weakened trunk muscles.

Nadia was very patient, especially on my bad days. When I was tense and anxious, my diaphragm didn't function all that well. After my first lesson, she played a piece by Handel as I gazed out the window at the patio and the towering palms.

I always looked forward to hearing Irma call out "Na-ajia está aquí!"

While studying the flute, I made another discovery: I was able to let go of my fear of failure. Either I allowed myself to be comfortable with the fact that I lacked talent for this sort of thing or I simply let go of any expectation of results and resigned myself to enjoying the process.

I started to feel a growing awareness of inner strength and a healthier sense of self. When Bill died, I realized that my self-image had always been defined by my relationship with him. Now, I was beginning to come into my own. Father Moretta was right when he told me I was a strong, independent woman. That person had always existed but was suppressed because my half-British upbringing had taught me that assertiveness was impolite. "Never complain, dear, just get on with it," my mother would remind me when I was about to disagree with her.

I felt Sigrid was right when she told me my husband had transferred some of his feelings for his mother onto me. In my moments of exuberance, he would fall silent and turn away. Now, I could be everything God wanted me to be, and, when his Son healed me, I would work on his behalf.

May came, and with it the first anniversary of my paralysis. On the first day of May, I awoke with fear borne of remembrance, but deep inside I knew I would conquer my fear slowly but surely. I took solace in reading my Bible, searching for something to hang on to. *God has put me on this path for a good reason, for the good of those around me,* I would tell myself. I would do his will, and, when I retreated from this world, He would be there with me to patiently coax me back again. Also, I promised Mother Mary that I would pray the rosary every day; it was through her Immaculate Heart that I was converted to Catholicism at seventeen years of age. I did try, but she knew the monotonous recitation bored me. Still, I slept with the rosary wrapped around my hand every night.

I began to feel a greater sense of contentment. I was content to clean out Bill's desk and put my new desk—a desk made to accommodate my wheelchair—in order. I was content to welcome Julie into my home and, with her help, to organize my clothes.

I started a new painting. The mornings—those once dreaded mornings—now had me feeling full of optimism again.

Arne came to visit. An artist I had met through Damian and occasionally worked with, he was also my instructor from time to time. How is it that one can feel love for someone upon first meeting? Yet that is what happened when I met that bearish, slightly balding, sweet man for the first time. Was it the Christ present in him? Was he religious? I didn't know, but sweetness clung to him like honey to a spoon. And, he was an exceptional artist. Sadly, he was still deeply affected by the breakup of his marriage; his pretty, German-born wife had walked out on him.

After a tour of the house, we sat outside under the wisteria.

"This patio reminds me of the one in St. Lo. Whenever I think of you, I always picture you there," he said. Sipping some wine he continued, "You are very beautiful. I would like to paint you." I smiled.

We spoke about our present lives and about Damian. I confessed of my brief affair with him.

"I could sense there was something between you," he commented, then continued to talk about Damian's many girls.

"One of them has become a treasured friend of mine, Arne," I said. "She phoned me just this morning to talk about Damian. She's married, Arne, and happily so, but she said to me, 'Those days I spent with Damian were so special. I don't talk about him with my husband because he wouldn't understand.' I really identify with her Arne, because that time in my life was so unique, so wonderful. My involvement with him surprised me, and I'll never feel quite that way again."

"I can't have sex with someone unless I feel something truly deep for that person," said Arne. I agreed with him. Then he asked me if I thought he should be going out with women twelve years younger than himself.

In my new role as counselor, I replied, "There are no rules where love is concerned."

Chapter 12

A Family Again

Jennie kiss'd me when we met,
Jumping from the chair she sat in;
Time, you thief, who love to get
Sweets into your list, put that in!
Say I'm weary, say I'm sad,
Say that health and wealth have miss'd me,
Say I'm growing old, but add,
Jennie kiss'd me.

—Leigh Hunt

Chapter 12

Jennie came home to stay on May 18, 1982. I could only hope that I was strong enough to be the mother that I wanted to be for her, but that May morning I was nervous and teary. Nevertheless, I made a decision to let go of my anxiety and to be happy. After speaking with Jennie over a period of days, I knew she was ready to come home. Julie went to pick her up in the afternoon.

Irma was excited about Jennie's return. Her help with my routine in the late morning made it possible for me to be ready when Jennie walked in the door.

When Jennie arrived, I was in good spirits. I felt strong. With Irma to help me and with Julie as a young companion for Jennie, the day passed peacefully as Jennie played with the cat, put her belongings away, and settled into her new life.

The following evening, I kept a dinner engagement with friends. Rather late that night as I got home, I was pleasantly surprised when Jennie ran out to greet me. We went to my room. She then stretched out beside me until midnight, at which time she sleepily shambled off to her own bed.

Soon after, Irma came to tell me that, while I was out to dinner, Jennie had run into Irma's room because she heard noises that scared her. It turned out that the noises were the result of the cat, who had been shut in her closet by accident. Now that Jennie was home after a five-month separation, I was a little jumpy. I felt some anxiety around taking on the responsibility of a young girl.

When Jennie attended her school carnival with Julie, I was reminded of the past again. Bill and I had never missed a school function. Now, I would need to strike a balance in my daily routine in order to conserve energy if I was to feel strong enough to accompany my daughter on these special occasions. I was unsure as to how I would achieve such balance. At the same time, I hoped that my lack of ability to accompany her would end up becoming an opportunity for Jennie to develop a strong sense of independence, self-reliance, and a healthy self-esteem. There were no siblings around and no father to rely on, only a handicapped mother who wouldn't always be available for her.

Jennie came home from the fair with paint on her face, several banners decorated with the school logo, and a bag of goldfish. My God, how that bag of fish reminded me of the last fair I had attended with Jennie and her father. Her dad had won a bag of fish for her at that time. How long ago was it? I couldn't remember.

Watching Jennie grow up tended to throw me into the past a great deal. Those constant reminders of the past would be something I was going to have to get used to. So I prayed, "Jesus, I long to feel joyful and happy hearted. Please let me bear my cross with strength, grace, humility, and humor, always remembering that you are bearing it with me."

On Mother's Day, I took my mother, Uncle Phil, Irma, and Jennie to see the film *Chariots of Fire.* Thinking my mother would enjoy seeing the England of that period, I was optimistic that the day would be a success.

My mother showed up in one of her ungracious "show me" moods. "This movie's about men running around," she said disparagingly.

"Oh no, it's much more than that," I said.

Jennie, not unaware of her grandmother's starchiness, jumped in excitedly with "You'll love it, Mimi," using the name all my children reserved for their grandmother.

Then later, "The Duchess"—as some of Mother's friends called her— immediately got on her high horse when I asked Uncle Phil to drive.

"But he's not supposed to drive," she announced.

"Well, he's going to," I insisted. "It will be fun for him to drive my new car."

"Then I'm not going," she snapped.

The rest of us went to the garage, and, as Irma helped me transfer to the passenger seat, Mother joined us and, without a word, climbed into the back seat. As we drove off, I peered at her in the mirror on my visor and noticed that her right hand was clutching the door handle while her left wrist nervously jangled her bracelet. Suddenly, I had a flashback.

I remembered that my mother never let anyone, not even my father, chauffeur her around. Surely it was a control issue.

The film was so beautiful. As we watched the Gilbert and Sullivan operetta being performed in the movie, I was certain this would take Mother back to the D'Oyly Carte productions and the pantomime performances she had attended as a child. As we left the theater, her face was expressionless.

"Oh, wasn't it superb!" I declared.

"I remember reading about all those American athletes in the paper when I was a young man," said my uncle, who was approaching ninety.

Mother said nothing. Uncle Phil drove us home.

Everyone came inside for tea. Jennie lit the fire. Mother sat on the edge of her chair—her back ramrod straight, her lips thin as a pencil line. Uncle Phil, with his eyes all a-twinkle, relaxed against the sofa pillows, musing over the American athletes portrayed in the film. I played the flute for a while. And then, feeling fatigued suddenly, I told everyone I needed to rest before we went out to dinner.

The Jell-O and custards my mother brought from time to time weren't going to make up for the fact that she was who she was. She was never going to change. Whatever her demons were, I could no longer handle them; I *would not* handle them.

Jennie was noticeably uneasy with Mother's behavior during our Mother's Day dinner later that evening. She burst into tears when we returned home.

"May I sleep with you?" she asked.

"Of course," I replied. Jennie made up a bed on the sofa, but, around four or five in the morning, she slipped into my bed.

Holidays were not as they used to be.

The following day, I talked to Sigrid regarding my concerns about Jennie: "She went into the garden and picked flowers for the house in an effort to make Mother's Day seem festive. Her sister Dana phoned, but her other siblings did not call. She makes such an effort to keep life as it used to be," I said with tears in my eyes. "With respect to Julie, I don't feel she is working out as the best companion for my daughter. Her boyfriend hangs around a lot, her room is almost on fire with candles, and she has a skin condition that leaves flakes of skin on Jennie's toilet seat. Frankly, I'm worried. Julie is sweet, but she appears to be without any family. She is emotionally needy, and I don't feel that she can give Jennie the support she needs." In that moment, I made a decision to find a more suitable live-in companion for Jennie.

~ ~ ~

With a referral from my physical therapist at the hospital, I was able to arrange for a new physical therapist to come to my home.

"There is some return of function in your legs, but how much more we can expect only time will tell," my physical therapist from the hospital said. "It will be slow. Your new physical therapist will keep us informed."

As I was preparing to leave, Lauren, my original P.T., spoke with me. "Berta, I had a dream that we were hitchhiking up north. In the dream, I turned to you and said, 'Berta, is that you?' You were walking. I was so excited to see you walking again. Now I hear there is some return of function. That's so wonderful," she said as she gave me a warm hug.

Please dear Jesus, hold me in your gentle arms as my healing continues, was my silent prayer. Years later, He partially answered Lauren's prophetic dream and my silent prayer when He moved me to Northern California, to the ocean, to the redwood forests my father had so loved all of his life—but *without* the use of my legs.

A letter from Sister Vicky offered some words of inspiration:

> *I try to stay aware of Victor Frankl's three fundamentals of human existence:*
>
> *1.There's a will of meaning*
>
> *2.There's a meaning to suffering*
>
> *3.There's a freedom of will*

Being human means continually being confronted with situations,
each of which is at once an opportunity and a challenge, that is,
each situation gives us an opportunity to fulfill ourselves if we
listen, respond, and meet the challenge to fulfill its meaning. Berta,
what we need is faith and surrender—to do what we can reasonably
do, and then leave the rest to God.

On a warm day that signaled the coming of summer, Irma wandered into my room to share with me that the weather was making her homesick. This would be my first summer away from the beach, and I felt I would need all the prayers I could get, and so would Irma. We spoke in Spanish about the trying weeks to come. Irma would miss her family, and I would think nostalgically of summers at St. Lo.

Once again, the future managed to take care of itself with a little effort on my part. Jennie was preparing to attend the summer camp her brothers had so enjoyed. We received an invitation to stay in Theresa's house in Aspen, Colorado, in July. And, most significantly, Leslie phoned me, which brightened up my day. She informed me that Riley would be going to camp with Jennie. She then mentioned how much she would treasure the letter I had sent her and assured me that she felt our relationship was mending.

In June, I took up pen and paper and started writing again. During Arne's last visit, he left me an essay that he had written, and I promised I would write a poem based on its theme. After reading and re-reading Arne's essay, entitled "Silent Communication," the following verse came to me:

Sad was the scene, oh yes!
An old man dying on the street.
The afternoon sun in cloudless caress
Forms a shadow on aging eye sockets,
And within the depths
That lie beneath the pupils
Those eyes, like dim stars,
Obeyed the man's last wish
To scan the heavens and infinity above.

Serenity was his expression,
And sadness turned to wonder
As those old bones communed his peace,
And the distance of his viewing ceased
When body and soul separated in unseen silence.

But the expression of frozen serenity
Remains, as the red river stops its flow.
The red becomes one with the setting sun,
Casting deep shadows amongst the living.
I continue towards my destination
With thoughts that I'd been witness
To death's peaceful journey on that April day.

Returning home without the sun
That was replaced by the cold rains of evening,
I passed the final resting place once more.
The memory of the old man's expression
Erased any trace of sadness
As stars shone through the storm
On my smiling face.

The poem remained true to the feelings he had expressed in his essay. Consequently, I had the joy of seeing into his sweet soul as I worked on the poem. I sent the piece to dear Arne but never received a reply.

During my next visit with Sigrid, she inquired about the possibility of her renting a house at St. Lo. I avoided the subject, directing the conversation to other topics, hoping she would forget about her inquiry, but she didn't.

"I would like to get a feel for the place," was her explanation. Did she believe that she would come closer to understanding the emotional intensity I felt about the place? The request had felt burdensome. Again avoiding the subject, I moved on to other things, but Sigrid soon asked me, "Did you find out about a house?"

"Nothing, there is nothing," I lied. Looking her straight in the eye, I continued, "I have asked people, and if anything comes up, they'll let me know." The task of calling around to see if there was a house available at St. Lo was too much for me.

She looked disappointed. However, I felt relief from not having attended to her appeal. Later, as Leslie and I discussed the situation, I felt I had done what was necessary to protect my privacy, even though I had to look Sigrid straight in the face and lie. "Her request is totally unprofessional," said my daughter, whose experience with psychologists was much broader than mine.

Norma was waiting for me when I came home. She had brought with her two dresses that she had purchased in Tijuana, as she had promised. The dress styles had suited me well in the past, and they would be even more comfortable in my present condition. Long loose cottons of bright color hung to my ankles, and colorful embroidery lightly tied the gathered yoke and sleeves. I could slip them over my head, and, with little assistance, I was dressed for the day. I thanked Norma for the dresses, and we chatted for a while.

On top of all my other physical problems, I was experiencing menopausal symptoms, and I mentioned this to Norma, as I felt comfortable confiding in her about such things. "Anger precedes my monthly menses and compounds the weeping, the depression—those ever-present demons," I said.

"I tend to have a bad temper," Norma said.

In talking with her, I discovered that both Norma and I were afflicted by some sort of pre-menstrual imbalance.

"My mother had a nervous breakdown during menopause. She was also a cripple her entire life," she explained. And then she went on to tell me about a lady who was suffering from Parkinson's disease. "There are so many sufferers," she concluded.

After she left, I looked at the little pottery plant holder in the shape of a lamb that she had placed on the patio table. If I had not become ill, I probably never would have had such an intimate conversation with Norma. Our moments at St. Lo had always revolved around fun and sun. Now, I was blessed to see another side of this truly lovely, intelligent woman.

~ ~ ~

There are times when even the best of company cannot guarantee an end to loneliness, and so, after dinner, I picked up pencil and paper and began to write.

After a few minutes, I put down the pencil and phoned Damian.

"You never phone me!" he remarked after I said hello.

"I feel silly. Like a teenager phoning a boy she likes. I'm definitely not a teenager."

"Oh come on now, we know each other better than that," he said, but there was a coldness in his voice.

"What are you doing?" I asked shyly.

"I'm working."

I wanted to tell him I was lonely. Instead, I asked him to do me a favor. "Please, could you get some acrylic paint for me? I need some white paint," I explained.

"Of course," he answered.

The remainder of the conversation was superficial, and, as usual, he told me about his current girlfriend. This time, it was a Japanese girl, called Yum-Yum.

After the phone call, I thought, *Berta, you have too much pride. Damian would have understood two simple words like "I'm lonely."*

Shortly after, Irma came in to announce that Fran, my new physical therapist, had arrived. "You need to get ready for therapy," said Irma.

Fran was a marvel. She was a dark-haired woman in her fifties—a real pro at her job. Under her care, I became stronger physically. On the days I broke down, she drove to St. Elizabeth's Church in Altadena to pray for me.

"I'm too full of pride, Fran. God hears you, so ask Him to make me more humble," I requested.

~ ~ ~

The next day, Damian came by after a run. In that moment, I knew, in spite of the distance in his voice on the phone the day before, that nothing had changed between us. Sweat curled his hair, his blue eyes sparkled with intensity, and his cheeks were flushed.

"I'm all sweaty. Where shall I sit?" he asked, settling himself on the sofa.

We talked about war—now over— in the Falklands. Then he saw my flute. As he walked to the table where the flute lay in its open case, I reached up, put my arm around his waist, and then gently rubbed his back with my hand. Sitting down on the sofa once again, he began to play the flute. And then, I took a turn at playing it. His mother was right: he was terrible. And I wasn't much better. But our efforts got us both laughing.

The phone rang. Damian hopped up to answer it. It was his friend, Christopher, on the other end. When Damian handed me the phone, Christopher said, "I'm coming to see you tomorrow. Keep Damian there for a few minutes. I'll have Arne phone you."

Almost immediately after the call from Christopher, the phone rang again. Again, Damian answered, mimicking the voice of a certain Mr. Blackwell, the gentleman who puts together a worst-and-best-dressed list of celebrities every year. "You've just won an award for the best-dressed man," he said to Arne.

Arne's clothes were always a joke. Unmatched, unironed, and sock-less would best describe Arne's *"haute couture,"* a look that said to me he was more interested in his art than his image.

When I finally spoke to him, he said, "Now I know I'll never make that list. I've lost my visor," referring to his black, plastic, sweat-stained headgear that he always wore. "Ask Damian if I left it at his house."

As I spoke to Christopher and Arne, Damian reached out for my hand, intertwining his fingers with mine. "I'm going to be having dinner with Edward. I'll go home and change, and then bring you your paint," he said, and then he bent over my chair to embrace me. I twirled the still damp curls with my fingers.

In the early evening, the two men showed up with tubes of white acrylic paint. It was good to see Edward, a man about Damian's age and a casual acquaintance from St. Lo. He was now a house painter.

"How are your children?" he asked.

"It's a struggle, Edward," I replied.

"I can imagine."

Odd, I never realized he had even noticed my family. Funny the things that are left unspoken for years, the missed connections between human beings. At St. Lo, one gravitated toward like-minded people. Edward's family was also from Pasadena, but I didn't know any of them very well. "Nodding acquaintances" would best describe our relationship in town and at the beach.

"I'm going to St. Lo this weekend. I haven't been down since last summer," he said casually.

Why? I wondered to myself. Well, he was a working adult, and it should have been clear to me by then that, once children are beyond their teen years, they move on, and family becomes less important. As the two men were leaving, Damian stopped to kiss the top of my head.

I was painting earlier that day when Irma came into the living room, knelt in front of me, and asked in Spanish, "Puedo decir algo a Usted? Can I ask you something?" she inquired, translating her own words into English.

"Yes, of course" I replied.

"Does Damian love you?"

"Yes, and I love him."

"I thought so, I can see it in his eyes when he looks at you," said Irma in English. "I can hear it in his voice as well. You will be like me," she continued. "After you walk again, you won't marry, but Damian will be with you."

Irma, Irma, she sees all, and oh, what fantasies!

It is an exquisite thing to love someone and to feel loved in return. I have fallen in love twice in my life. When Damian showed up so swiftly after my recent phone call, it seemed that he sensed my loneliness; I didn't need to explain. The difference in our ages was not an issue, and my illness had changed nothing between us. That love would give me strength throughout the years, and I would come to believe that Damian had been sent to me because of the compassion of Christ. "Get out in the world. Fall in love," Father Moretta had said, "only not in the physical sense." When I painted, thoughts of Damian would always be with me.

June 24 arrived. It would have been my thirty-second wedding anniversary. It occurred to me that young people who enter into marriage never think of how their lives as a couple will play out. To them, the future appears bright and everlasting. "Till death do us part" is the spoken vow, and a happy young couple is so absorbed in the present moment. Death is far, far away from their minds on their wedding day.

While praying to Bill as the day passed, I asked him to ask God to restore my health. I offered prayers of thanksgiving to God for the family and for the family life Bill and I had shared, and to Bill for his support, patience, generosity of spirit, his quality of refinement.

After reciting the prayers, I became calm again and recalled those days when I wandered through the rooms of St. Lo during my first year of widowhood. The aura surrounding that person was one of loneliness. She walked to the windows and looked out at empty streets and empty houses. The older children had already moved on to live their own lives, but the impact from this had not really hit until Bill passed away and a deep sense of loneliness took over. Continuing to gaze on the past, I saw Jennie and me eating at our favorite cafés before I would drop her off at school. Then, after picking her up from school, I would take her to Thrifty's for an ice cream cone and to the market, where I halfheartedly shopped for food.

Occasionally we wandered aimlessly around the local mall. With all those people around us, it gave me a false sense that life was as it always had been. At the mall, I would always notice the shoe store where Bill had bought his last pair of running shoes. I remembered how he had agonized over buying them. "I'll never wear them out," he had said. And he never did; they were on his feet when he died, and the hospital never returned them to me.

"Oh, go ahead," I insisted, wondering at the time why he was making such a big fuss. It was a fairly typical episode; Bill rarely spent money on himself.

Then, I reflected on Jennie's soccer games, when I sat in the stands by myself, watching her play soccer in a tentative manner. I was aware of the fact that she was feeling her father's absence.

The phone rarely rang anymore in that empty house, a house with large rooms and no one occupying them—just bare walls surrounding empty space.

Bill had left a very frightened lady behind, one who didn't recognize her fear. I buried it so I could be strong for Jennie.

I remembered that Damian suddenly showed up at the house a few days after Bill's death. He came to say goodbye before leaving for a painting trip to the Far East. We went out for dinner, but I felt distant, estranged.

"Are you all right?" he asked as we said goodbye at my door.

"I don't know, Damian," I replied. It was the first time anyone asked me that question. It wasn't until then that I actually began to get in touch with my own feelings.

Two weeks after Damian's visit, I was paralyzed. Would my health have remained intact if I had sat down with all my children to cry and rage over their father's death? "Our lives have changed completely. Please, please stay with me to sort out our financial situation. With your help, I need to make some big decisions concerning the house and Jennie": Those were the words I should have spoken but did not.

On this day, June 24, my wedding anniversary, I was left with questions that needed to be answered. The summer had begun. How would Jennie and I get through? We were so far from everyone and everything we loved. With Jennie going away to camp so soon after her return home from Anne's care, would she be homesick? Was I strong enough to plan a trip to Aspen, Colorado? I would soon have the answers.

Chapter 13

DEATH

Loss in all of its manifestations is the touchstone of depression . . .
The loss of self-esteem is a celebrated symptom
and my own sense of self had all but disappeared.

—William Styron, *Darkness Visible*

Chapter 13

"I don't think you found what you were looking for here," said one of the nurses when I left the psychiatric ward.

No, I hadn't. Instead, I had added another loss to my list: My daughters' assessment of my ability to be a mother did not fit with how I viewed myself as a mother. How did I see myself in my maternal role? As a nurturer and spiritual director—someone who kept a steady hand on the home front. It brought me great joy to plan and celebrate birthdays and holidays with my family. I encouraged my children to take their schoolwork seriously, telling them: "Do your very best. That is all I expect." I also saw to my children's spiritual development. All of my children had been baptized, went to confession, took Holy Communion, and were confirmed. I always made sure that they attended Mass on Sundays and holy days.

After group therapy with Leslie and Dana, I came to understand that I had failed as a mother. Bill, on the other hand, triumphed as a parent in their eyes.

Now that I was back home, things got worse. The doctors prescribed anti-depressants of every type to lift me out of despair. I was on and off estrogen therapy. One of the patients, George—a former alcoholic—suggested that I try lithium. So I gave it a try, but thoughts of death continued to plague me.

The words of Gustave Flaubert—in a book about Degas—perfectly summed up my feelings at that time:

> *I was born with little faith in happiness. When I was young, I had a complete presentiment of life. It was like a nauseous smell of cooking escaping from a vent. You don't need to eat it to know it will make you sick.*

I felt exactly like that every morning: sick and filled with dread. My eyes ached at the first sight of dawn. I struggled to endure my morning routine. Medications dulled my taste for food. Watching television and reading required concentration, something I lacked. Nighttime was a temporary escape from the terror I felt, but still, before I drifted off to sleep, I prayed for death. "I can't do this anymore," I cried out to the Lord. "Please come and take me away."

I imagined various ways to commit suicide: slitting my wrists with Bill's hunting knife; putting a plastic bag over my head and tying it around my neck; phoning the Hemlock Society for assisted suicide; swallowing every medication I had with a glass of Scotch.

At the time, I fooled myself into believing that I was a functioning human being. After all, hadn't I searched for and hired Katie to replace Julie as a companion for Jennie? I was successful at finding someone who had such verve and a happy disposition.

I felt deserted when Jennie stayed at St. Lo with her friend Lee, when Morgan traveled through Central America, when Leslie and Dana took off and hiked in Sun Valley, Idaho. Abandonment and dread were my constant companions. Paralyzed as I was, I felt I was a burden on my family and was in the way. In my depressed state, it made sense to me to end my life so that my children could go about their lives.

Jennie surprised me on the Fourth of July by coming home from the beach to visit. Jennie had made little American flags that we pinned to the clothes we wore to a party. In contrast to previous celebrations, Jennie seemed shy as she mingled with some of her classmates. I felt out of place as I paused to observe the perfect, beautiful hostess—a frozen smile on her face—perform her perfect little duties in her perfectly manicured garden. After all the years of casual beach living, Jennie and I felt we didn't quite fit in with the carefully coifed and mannered lifestyle of the city.

When the fireworks fizzled out, so did we. We decided to go home.

The following day, there was a glitch in the sale of the beach house. On top of that, the contract fell through on the RV rental for our summer trip to Aspen, Colorado. I was suicidal again. That evening, I wrote a poem that expressed the real reason behind my depression:

Fourth of July, 1982

Far from the sea
Living in a landlocked world
Closing my eyes
Watching yesterdays skip across the sand
Straining to see
The faces of my children, husband, friends.
We were happy
Wrapped in red sun, blue water, white sky,
Eyes focused upwards
Towards rockets blazing, spewing light.
The light goes out!
The ashes join the other ashes in the sea.
Opening my eyes
I am alone in the city, in my chair, in my heart.

I phoned Sigrid for help.

"It's the trip. It is overwhelming you. I'd be scared to death too, but it will be good for you in the end," was Sigrid's interpretation of my suicidal feelings.

Divine intervention came by phone and by mail.

"Mrs. Hees?" said a voice over the phone.

"Yes, who is it?" I inquired.

"This is Dale, the man who rented you the RV. I have a newer and better model available. Are you still interested?"

"Well, yes, I guess so," I replied with some hesitation.

"I'm positive you will be very comfortable in this vehicle," Dale assured me.

"All right then," I responded, after recalling Sigrid's words: "It will be good for you."

After I hung up the phone, I read a letter from Sister Wilfrid.

"Yes, yes, Berta, you will walk again," Sister reassured me in her message.

When Bill came over to help me prepare for our journey, my fear and dread subsided. Childlike and dependent in my fragile emotional state, I was relieved to have someone tell me what to do.

~ ~ ~

We left Pasadena in our rented motor home a little before 9:00 A.M. I stretched out on the built-in sofa next to the large windows, which gave me an unobstructed view of the scenery. Irma and Jennie sat across the aisle from me in swivel bucket seats with a table between them. Bill sat up front in the "cockpit." My son looked very comfortable in his overstuffed, oversized chair, the road stretching out before him. The co-pilot's seat was just as comfortable, and, from time to time, Jennie or Irma would sit there. In the back of the motor home was a sink underneath a large window. From the window, we could see the road just traveled, unraveling like a gray ribbon. A shower, toilet, stove, refrigerator, tape deck, air conditioner all added up to a comfortable and convenient way to travel.

At one point, Jennie climbed the ladder to the upper bunk above the driver's area. Later, she pulled the curtain closed and hung a sign that read, "Do not disturb, is sleeping."

Rolling through Barstow, Needles, and the desert, Bill played some cassettes. The country and western music that filled the air blended in well with the environment. Not my favorite style of music, but it suited the scenery, and we had a lot of fun humming along as we discovered the joys of this new way to travel. After passing through Flagstaff, Arizona, we finally stopped at Winslow and decided to rent a motel room for the night.

Irma said that when we drove through Cucamonga, it reminded her of Nicaragua. The scenery stirred up memories for me too. My dad owned an orange ranch in Cucamonga. Barefoot and free, my sister Jeannette and I used to splash around in the irrigation ditches when we were children. We always looked forward to visiting the ranch.

Then I looked up at Jennie nestled in her bunk.

"Hey, Bill," I shouted, "when you turned on the air conditioner, Jennie's hair stood straight up."

Eyes wide with surprise, Jennie sat up in her bunk with a big grin on her face. We both broke into a giggle like two little girls.

Irma announced that she was hungry. "Let's stop at Taco *Bill's*," she suggested.

We all cracked up.

My favorite part of the day was the evening after Irma and Jennie left the van to prepare for the night in the motel. Bill and I had a cold beer as darkness settled. The soft lights inside the van provided us with the perfect atmosphere in which to relax and laugh about our adventures. I told Bill that, when I looked at the back of his head while he was driving, I thought of his father and how much his father would have enjoyed this experience.

"I'd sure like to get a group of friends together and rent one of these things someday," Bill said.

It was quite warm the following morning, making it easy for me to dress and be ready to leave by 7:00 A.M. Irma, anxious to see all the sights, had already taken a walk before I woke up. We stopped at a fast-food place and picked up some breakfast. We made another stop for donuts, and, when Jennie returned with the purchase, she said, "The man didn't give me enough change. He only gave me a dollar. I said that wasn't enough."

Smiling to myself, I thought, *Good for Jennie. She's looking after herself.* I saw her thinking for herself, becoming more self-motivated and responsible, and contributing in any way she could. She involved herself in all aspects of the trip without asking "Are we there yet?" For example, adorably helpful, self-confident, she would wash the windows without being asked each time we stopped for gas.

The country music was playing as we glided through New Mexico, and I laughed when the song *Let's Do Something Shabby and Insensitive* reached my ears. I laughed even harder when I discovered that Bill actually knew all the words.

It was cooler now. The morning air swept across my face, and I started humming *Gracias a La Vida, One Hundred Miles* and *Errores y Defectos.* The tunes made me think of Damian and of the letter he wrote to me while traveling to the Grand Canyon in '79. I saw myself sitting by the dining-room window, reading that letter over and over. It was the first acknowledgement of how he felt about me. The memories were sweet.

I'm sure Theresa meant well by suggesting we take the scenic route, but the road seemed to go on forever. Tempers flared, and everyone got a bit edgy as the motor home lumbered up steep grades and around hairpin turns. The scenery helped to keep us occupied and calmed our nerves. Bill, the geology major, provided a running commentary on the minerals he recognized in the rocky outcroppings. His whistling told me that he was a bit nervous driving our rented behemoth. All the same, the scenery made it all worthwhile. Passing through Durango, Colorado, we saw people whitewater rafting on the river that ran through the town. As we drove through Ouray, Telluride, and other towns along the way, the Old West came alive. Wildflowers and waterfalls were everywhere. Though spring was in full bloom, patches of snow stubbornly clung to the ground beneath the tall pines. Bill pointed out the presence of iron ore in the snow where it was streaked with brilliant red.

Jennie spent most of her time in the upper bunk on her tummy, her chin propped up in her hands, taking in the view. Occasionally, she sat in the co-pilot's seat sharing jokes with her brother, enjoying his dry sense of humor, his imitations, and how he whistled through his teeth. I thought of his father who used to do similar things as he concentrated on some task at hand.

Irma was totally overcome by the beauty of the landscape as we passed from California to Arizona, New Mexico, and Colorado. Never having traveled outside of Nicaragua before she came to California, she had her first glimpse of snow and majestic mountains. The mountains of Nicaragua were not at all like the immense, rugged Rockies.

As we headed toward Aspen, I was quite cozy and comfortable. Stretched out on the sofa as the night fell and the stars appeared, I contentedly hummed *The Red River Valley* as we drove into town. Bill, fatigued from all the driving, parked near a streetlight in the town of Aspen to the loud applause from exhausted but happy passengers. We phoned Theresa to let her know we had arrived. She said she was on her way to meet us and then led us to her home. Bill and Jennie's company was a great comfort to me, and Irma carefully attended to my needs, both of which contributed to my enjoyment of this very long trip.

When we got to Theresa's redwood and glass home, Jennie, Irma, and Bill bounded out of the RV. *What a pretty home*, I thought. *Too bad the living quarters are upstairs.* I waited while everyone stretched their legs and explored the accommodations. Meanwhile, I tried to figure out how they were going to get me up to the master bedroom. Finally, Bill carried me upstairs.

The living room sofa was my first stop. Even though it was late, Theresa set a tray of beer in front of us. Theresa and I toasted the driver, while Irma and Jennie settled in for the night downstairs.

"I'm not a beer drinker; I don't really like it. But, on this trip through the Southwest, with country music playing, beer seems to be just the thing," was my sole contribution to the conversation.

Too keyed up to go to bed, I listened as Bill told Theresa how excited he was about the geologic formations in Colorado. When Theresa discovered that Bill was making a living in construction while he was attending university, she asked him if he would come back in the fall to do some remodeling on her house. Then, overcome by fatigue, I called to Irma. After Bill carried me to my bed, Irma settled me in for the night.

The first thing I saw when I awoke in the morning was the sight of aspen trees outside. Small birds darted in and out of the golden leaves.

"Are you ready to get up?" Irma asked after she entered my room.

"Yes, thank you," I replied. After helping me into my chair, Irma wheeled me to the bathroom, where I was greeted by a framed pastel sketch of the sea that hung on the wall. It was Damian's work. Theresa and Damian knew each other at St. Lo. I smiled to myself and said hello to the artist.

After breakfast, Theresa took me out on the deck, which wrapped around three sides of her house. In the distance, the snow-capped peak of Mt. Sopus rose above the treetops. Like snowflakes, white wisps of seed pods from the cottonwoods floated through the air.

Irma put a pink flower in my hair and said, "God likes you very much. He will help you with everything."

Theresa, Jennie, and Bill went out for a drive. I sat on the deck admiring my surroundings. A tiny finch popped in and out of a birdhouse while hang gliders soared in and out of the mountain passes. Theresa's new wind chimes filled the air with their sweet, tinkling song.

I sat quietly. The beautiful view expanded my spirit. Now that I was resting and at peace—while everyone was out playing—the dark cloud that usually hung over me lifted. I began to pray: "May He be present on my continuing journey."

I looked at the house next door. Theresa had informed me that the young married woman who lived there—mother of an infant son—was hospitalized with spinal meningitis.

"Jesus, put your arms around this family," I implored Our Savior.

Life isn't perfect here either, I thought.

~ ~ ~

In the evening, Bill, Theresa, Jennie, and I went out for dinner. I wasn't in the best of spirits nor in the mood for conversation. I was exhausted and felt that I was on the verge of an asthma attack. The cold draft from the air conditioner that droned above our table caused me great discomfort. While Theresa went to see if something could be done about turning down the air conditioner, Bill shared his thoughts with the rest of us.

"I really enjoyed hiking with Theresa, but I felt so awkward and said all the wrong things. Maybe I have some growing up to do," Bill confessed.

"So do I, dear, so do I," I said as I gently touched his hand.

~ ~ ~

The following day, Sunday, the clouds brought summer showers. But the showers didn't stop Bill and Theresa from hiking again. After breakfast, Irma took care of my needs. Then she took Jennie to town to go shopping.

I read for a while until I became restless. I wanted to go for a walk, and was unable to shake the feeling of anger and resentment that took hold of me.

When Theresa and Bill came home, their arms were full of groceries.

"I need to stretch out on my bed, Bill. My spine is tired," I complained.

"Sure, Mom," Bill responded. He carried me to my bed.

Grumpy and impatient, I waited for Irma to return with Jennie. Within moments, the two of them came home. Irma bore the brunt of my pent-up anger.

"I'm overdue for my catheter," I barked at Irma.

"Jennie was hard to keep up to—she was going this way and that!" Irma groaned.

"I'm sorry, Irma," I apologized. "Go ahead and take a rest." Pausing for a moment, I confessed, "It's just that I hate being left behind."

Trying to keep my emotions in check, I listened to Jennie and Bill joking with each other as Bill and Theresa did some measuring for a possible remodeling job. I felt distanced from everyone, just as I had felt in Idaho during Christmas of 1980. Like Bill, I needed to grow up, but I also would have to find the strength to separate myself from those who had once looked at me as the center of their lives.

Changing myself would include living without an audience—my family audience. Like most parents, I felt a sense of loss because I could no longer share the day-to-day lives of my older children. If my husband were still with me, would the loss have seemed so severe? Probably not, but my present circumstances would have made me even more dependent on my husband, and I am certain that my resentment would have been destructive to our relationship. *This journey is like a crucible, but it will be for the best*, I thought during a night of loneliness that even the bright morning light could not alleviate.

When I showed up on the terrace for breakfast, Bill and Jennie were preparing to drive Theresa to the airport. Her plan was to leave us as soon as we were settled into our new surroundings. We celebrated our arrival and her departure at dinner the night before.

The children have each other, I thought when I awoke that morning. I sat by myself on the deck, no longer enchanted by the view. I saw myself as a wraithlike figure looking for a place to land, a place to call home. Confinement bred frustration, and frustration manifested itself as a long, protracted scream. Jennie heard me on that day and broke down crying.

"God!" I yelled. "Can't I ever express my feelings without having to worry about how it's going to affect those around me?"

"I'll take you out, Mom. Just say the word," offered Bill.

We went for a drive to the place where he had hiked with Theresa. The Marron Bells was an area of interesting geological formations, and I had the perfect guide.

On the way home, I burst into tears. "I'm so sorry, Bill. Everything overwhelms me," I admitted.

We ended our stay in Aspen with dinner at a restaurant. The summer evening was so pleasant that the three of us—Bill, Jennie, and I—decided to go for a little stroll. The sidewalk was rather bumpy, and I was about to suggest we go home, but instead I cried out, "Stop! I want to read the sign on that chalkboard." *Snow Melts, Men Die* were the words written on the chalkboard announcing a reunion of Aspen ski instructors.

"Hmmm," I muttered, "everything can change in an instant, even for ski instructors."

~ ~ ~

When we finally returned home to Pasadena from our long journey, Bill and I hung out in the van enjoying our ritual of sharing a can of cold beer for one last time.

During our brief time away, the RV had transported me into a different world. With the help of country music, beer, and the ever-changing scenery of the West, I had barely noticed the daily routine of my physical care.

Twenty-four hours later, I was sad to watch Bill drive away to his home in Santa Cruz. He took with him his father's beauty—caring, humility, and charity.

Irma, Jennie, and I were content to be home. My only goal at that time was to rest while Jennie prepared herself for camp.

"I burned my arm," Jennie said, pointing to a bright red spot on her forearm. "It's nothing. I was ironing name tags on my clothes."

After a few days of rest, I resumed my physical therapy. The effort brought tears to my eyes, but I noticed some physical improvement, which gave me hope.

Some friends stopped by. I thought they were coming over to hear about my trip, but instead, they told me about their own concerns. *Is everybody sad?* I wondered, when one wife confided that her husband hadn't slept with her for two years, and another, bored by the prospect of her husband wanting to sail to some "barren rock" for their summer vacation, was frustrated by the fact that, as far as she was concerned, he would just be moving her from one sink to another or, in this case, the galley. On and on the stories continued. Another friend found out her husband owed the government $100,000 in back taxes and then discovered that his health was failing as well.

Criticism came my way about my plans for sending Jennie to summer camp. "Won't you be lonely without her?" was the sort of comment I heard. Actually, I believed that the decision would help us both. The camp was at Huntington Lake, the same camp her brothers had so enjoyed. I knew Jennie would be just fine, and I would enjoy my time alone to continue working on myself.

Because she had to grow up without a father, I wanted to give her a life as close as possible to what her siblings were able to enjoy. Her father had provided her with the means, and I'm sure he would have loved to see her experiencing new things.

When fear and dread took over again, I phoned Damian for solace.

"How refreshingly sweet and straightforward you were about your feelings for me, Damian. I wish I could have been as honest about my own. My natural reserve, the difference in our ages, and the love I had for my husband made it impossible for me to do so. I want to say to you now that I fell in love with you," I stammered.

"I'm hearing some very nice things over this phone," he said. "I still feel the same way about you," he added.

"I'm still your friend?" I asked.

"Yes, you always will be," he answered solemnly.

"Damian, the memories of the winter when we worked together, the memories of family life, and the presence of Jennie are all that keep me going now," I said.

"We'll talk again soon," he promised. "Kiss, kiss, goodbye."

When I resumed my sessions with Sigrid, I told her about my conversation with Damian.

"Before we get to that, I want to tell you that the trip was a magnificent accomplishment," Sigrid offered. "As for Damian, you have an awful lot of guilt in regards to your relationship with him."

"No, I never felt guilty. After becoming paralyzed, I felt the relationship was like a gift from God. And the memories have helped me to get through this terrible time," I assured Sigrid. "But, I don't want to be in love again—never, ever again."

~ ~ ~

August began with another serious bout of depression. Sister Wilfrid came out of retreat to help me. I was in the garage strapped to my tilt board when she arrived. She knelt by my side, with Irma kneeling next to her. Then Sister stood up to administer Communion to Irma and me, and then she resumed her kneeling position. The three of us remained in silent prayer for several minutes. After reciting the Our Father, the two women stood up. Then, Sister asked us to pray for a young man who had been badly burned.

"Don and his wife recently phoned from the beach. We should pray for them too. John can't go to the beach anymore because of his deteriorating health," I said, as I thought of those wonderful September mornings John and I had spent on the beach. How self-satisfied John and I used to be, sipping our coffee and reveling over the vacant beach stretched out before us. Now, we were ghosts like Bill—two people from another time.

To break the solemnity surrounding us, Sister Wilfrid related a story of what her nieces and nephews had said when their mother told them they were going to visit their aunt: "'Which one? The one who gives us ginger ale or the one who wears the same dress all the time?'" Irma and I looked at Sister's dress and had a good laugh.

Then Sister added, "It was a long time ago when nuns were required to wear habits all the time, and they were allowed only stiff and formal visits in the convent parlor once a month with friends or relatives. How silly all those rules were, so inhumane and stifling."

After giving me a book to encourage me to continue writing in my journals, Sister left. I then took a look at George Simons's *Keeping Your Personal Journal.* It read:

> *Journals are often begun at life's turning points when one begins to veer away from the roles one has been identified with, and thus begins to move counter to the expectations of most of those around us.*

Sister returned the following day, and we prayed for the father of one of young Bill's childhood friends. Sister commented on my journey, saying, "Your trip to Aspen sounds remarkable. It may have set you back a bit physically, but the emotional rewards of being with your son made up for it, I'm sure." She continued, "It is only a matter of time, and you'll be walking again, Berta."

"Sister, are you happy to be a nun?" I asked.

"Oh, very! I hadn't really planned on becoming one, but that is what God wanted," she replied.

"Did you ever want to get married?"

"Yes, I was in love, but when he asked me to marry him—" Sister paused to smile at the memory. Continuing with her story, she told me, "We parked by Lake Michigan. When he handed me the ring, I told him I wished to be a nun. Soon after, he became a priest."

I was glad to hear about Sister's own relationship experience, and I felt she was sympathetic to my relationship with Damian.

When the day came to a close I completely broke down. Clutching Jennie's first letter from camp, I phoned Dana to read her the happy words Jennie had written. Then I explained to her, "I can't seem to get a grip on my life. Jesus must want something from me, but what is it?" I asked, as if she would know the answer.

"I realize how difficult it must be for you to have patience as you wait for an answer to come," she replied.

"Please pray for me," I asked.

"I do. I think of you all the time. I'll call you—" she said, but I spoke over her words.

"Jennie comes in to say goodnight carrying her teddy bear, and, when she leaves the room, I cry. I cry at everything!" I broke down sobbing.

The sorrow never seems to leave, the memories never go away, the wounds won't heal. Christ will give me the grace to bear my cross, but for how many years to come? I am weak. I feel unable to endure this kind of future. My legs are everything to me. How they used to love to dance, to swim, to walk, to take me to new places. I am ruined!

~ ~ ~

When things got me down, I lacked the courage to pull myself out of depression. But every now and then, I'd have a reprieve. At the end of the first week of August, I rejoiced. I actually had a good day! Even though my body felt like it had been in the washing machine on the spin cycle, and it was 100 degrees outside, I felt tranquil on the inside. That day, I received another sweet letter from Jennie, I wrote some letters, did a few exercises with Katie's help, took a rest, and watched a touching film, *The Majority of One*. I found myself identifying with the widow in the film.

The day was rather quiet until Irma came home from her weekend off. She was slightly inebriated.

"It's okay, Irma. Go to bed," I suggested.

Suddenly, a loud crash came from the kitchen! Irma ran to see what was the matter. She returned to my room and groaned, "The cat knocked over the wastebasket. A jar of mayonnaise I had thrown away fell out and broke. There's mayonnaise all over the floor!"

"I can see that," I smiled, as I noticed that Tom's whiskers were covered with mayonnaise.

Then Tom threw up and defecated in the fireplace.

"Damn it!" I yelled and burst into tears. Was I crazy crying over a simple mishap, crying over the phone with Dana one day and then laughing with Leslie the following day? I clutched Jennie's note and yelled, "This is all I have: the little girl that wrote this note!"

Coincidentally, Damian phoned at that moment and asked if I was all right.

Not knowing what else to say, but knowing that relief was on its way, I cried out, "Morgan is coming home. Morgan is coming—" and I burst into tears and hung up.

~ ~ ~

After returning from his travels in Central America, Morgan came by the house unannounced. He brought with him a bouquet of tiger lilies and many stories about his journey. He related the story of his one disappointment: "We were delayed and harassed at the borders. It cost us money and time. My friends had just enough money to get home. I decided not to go on to Buenos Aires and to Rio without them, so I came home via Miami, New Orleans, and San Francisco. I wanted to ease my way back and minimize culture shock."

It amazed me how, whenever the children were around, I regained my emotional balance. My fear and anxiety were quelled.

Katy, Morgan's girlfriend, was sitting quietly by his side while he spoke. When he told me he had gone straight to her home after he returned from his trip and had spent the day with her before showing up at my house, I was the hurt mother for a moment, but quickly took control of myself. I understood the power of being in love.

Later that same afternoon, I had a session with Sigrid. We discussed a recent dream I had that clearly had to do with my enormous mood shifts between tranquility and dread. Sigrid interpreted the dream as a representation of my repressed sexuality. "You are a very sensual person, Berta," she said. "I think in the past, you developed the serene side of your nature to protect yourself. It was a place where your mother couldn't reach you. In your teens, you probably didn't allow the strong sexual side of your being to express itself, because it would not have pleased your mother. You subsequently became a Catholic, and the Virgin Mary became someone to emulate. There is no one as spotless as the Virgin Mary."

I found her analysis revealing, but it left me feeling sad. And it made me question all my sexual experiences since my wedding night, when I was nineteen. That night was my first time and was totally satisfying for me. The following morning before I got up to prepare for Mass, I kissed my darling Bill. As I descended the elevator of the hotel, I wondered if I looked any different to the other occupants. At Mass, I thanked Our Lord for finding me such a tender and loving life partner. My serene side was probably responsible for the reason why so many of my friends called me the "Madonna."

In the course of almost thirty years of marriage and five children, not every night was as blissful as the first. The seasons of marriage change a relationship, but I was always content with what Bill and I had. The sensuality Sigrid spoke of began to bloom when we moved to the beach. Religion, art, music, poetry, the beauty of nature delighted my senses. As my family responsibilities eased up, with St. Lo as the setting, I felt more passion for these things that fed my soul.

After Bill's death, I had felt unprotected. Did I become paralyzed to protect myself? No, I wanted my body back. I did not want fate to make that choice for me. I didn't necessarily want another relationship; I was too protective of my independence. And, there was a child to raise. "I wonder if I can raise another child? I feel so broken," I said to God.

~ ~ ~

Morgan paid me another visit before he left for a wedding in Oregon. We discussed the changes in our lives.

"It took me months to get over the loss of our home. I don't think we'll ever get over it, Mom," he said.

"No, we won't," I agreed.

I shared my feelings with my son by reading him some of the poetry I had written since my paralysis took over. Those words helped him to have a deeper understanding of my plight.

We talked about his relationship with Katy. He informed me that they would be married within the next few years. Morgan was looking forward to his future. His healing had begun. "We lived together for a while last year, but now I prefer that we live separately until we get married," he said.

My mood lifted when Jennie came home from camp before leaving for Sun Valley. Her time at camp had been a great success. "Riley went to Mass while we were at camp," she said, and I enjoyed hearing that bit of news. My granddaughter had yet to be baptized.

After Jennie left, I drifted into depression again. I saw nothing—absolutely zero—in my future until Sister Wilfrid came over to give me Communion one afternoon. I told her about friends and acquaintances who visited me to unload all their woes. "I always believe that they are interested in how I am doing. Instead, they reveal the difficulties in their own lives. Divorce, love affairs, abortions, debt, and illness are the common themes among my contemporaries. Young adults speak about surviving alcoholic or workaholic parents or philandering fathers. Sister, when did life become so messy!"

Sister Wilfrid responded, "You are performing your ministry. What is happening in your life has an effect on many people, Berta. Through your suffering, you are helping others. Every second of your suffering is shared by Our Lord, so you must continue to do your part: be strong, and don't sink into depression, so that you can give courage to the people who come to you with their stories." I felt that, with Sister's remarks, the gate had opened a bit. I started to gain an understanding of what my purpose was.

Sister Wilfrid and I prayed together. At the time, I didn't understand the deeper meaning of what Sister Wilfrid told me. I didn't understand how I could follow my ministry without the use of my legs. So I bargained with God: "Return my legs, and I'll know what to do with my life. With your help, I'll help other people."

This bright spot was short lived, however. The very next day, I once again felt the familiar heaviness of dread upon me.

I longed for death to get me off this emotional roller coaster. *Now is the time*, I thought, as I went to the kitchen to get a bottle of Scotch, to round up every pill in my bathroom, and to fill the sink with water. My plan—as impulsive as it may have seemed—was for my head to drop under water in the hopes of drowning, once I was knocked out by the pills and Scotch.

Once and for all, the anguish will be no more!

Suddenly, the doorbell rang. I could hear Mary Jane talking to Irma.

"Go away, please!" I yelled.

The bathroom door opened, and Mary Jane, her daughter Amy standing beside her, cried out, "What are you doing?"

"I'm tired. Please go away, and let me go," I said between sobs.

"Come with me," she said. She steered me into the living room. Mary Jane and Amy held my hands. I wept and wept.

Chapter 14

AT THE GATE

Perhaps nothing can be sole
Or whole that has not been rent.

—W. B. Yeats

Chapter 14

W hen I lifted my head and saw Sister Wilfrid standing there before me, I swore out loud, "Holy Mary, Mother of God." My bladder began to leak all over the floor. Ignoring it, I told Sister Wilfrid exactly what was going on. Her face turned so sad, it was beyond description.

"Have you asked your psychiatrist why you have these black moods?" she inquired.

"Sister, doesn't anyone around me understand that what I am going through are not simply mood swings? I'm in perpetual darkness. It's like being in hell! I want to take a knife and cut it out," I screamed. "The only friend I have is the night. That's the only time I find peace. Daylight comes, and then terror and dread stalk me all day long. As for Sigrid, she says it's cyclical, perhaps menopausal. My body has been the repository of various types of antidepressants. Never having been a pill taker, I find it difficult to stay with a regime, and I do not enjoy the side effects. Those pills make me drowsy, constipated, and forgetful."

I continued, talking about my "calling" as a wife and mother: "Bill and I were called to be parents, just as you were called to become a nun. In our marriage and family life, we found the love and stability that had been missing in our childhoods. The move to the beach was my husband's decision. Later, it became a transformative experience for me. Another aspect of myself came into being, one that had been denied for a long time. I became free spirited and deeply spiritual at the same time. I overflowed with joy back then. St Lo was my secret garden. Well, that's all I have to say about it, Sister," I said angrily. "You know the rest of the story."

Sister sat quietly, tears running down her cheeks.

"Your life there was more beautiful than most people *ever* experience," said Sister, attempting to comfort me. "Please try to get some joy from that. This house is lovely and so right for you. How fortunate you are. There are many patients who go home to one room with *no one* to help them."

"I've heard it all before. I've been told to 'just snap out of it' and been told that I'm such a strong person. Well, apparently, no one has ever experienced—at least no one I know—this state of pure emotional dread. I don't even understand it myself," I fumed.

"Irma, come and help me to bed," I shouted. Mary Jane, Amy, and Sister quietly left. I felt more peaceful after Irma settled me in my bed.

The phone rang, startling me. I was reluctant to answer it, as it took a great deal of struggling to get my body in position to pick up the receiver.

"This is Sister. Are you all right?" she inquired.

"I had to lift my legs so that I could roll over to answer the phone. And, the ringing made my nerve pain flare up. Even so, I felt a sense of peace come over me when you were here, and it's still with me," I explained.

"That's Jesus. The peace of the Christ Presence," she said.

After I said goodbye to Sister, the phone rang again before I could reposition myself on my back.

"Hi, this is Damian," said a familiar voice. "I'm at the beach."

"Yes, it's August. I guess you would be there," I pointed out.

"My show went very well. It was my birthday, too," he added.

"I know," I acknowledged flatly.

"The beach is . . ." but I didn't hear his words.

"I have to go now, Damian," I told him, and hung up.

I thought to myself: *How coincidental that Damian would call me on such a day? Why did Mary and her daughter show up? How is it that Sister Wilfrid came by unannounced at the same time?* I didn't have the answers to those questions, but I now suspect it was the hand of God.

Then, Mary Jane phoned me. "You're feeling deserted," she said. "Morgan went to San Francisco to meet Dana. Then they are going to Santa Cruz to see Bill." That was her explanation for my suicide attempt. "Where is Jennie?"

"She's in Sun Valley with Leslie. I haven't heard from her."

"Well, there you go, Berta," Mary Jane pointed out.

It was August. I was not at the beach. I was completely alone. All of these reasons were part of the puzzle, but my emotional breakdown began as a result of paralysis and my move from St. Lo. "It is a sign of weakness to ask for help," my British mother always used to say to me. I was unable to articulate my feelings of vulnerability as an adult because her Victorian stoicism had been instilled in me at an early age.

For the remainder of August, I wrote and wrote to make the blackness bearable. Our cat, Tom, died, so I wrote about him and the pleasure he had brought to our family. He was born long ago on April Fool's Day, hence his name, "Tom Fool."

"I miss him," Irma cried. In spite of his *pulgas* (fleas), she and Tom had developed a relationship—a sort of love-hate relationship. So, she was very upset when he hadn't eaten his breakfast and died soon after. For me, he represented the years my children were growing up, and now he was gone as well.

~ ~ ~

Labor Day came and went. The weekends and holidays continued their pattern with the phone not ringing, and, at my request, only a few visitors coming over. I couldn't bear to hear any more stories about broken lives. Jennie, home from Sun Valley for a brief visit, left for St. Lo with friends, and Morgan spent some time with me after he returned from Oregon. I was encouraged by his visit when he again expressed that he was not going to live with Katy until they were married, and "I spoke to Dana about having the family live closer together again. She told me she agrees that this should happen, and probably will happen in time."

Jennie came home on Labor Day.

"Your friends said to say hello. I swam in the sea a lot. Oh, I almost forgot—Charles was there too. He told me to tell you that he missed you," Jennie related and then went to bed.

I wanted to scream out loud: "I should have been there with you, dear Jennie!"

Oh blessed night, I thought, after Irma settled me in for the night, and then I said a prayer: "Help me remember the better place is here with You, getting well."

Suddenly, I heard a voice, as if someone were addressing me. I looked around the room to figure out where the voice was coming from, but I didn't see anyone.

"Stay with me a little longer. I will not keep you here forever. You will walk again, and it will be soon. You will be free to live your life as you wish," the lyrical voice whispered.

At first, I wondered if the Devil was playing tricks with my mind. Delight surged through me after the voice delivered its message. My whole being was enveloped in sweetness, and I fell into a blissful slumber. After a trance-like sleep, I awoke and pulled myself up into a sitting position, hoping to find the sweetness still there, but it was gone. Dawn was breaking.

I picked up a pencil and paper from the nightstand and began to write:

Novel, *The Second Journey*—B. Hees, Wed., Sept. 8, 1982.

How to begin? I picked up the book nearest my bed and began to read the first words that I laid eyes on.

Thou hast enlarged me when I was in distress, – PSALM 4:11.

Then, the text expanded on the theme of the Psalm:

This is one of the grandest testimonies ever given by man to the moral government of God. . . . He declares the sorrows of life to have been themselves the source of life's enlargement. . . . It is written of Joseph in the dungeon that, "the iron entered his soul." . . . He had been rejoicing in youthful dreams, and dreaming hardens the heart. He who sheds tears over a romance will not be apt to most help reality; real sorrow will be too unpoetic for him.

That was I, the dreamer, the romantic always searching for gold and not the iron.

The gold is but a vision; the iron is an experience . . . unites me to humanity . . . not joy, but sorrow; gold is partial, but iron is universal.

Thou canst not lift the iron load of thy brother if the iron hath not entered into thee. . . . Say not that the shades of the prison-house have fettered thee; thy fetters are wings—wings of flight into the bosom of humanity. The door of thy prison-house is a door into the heart of the universe. God has enlarged thee by the binding of sorrow's chain.

GEORGE   MATHESON

Then, from the same book:

If Joseph had not been Egypt's prisoner, he had never been Egypt's governor. The iron chain about his feet ushering in the golden chain about his neck. – SELECTED.

Mrs. Charles E. Cowman, *Streams in the Desert*

The words stunned me. I had opened the book at random to a place where everything was spelled out for me.

The phone rang. It was my mother.

"Thank God a year has passed," my mother said on the phone. "Nobody knew what to do." We were talking about last year's move to Pasadena, and I found her unusual frankness refreshing.

Still, Thanksgiving was on the horizon to be followed by Christmas, and what would the New Year bring?

Emotional stability continued to elude me. Fear and dread haunted me constantly. The light of day hurt my eyes. After Labor Day, I told Morgan that I couldn't live through another summer. He stormed angrily out of the house. I thought of the day in August when suicide seemed to be the only answer, so, I guess my son worried that my words meant that I would not be around for any more summers.

When October arrived, Jennie already spent one month in school. Damian and Christopher came to assist Fran with my therapy. After they put my shoes and socks on, they lifted me to a standing position. As I made some attempts at walking, they jokingly argued about which leg had performed better. There I hung, suspended in mid air, as they were trying to decide who would put me on my bed.

"Damian, Damian, I'll take her." Christopher gently put me down to rest.

During Thanksgiving, the house was full of noise and laughter. Fires burned brightly in the living-room and dining-room fireplaces. Reflections from the flames danced on the silverware on the dining-room table. Jennie had polished each piece while Bill helped Irma with the cooking, and I arranged the flowers he brought.

Gathered that day were Morgan, Bill, Jennie, Katy, Aunt Alice, her grandson Richard, my mother, and Uncle Phil. Before we ate, we raised our glasses of champagne to the loved ones who were not present. Damian stopped by to say hello and to bring his Christmas card.

Morgan's twenty-third birthday had come and gone as the year was drawing to a close. We talked to each other on the phone that day and laughed as he recalled the terrific finish of the Cal Stanford game. Cal had plowed through the Stanford band, knocking the trombone players right and left as the team made the winning play.

The years are flying by, I thought, as I sat in a spot of sun, writing a poem for Jennie's thirteenth birthday. I wrote:

Gifts

All your dreams fulfilled
(If I could give them to you)
would be yours.
All the tossing of the waves,
(If I could give them to you)
on yesterday's forgotten shore.
All the years to come,
(Only God can give you)
say "Yes!" and they are yours.

I completed the poem at sunset. At that moment, I could have gone into the house, but who would have greeted me there? Only silent possessions that stood like sentries guarding another life. There was no future here; there was no past in this house, only rooms shared with Irma—a stranger to my former way of life—and Jennie, whom I knew would move on in a few short years. So I listened to the fish making an occasional splash in the pond, the cars going by outside the walled garden patio, and the birds chirping until the darkness of night fell. Irma came out to wheel me into the house. "It's too cold out here," she said.

At my desk, I reread a letter that was intended for my older children. I wrote it in late September, 1982, but I never mailed it.

> *I am in much distress. I have tried my very best to make a home for my darling Jennie, but my wounds just won't heal! I live constantly on the brink of falling into a total void. The events of the last two years have ruined me. No matter how much I try, I cannot recover. It is my desire that you put me away somewhere so I cannot harm myself. I am worn out from my physical care. I am so longing for the sea again and wish to rest there as your father does. Oh, how I envy him his swift, painless death. God has been less kind to me.*

> *I don't know where such a place exists, for my care I mean. I would hope that together we might find some Catholic home where I might receive care for my body and soul. There must be such a place.*

> *I cannot continue to live in a world where I don't belong. I feel as though I were buried alive.*

> *Jennie, dear Jennie, is the only light in the darkness. The house shines when she walks in the door. But I don't want her to remember me as a sorrowful grieving mass of pain. God only knows I miss the things we used to do together: the breakfasts before school at some diner in Carlsbad; running along the beach after school in September to splash in the tide pools; waiting for your father to come home on Wednesdays. I always, always met him at the gate to put my arms around him, as did Jennie.*

Children, I miss the person that I used to be and detest what I have become—a wretched being that no one sees, trying to smile, trying to write, trying to paint, trying to pray, all in an effort to make the days go by. All these activities serve only as band-aids to cover wounds that will not heal, the wounds that no one sees.

When Leslie said in her note to Jennie, "I am sitting at my desk in my room," my mind instantly escaped to my bedroom at St. Lo, where I used to write as I watched the gulls soar, the changing moods of sea and sky, the dolphins passing by. Images of feet in the sand, sailing paper boats with Jennie and her dad as the weir overflowed into the ocean came to mind. That place, those days, will forever remain in my heart. Those were the happiest days of my life.

The problem is that I cannot feed off memories for the rest of my life as a way of keeping myself alive. As the days go by, I have too much time to sit and think. There are few things to distract me. Friends gradually drift away, and the house, pretty as it is, feels like a tomb. God has imprisoned me. Although He is surrounded by saints who were literally imprisoned during their lifetimes, I am, try as I might, unable or unwilling to accept the grace He would offer me in my situation. My cross breaks me. I am not a saint, nowhere near to the perfection of God. Nonetheless, He has helped me in many ways.

Long to run free down the hill at St. Lo in the fall, in the winter. My spirit, my soul felt so free there. Why Jesus took that away from me, I don't know. It isn't that I didn't appreciate it, as I used to thank Him each day for the joy I so keenly felt.

Waiting, waiting, always waiting,
I smile "hello," I smile "goodbye,"
But underneath, my heart is breaking.
Oh, but—where?—to go for a little while.

Your loving mother.

Oh, to go for a little while and to leave it all behind. But go where? To my death? But where would I end up? The choice was up to me. And, after reading this letter, I understood the lack of emotional and physical progress that I could claim for myself despite my efforts. And now, another year had gone by.

The early months of 1983 went by like a drunk veering down the road to oblivion. But before I crashed, the gate to the future opened a little bit more. No, the physical pain, along with the depression, did not recede. Still I courted thoughts of death. Slowly, I began to look beyond myself, beyond the gray curtain that enshrouded me.

Morgan called one afternoon to check up on me. "How are you, Mom?" he asked on the phone after consoling Jennie upon the death of her friend's mother, Caroline.

In total honesty I said, "I've had some difficult days since the year began. I either want to walk again or self-destruct."

"You made that decision months ago," he replied, "so, I guess you'll just have to walk again."

A few days later, Bill phoned me, and I recall how I had expressed my despair to him. "If I had a gun, dear Bill, I'd blow my brains out," I told him. I certainly had no intention of alarming him or hurting him. I suppose I was just trying to reach out; I needed someone in my family to understand the emotional turmoil I was going through.

"Please call me," Bill said. "I'm home every evening." He was sure I would walk again. "But, even then you'll have to make it on your own." I suppose that meant I would have to carve out a new life for myself apart from my children.

Lying in my bed as the household settled into slumber, I gave voice to all the feelings that had assailed me during the day. Sister Wilfrid knew the only way for me was to rise above my suffering and pray for all those in distress. She taught me by example. She was physically suffering herself, but at the same time she reached out to all kinds of people through her prayers. But I was a slow learner.

The strained relationship with my children was always foremost in my mind. I didn't see them as being especially helpful. Perhaps it is unreasonable to expect your children to help you once they grow up. But I believed that, out of respect and admiration for their father, they would have treated me and taken care of me the way he would have. They did send me flowers on my birthday, but I expected more from them after I suffered so many losses.

Anger gnawed at me despite all my prayers. Was Irma right when she said, "Your illness is pure nerves, anger turned inward"? She had read my horoscope from a Spanish magazine that said anger would affect my spine and, even worse, cause me to go crazy.

"You must change," Irma cautioned me over and over again.

I continued to pray that I would be rid of all past anger toward my mother, husband, and children. I turned to Jesus, hoping that He might heal me of my self-destructive behavior.

My relationship with Damian began to change. One morning, Damian stayed with me after physical therapy. When we were alone, he sat beside me on my bed.

"I do not love you as I used to," he said. "I do love you as a person and a friend. All love turns into friendship." Then he gave me a gentle kiss, and left.

I wasn't so sure about this. But in a way, he was right. Long married partners do become best friends. They have years of shared experiences as a foundation. Now that Damian and I had formed a lasting friendship, it was easier for me to call him whenever I needed emotional support. We spoke on the phone from time to time reminiscing about our past relationship. During one conversation, he referred to the day we first made love— the day he left the beach. "It's amazing we weren't involved before," he remarked.

"Damian, when we began to work together, I saw myself as a woman twenty years older, a woman in love with her husband, and the mother of five children. I thought you were very kind to take me on as a pupil," I explained. "As far as I was concerned, the possibility of a romance never entered my mind."

"Well, it was inevitable, given the beauty we were surrounded by and the intimacy we shared during our lessons," he said.

"You had your young friends who visited from time to time. I remember one in particular who said, 'Ah yes, the older woman.' I felt embarrassed that he might be thinking there was anything between us," I recalled.

"I liked your family. You were all so attractive. Your husband was a fine man. I really liked him, and I knew you loved him."

"You understand, Damian, I was serious about painting. My life totally changed when Bill insisted on moving to the beach. I wasn't happy about the move until I discovered that I now had time to pursue my own interests," I admitted.

Sometime after that conversation, we spoke about the moments when the "inevitable" attraction began.

"Do you remember when we were working on the eyes in the first drawing, and you looked directly at me and said, 'Let me see your eyes.' I thought then, as you gazed at me, how much I wanted to kiss you," Damian confessed.

"I'm surprised. We were just getting to know each other. I recognized my attraction for you much later."

"When?"

"We were working one afternoon, and you got up and went to rest on the little sofa bed that your father enjoyed so much, you know, the one that pulled out from beneath the bookshelf. I wanted to follow you. Instead, I ignored those feelings. After grabbing my paints, I left in a bewildered state."

Damian said, "I was hoping you would follow me then." His voice trailed off.

"Why didn't you tell me how you felt?" I asked.

"Why didn't *you*?"

"I was married. I was also afraid of making a fool of myself."

In another conversation, Damian said, "When you and I meet in Heaven, and we appear as our souls really are, I'm going to look like Dorian Gray, and you are going to be so pure. I think I might try celibacy. I wonder if it would be possible. I don't want to be in love anymore. It takes too much time, too much energy. I don't write poetry anymore. The poems I wrote to my recent girlfriend were revised verses." I wondered if the ones he had written me were among those revised verses originally written for someone else.

"Do you love this girl?" I asked.

"No I never loved her," he said. "She asked about you and me once. We talked about the possibility of your paralysis being caused by guilt over our relationship and by Bill's death coming so suddenly during that time. Or, perhaps, it was stress or just medical reasons. You know, Berta, many people knew or guessed we were involved with each other."

"No, I didn't know people were speculating on our relationship. I never gave it a thought. Winter is quiet at St. Lo. There aren't many people around," I pointed out. "Well, Charles speculated on the relationship. I told him he was crazy. 'I'm forty-eight and I'm married to your cousin,' I said to Charles."

"How about the day of Leslie's divorce? Remember? We went for a walk," he reminded me.

"I was in shock. I had no one to turn to that day. Bill wasn't there to support me, and he never phoned me. He should have phoned me. Weren't you seeing Dana at that time?" I inquired.

"Yes," he answered.

"I was happy you were seeing her. I wasn't in any way going to compete with my own daughter or anyone else for that matter," I declared.

~ ~ ~

I went over and over in my mind about what could have caused my paralysis. My doctors didn't have any answers. Even though I was a practicing Catholic, I felt no guilt over my relationship with Damian. I was convinced that guilt had nothing to do with my sudden paralysis. Back problems had haunted me since my thirties. I had considered surgery back then, but my doctor advised me against it: "Berta, too many people leave the hospital in wheelchairs." I wore a brace instead. The brace helped me for a while. The discomfort eventually went away, so I tucked the brace into a drawer.

The financial problems that my husband had left me with, Leslie's divorce coming so near the time of Bill's death, the depression that followed, and, possibly, a bad spill experienced in Sun Valley that first Christmas all contributed to my paralysis. I was sure of that. On that day in Idaho, as I came off the chairlift, I fell with such a force on the ice that my teeth clenched together. For years, the doctors told me that my spinal cord was gradually deteriorating, and I'm convinced that the fall further weakened my condition and set the stage for paralysis. After all, I did go into the hospital with my right leg out of commission after an emotionally and physically draining move to the beach, and that same leg tingled when I propped it up on the coffee table as I was watching the television.

A week passed since my conversation with Damian. He came over with Christopher one afternoon, and I saw more in Damian's eyes than just friendship. He shot me a piercing look from those blue eyes that could never be mistaken for mere friendship. My heart told me that my feelings for him had not died.

On a beautiful February morning, Damian picked me up to take me for a ride to Mt. Wilson. That particular route was new to him, although he was familiar with most of the trails. From time to time, he would pull his van to the side of the road to point out the river below and the hiking trails he liked.

"I wish I were Morgan and had just one girl, or I wish I were you, so I wouldn't have to bother with relationships," he said.

He asked me if I was capable of having sex.

"No, the body I once knew no longer exists," was my reply.

Damian parked the van near a patch of snow. I watched as he walked over to the snow, made a snowball, and threw it into the canyon below. Then, out of nowhere—or so it seemed—a snowball suddenly hit me smack in the face.

"Where did that come from?" I laughed when he returned to the van.

"I just had to do it," he grumbled.

Was he being playful, mischievous and flirtatious, or was he frustrated because I could no longer have sex? I believed it was the latter.

As we headed toward the pavilion for tea, he said, "I'm fasting today," as he pushed me up the ice-covered path to the viewing deck. "Let's go sledding," he said. Slipping and sliding over the ice, I began to laugh and couldn't stop until we pulled up to a table on the deck. We were both hungry, so Damian got some sandwiches and something to drink from the food concession.

"I guess I'm not fasting after all," he remarked as he devoured a sandwich and watched me eat mine.

A few hikers came off the trails and joined us at our table. A young man from Colombia spoke a little English, so the conversation alternated between Spanish and English. He was traveling with a Japanese boy. Then Steve, a married architect, joined us at our table. The men traded trail stories. By the time we parted company, we were all on a first-name basis. It surprised me that such a cosmopolitan group could be found right in my backyard. It was exhilarating to be with Damian again and to share stories with these people we met along the trail. What a wonderful experience to feel the same sexual attraction for Damian which had not disappeared because of my paralysis. I enjoyed his sense of humor and love of life. I was touched that we still cared so much for each other. Damian held my hand all the way home.

~ ~ ~

The mood at home was bitter. My mother was mad at me—again. Sigrid was mad at me. Sister Wilfrid was mad at me. They were all down on me for complaining all the time about not being able to help myself. But, it was true: I could not help myself. The tedium of my bodily care, combined with extreme, unceasing nerve pain that no one took into consideration—not to mention my depression—affected me in ways they couldn't possibly understand. All they saw was a woman sitting in a wheelchair or lying on a comfortable bed. But "comfortable" was not a word that would come to mind were I to describe how I felt. I wanted to cry out: *"Look around. Is my husband here? And is my sister here? Are my children here? No! Except for a thirteen-year-old girl who is totally dependent on me!* Complain? No, I didn't complain. Instead, I was stoic.

Ignoring everyone around me, I advanced at my own pace. I attended an AA meeting. Then, I had a joyful reunion with three dear friends—Sally, Marta, and Maureen. We had all attended the same high school together. I also signed up for a positive attitude class.

Soon after, I was fitted for leg braces. I began a new physical therapy regimen in my garage. Morgan swept out the garage and moved my car, and Bill made exercise bars for me so that I could brace myself as I attempted to stand up. After Fran helped me with my range-of-motion exercises on my bed, which loosened up my legs, Damian carried me to the garage. There, I sat on a chair, grasping a bar with each hand, while Fran put on my leg braces. Then, with Fran's help, I hoisted myself up into a standing position. Fran locked my knees into position.

Morgan and Damian were excited to see me standing.

"I haven't seen the world from this height for a long time. Everything looks so small!" I exclaimed. I always took pleasure in being tall—over five feet eight inches tall.

The expression on Fran's face told me how well I was doing, especially when she slapped my right leg and was rewarded with a step. With a smug little smile, she said, "You are going to be just fine." That is the thought I would keep in my mind.

While I attempted—and finally succeeded—to stand on my braced leg, Damian slipped away to hang a picture over the sofa in my bedroom.

A few days before I stood up for the first time, Damian joined me for dinner, bringing with him a painting I had purchased from him. The painting had been realized during the time we worked together. In fact, the first time he showed it to me at St. Lo was quite an event.

Back then, Damian phoned and asked me to come down to his garage studio. He was waiting at the edge of his driveway when I arrived. "Close your eyes," he said, "I have something to show you." He took my hand and led me toward the garage door. "Now stay there a moment," he said, and then I heard the garage door open. "All right, you can look now."

Before me was a large canvas with an image of Damian and me in a gentle embrace. The painting beautifully depicted our mystical, sensual, feelings for each other.

"Where is my hair?" I asked him. The woman in the painting had short hair; mine was down to my waist. He grinned, but gave no explanation about the woman in white. Damian had depicted himself as an angel with wings that were drawing the woman toward him.

"You make me feel like a little girl," I said, smiling, as I took the painting.

"You look like a little girl to me," he said.

Now, the picture was mine. Any night, lying in bed, I could turn my head and look at those two figures and find joy. During the day, I enjoyed hearing people's reactions.

Irma once commented, "That is definitely Damian, but the woman looks like Leslie." No, it wasn't Leslie, although she and I did bear some resemblance to each other.

Morgan looked at it, but said nothing. He knew it was me.

Jennie asked, "Is that anybody in particular?" And then, not waiting for an answer, she lost interest.

Sister Wilfrid kept glancing at the portrait whenever she came to visit, but I said nothing and left her to wonder.

Christopher said, "Arne thinks it's sacrilegious." Yes, it could have been seen as a depiction of forbidden fruit; however, when I looked at it, all I saw were the joyful days Damian and I had shared together.

~ ~ ~

My thought-dynamics sessions were beginning to have an impact. One morning, I woke up and decided to have "positive thoughts" direct my behavior. As a result, when Damian phoned and asked me how I was doing, I cheerfully replied, "Just fine!" My stomach twinged for a second, as I was so used to coming back with my usual "Oh, I'm all right" response. But I was determined to change that. And, ultimately, it was much easier to feel happy. Why had it taken me so long to untie those Victorian laces that reined me in when I was feeling too much joy?

~ ~ ~

In March, the anniversary of Bill's death came and went. I approached the day with acceptance. But, *"Beware the ides of March,"* I thought, when Jennie brought me her report card. She was crying. However, there was more to the tears than an unsatisfactory report card. Things were not going well socially at school either. She had not attended Mayfield since kindergarten. The inevitable cliques had been formed, and she felt like an outsider.

Sitting on my bed, she emptied her troubled heart: "I talk to my friends about St. Lo, but they clam up when I talk about the things you, Dad, and I used to do. It makes me feel like I'm different. Why did we have to sell the house? I don't feel like I belong here most of the time. I've felt this way ever since we left Pasadena and moved to the beach. It is as if I were two different people. I didn't like it when we moved to the beach. Then, I got used to it. Now, I'm back in Pasadena, and I don't belong here either. I talk to myself a lot because no one wants to talk to me. And, when I'm with Morgan, all he talks about is Katy's family." She stopped to cry for a moment, and then continued. "I'm having trouble with two girls in my class. They deliberately ignore me. I'm not very happy in this house. I'm frightened."

We went to the kitchen, and, over juice and cookies, we tried to sort things out, but she seemed to have lost her foundation.

"You have been through some very difficult circumstances. You had no choice in the matter, and neither did I. We are both struggling to carve out a new life, but memories of the old life keep intruding. In time, the past will recede, and the present will bring acceptance. We'll do it together. I love you," I told her.

"I love you too, Mommy," Jennie cried as we hugged one another.

That evening, she returned home after a school dance looking very happy. It was clear that Jennie did not only have to navigate through the rough seas of adolescence and puberty, but she also had the added challenge of having to deal with the recent upheavals in our family situation.

On Holy Thursday, a letter arrived from Dana:

Dear Mom,

I had a nice chat with grandmother Mimi today. She sounds well and was very sweet when I told her that I am getting married. I spoke with Morgan last week, and he told me that you are making a great deal of progress with your physical condition. I am very happy for you and look forward to your continued improvement. I know how important it is for you to get back on your feet.

I'm sorry you are so disappointed about not being invited to my wedding. But I want a day free of anxiety and worry which would not be possible if you were here. Please try to respect my decision, as I must think of myself first.

I'm looking forward to a party with other relatives and friends at the club in September. We can work out details as the time gets closer.

Kevin and I went to a couples workshop last Saturday. It was a very rewarding experience, and I came away with an even deeper love for and understanding of Kevin. I'm thrilled at the prospect of being married to him.

Please let me know the details of Jennie's arrival in Sun Valley next week.

Love, Dana

Crying and upset about not being invited to Dana's wedding, I phoned Sister Wilfrid and read the letter to her.

"Tear it up and throw it in the wastebasket," she advised.

A few days later, I destroyed the original, but I didn't entirely take Sister's advice. I made a copy and tucked it in my desk. Maybe, someday, I would understand why Kevin and Dana hadn't gotten married in Pasadena.

To temporarily escape from the difficulties we were experiencing, Jennie and I accepted an invitation from the artist, Jerry, who had painted portraits of the children, my husband, and me. Damian had put me in touch with him again.

It was a magical evening for me, for Jennie, and for Morgan, who drove us to the ranch above Altadena. As we approached the old adobe house, we stopped to look at the rhesus monkey in a cage by the front door. "She reminds me of E.T. when she pulls the shawl over her head," said Jennie. The house hadn't changed a bit since my last visit many years before. Inside the house, mustard-yellow grime coated the walls and some very valuable paintings. The atmosphere had an eerie enchantment from the flickering of a fire and candles. Jerry's beautiful wife, Chloe, was sweet, gentle, and welcoming. She reminded me of a startled fawn, about to run away at any moment.

We soon sat down for dinner—delicious lamb, onion gravy, rice pilaf, salad, Turkish coffee, cheese, and some wonderful spiced fruit. Morgan mentioned that he had sampled a similar type of fruit on his travels through Central America. The man who helped take care of all the animals ate with us. After our meal, he took Jennie and Morgan to see the pigs, goats, and horses.

Chloe was writing poetry, and rented an apartment in one of Pasadena's oldest and most picturesque hotels, where she could do her work. As we discussed our various works in progress over a glass of wine, Joseph—a Great Dane—and Obeynot—so named because the Chihuahua wasn't very good at obeying—would come to the table from time to time looking for scraps. By the end of this glorious evening, I felt as if I had traveled to some distant land even though the lights of Altadena and Pasadena shone below. Dark mountains rose behind the ranch. The studio where I had sat for my portrait looked the same as before. New sculptures made of various throwaways had been added here and there, announcing the fact that, to Jerry's eye, there was no such thing as junk. After some twenty-odd years, it warmed me to see that some things never change.

"You were sitting in a car," Jerry reminisced, as I sat staring into the darkness around me. "You were reading a book," he continued, describing the morning I was there to sit for my portrait. "I asked why you hadn't come to the house."

"Because," I explained, "I had never posed for an artist before, and I was nervous and feeling shy. Besides, you and Chloe were having one hell of a row, and I didn't want to intrude."

The evening sadly came to a close. None of us wanted for it to end. It was an enchanting evening, one of those memorable moments that you know would never come again.

~ ~ ~

One afternoon, Morgan phoned to say he would be over for dinner. He had found work. In the evening, he showed up looking very handsome in a new suit. "Oh, qué guapo!" cried Irma when she saw him at the door.

Jennie sat beside her brother on the sofa, as he told us about his new job with an advertising firm that was hooked up to all the computer networks across the nation. Among the many accounts they handled were Toyota, Hamm's beer, Peter Paul, and Procter & Gamble. His boss was a woman, and most of the other employees were women, with the exception of my son and one other man.

"Is your name on your desk?" asked Jennie.

"Not yet, but there will be a plaque with my name on it outside my work area," he answered.

Tired, his head swimming with facts and weariness, I knew my youngest son had moved on from those carefree days of school and summer at the beach. *Bill, are you watching?* I asked the spirit of my husband.

In a conversation with Sister Wilfrid, I told her how much Morgan's decision to live nearby had meant to Jennie and me. "He took Jennie and my mother to see his office. Because Jennie was interested in attending his prep school, he drove her to Carpinteria to see the place, even though she had attended so many events there with her father and me. He was even brave enough, considering my still shaky emotional state, to drive Jennie, Jennie's companion Katie, and me to St. Lo for a day. I was fine emotionally, and I know it was because he was with me. Your prayers asking God to send one of my children to live nearby have been answered, Sister," I remarked.

"He is your son, Berta, and he has been especially blessed to play this role. God will see that his life is full of rewards. Be grateful you produced this special person," she said.

On an afternoon in May, Morgan, accompanied by Katy, came by to talk about Dana's wedding day in July. "What are you going to do about Dana's wedding day?" he asked.

"Well, Mother and I thought we would go out to lunch and toast the newlyweds," I answered.

"I really don't understand Dana's letter," he said, his eyes glistening with tears. (Yes, I showed him my copy of the letter.)

Before the wedding day arrived, Jennie honored me on Mother's Day by putting flowers on the outdoor table and serving me orange juice and croissants for breakfast. The following day, Damian and I visited several galleries and had lunch with his mother in her home.

These moments with family and friends were like a lifeline to me and gave me strength before the day of Dana's wedding in Sun Valley, Idaho.

Jennie, who was already in Sun Valley, phoned to give me an update on the events leading up to the wedding. "At this moment, Dana and Kevin are talking to the minister," she told me the day of the wedding.

Although my mother and I had decided not to go out for lunch on Dana's wedding day, my mother and uncle dropped by. "We didn't think you should be alone," my mother explained. The three of us sat together in my living room. The clock ticked away. The wedding ceremony I wasn't invited to came and went. I contained my sorrow, shedding only a few tears.

I read a note from Kevin's mother, who lived in New York. She was unable to attend the ceremony:

> How very fond we all are of Dana and how happy we are about their decision to marry! It is regrettable that you and I have not met.

The matter-of-fact tone of her note helped me deal with my sadness about not being able to go to the wedding.

Jennie's godmother, Judith, also wrote me a consoling note:

> *Dana's wedding was this month. I'm glad your mother and uncle*
> *were with you, and I hope you adjusted emotionally to not being*
> *with Dana. Strange, the ways of children sometimes!*

Judith understood the pitfalls of being a parent. One of her sons had fallen in love with and married a girl of a different faith. He converted to his wife's religion, which required him to renounce his mother. Judith didn't hear from her son for years.

~ ~ ~

Jennie went to summer camp again, and August drew me into a golden haze of summers past. Then, another jewel came into my life—my new physical therapist, Larry.

Larry was young, hard-working, ambitious, married, raising a family, and Catholic. He held a somewhat progressive view of the Church. We shared the same irreverent humor about family members and human foibles. I was his counselor as he struggled through the minefields of family life, and he was mine as I struggled to walk again. I was thinking that, if I could walk again, my family would be as it was before Bill died.

Therapy was fun. Larry would come to care about Jennie, and I would come to care about his family. I got to know them initially through his stories. Birth, death, struggle, education of children, and eccentric relatives were the topics of our conversations, which were laced with laughter. I looked forward to our activities, and definitely missed him when personal commitments, though rare, kept him away.

On one of my better therapy days, I phoned Damian to tell him it would probably be unnecessary for him to come anymore.

"Oh no," he said, "I can probably still be useful, and besides, you need someone to speak up for you. You don't speak up for yourself."

He arranged for Christopher to come on Thursdays (Damian would come on Mondays). Fran trained Larry during the course of several sessions until he was able to manage on his own. When Larry took over, it wasn't necessary for Chris and Damian to assist me anymore. The day

Fran left for good, Damian kissed her on the cheek. It was his way of saying thank you for taking care of someone he loved.

Music, therapy, running a household, along with the occasional support from Damian, carried me through the summer. "Love doesn't care how old you are or, for that matter, what you are, I might add," he remarked when he had phoned me to say thank you for his birthday present. Thinking about his upcoming trip to Tibet, I had sent him Thomas Merton's *Asian Journals*.

One lesson I began to learn during this time, during this very, very hot summer, was about love. It is fleeting, changeable, and not something we should rely on to make us happy. Somehow, we must depend solely on the God within us, the Spirit who remains our lover throughout life. When human love ends, He fills us up. The steps to get us there are lonely, hard. Turning my life over to God each morning took practice. I had many lapses. I patiently persevered in trying to stay out of my own way, which eventually made life less stressful.

Books were great comfort—newspapers too. The obituaries made me envious of the deceased, and I would carefully note the age of each person and the cause of his or her demise.

The actor, David Niven, died, and a long forgotten memory came to me. When I was a new bride, I would walk to a small market where the produce was brought in fresh each day. There, I met David Niven over a head of lettuce that we reached for at the same time. He was a gentleman, and he let me take the lettuce.

Another obituary caught my eye. Luis Buñuel, author of *That Obscure Object of Desire*, had spoken of life after death:

> He'd like to come back from the grave and buy a few newspapers every decade or so. Ghostly pale, sliding silently along the walls, my papers under my arm, I'd return to the cemetery and read about all the disasters in the world before falling back to sleep, safe and secure in my tomb.

Amen, I thought. I went to see the film of Buñuel's book and later read the review:

In addition to the theme of the impossibility of ever possessing a woman's body, the film insists on maintaining that climate of insecurity and imminent disaster — an atmosphere we all recognize, because it is our own.

Amen again, remembering how often I peered out the windows at St. Lo and felt separated from the life going on around me. It had been the same in Pasadena as Bill and I raised our children. Back then I thought, *This is all too good to be true?* I was wondering when it would all end.

Music also played a major part in my life. My mother had a lovely soprano voice and accompanied herself on the piano, my father composed, and I studied piano—all of which contributed to my love and appreciation of classical music. When I listened to certain harmonies, I was able to reconstruct aspects of that other life. On occasion, music made me sad because I could no longer move to the rhythms or play the piano unless I used my right hand while my left provided support for my upper body.

~ ~ ~

Finally, in September a note came from my new son-in-law:

Dear Berta,

Dana and I are looking forward to seeing you. There is a touch of fall in the air these mornings when we get up, which reminds us that another cycle has come to a close — the end of summer, the start of a new school year, and all that goes with it. It seems that long after we are students, the rhythms of fall still remind us of starting a new school year.

I hope that the dull lonely times of August are behind you and that this fall can bring some hope to you both physically and in terms of renewed interests in life's pleasures.

He continued, thanking me for their wedding gift to them:

. . . but since it arrived during the height of my enthusiasm for all the wonderful thoroughbreds out at Santa Fe Downs, Dana was careful to deposit it into some discreet account. I only wish I had some money. I would give it to my sweet wife, who happens to be extremely pragmatic when it comes to financial matters! We are so looking forward to our visit with you.

Love, Kevin

Would I ever travel again? I wondered. Two postcards arrived from Amsterdam. One of them said:

I remember you said on the beach at St. Lo that there was a chance you would go to Europe, particularly to Amsterdam. Promise that now to yourself, lieve Berta. Let me look after you here, and let us look forward to that! When will you come?

All my love, Laura.

A seed was planted.

Then the black hole of depression swallowed me up again for an entire week. Morgan came to check on me every evening. I told Morgan and Jennie, "I don't believe in God anymore."

"He didn't do this to you," Jennie said, with a sweet smile on her face. At night, she brought me M&Ms and flowers. When friends phoned, I would start sobbing the moment I said hello.

"I heard you were so much better!" or, "Now you just stop that!" were the phrases I heard over the phone.

My friend Annette suggested, "It's probably because the children are coming home, and you're worried about how you will handle it. I'll take you to an art exhibit. I can always tell the kids I lost you at the art show and that's why you didn't show up for dinner."

Sister Wilfrid called to say, "I'm going to pray hard for you, and I will pray that you get a good night's sleep." I did sleep that night, but by Friday I couldn't get up off the bed due to depression.

Mary—my friend, neighbor and accountant—left her office to be with me. She got Sigrid on the phone. "Don't try to tough it out, take your antidepressants," Sigrid commanded. From a tree limb out in the patio, Jennie hung the basket of impatiens Mary had brought me so I could see them from my bed.

The following week of physical therapy went better than ever.

"Okay," said Larry, "think about the progress. You are down to only one person helping with therapy. You don't need anyone else helping you now." After the range-of-motion exercises, he said, "The level of your paralysis has gone down—it's now down to T8 or T9—and that is another positive. The changes in the last two weeks have been very rapid, Berta." Larry was referring to my level of paralysis.

Damian and I went to Aunt Alice's to go swimming. On the way to Aunt Alice's home, Damian stopped at a drugstore and bought me some yellow floaties—the kind you put on your children's arms when they are starting to swim. At the pool, he put them on my ankles. With my legs afloat, I could kick and swim! The water made me buoyant and free. It was excellent for my well-being emotionally and physically, even though my legs remained immobile after I was taken out of the water.

Before I was lifted into the pool, Alice and I had a chance to talk while Damian changed into his swimming trunks.

"Just think how lucky you are," Alice said, in reference to Damian. "He loves you so."

When Damian returned, he swam a few laps while Adolph—our former dog, who now belonged to Damian after proving to be too much for us to handle—ran around the pool barking.

After our swim, Damian placed me in my wheelchair. Alice said, "Now you watch Damian while I fix a little sandwich." As I watched him swim, I thanked God for Damian's presence.

Alice, who had known Damian's aunt before her death, talked about her as the three of us ate our lunch. "She was a women's libber before anyone had heard of such a thing," she said. Damian agreed—yes, his late aunt was quite the bohemian. She was a sculptor and had a black lover, which was quite unheard of in the days of her youth. I imagine it must have been rather shocking even to the young women of Pasadena who led fairly free-spirited lives in the '20s.

On the way home, Damian surprised me when he took me over to the house, the house where his late aunt had once lived, the large brown-shingled Craftsman-style house that tilted toward the street. Now Damian occupied the place. When he set me on the front porch in my chair, I immediately rolled toward the front railing before I had a chance to put my brakes on.

Damian wheeled me inside. The interior of the house reminded me of the genteel shabbiness of Miss Havisham's house in *Great Expectations*, by Charles Dickens. Faded wallpaper was peeling off the wall. The once beautiful tapestry rugs, the upholstered chairs and sofas were covered with dust.

"It's fascinating, Damian. I feel as if I've walked into another era. Your aunt should be walking down the staircase with a long strand of pearls swinging from her neck," I said excitedly.

We reached the room that was now his studio, where he had works in progress everywhere. He handed me a faded newspaper clipping.

"I had to remove the mattress from my aunt's bed. I found this underneath," Damian explained.

I read the announcement of her marriage. "Did she have children?" I asked.

"Yes, two, but the marriage didn't last," Damian replied. "I found some cocaine under the mattress as well." Suddenly, he blurted out, "Let's go see the garden."

The garden was wildly overgrown, with sculpted figures visible in the weeds and thicket here and there.

On the way to my house, I took his hand and kissed it as I said, "Thank you." I was touched by the fact that Damian had given me a peek into his family's past.

"I'll always be there for you," was his response.

The mail was piling up on my desk. No doubt refreshed by my swim, energized by the exercise and the time spent with Damian and dear Alice, I began sorting through the bills, junk mail, and letters. My dear friend Liz had died from cancer. Her sister wrote:

What a real help and joy it was for her to have you to bum around with. She always loved the Del Mar outings, tennis, and having Jennie to care for occasionally. You helped her live through those dreadful first years when her need was so great. Her last years were really quite happy ones.

Although her funeral was held nearby in the pretty Episcopal church where I was first baptized, I could not attend. Instead, I prayed for this beautiful, funny lady and thought of our shared laughter. I recalled how, one Friday evening, I saw her and her husband embracing and sharing a long, lingering kiss. A few months later, he left her for another woman. I remember the image of Liz walking toward the sea, the collar of her white raincoat pulled up around her face, tears mingling with the rain. Later, I was told that the minister presiding at her services had read a note she had written in which she forgave everyone.

Next, I opened a letter from Leslie that expressed her desire to have something written down, rather than a lengthy phone call:

Your last two letters to me have left me quite troubled and concerned—your emotional health seems to be stretched very thin.

The letter continued, stressing my need for psychological help and urging me to "stick with it." In the letter, she said:

Everyone knows you've had terrible times, Mom. And we--your children—have had to share in some of your suffering. But, there comes a time when the support of friends and family is not enough. You're the one who needs to take care of your own mental well-being.

Rather than a birthday present for me on October 8, the only gift I want from you is your word, and follow-through, on seeking, finding, and committing to a good psychologist, and sticking to therapy. It takes time, but you have that. I love you, and I want a healthy, happy mother again.

Hugs, Leslie.

I decided to heed her advice.

Chapter 15

CHANGING COURSE

*You can't improve
on your own functioning;
you can only interfere with it,
distort it, and disguise it.
When you really get in touch
with your own experiencing,
you will find that change
takes place by itself without
your effort or planning.*

—John O. Stephens

Chapter 15

"Let it go, let it go," Sigrid advised me at our next session. With tears rolling down my cheeks, I had just told her about Dana's letter. "The wedding has taken place, and you have survived. Learn from the experience. It will make you stronger," she continued.

"Sigrid, Sigrid, Leslie told me that I must stick with our sessions," I said.

She agreed with me at the time, but in December of '83, she reassigned me to a different therapist.

I met Carter two days after my fifty-third birthday. He was a young man with dark, curly hair and a cherubic face. He peered at me intensely through his black-rimmed glasses.

"Do you mind being fifty-three?" he asked me with a smile.

"No, I would not mind it at all if had my legs back. In fact, I'd rather be sixty-three or seventy-three. I would be better able to deal with being in a wheelchair, Carter. Is it all right if I call you Carter?" I asked.

"Sure."

"My entire family is coming over for Christmas, Carter. We are actually celebrating my daughter Dana's wedding. I'm looking forward to seeing her and her husband, but I'm nervous about it too," I told him.

"Why are you nervous?"

"Because I am not comfortable with myself since my paralysis," I replied. "So as not to draw attention to the fact that I'm in a wheelchair, I feel that I need to make a great deal of effort to be relaxed and appear happy. I am nervous about seeing the children because they have seen me sad and crying for so many years, and I want to show them that I am making progress."

"Try focusing on those around you," he suggested. "Listen to them and watch what they are doing. I think you'll find they are much more interested in their own lives."

And so it was, exactly as Carter said it would be.

~ ~ ~

"Merry Christmas, Mom," said each of my children, hugging and kissing me when they came over to celebrate the holidays. Soon after this initial display of affection, the children distanced themselves from me and chatted amongst themselves. I became invisible.

"I've just broken up with my girlfriend," I heard Bill explain to Morgan.

Jennie was telling her sisters about how she had just served breakfast to the eighth graders. "Next year, it will be my turn to be waited on," she said excitedly.

Listening to the conversations around me, I realized how my role in my children's lives had diminished. What I was experiencing has happened to every parent, regardless of his or her physical condition.

When the moment presented itself, I congratulated Dana and Kevin on their marriage.

"I'm very happy you have each other. Take care of Dana, Kevin. She's been through a great deal," I offered. "Oh, by the way, will your anniversary be the day you moved in together or your wedding day? I'm not up on all of the latest social trends," I explained.

"July 10, the day we were married," replied Dana matter-of-factly.

Kevin and Dana were very sweet, very attentive to me through the New Year. After we came home from a party at Jerry's ranch, Dana offered to help me to bed. I accepted and appreciated her offer; it was cold at the party, and my spine hurt. As if it were part of her normal routine, Dana helped me up onto my bed, took off my clothes, slipped my nightgown over my head, emptied my urine bag, and then tucked me in under the covers.

"Goodnight, Mom," Dana said as she embraced me and kissed me before retiring. What a wonderful moment that was for me! I felt much less self-conscious about my disability than ever before.

Kevin, Dana, Morgan, and I tried a new restaurant on New Year's Eve. There, we put on paper hats, threw confetti, and blew little horns when the clock struck midnight. We found ourselves bringing in the New Year with a group of Armenians who sat at the table next to ours. Their unabashed enthusiasm was contagious. The notes of a strolling guitarist who sang *Solamente Una Vez*, cheered me. Oh, yes, that song again!

On New Year's Day, while everyone went to the Rose Bowl Parade, I stayed in bed, trying to move my legs. I was hoping that I would have some return of function with the beginning of the new year. I tried to coax my legs into a standing position. They refused to cooperate. My legs and feet hit the floor with a thud. My spine was contorted into an uncomfortable position as a result of my attempt to move my legs. My hopes were dashed.

"Irma, Irma, come and help me!" I shouted. I was afraid that the weight of my legs would pull my torso off the bed too.

"Yo vengo. I'm coming," she answered.

As Irma placed my legs back on the bed, I asked her, "Irma, while the others are at the parade, would you help me dress so we can dismantle the tree?"

Jennie returned from the parade as Irma and I were removing the decorations from the still fresh and fragrant green Christmas tree. "Couldn't we leave the tree up for just a few more days?" cried Jennie.

I would leave the tree up for the rest of your life if I could, I thought. But I said, "No, trash removal is on Wednesday, and Irma and I have the time and the energy to do it now."

Jennie silently retreated to her room. She was worn out emotionally from the holidays.

Dana and Kevin came to say goodbye before leaving for Santa Fe.

"We went to the club for brunch after the parade," Kevin grumbled. He had few kind words to say about old acquaintances he had encountered there. I noticed Dana's face harden in disapproval.

"Kevin," Dana growled, "you're over-generalizing."

Considering that he had spent a good part of his former married life playing tennis on the courts, dining, and socializing at the club, I couldn't understand why Kevin was being so judgmental. Perhaps his past sprang up in front of him like a sign on an old cash register that read "No change." The people, the sites, the sounds were all too familiar, I suppose.

When I saw Carter for the first time since the holidays, I broke into a wide grin. "Why am I smiling so?" I asked him.

"How would I know?" Carter replied.

"Bill never entered my mind at all. It's the first Christmas since his death that I didn't think of him. As the children socialized among themselves, I came to the realization that I was no longer the center of their lives—which was a kind of victory for me. Actually, I didn't really even mind at all."

"It is normal for you to feel tired and weepy after all of the commotion of the holidays. Congratulations, though, you've made some progress," Carter said, encouragingly.

"The best present was the phone call from Michael and Leslie announcing their engagement. They went to Maui after the holidays. Anyway, I was ecstatic, happy that my daughter had found herself—as she put it—out of the position she despises. She used to say to me: 'It's just not for me to be in a relationship outside of marriage.' Leslie and Michael are a good match. Michael has the same caring civility and sweetness that her father possessed," I observed.

A day or so after my visit with Carter, Larry came over to resume my physical therapy. I was in a terrible state, because the nerve pain in the paralyzed part of my body was intolerable. But I wiped away the tears while Larry exercised my legs. Then, he put my braces on my legs, helped me into my chair, and wheeled me to the garage. With a belt around my waist, Larry lifted me into a standing position between the parallel bars.

Trying to hike up my hip to take one step would have been impossible without help. I grew tired almost immediately. Larry would push my chair forward, and I would collapse into it. This was how it went, week after week after week. God only knows where the strength came from. At least, my conversations with Larry served as a pleasant distraction.

After Larry told me a story about Mother Theresa, he shared some news about Fran, my former therapist. Fran had the same level of dedication as Mother Theresa. Now, she returned to her work as a lay missionary in Nicaragua. When I later spoke with Irma about Fran's new work, we both agreed that there was something special about this lady in her dedication to the body and soul.

Sister Wilfrid continued to bring me Communion. We gave thanks for a successful family reunion.

"But Sister," I confessed, " I no longer believe in God."

"Oh, you know that is not so. You are angry. We all have our moments of doubt. As soon as you've grown stronger, you'll be skipping down the sidewalk."

"I told Jennie that I no longer believed in God because He had done this to me. Jennie told me that God wouldn't do such a thing."

"She's right," Sister said, embracing me. At that moment, her veil slipped off her head. She waved it at me as she left the house.

~ ~ ~

Jennie made a court appearance to serve as one of the witnesses in a case of indecent exposure. I was against the idea. "He'll know your name and where you live," I cautioned.

"It's my duty. I *want* to do it," she countered, and went ahead and did it anyway. Unfortunately, the defendant ended up being set free. *My, how strong my daughter has become*, I thought. I felt very proud of her.

I certainly wasn't smiling on my next visit with Carter. "I've had a very disturbing dream," I explained. "In my dream, I was in a new home, which seemed to be at the beach, although the architecture was unlike St. Lo. I was feeling very happy. There was a man present, but I don't know who he was. Then Jennie showed up with a friend and spread her games all over the floor. Suddenly my mood changed from joyful to gloomy. I looked up and saw paint peeling from the walls. Friends came by. They were smiling, but they looked concerned. Bill appeared in the dream, looking as I remember him before he died. I woke up sad and gloomy."

Carter suggested that the first part of the dream represented the new life I was building, and the latter part of the dream represented the past. "Perhaps you will live happily in a different house by the sea. Your former home will not matter anymore," Carter suggested.

"I've just read a book that affected me greatly," I told Carter. "In it, there's a passage where a woman sits alone in a restaurant and looks at the second place setting. As her husband is dying, she knows that, on her travels after her husband's death, that the waiter will remove the extra place setting. The emotions she felt when she closed her home were the same as when my home at St Lo was being emptied and I watched the van pull away through the gate."

~ ~ ~

Leslie immersed herself in planning her wedding. Between her mental and physical therapy sessions, Leslie would phone to tell me about her wedding plans. She envisioned it as a simple and intimate celebration with family and close friends.

"We'll be married in Michael's house with candlelight everywhere. Kevin, Dana, Bill, Morgan, and Jennie, along with a few friends—including the elderly ladies who live here and who each think of themselves as Michael's mother—will be present," Leslie said jubilantly.

"My little granddaughter too," I added.

"Yes, of course. I'll be very happy to be married. I never liked living as I have been. It just isn't for me," she said, repeating a comment she had made not long ago. "I'll call you from time to time to keep you posted about what is going on," she promised.

Morgan phoned later that week to see how I felt about his sister's news. I told him I was fine, as I realized that the real reason he had called was to check on me, to make sure I was all right emotionally.

Jennie was getting cranky and irritable now that her body was going through changes and as she worked through her own healing. But, on a day in early February, she reached out to me.

"Would you like to talk?" she asked as she came into my room. She was sensing my need to open my heart.

"I'm tired of hoping that I'll be well again—the endless waiting for something that may never happen," I wept. I told Jennie of my concern about her being away at boarding school. I felt this to be a good thing, but told her that the house would feel so empty without her. It was a relief to share my concerns with her.

Her face told me that she was fighting to control her emotions. Before she left, her voice was strong and sure as she asked me if there was anything I needed, "a glass of juice or some cookies?"

"No thank you, my dear," I replied. Later she brought me flowers for my room. Like the time that Dana put me to bed, I allowed Jennie to see how vulnerable I was. It was healing for me to drop my guard and expose my weakness to my children.

Still, I was able to find something to worry about. The black hole of my depression thrived on worry. My mother had cataract surgery, which stirred up a great deal of fear in me. So many of the people I depended on were getting on in years—Aunt Alice, Sister Wilfrid, Mother—and I was terrified that they might die and leave me all alone. Thinking about it caused me to slip into depression again. I turned to alcohol to dull my suicidal thoughts.

Morgan sat with me as I drank one Monday evening. Sweetness, understanding, and compassion flowed from my son's heart. Drinking gave me pause, because I was never anything but a social drinker until recently. My husband and I never sat down to have a drink together when he came home from work. That night, liquor, combined with my medications, erased everything from my mind.

I had no memory of going to bed that night. Irma told me later that Morgan had said, "Mother has everything, so why is she so depressed?"

"I told Morgan it was because you don't have your health," said Irma.

Valentine's Day was a very bad day for me. I talked to Carter for more than an hour, trying to get beyond my suicidal thoughts. After our session, I went home and watched the Winter Olympics on television, or at least the figure skating and ice dancing. It wasn't so long ago that I could feel the pulse of music in my body and danced gracefully to its rhythms, just like the skaters. Now, I felt trapped in my paralyzed limbs, unable to experience the freedom and joy of movement that I had once known.

Carter took my thoughts of suicide seriously. At the end of my next visit, he asked me if I would see a Dr. Gerstein at U.C.L.A. "I would like your children to come with you." Then he inquired, "Did Leslie ask you to come to the wedding?"

"No," I answered sadly.

"Certainly it could have been arranged. You could have arrived a few days in advance to give yourself time to recover from your journey.

Perhaps they could have been married closer to home." I had wondered the same thing about the latter arrangement.

As I started to speak about the early months of paralysis, I began to weep uncontrollably.

"Don't," said Carter. "We needn't continue this."

At the end of the session, Carter said gently, "I have two questions to ask you. Has the change over from Sigrid affected you in any way, and would you be willing to see Dr. Gerstein with your children?"

I answered "no" to the first question and "yes" to the second.

"Great, at least that's taken care of," said Carter.

Then I called Carter "Damian" as I asked him a question. "Oh my, I just called you Damian! Well, we were just talking about your cousin, whose name is Damian." Nevertheless, there was still the question that my relationship with Carter may have reminded me of my Damian? Did it remind me of the open, frank conversations that Damian and I used to have in 1979 when we were painting together?

~ ~ ~

On February 22, at 6:30 P.M., Leslie and Michael were married in Sun Valley, Idaho. Her brothers gave Leslie away, and Dana was her matron-of-honor.

I lay in bed at home with Aunt Alice by my side consoling me. "They all seem so far away, and I feel excluded," I sobbed.

A few days later, Morgan dropped by to describe the event: "When the minister asked if there were any objections to the marriage, all the people who had gathered in the room shouted a resounding 'No!'"

Morgan informed me that Paul phoned Leslie to wish her and Riley well. My heart was happy to hear that.

A few days passed, and the newlyweds came to visit. They brought a bottle of champagne for Irma, a necklace for me, and earrings for Jennie. In the evening we all went out to dinner.

The fun began after we all piled into the limo. Aunt Alice, my mother, and I were in the back seat with a fully stocked bar. "Too bad it's such a short trip to the club. We don't have time for a quick one," I remarked. We turned on the television for a little while instead.

As we pulled up at the club, Alice said, "I hope someone I know sees me step out of this thing."

At dinner, Michael spoke sweetly about my children, and I told him how much Leslie's father would have liked him. Michael and Bill shared similar childhood experiences, which probably accounted for their character development—both were compassionate, sensitive and somewhat insecure. Alice, bless her, was flirting with my new son-in-law. "If I were younger, I would have nabbed him," she told me later. While the newlyweds were in town, Alice told them they could use her house at St. Lo whenever they wished because Leslie told her that she had no place to come home to.

A few days later, I had another session with Carter, and I broke down again.

"It's just your day to cry," he said.

But why? Was it a reaction to all the excitement? Perhaps it was a combination of things: the fact that Jennie was going to Maui with Riley, Leslie, and Michael; listening to Morgan describe his brother's house up north, telling me about his time spent in Sun Valley; perhaps it was observing Mother and Uncle Phil, both in their eighties, getting up in the morning after the dinner celebration, so spry, so ready to get on with the day. As for me, it always took me a long time to get up, to clean up, because my bed was usually wet in the morning. *What a pathetic contrast with these eighty-year-olds!* I fretted.

"I know I won't make it if I don't walk again. Sometime, somehow, the time will come for me to go," I told Morgan, a day or two after my conversation with Carter.

He calmly tried to reassure me, "Even if you are sixty-five before you start walking again, you'll still have a good ten years," and he patted my knee.

On the phone with Carter one evening, I said, "I'm all right now. I'm tucked in bed, and at the end of the day, I feel unburdened. I can relax now. I've made it through another day. I don't feel I have to accomplish anything. I'm safe."

In the darkness, the radio played *Love for Sale*. Bill had often sung that tune. "Hey, Bill," I whispered into the night, "that song became a reality for you. If you were here, would we be struggling with lapses in fidelity? Were those lapses just speed bumps on the marital road? Do you want to hear about my struggles with my health, bringing up Jennie, our daughters' marriages, the death of our friends? I know that our marriage would have prevailed. Many, many happy memories of family life still console me. So, good night, Bill. You are dead, I might as well be!" I had endured so many losses after Bill's death, and I felt I couldn't take it anymore.

~ ~ ~

Carter took Morgan, Jennie, and me into group therapy with Dr. Gerstein. The doctor sat behind a one-way window, in front of which the family members, along with Carter, were sitting. The session began with Morgan. Carter asked him about his work and his education. My son conversed in that easy, relaxed, clear-thinking, likeable manner that would win over the most obstinate listener. And he was being sincere: that's just how Morgan was. Jennie lowered her head as she was questioned. Was it shyness, or did she resent the prying? Her answers were barely audible until the subject of school came up. Then she lifted her head and spoke very confidently about her hopes and aspirations.

"I want to go to boarding school," she stated.

"How do you feel about leaving your mother?" asked Carter. Her head went down and her eyes filled with tears. The reply was barely audible. "What concerns you most about leaving your mother?" Carter repeated. Jennie started to cry. With some prodding from Carter, she said that she was worried that I would kill myself or die while she was away.

"Morgan, how would you feel if your mother committed suicide?" asked Carter.

"I could handle it, but, yes, it would bother me." Morgan would understand, but Jennie was too young.

Dr. Gerstein came into the room, stood behind me and put his hand on my shoulder. Dr. Gerstein asked Morgan about my drinking. "Yes, my mother drinks. I worry about the combination of alcohol and pills." The doctor looked at Carter and, with a gentle smile, asked if Carter's hair was turning gray because of me. Carter tilted his head to point out the gray hairs amidst the dark curls.

"I doubt that I am responsible for all of them. They were there when we first met," I volunteered.

Then Dr. Gerstein said to Carter, more as a statement than as a question: "You like her very much?"

Carter glanced at me and replied, "Yes I do."

"And you are very concerned about her?" the doctor continued.

"Yes. Yes, I am," said Carter. I was very moved by his caring.

After the session, I asked Carter if I would see him at three o'clock that Friday. He looked at me with surprise, smiled, and said, "Well, we'll have to see about that. I'll be in touch." I had a foreboding that our doctor-patient relationship would no longer work, and I thought, *If that's the case, I doubt that I could work with anyone else.*

On the way home, I remembered what Carter said about my children, "They're exactly as you said they were," meaning they were handsome, sensitive, beautiful, and without affectation.

Dr. Gerstein's remark to Morgan and Jennie had been, "Don't you think it's time your mother got over this?" Did he mean my depression? I wasn't quite sure, as there were a number of things to "get over."

Carter phoned me a day or two later. "I hope you weren't too tired after the session."

"Of course I was," I replied. "I didn't sleep at all that night because my mind wouldn't quit. The next morning, I was drenched with sorrow, but around five in the evening, I dried my tears, dressed, and enjoyed Jennie's confirmation ceremony."

Jennie was confirmed at our church. Mary Jane was her sponsor. Jennie assumed "Margaret" as her confirmation name. After the ritual—which Jennie had handled with grace—Mary Jane, her husband Jim, and I enjoyed dinner in the church auditorium with the other families. Compared with the first part of the day, the evening went very well.

Jennie and I had a conversation about her Dad two days before the anniversary of his death. "I'll miss you, Mom, when I go away to boarding school," Jennie confided.

"When you are away at school, and if things are difficult at times, remember the best things about your father: his generosity of spirit, his humility, his patience, his caring and compassion for his family," I replied.

"I do want to go away to school, Mom," Jennie stated firmly, and then added, "I'll always remember Dad."

"Me too," I said.

For a moment, I thought about Bill's death. It was such a sudden and significant event. Time didn't stop. Seconds ticked on into minutes, days, weeks, months, and years.

Overall, at this moment in my life, I was contented for days at a time.

Jennie came home the next day from school feeling upset. "I don't want to be driven to school anymore; I want to ride my bike!"

"All right, it's done," I said, though I knew I would be worried about her safety. So, mentally, I would try to picture her pedaling to school with her guardian angel perched behind her.

I was trying to reach a decision about which boarding school would be the best choice for Jennie and consulted friends about the possibility of having her attend the same school that Morgan had attended. It was closer to home than the school Dana had attended, so it would be easy for me to visit her on Parents' Weekends. The issue was the steep tuition. It had gone up substantially since the time her brother lived and studied at that particular campus. Even though Jennie's inheritance would provide for her education, I didn't want her financial base to be depleted. As fate would have it, the school turned down her application, so we had to look at other alternatives.

~ ~ ~

Like Damian, Carter told me during my next visit that I didn't stand up for myself, that I let the children run all over me. Leslie and Michael were in and out of California all the time without so much as a phone call. They would visit Aunt Alice, but they didn't visit me. If they were staying in West L.A., the news would come through a third party. It broke my heart.

On the day before the anniversary of their father's death, Kevin, Dana, Leslie, Michael, Jennie, and my granddaughter all left for Maui "for a rest." (That is how Dana explained the reason for the trip.)

Carter insisted that we persuade the children to stay over when they returned. "Leslie has told me twice that her psychologist has said the family should have gotten together two years ago. I think she is afraid, and so am I," I said, pointing out one case of resistance.

"Well, we've got to do something," replied Carter.

"But what?" I asked.

"Call your children and tell them we must have a meeting when they return. Do it! Call Morgan and tell him to talk to Leslie and give Morgan your husband's hunting knife for safe keeping. Can you do that? The knife worries me. It should worry you too," Carter scolded.

Yes," I complied, though I knew I had no intention of doing so.

~ ~ ~

The children phoned from Maui to tell me they had taken flowers down to the water in memory of their dad. I had lunch with Alice, and then we went to the cemetery and put flowers on the family plot.

Even though I missed Jennie, I enjoyed having time to myself. Once again, with no reason to keep up a brave front for my daughter, I discovered that I was happy spending time alone! In a moment of inspiration, I picked up the phone and called Sister Maria, who was the head of Dana's former school in Northern California.

"Would you have room for Jennie in the fall?" I asked her.

"Of course, we would love to have Dana's little sister," she replied without hesitation.

Now the issue of Jennie's schooling was settled, and it was as easy as a phone call. I felt great peace about the outcome of my stroke of inspiration. Without hesitation, I phoned Jennie in Hawaii with the news. I also informed the rest of the family. And everyone, especially Jennie, sounded relieved.

While everyone else was "resting" in Hawaii, Morgan came for dinner to talk to me about his future. He was trying to figure out how to support

Katy while continuing their education after getting married. Morgan wanted to get his Master's in Business Administration. Katy wanted to become a graphic artist, which would mean attending the nearby Art Center of Design. Morgan had a full and expensive plate before him.

"We will continue to live nearby," he assured me.

The family was healing. I felt more comfortable with respect to my physical limitations, and I began to think about how I could live my life with Jennie away at school in the fall.

"Thank you, Morgan, dear, for all you have tried to do to help me through this terrible time in our lives. Now, I want to do something for you," I proposed. "Here, take your father's hunting knife. I don't need it any more."

Chapter 16

BECOMING THE NEW BERTA

My Silver lady, my birch tree fair!
Teach me your patience, my faults to
outgrow
How to discard and how to become,
Where your Winter is over and Spring
begun.

—Rachel Beresford

Chapter 16

Without fear, I took on a new approach toward my physical needs. I gave up on the tilt board in the garage—the garage felt claustrophobic, and it was too cold in the winter, too hot in the summer.

Three years of bladder accidents and having to catheterize myself every four hours left me exhausted (I was often deprived of a decent night's sleep) and made it difficult to arrange time away from home. I now wore a diaper when I went out and at night.

I was hesitant to give up my program because I didn't want any setbacks, and I came to the realization that the hoped-for improvements were not forthcoming. So, I decided to simplify my routine.

I pressed Larry for the truth about my progress. He said he really didn't know— couldn't know—how much return of function there would be. Sister Wilfrid lost some of her optimism around my recovery: "Nobody knows Berta, nobody knows, not even me."

It was all right to hear the truth. I was beginning to accept that I would have to live with useless legs and a great deal of pain for the rest of my life.

Once I reconciled myself to the fact that I was probably going to live with paralysis for the rest of my days, I found a new role in life that gave meaning and purpose to my existence: I became a counselor of sorts, a sounding board for others, someone who could lend a compassionate ear to people from all walks of life. Where were all these people coming from? Why did people I hardly knew think that I had the answers to the questions they had about their personal issues? Was it my destiny to be available to others? Had a gate opened, directing me to a new life, a life of ministry to others? Taking time to reflect on these questions, I felt motivated, useful, and free from my physical burdens. Focusing on others helped to distract me from my daily routine. It was important for my emotional health to feel needed by others.

Louise was a good example of one person who I was able to help in this way. She was a young woman I had met briefly at St. Lo. She had written to me about Joseph (the man she had fallen in love with). Her parents disapproved of him: he was married, a father, and considerably older than she was. I wrote Louise back, inviting her to come to my home for a visit. She accepted. We made plans to have lunch together so that I would have the opportunity to learn more about her.

Holding her letter in my hand, I asked her, "Are you Catholic? In your letter, you describe a Mass you attended."

"No," she replied. "In fact, my parents don't approve of Joseph, in part because *he* is Catholic," she answered.

"What are your parents like?" I asked. I didn't know them well, as they bought their house at the beach around the time my life became tumultuous.

"My father is a successful businessman," she replied. His work is his life; he has no other interests. My mother has no money of her own and hates to ask my father for every cent."

"I know how that feels. I was financially dependent on my husband. However, neither my husband nor I made an issue over money. What little I had was his, and what he had was mine. Our main focus was the family," I declared. "As for the fact that the two of you are of different religions, that's something you'll have take up with a priest. I don't know how to help you, Louise, except through prayer."

"Yes," Louise nodded, "I understand."

"The age difference is not significant enough to be of concern," I offered.

"I've talked to Joseph about you. Would you meet him?" Louise inquired.

I received a postcard from Joseph soon after my lunch with Louise. It was postmarked "New York," and the message was brief:

> *I admire your courage. I am a friend for life. I am coming to the West Coast for my darling's birthday. Would you celebrate with us?*

I did not attend Louise's birthday party, but Joseph came over for dinner one evening. Later that evening, after I had listened to Joseph's story, Louise joined us.

Joseph was a small, gentle, soft-spoken man, and a professor of French literature. He was surprised and disturbed by his unexpected love for Louise. I related to him my own story about Damian: "Love catches one by surprise when one is neither looking for it nor expecting it," I explained. "I suppose I should have walked away from love, but I chose not to."

"How were you affected by your decision?" asked Joseph.

"I never felt guilty, but I confessed to a priest anyway. You may not understand, but, when it recently seemed that my life was over, I had the joy of remembering that period of my life which would help me get through the day. I will always be able to recall those sunny days," I smiled.

Louise and Joseph made it clear that—one way or another—they would get married. They continued to pay me visits, and I listened as they talked about their situation. What the two of them were searching for was someone's approval.

Another phone call and another visitor. This time it was Jane, a young woman I had seen only occasionally over the years.

"I woke up at four this morning and thought about you," she told me on the phone.

When Jane came to visit, I noticed how strikingly attractive she was. Artistic, with the endearing voice of a child, the abandonment of a child, a slight carry-over from hippiedom was reflected in her attire. She wore sandals on her feet. A tablecloth skirt with a peasant blouse looked like they were from another era. Jane, now a wife and mother, possessed a very good mind belied by a peculiar ethereal vagueness. She had experienced an epiphany the time her son revived after nearly drowning.

About to give birth to a third child, she looked radiant and joyful. As I sat in my chair, she stood behind me with her hands on my head. She invoked the Holy Spirit. "Just let Jesus carry your yoke from now on," she said as a blessing.

That was her gift to me. My gift to this young woman was lending an ear to her over a period of twenty-five years as she struggled with her spiritual life, her marriage, and her parents' efforts to control her life. Her parents owned the home she lived in, and everything in it. She seemed unable to give up the life this provided for her family. The best I could do was to listen, and to keep her on the imaginary Tibetan prayer wheel in my head.

~ ~ ~

On my next visit with Carter, I sorted out my attitude towards sexuality. We started with my relationship to Damian. Was I just trying to reassure myself that I was still young and desirable, wanting a beautiful fantasy in an equally beautiful setting? In my mind, it was not the sort of thing that a Catholic striving for spiritual perfection would do. I gave myself to Damian. I wanted him to know how much I loved him, how much I was in love with him.

The topic of the affair had come up after Bill's death, when Morgan admitted, "I was worried about the situation."

I had explained to the children about how depressed I had become after Leslie's divorce, about their father's concerns about my well-being, and about my bumpy marriage. All of those reasons had something to do with why I had an affair with Damian.

Continuing on, I related a very recent experience I had had with a married man.

"He came to see me, to tell me he could help me," I told Carter. "The man said to me, 'I've heard about your despair, and, as I've felt that kind of despair myself, that is why I am here.' I thanked him for his concern.

"Over the next few weeks, he visited several times until I became embarrassed by his unsolicited attention. I felt he was getting overly familiar with me. He asked me to read a poem I had written long ago, and then he phoned to say, 'You wrote it just for me, didn't you?'

"'No, no, no, I didn't,' I replied.

"He was suicidal. I couldn't help him. I was still too close to that dark place myself. His family must have suffered a great deal. As the years passed, his life evolved to a more peaceful place, as he gave up prescription drugs and alcohol."

Carter asked me how I felt about the situation.

"Well, it was not welcome. It was frightening. I am, as you know by now, a perfectionist and a romantic who truly believes in happily ever after. As soon as I became a widow, I was approached by a number of married men. I found the attitude of these men both confusing and amusing. I was beginning to feel like a piece of meat in a meat market. It was demeaning to me. How disrespectful and insensitive of them during my time of grieving!

"I now fully embrace celibacy. I did not choose it, but I am free to develop a closer relationship with God and his Son. Perhaps, as Father Moretta once suggested, I'll become a saint."

I paused, and with a smile, I said, "I guess not today, Carter! I am staring at your legs, for heaven's sake!" We both laughed.

~ ~ ~

Three days after my talk with Carter, I was awakened by what I thought was someone whispering in my room.

"Who is it?" I asked, as I looked at my bedside clock. It was 6:30 A.M.

"Your biggest enemy is fear, fear of life and of your own potential for change," were the words I heard. "Your tears will go away. Life won't be the same as it was for you, but nevertheless beautiful and joyful."

The message was clear. I turned onto my back, untangling my legs in the process, so I could see who was in the room. Frightened, I called Irma. "Please come, Irma!" I cried over the intercom. When Irma came to my room, I told her what I had heard.

"Querer es poder. To want something is to be able to have it," Irma pointed out.

I had been praying my rosary regularly and attending Bible study in order to prepare myself for the enormous undertaking of giving control of my life over to Our Lord. Had He spoken to me this morning to set me on the path He desired for me to follow?

~ ~ ~

Now that I could see a future for myself, the dreadful sadness of the past few years would sweep over me only on occasion. By the grace of God, I could help people. They sought me out, and, with his help, their burdens would be lighter.

I discussed this with my son Morgan when he dropped by with some literature from the Spinal Cord Society.

"I flagged down their truck as it was going down the street," Morgan grinned as he handed me the papers.

"Oh, how dear of you, Morgan," I cried. He repeated the words he had said fairly recently: "Until you help others in need, your life won't change."

"I would like to go to Central America and help people in those countries," I said to my son.

"Maybe people here need you more," he suggested.

"Americans are so sanitized that I don't think I would have the patience. I'd rather die in Central America helping children there. The families of my caregivers need a great deal of help. The situations in Nicaragua and El Salvador are terrible."

Jennie was sitting in a nearby chair during this conversation. She drew up her knees and clasped her arms around her legs. Resting her head on her knees, she peered up at me as I spoke.

"First of all, I must see to Jennie's education. We are going to Mayfield, where the director of admissions will intervene in case she changes her mind about boarding school," I said to Morgan.

The sounds of an active school on the day of the interview remain with me still. While the director of admissions spoke with Jennie, I sat in the library reading *On Death and Dying*, by Elizabeth Kubler Ross. I heard the sounds of a student crying in the principal's office and the responses of the students to a Latin Mass being said in the large reception room. "Kyrie eleison, Christe eleison" they sang, which caused me to look up from the book I was reading and to remember how much I missed the Latin Mass. *Kumbaya* accompanied by guitar just didn't do it for me. The mysticism that had attracted me to the Church wasn't completely gone, but it had been diluted.

Following Jennie's interview, I was wheeled to the office of the director of admissions, where I was asked to expand on the answers Jennie had given to her interviewer.

I thanked the young student who had pushed me to the office.

"Oh, that's okay, I'm used to it," she said. "My brother's in a wheelchair."

Alone with the director, I heard her repeat Jennie's answer to the question "How do you view yourself?"

My daughter had answered, "I am caring, compassionate, independent, and I never quit."

As a mother, I thought, *How fine her suffering has made her.*

The director continued: "She sees herself in the future as a writer and hopes to publish before she turns thirty, but her dream is to be an actress. She told me that in sixth grade she discovered how much she enjoyed performing. She said she wanted to marry, not a doctor or a lawyer, but an architect or a designer. Then she added that she felt the money for the poor wasn't really reaching them."

"Yes, that is Jennie," I said. "I can hear the creative side loud and clear," I added before leaving the interview.

I rolled across the marble floor to the entrance of the school. Looking up at the carved oak stairway, I imagined Leslie standing there in her white concert dress, a wide, red satin ribbon tied around her waist, a lighted candle in her hand. She was singing Christmas carols along with her identically dressed classmates. Oh, how beautiful, how innocent the family was then!

~ ~ ~

Jennie's approaching birthday made me realize what a young lady Jennie had grown into; the little girl I knew was gone. I tried to write a poem for Jennie, one that would express the importance of that day. But, I had such a difficult time with it that I finally decided to give it up. Besides, the words of Thomas More in *An Advent Rose* said it best:

Let Fate do her worst: there are relics of joy,
Bright dreams of the past, which she cannot destroy,
Which come in the nighttime of sorrow and care,
And bring back the features that joy used to wear.
Long, long be my heart with such memories fill'd!
Like the vase, in which roses have been distill'd—
You may break, you may shatter the vase, if you will,
But the scent of the roses will hang 'round it still.

~ ~ ~

Dinner with my friend Margaret brought up some serious concerns she had about her life. Amidst the tears, she told me her ex-husband was getting married again, and her daughter was causing her a great deal of concern.

She began, "I went to see a psychologist. He said the same thing your psychologist told you: about letting children make their mistakes while getting on with your own life."

The next morning she phoned to tell me, "I went home, had a good cry and feel a lot better today." I felt better too, because I felt my new role as counselor was being validated once again.

I received a postcard from the professor of French literature. It read:

> *Dear Berta, this is my favorite card. I have kept it to myself all*
> *these years. Now I send it to you as a token of thanks and a sign of*
> *love. Please show it to Louise when she comes to see you again.*

The picture on the card was that of a lovely, red-haired, modestly dressed woman holding a patterned scarf against her left breast. The original painting, *Innocente*, hangs in the Uffizi Gallery in Florence, Italy. From our talks, Joseph had recognized my strong attraction to beauty and innocence.

Come October, the story of Louise and Joseph would have a happy ending. These two dear people joined as one in New Orleans, Louisiana. I would receive a note from them thanking me for my love and support that they felt so contributed to "that most wonderful of days." Enclosed with the note was a picture of the two of them on their wedding day. Apparently, the bride, to my delight, converted to Catholicism.

~ ~ ~

In 1984, a new development required my attention: Jennie had started smoking! Confining the activity to her bedroom did not conceal the fact; the odor seeped through all the air vents and into my room. The smoke caused my asthma to flare up. So, I decided to have a talk with her. Speaking gently but firmly, I told her she was much too young to inflict such a habit on herself. Besides, I could not tolerate her secondhand smoke. As I pointed out to her the various consequences of smoking, I knew that what I was telling her was not something she didn't already know. Would marijuana be far behind? That was another question to consider. It was hard, very hard, after raising four children, to go through all this again— some of my other children had tried smoking as well. Jennie apparently was starting the experimentation stage of adolescence much earlier than the previous four.

I attended Jennie's senior play. She was so, so happy to see me there, and, yes, she did have a talent for performing. She played the role of the Russian countess so convincingly up there on that stage that I could hardly recognize my own daughter.

Soon the door would close on Jennie's childhood and another would open far from home come September. I would be alone with an uncertain future. Together we decided not to go to the eighth-grade mother-daughter luncheon; we wanted no more goodbyes!

Jennie's eighth-grade graduation and the celebration of Morgan's engagement to Katy brought peace and harmony to our lives. Time to grieve and new beginnings had brought the family closer together.

It was the beginning of spring, when new green shoots emerge from the ground to blossom into an array of color. The miracle of my new beginnings became more apparent when a close friend said, "I couldn't take my eyes off your children when I saw them the other day. I just kept looking from one to the other."

I felt Leslie and I were growing closer to each other when she said on the phone, "You're our mother, and it doesn't matter where you live. Wherever you are, that's home to us."

In a note to me, she wrote:

> Thank you for all your thoughtful words this week! It really helped to talk to you, Mom. It's been too long! I can see you're getting much healthier all the time, and I feel you are more available too. Good for you!!

Feeling well and remarkably content, I realized that, with the record-setting heat wave of the past summer, I had not missed the beach. The few tears that did fall resulted from the emotions that came up around Jennie's graduation, the dinner to announce Morgan's engagement, and the visit to the psychologist with all the children—events that would have put emotional stress on anyone.

I had to face the fact that I would have to grow old all alone. It was difficult. I began to understand that life was about change, and, for me, change was never easy.

Jennie had returned from camp in the Northwest, a different camp than the one she had attended in the summer of '82. During her summer in the new camp, she fell in love with the area, a place where paddling a canoe amongst a pod of Orcas was not uncommon, and where writing poetry was encouraged. Ten days after her return from camp, Dana and Bill drove her north where she would begin boarding school.

After Dana flew back home, she sent me some pictures of the time she and Bill spent on the campus with Jennie. Searching through old albums, I found a picture of Dana that was taken in the same location where Jennie had posed in the most recent photograph. Setting these by my bed gave me a sense of continuity and security. I prayed that Jennie would experience similar feelings during her four years at boarding school and beyond.

With Jennie away in boarding school, I felt I could relax. I no longer had to worry about how Jennie would be affected by my emotional ups and downs, day in and day out.

This sense of ease reflected in my physical therapy. At Larry's suggestion, I tried to use a walker. Progress was slow, but I received an emotional high from being upright. All of the struggles I had endured in rehab—the range-of-motion exercises on my bed, the vertical standing board, putting on braces and attempting to walk through the parallel bars—had brought me to the shaky place where my muscles would go into spasm with each step.

One day, as I was waddling through therapy, a phone call came from Jennie.

"I'm up on my feet," I cried into the receiver that Larry was holding. My remark was a timely one, as Jennie had told me that she was quite homesick, and my progress report seemed to cheer her up.

After a brief conversation, I gave the receiver to Larry, and he said to her, "Don't worry, your mom is fine."

In October, Jennie came home for her first break from school. Michael and Leslie accompanied her, making the visit even more special. When they walked in the door, I was sitting at my desk as music played in the background.

As I listened to my daughter talk about her new experiences away from home, I could hear that adjusting to her new world was not so easy for her. However, she was not unhappy.

When I had a moment alone with my son-in-law Michael, I asked him, "How do you like being a husband and a ready-made father?"

"The only thing I don't like is when your granddaughter says she is bored." I smiled, remembering how my own children were at my granddaughter's age—age eleven—and I thought to myself, *That's normal.*

One evening, when the four of us dined together, I felt the tug of war between duty to family and my devotion to God. The youthful concerns of those gathered with me seemed very distant from the spiritual path I was on. I felt that the inner changes necessary to prepare myself for a life dedicated only to God isolated me from those I cared about. For a moment, sadness overwhelmed me as I looked at the faces of my loved ones, who were gathered around the table. I heard the gate clang shut behind me. And I felt strong.

Morgan and Katy's upcoming wedding was celebrated with dinner parties, showers for the bride, and teas. The plans for Morgan's bachelor party hit a snag when his friend, Will, who was giving the party, phoned to say, "There seems to be a lack of interest." However, the twenty-some-things eventually managed to get it together, and the evening turned out to be a great success.

Bill, whom Morgan had chosen to be his best man, came home to take part in the wedding. Sitting in the living room armchair, he informed me that he had picked Jennie up at school to drive her around the area where she would be studying for the next four years. They went to Big Sur to eat lunch at Nepenthe, took a stroll on the beach at Carmel, visited Scotts Valley where he had once lived, and hiked through the redwoods in Big Basin.

With a groan, he rested his head on the back of the chair and explained how upset he was with his sisters. During the past summer, while they were on the river in Idaho, they had genuinely insulted his girlfriend with unkind remarks.

"I almost brought her home," he said sadly.

In an effort to console my son, my heartfelt words to him were: "I don't think they give you enough credit for buying a house and working faithfully in construction, a job you are very good at and enjoy. While your sisters are traveling in New York and the Caribbean, you are laying a solid foundation for your future and for the person who is lucky enough to share it with you."

~ ~ ~

Parents' Weekend at Jennie's school proved to be a test for me. I made my first plane flight since paralysis. Wheelchair bound, I was the first person on the plane and the last person off. Morgan and Irma accompanied me on the flight. It was exhilarating!

Before leaving, I spoke with one of Jennie's teachers on the phone.

"She is doing well now that she's gotten accustomed to life in boarding school, which is to be expected and very understandable," she said. She mentioned Jennie's performance in *Bye, Bye, Birdie.*

Still performing! I thought. I knew my daughter was happy.

I attended every one of the weekend events with the exception of an early morning lecture and two teacher conferences. The teachers I spoke with assured me that Jennie would be able to overcome the difficulties she was having with algebra and ancient history.

Jennie gave me a tour of the campus and introduced me to her friends. She seemed quite self-assured. In the evening, we returned to my room at the hotel nearby. Sprawled out on twin beds, we ordered room service and watched television. There, I recuperated from my journey and the day's activities. Michael and Leslie came to visit, so, along with Irma and Morgan, I felt I had plenty of support. Before leaving Northern California, I had the additional pleasure of seeing Bill's home for the first time.

~ ~ ~

Back in Pasadena to face the preparations for Morgan's wedding, I had to deal with an outburst from Leslie. Leslie—always very easily upset and very sensitive—was dissatisfied with the plans that were made for Thanksgiving and the preparations for Morgan and Katie's prenuptial parties. I talked to my psychologist about it.

"Something is wrong in her life; she's taking it out on you. Laugh, Berta and put it aside," he advised me.

Morgan's wedding took place in a lovely cathedral-like church. It was not a Catholic service, but I was accepting of that. The only moment of pique I felt was in the vestibule of the church before the wedding when Morgan's mother-in-law-to-be straightened his tie. I thought, *I should be doing that.* Guests and family dined and danced at the reception. I was content just watching.

Morgan could be very proud of himself since his father's death. Honoring the Hees' Family Trust, he regularly sent me a check until I no longer needed the money. After completing his education at U.C. Berkeley, he traveled through Mexico, Central America, and throughout the United States, and then returned to Pasadena to receive his MBA from Claremont Men's College, to work, and to be supportive of Jennie and me. The "family tease,"—the little boy who stuffed gravel up his nose and ate snails from the garden—was also the one with a loving heart, a wicked sense of humor, and plenty of patience, all of which helped to ease my pain over the months and years since 1980. With all my heart, I wished him well.

Morgan was twenty-three. His father was the same age when he and I got married. For Morgan's generation, he was marrying young, but I suspected he liked the stability that a family brought to his life. Like the rest of my children, he wished to recreate the home he had so abruptly lost.

~ ~ ~

I encountered some good things as I traveled my new path.

During a conversation with my mother, she told me she had been struggling with fear all her life. Her guard came down in that moment, and I loved her for it. From that moment on, I consciously made an effort to remove the word "perfect" from my vocabulary. Perhaps Leslie's divorce would not have been quite so painful for me had I seen myself for what I was at that time—a perfectionist like my mother.

So, I allowed myself a moment to reflect on the recent past with a sense of joy. Dana had been married for a year; Leslie was married in February; Morgan, in November. After graduation, Jennie went away to boarding school, and, much to Carter's relief, we all went to therapy, and we survived. We stopped the finger pointing, stopped looking for someone or something outside of ourselves to blame for the chain of events that had shattered our lives and caused me to have a nervous breakdown.

With time for myself, and with some caution, I would go where He would lead me.

"What is it? What is it you want of me?" I asked Him again and again in the hours before sleep. Finally, the whispery voice came back with the answer, "It's time to begin living your own life."

Chapter 17

LIFE'S a "BEACH"

So long to all I loved and
will not hunt for anymore, adios.

—William Goyen,
"Tongues of Men and Angels"

Chapter 17

One January morning, I woke up singing *Street of Dreams*: "... dreams broken in two can be made like new on the street of dreams." But I didn't want to retreat into a dreamlike state anymore, at least not permanently.

In a conversation with Leslie, I heard her say that my little grand-daughter had been dreaming all the years since her parents' divorce that they would get back together, and that they would all go back to live in Pasadena. "I want to live in my old room again," Riley told her mother.

"It was devastating to me to hear her express her desires," Leslie commented.

But that was not all, as Riley had added, "I love Michael, but I'll always love my daddy best of all."

"Her father never paid any attention to her. I'd go to the market, and he would watch TV without ever knowing where she was," Leslie told me.

All the things I feared about the divorce were coming true—primarily Riley's unspoken pain. At a very young age, she was separated from her father, grandparents, aunts, uncles, and cousins. I could sympathize with my daughter and granddaughter; my tears had already been shed long ago. Leslie was lonely, looking for support.

"I miss my father all the time. Sometimes I feel his presence. It is as if he is nearby or watching me. Oh, it's difficult to explain. He and Michael would really have gotten along so well, and I regret the fact that he's not here for my daughter and Michael."

"I hope you have a baby, dear," I unwisely blurted out, trying to say something consoling when I didn't know what else to say.

"Well I'm still tossing that idea around," she replied. And then we said our goodbyes.

My friend Esther drove me to a reunion of Mayfield alumnae mothers. On the way to the gathering, she spoke about her retarded son who was reaching adulthood and about the sorrow she felt.

"On New Year's Eve, when all the children went off to parties, he remained behind to help me with the dishes. He loves to dance, Berta, and, while we were alone, I could tell he felt left out. His chin began to tremble." She wiggled her chin with her fingertips to show me. I put my hand on her shoulder to console her until we arrived at the school.

There were a few other brave women present that afternoon. One woman with multiple sclerosis looked particularly radiant. She had fallen in love and was marrying again. Her first marriage had been annulled, and now she would soon marry a Catholic widower.

"No one has ever treated me with kindness in my entire life. At last I have found someone," she told me.

Another woman and I agreed that the best years of our lives were the ones we spent carpooling. "But, Berta, if someone had told us then that those were the best years of our lives, we would never have recognized it."

Most of the women at the gathering had a look of tired resignation in their eyes. But we were not old—not *really* old. I was fifty-four. Yet illness was stalking my generation. A friend had a mastectomy, and her husband, once so vital, was paralyzed due to a stroke.

Even my staunchest supporters no longer believed that I would walk again. When I told them how well my physical therapy was going, I was greeted with silence. The only support came from my children, Irma, Mother, Uncle Phil, Sister Wilfrid, and God.

Because of physical therapy, I became stronger, but the most significant changes were not so obvious. These changes took place on a soul level. Every morning, I would talk to Jesus about everything. When I felt fear or sorrow, I would ask Him to take them away. Help often came in the form of a phone call. Dana phoned to tell me: "Leslie phoned Bill to explain a letter she had written to him. She doesn't want to alienate him." Later, Jennie phoned to tell me she would be home on a school break and would be bringing a friend. I was grateful that Jennie felt comfortable enough with her home life to share it with her friends. These were the events, the connections that kept me going.

Physically stronger, I was now able to walk with braces on my legs and with a strap around my waist that Larry would hold onto when I tried to move my legs. I was now able to sit on a chair without losing my balance and to turn over in bed. Irma would massage my abdomen in a continuous motion with a vibrating massager because my muscles were more toned now and could handle the treatment. With each change, I expressed my gratitude by saying a prayer of thanks.

However, life doesn't quit or "allow us that free ride," as Rilke so poignantly says in *The Widow's Song*. Leslie's husband, Michael, was in the local hospital undergoing gall bladder surgery, so I prayed for him: "Jesus, you must make this right! I can't stand to see my beautiful family so mistreated. Take care of Leslie and give me the strength to help her."

My prayers were answered: Michael went home to Sun Valley to recover. Bill went with Michael, Leslie, and Dana to celebrate his twenty-seventh birthday. His sisters, Leslie and Dana, enjoyed spoiling him to pieces. Bill and his sisters skied together while my son-in-law rested. Young Bill, like his father, asked for very little. His sisters understood that he wasn't one to keep in touch, so they reached out to him.

In March, I went through severe depression again. Bill phoned to tell me he would come over on a Thursday to take me out to lunch.

"I'm not doing well," I said.

"So I heard," was his reply.

Then Leslie and Michael came over.

"I'm only happy when you are here," I told them all.

"That's not good," Michael replied.

"I know it's not good," was my answer. Everyone was silent. No one offered a solution.

At lunch, I told Bill about my discussion with Sister Wilfrid on the subject of suicide:

"'Yes,'" she said, "'He will understand because of all you've been through.'"

"'Will I see my husband again if I take my own life?'" I had asked her.

"'Yes. He will not deprive you of this. The only thing is you will not complete the mission you were supposed to fulfill in this life if suicide is the choice you make,'" she replied. (Sister believed in a loving God who gives us all a certain path to follow. If I decided not to finish the journey He had laid out for me, I would still be loved, according to Sister.)

When Bill, Leslie, and Michael left with Riley to go to Disneyland, I wondered if I should open the bottle of Scotch that Michael had brought me, drink it all and slit my wrists. Fighting to protect one's soul never stops. It is a constant battle between good and evil. I believe in the Devil's power and the forces he brings to bear when we are at our weakest.

Later, I spoke with Jennie about my depression and added that perhaps it was inappropriate of me to talk about such things over the phone.

"No, I want to hear how you feel," she said.

She had just finished a two-day religious retreat at school, and we talked about how spiritually refreshing retreats can be, how they give one the strength to go on in the world.

There was also some very good news. Jennie had received an "A" on her algebra test, and she had a part in the play for Father-Daughter Weekend.

Morgan drove all the way to Camarillo where my mother was visiting friends, picked her up, and brought her to my house, where she was to stay for two days. When they arrived, Morgan put her clothes away, pinned her eye-drop schedule on the kitchen bulletin board, and generally helped her settle in. The next morning, he took her to a doctor's appointment in Los Angeles and to her home nearby. He then returned her to my house to settle her in again. At 7:00 A.M. the following morning, she came to my room fully dressed and asked me to call Morgan to come and take her home.

"Please tell Morgan not to be angry with me," she cried.

Confused and disoriented, my mother was not managing well. At first, I thought it was the result of her cataract surgery, but, after our brief time together, I realized that, at eighty-seven years of age, she had reached the point where she could not live alone, nor could she live with Uncle Phil because he was ailing as well.

"I don't want to take care of people any more," she had mentioned during her visit. She must have been uncertain about her immediate future, as I was out of commission and my sister lived far, far away. She was afraid that there would be no one around to take care of her.

Irma told me she had heard my mother rattling around in the kitchen at 4:00 A.M. And then at 7:00 A.M., when Irma arose to boil water for tea, she discovered that the stove was still on and the kettle had been burned. This helped to confirm for me my mother's state of mind.

I phoned my sister in Virginia, as she was planning to come out to California in the next few weeks.

"I found a very strange message on my answering machine," said my sister Jeannette when she phoned me from Virginia. "I understand the seriousness of the situation with Mother."

"Jeannette, her friends phoned me to ask, 'What are you going to do about your mother?'" I explained to Jeannette. "And I don't even know what to do with myself, never mind with my mother. It upsets me that the callers don't understand the situation."

Before we said goodbye, we came up with a plan to get mother to Virginia, where my sister would care for her. My sister had graciously accepted the task, although she was already taking care of her aging mother-in-law—who was now in a full-care facility and made no secret of the fact that she didn't like my sister.

"How do you handle that, the fact that your mother-in-law dislikes you?" I asked.

"I just tell her that I'm all she's got. Her son doesn't want to visit because she's so difficult."

I called Sister Wilfrid for her advice about the situation with my mother.

"Sister Wilfrid, what am I supposed to do?" I asked over the phone. Realizing in that moment that my mother's situation was a family responsibility, I didn't wait for an answer. Instead, I asked her if she had received the flowers I had sent and if she had read my essays.

"The flowers are underneath the crucifix in the chapel," she replied.

"Oh, that is why I woke up this morning and clearly heard 'The church is your home,' and then, *The Narrow Gate* came to me as a possible title for a book. It is from St. Luke."

Sister Wilfrid told me she had read my essays.

"Which one did you like the best?" I asked her.

"The one about Damian. It is so poignant that I wanted to hear more." I had gotten similar comments in my writing class. "The essays are all so different. It is unusual for one person to write in so many diverse ways," she added.

A few days after our conversation, Sister and I were driven by a caregiver to U.C.L.A. for a visit with Norman Cousins—well known for his writings on dealing with illness, particularly his own. After Dr. Cousins greeted us, Sister immediately asked him to autograph the copies of his books that she had brought along. The request embarrassed me, but he politely obliged her.

I told him as briefly as possible about the circumstances of my life. After listening to my story, he attached something rather like a black plastic clothespin with wires to the end of my index finger. I imagine they were electrodes. He then told me to concentrate on the end of my nose. With his direction and my concentration, it was possible to circulate my blood to the injured part of my body by simply willing it to do so. A monitor indicated that this was occurring. The atmosphere was calm and relaxed. When the experiment was over, Dr. Cousins said, "I cannot promise you a cure."

"Your honesty is enough for me," I responded.

A few days after my visit, I wrote Dr. Cousins a thank-you note:

Dear Dr. Cousins,

The moment I remember best was the embrace. It was genuine, heartfelt, and reminded me of my husband Bill. Or was it the smell of your tweed jacket? There were many times during my thirty-year marriage that I reached out to touch an arm clothed in just such a jacket. I didn't want to let go! It brought me security, like a pat on the head—something to remind me that everything was okay.

But everything is not okay—at least, not yet. I have found the answer to the question you asked me—"Would he want to see you this way?" I now think of my recovery process as getting well for Bill.

After returning home, I spent time taking in all that you said and found it healing. It is impossible to describe the peace I felt

Thank you for seeing me and letting me share some of God's love, which has filled the space that suffering once occupied

Gratefully,

Berta Hees

On April 23, 1985, I received a note from Dr. Cousins. I was surprised that he would take the time to write to me. The note summarized his feelings about our meeting. I now understood that my own spiritual perceptions about my illness were penetratingly accurate. At the same time, that spirituality enabled me to create an inner environment; this aligned with medical science became a powerful combination. I had a strong inner life that I often escaped to. There, I found the peace and contentment that often contrasted with the events in my life. I expressed beauty in my painting, my love of music, my love of beautiful surroundings, my friendships, my home, and my garden.

~ ~ ~

I had decided to give my home a facelift and hired a crew of contractors to paint the exterior. These young men shared their tales of suffering with me, but, this time, *I* was the one receiving advice.

Bobby, who was in charge, asked me about my paralysis.

"I've been through something as well, and I'm not the same person as a result," he declared after hearing my story.

"It's so unfortunate to have something like that happen. You shouldn't have to go through great changes at such a young age." I shot back.

"I don't share this with everyone. I have herpes. At first, it destroyed my life. My girlfriend left me, and I didn't feel it was possible to start any new relationships or even get close to someone. I ran around looking for help from anyone and everyone. It wasn't until I accepted myself and my affliction that life began to change. They now have medication to control the virus. And, I now have a wonderful girl in my life. She understands and cares for me in spite of everything. You must do the same, I mean, you must accept what has happened to you, and you will get out of that chair. You can do it," he smiled. He walked over to me, put his arms around me, and said, "I love you."

"You're still young, Bobby. You have youth on your side. It's harder for me at my age," I pointed out.

As he opened the door of my walled garden, I heard him say, "I'm not young anymore after what I've been through," and then he left.

I was comforted by the fact that he trusted me enough to confide in me.

~ ~ ~

I changed psychologists. Daniel, my new therapist, resembled my husband, not only physically but also in his quiet manner. His office was not wheelchair accessible, so he came to my house for sessions. I told him about Bobby.

"He's right," Daniel said. "Accepting yourself as you are is the beginning of your emotional and physical healing."

He started a grief group, which I participated in. The meetings were held in an enormous, square, white church several stories high—a relic from Pasadena's past, when it was being settled by Midwesterners.

When I went to my first meeting, I found the building scary. As I rolled through the long, empty corridors, I heard the echo of my wheelchair. I found an ancient elevator and pressed the "up" button. Its creaky doors slowly opened, and I went in. I hit the button for my floor, but nothing happened right away. Then the doors slowly closed, and, with a sudden lurch, I began my ascent to the fifth floor.

The room where our meetings were held was comfortable and spacious and had a blackboard on the wall. Daniel had outlined on the board the various stages of grief.

People introduced themselves. The ages of the members in the group varied widely. Twenty-somethings to fifty-somethings, and all were women. I wasn't surprised. In my experience, men who had lost their wives usually didn't express their grief openly. The older women were widows like me, probably harboring the same fears, anxieties, and anger that I was so familiar with. One or two had cancer. Like me, they spoke of how terrible the weekends were when the phone never rang and their married friends were too busy for visits. One widow said she used to plant flowers on the bad days but doesn't want to do it anymore. Another widow said she went to the movies alone and found it comforting to see other lonely people like her in the theater. One young woman was inconsolable after taking a trip to Rosarita Beach only to find it didn't help her much with her grief. Her father had died three years ago. Then she had nursed her mother until her mother died of cancer. On top of all that, her eight-year relationship had ended.

After our introductions and a brief explanation of the circumstances that had brought us together, Daniel said a few words about what we could expect as the meetings progressed. He passed out some papers at the end of the session. It took me longer than the others to assemble my belongings. I suddenly noticed that the room had cleared out. Everyone was gone! I became frightened, though I managed to wheel myself to the ancient elevator, where, after pressing the button, I listened to the wheezing and groaning of the lift as it ascended the shaft. *If it breaks down,* I thought, *I could starve to death in this cavernous place before anyone would find me. Oh well, what an ironic end this would be after all my travails.*

One day, as I was leaving a session, I pushed open a door leading to a huge auditorium where the Sunday services were held. The room was half the size of a football field. There was a stage where the minister must have stood to deliver his sermons. There was no center aisle, just rows and rows of benches. A two-tiered, horseshoe-shaped balcony rose above it all, like box seats at the opera. Who sat in that space? This was not the era of serious Bible-thumping churchgoers. They could stay home and watch the service on television.

Jennie phoned, bursting with news about Father-Daughter Weekend at her school. Her brother Bill assumed the role of father.

"We went to the Highlands Inn for breakfast, and the view was so beautiful I didn't want to leave," she said with much excitement. Bill didn't take her dancing. He didn't bring his camera, as her father would have done. And, he didn't go to Mass.

"But I went," she said. "I thought of my father the whole time."

"Sister Wilfrid said his spirit would be with you," I commented.

Before saying goodbye, my happy daughter said, "They have a psychologist here, and I think I will go see him."

"I agree. It is a good idea," I replied, aware of how much my attitude towards psychologists had changed over the years.

~ ~ ~

The Smiths were having a big black-tie bash to celebrate their fortieth wedding anniversary, and I couldn't decide whether to go to such a large event. So many people—one hundred ninety-seven—all dining and dancing. I discussed my fears with Sister and Daniel. They both encouraged me to go.

As my interim caregiver, Susannah, drove me to the party, my nerves were on edge and burning with pain. But once I was there, sitting with people I knew and genuinely liked, I had an absolutely delightful evening. Les Brown's band played music that evoked happy memories. I didn't even care that I was not able to dance.

I don't recall who it was, but someone wheeled me over to visit with Damian's father, who was looking unwell because of the radiation treatment he was undergoing for cancer. We held hands and joked about our trials.

As I moved among the guests, I heard phrases like "You are going to walk again," or "You look better than I've ever seen you look." All sorts of friends offered me a sign of encouragement by giving me the thumbs up sign. But the best moment came when Jack—who once lived in St. Lo but who now lived up north—knelt down beside me, kissed me on the cheek, and said, "There will be other beaches, Berta."

"Of course, Jack. How dear of you to remind me."

The reunion with my sister Jeannette brought indescribable joy. Terrified of flying, she never visited me on the West Coast. The last time we saw each other was twelve years ago when Bill and I were in New York City and later stopped in Virginia for a visit with her family. Now she was here, singing in my kitchen each morning while she prepared tea and toast for the two of us. I felt loved, safe.

Jeannette was an artist, a writer, and the mother of three grown sons. Happily married for many years, she and her husband enjoyed the Virginia countryside, where they walked their dogs and fished from a canoe on their pond. "But I'm still painting and writing. My husband refers to those moments as my 'creative fits.' I become so engrossed in my work that no one comes near me," she said with a laugh.

The letter she wrote to me after her return to Virginia got straight to the heart of her visit:

Berta Dear,

I always need time to sit and think before writing a letter. Words and their meanings have such a great deal of influence on all of us—at least in my mind—so I feel that one should always be as precise as possible.

You sound hopeful but weary—feelings not necessarily mutually exclusive, of course—but I wanted so to reach out and touch you, to do something comforting. A letter is such a poor substitute for a hug, but it's the best I can do.

Visiting with you, getting closer to you, sharing my feelings with you, and realizing that you feel the same way about "Manipulative

Mum" was one positive thing that came from my trip—and for this, I am extremely grateful.

. . . Do so hope that things are improving for you. I know it's an agonizingly slow process, but I am sure that you will eventually be on your feet again. I pray all the time and think of you while I'm singing the Mass—storming heaven, so to speak—I look forward to the time when we can sit on the terrace here together and look out across the water and be at peace. Anyway we've made a beginning; being at peace with oneself can be the start of the healing process. Do give my love to Jennie and to dear Irma. You are fortunate to have them both. Try to give up judging yourself and try loving yourself a little more. You are loveable. I know that.

I love you,

Jeannette

The visit with my sister left me emotionally wrung out. We had discussed all the past and present pain in our lives, and we discussed in detail the ways in which we could help our mother emotionally and physically. Uncle Phil was made aware of our plans, and he supported us. Now, it was up to Mother as to where and when she would like to spend her remaining years.

Unlike my sister, I had not heard a word from Mother since my sister's return to Virginia. I could not bring myself to pick up the phone and be greeted only by "Well, how are you?" in her cold, clipped tones. Again, I felt that it was a form of punishment for some imagined slight. I decided that I had gone through my life tiptoeing through enough of her emotional garbage to fill the dump of the world.

Dana had recently spent a few days with me. During that time, she visited her grandmother.

"How did that go?" I had asked her.

"You can get so close and no closer," she replied. "Too many protective barriers. When I have children, I want them to know how much I love them."

A phone call from Leslie confirmed that the family had finally made an emotional break with St. Lo.

"We saw the best years, Mom. There are strangers moving in, and the place lacks the closeness we felt as children and teenagers. I'm glad we have the memories, but the place doesn't have the importance it once had in our lives," she explained.

I had made a short visit to St. Lo, and I agreed with Leslie's comments. "It's full of ghosts for me," I told Leslie.

"Some of my contemporaries from St. Lo came to visit over the Fourth," said Leslie, "They came to the house for a drink. It was almost like being at the beach. You know, Mom, I still think of all those Fourths, Augusts, the parties, the tennis tournaments. I was glad to go back this year, but it has changed for me too. I have changed.

"It's the summer, Mom, it's the summer. I have a view of the pond with the mountains in the background. I'm still in bed, and I can see two deer drinking at the pond. The air is brown with smoke from the fire that is burning at the place where we went rafting last summer. It's just as well we aren't going this year."

Before we said our goodbyes, she told me she was happy that Riley and Jennie were at the same camp. It made me feel good to know they were together. "I'll send the care packages—cookies and stuff—because it's hard for you," Leslie offered.

~ ~ ~

My son Bill came to visit me in Pasadena in August with a whole new attitude. He was also now emotionally ready to return to St. Lo for a visit. It was the first time since 1981 that he'd been back to St. Lo.

"I want to take Sam home one more time," he told me. Bill took off with the dog in his truck to spend the day in St. Lo. It turned out that Sam, who was getting on in years, wandered into our former home. Morgan and Jennie—who also happened to be at St. Lo—had to go into the house to retrieve the homesick pup. "Sam acted just like a baby. He was chasing gulls and dropping rocks he found on the beach by our front gate," Jennie told me later.

Bill returned to my home in Pasadena, and he shared with me his new perspectives on life.

"I've sowed my wild oats. I want to go back to school and lead a *different* life now," he said. He told me that he was looking after his ninety-year-old neighbor, Grace, and how much he enjoyed backpacking in the wilderness of Idaho and Northern California.

Bill was finally getting on with his life and making plans for the future. His father's death and my paralysis had hit him so hard that he even dropped out of university one semester shy of getting his degree. Now I felt that he was coming to terms with his losses and getting stronger emotionally.

"When you are well, Mom, you can come and live up North," he told me before he left for Santa Cruz.

While everyone was engaged in his or her summer activities and Irma was on vacation, I was free to create my own agenda each day. My temporary caregiver rented videos for me. I read books, ate lunch on the terrace at the club, and continued to practice the flute as the evening hours drew shadows over the house. Physical therapy and psychotherapy continued to drain me, but I slept well. Each day there were messages, either by phone or by mail.

The young woman who had arranged my visit with Norman Cousins phoned to find out if I was making any progress. After our conversation about my condition, she said, "I hear too many 'maybes.' Remember what Norman said: 'You have the ability to heal yourself. Depression is known to release a chemical that prevents or slows down healing.'"

I continued my ministry in a different manner: praying for those in need in the quiet of my home. Sally, my high school friend who had returned to my life to help me was now dealing with lung cancer and problems with her sixteen-year-old daughter.

"You'll love your baby, Berta," she had written to me when I discovered I was going to be a mother again at forty, just as she had been. And now, she was haunted by fear and anxiety due to nicotine withdrawal as much as the cancer. She drew great strength from her faith, so I tried to return some of what she had given me through her meditation and prayer. Eventually, dear Sally returned to her Father. Oh how I envied her going home.

The news that one of my husband's friends from the firm he had worked for was dying of cancer prompted me to pray. I spoke to Bill's spirit, telling him: "Bill, you will soon have a friend to greet."

One of my "knights," as I called them—the men who had taken me to an AA meeting—phoned, berating me for not keeping in touch. To me, that was a positive step forward. It meant, in spite of some serious depression, I was making it on my own. When I told him I still had to fight fear, he said, "Lots of people feel that way. I saw two women at the club sipping wine, and their eyes were dead. They're our age, and they've probably got twenty or thirty years ahead of them, but they are already dead."

As another summer came to a close, I was engrossed in a book entitled *Tongues of Men and Angels*. Its words spoke to me about my life:

> *I have in my long time noted—and wonder if you have ever—the turning around of some people's lives, as if some force moved in them against their will.*

And a quote from a father to a son resonated with me:

> *Life is a fight, a glorious fight. We should teach our children to be prepared to fight all of their lives.*

Chapter 18

STANDING ALONE

*So strengthen your drooping hands
and your weak knees. Make straight
paths for your feet, that what is
lame may not be dislocated but healed.*

—Letter to the Hebrews 12:11-15

Chapter 18

D aniel advised me not to depend on Irma. Her pregnant daughter had come to the United States without her husband. Irma would be distracted. He also told me not to depend on Sister Wilfrid. Sister had told me not to depend on my children because she said they were not interested in my problems. "So, it's just you and me, God. Try to remember that I'm a novice," was my prayer.

Sitting at my desk doing catch-up work, I read a letter from Jennie. In the letter, she mentioned, "I prayed for you at Mass." Putting the letter aside, I listened to the lyrics of a song on the radio: "When your heart is open, it's never too late to find love. Put the past behind you, and love will find you." *Is this a message from Jesus?* I asked myself.

There was a box of things in the front hall—Jennie had reorganized her room that summer. Her little Indian bowl was discarded—we had bought it on one of our weekend excursions when we were living at the beach. I was sad to see all those keepsakes in that box; she was discarding the mementos of her childhood.

We spent less time together than usual during that summer. Before she went away to summer camp, Jennie's days were very full. She had a job at Mayfield, went to concerts with friends and brought them home to spend the night. One evening, we listened to tapes we both enjoyed while we fell asleep.

Jennie, the candle in the darkness, was growing dim. When I was feeling down, I would turn my thoughts to my youngest daughter and my heart would be uplifted, and I would have a reason to struggle on. Now, she was seeking her independence. Sometimes, I wondered how the human heart manages to survive with all the adjustments it has to make.

When Daniel arrived for my next therapy session, he asked me straight away, "Are you angry about something?"

I replied in an instant, "My children, it's my children." And then all of my feelings poured out. "They are whitewater rafting on a river in Idaho now, and I feel cut off from them. I don't feel they have helped me as much as they should have throughout my ordeal. When they do visit, it is usually with some other purpose in mind, and I might only get an hour or two of their time.

"My son-in-law Michael's generous offers to pay for expensive trips for everyone are very seductive, but it is spoiling some of the children and their spouses. Morgan should be out looking for work, and he isn't. And Dana is not entirely happy in her marriage. Her husband seems to lack direction as far as work is concerned. At the same time, Dana and Kevin enjoy the company of Leslie and Michael.

"According to Leslie, most of the friendships she enjoys in Sun Valley are with older couples—friends of Michael—so I suppose it is livelier for her when her brothers and sisters are around.

"My concern is that they are spending too much time with frivolous activities and not taking life seriously enough. Our first priority—my husband's and mine—was to educate them well, so they would be able to take good care of themselves. I feel they could be using all the tools they were given to better advantage."

When the session was over, I was so worn out by it that I went straight to bed. But before falling asleep, I wrote down my spoken thoughts about my divided family. After reviewing what I had written, I prayed that if my children ever read my words of criticism, they would understand.

When I awoke from my nap, I felt another message had been given to me in a dream. In the dream, I was visiting my former Pasadena neighbors. Their home was not like the one I knew in real life, and it didn't seem to be at the beach either, although, perhaps it was, as there were many people around. My neighbors asked me if I would like to go somewhere. I accepted. When we arrived at an unrecognizable location, they told me they were going to stay there and that I would have to take the bus home alone. I felt dumped and deserted, lost, and unwanted. The message of the dream was clear: *You'll have to make it on your own.*

I took a small job at Mayfield School. Angel, the groundskeeper, made a ramp into the office, where I sat looking out at the front garden as I sorted and refiled index cards. The work was monotonous, yet calming. Unfortunately, my condition affected the quality of my performance.

I listed towards my right side, my weak abdominal muscles caused me to fall forward when I had to reach for something, and the radiating nerve pain sapped my energy. While the job lasted, it made me feel that I was taking care of myself.

Irma's dream was coming true. She purchased a new red truck for her nephew after he arrived in the U.S. He now picked her up on her days off and drove her to a small apartment in a nearby town.

I felt threatened by her progress. And even though Sister Wilfrid kept reminding me I had made it possible for Irma to begin a better life, it did not console me.

After recovering from cataract surgery, my mother, accompanied by Uncle Phil, came to see me. Suspecting how she must have felt lonely and how she dearly wished that one of her daughters would take care of her, I said, trying to elicit some kind of response, "I feel very lonely sometimes."

The expected response was not forthcoming. The silence was palpable.

Uncle Phil, contributed, "I also feel lonely sometimes. We all do."

Nothing, my mother said nothing.

Mother had brought some rolls that simply called for a cup of tea. We drank and ate in silence even though I had made it possible for her to express how she surely must have felt. It was my wish to comfort her, to let her know that I was concerned about her.

As she was leaving, she said, "Your bedroom is very attractive." It often took her a while before she complimented her own children.

The following month Morgan came to visit on his birthday.

"I treated myself to a massage on my birthday," Morgan said on that special November day. "The blind masseur remembered all the men he had massaged before my wedding a year ago." Jennie had written Morgan a birthday letter. It was cheerful and optimistic. And Morgan liked my present—the etchings from Holland that Charles had sent Bill and me as a wedding present.

Leslie, on her thirty-fourth birthday, said, "I remember when you were my age, Mom. I used to think, *Wow, she's a woman*. And now, *I* am that age."

Dana turned thirty a few days later. She and her husband were to come for a visit soon, or so I thought until Morgan phoned the day of their expected arrival to tell me that Leslie and Michael were flying them someplace as a surprise.

"Why didn't Leslie tell me about her plans? We had a conversation just a few days ago," I inquired of Morgan.

"Leslie doesn't want to be any closer to you than necessary. She said you are too manipulative," Morgan explained.

Manipulative? That word really stung!

I spoke to Daniel about the whole incident. "There's a lot of guilt there," he stated. He had said this before in reference to Leslie.

"Daniel, she could have told me about her plans for Dana. I would have been disappointed, but I wouldn't have made an issue of it. I don't know what Leslie's guilt is about. Leslie is sensitive to questions about how she feels, so I never ask if she is bothered by guilt."

And then, I related to Daniel about the time Dana had remarked about the picture of her with her classmates, which was taken when she was at the same school Jennie was now attending. I had the photo framed and gave it to Dana for her birthday. "I don't know what to do with it," Dana said. "All those girls running around in plaid skirts—I'm not into nostalgia." Didn't she understand what it meant to her parents to send her away to a school where she would receive the advantages of a good preparation for college and for life?

Leslie and Dana's indifference was making it easier for me to depend only on Our Lord. "They're not interested in me or my life," I said to Him. I began to take Sister Wilfrid's advice: "Let go."

~~~

During my visit up north with Jennie on Parents' Weekend, I was keenly aware of her struggles with school and adolescence. She was well aware of her problems and trying her best to overcome them.

When I returned home, I phoned Sister Catherine, the principal at Jennie's school. She informed me that Jennie's grades were poor and that her participation in class was unsatisfactory—no different than the year before.

"She is well behaved, so much so that she never needs to be sent to the principle's office like the other girls," she said.

"Do you mean she's *too* controlled, *too* good?" I asked.

"Yes. The other girls are in and out of here all the time. Jennie stands out from the other girls, lacks energy, and looks defeated." The news made me cry. "She has some good friends," continued Sister, trying to console me. "I'm so glad to talk to you, Mrs. Hees. I've wanted to do something for quite some time now, but I hesitated. Now, I'll get right on the situation. Sister Helen, Sister Marie, and I will do everything we can for Jennie."

"Thank you, Sister."

"That's what we're here for, Mrs. Hees. We pray for you all the time. When Jennie gets some help from the psychologist, things will change."

A day or so after my conversation with Sister Catherine, Jennie phoned me.

"Last night the loudspeaker blared across the campus calling me to Sister's office. I was terrified. It usually means trouble," Jennie said. "I told Sister that sometimes I want to answer in class, and I get angry with myself when someone else gives the answer. I think, *Oh, I know that. Why didn't I speak up?*"

Jennie agreed to see a psychologist to shore up her self-confidence.

We talked about how much we had enjoyed visiting the Monterey Bay Aquarium on Parents' Weekend. I did not tell her, however, how much I missed her father when I caught a glimpse of a man in a windbreaker with a camera slung around his neck. I did tell her about the dinner I had one crisp, starry night at a restaurant overlooking the sea, and how seeing the rocks below and the lights of Seaside in the distance made me long to live by the sea again.

Jennie began dating when she came home for Thanksgiving. When we went out for dinner to celebrate Thanksgiving, she met a young man at the club who phoned her at midnight that night. I told him it was too late to be calling, and he apologized.

He dropped by the next morning to take Jennie out for breakfast. I interrupted my therapy session with Daniel to ask Jennie how long she would be.

"About a couple of hours," she said, and then handed me a note for Morgan.

When Morgan and Katy came by to return my hair dryer, I handed him the note.

After Daniel left, I asked Morgan, "What's in the note?"

"She's just explaining where she has gone."

"I'm very angry Jennie went out with someone she just met, and that she left you a note explaining where she went! Why didn't she give it to me?"

In so many words, Morgan told me to bug off.

Katy came to my defense. "Wait until you have children of your own, Morgan. You have no understanding of the problem."

Morgan shoved her aside and said to me, "Talk to Daniel."

"I already have, and he said to get angry. So I'm angry."

Damian's advice also ran through my head: *"You don't stand up for yourself."*

Morgan continued, "Well, go talk to Sister Wilfrid then."

"I already have, and she's coming over," was my answer. When she arrived, I received the Body of Christ, and with it came peace. It had been a rough morning.

At 5:00 A.M., with Irma's help, I got up to put buckets under my leaking roof. Before returning to bed, I turned on the television and noticed I had double vision, no doubt caused by the combination of the alcohol and tranquilizers that I took a while earlier.

Did I want to die again? Could I deal with a dating teenager who had tobacco on her breath? It made me wonder. Was she ready to experiment sexually? Was she drinking or taking drugs? I felt helpless and stressed. But I didn't really want to kill myself; I just needed support. "Bill, where the hell are you?" I called out to my husband's spirit.

Sister Wilfrid told me not long before, "Your suffering is redemptive."

"What does that mean?" I had asked her.

"You are filling up the holes for Him. He is asking his dear friend Berta to help those around her. Your children will be helped so much! Eventually, they will learn a great deal from your suffering. Why, already you have found the strength to fly up north and talk to Jennie's teachers. Just think what that did for Jennie."

Once again, I had fallen back into a place I thought I had freed myself from that past year. Throughout the month of December, tears and depression were my companions again.

At the suggestion of a friend, I made an effort to record books on tape for the local community college. After receiving and setting up the necessary equipment, I found that I was not quite up to task, as the depression sapped my energy. My weakened diaphragm muscles affected my voice. Too much time spent reading aloud reduced my voice to a hoarse whisper.

As a way to distract myself, I decided to look into the situation with the leaky roof. I was told that it needed an overhaul, which would cost me $13,500. Instead of getting my mind off my problems, I found that I had yet another. My thought was that I might not live long enough to enjoy a non-leaky roof.

Retreating to a corner of my living room, I practiced my flute. Because of my health problems, the notes barely squeaked out. I looked down at my abdomen. Were my kidneys giving out? Kidney infections were a constant problem. Bedsores had broken out on my behind. So I set down my flute and went to my room. Resting on my stomach in my bed, I aired out my bedsores.

Oh, Jesus, what am I doing here in this foreign land?

~~~

Since Jennie was away at school on her sixteenth birthday that December, I had given her a present during Thanksgiving. Apparently, I struck out again as far as presents were concerned.

"Thanks, Mom," Jennie had said politely when she saw the wristwatch I had gotten her.

"It's all right," I assured her. "You can exchange it for something you like better." She kept looking up and down between the watch and me. "Put it in the drawer," I suggested. After Jennie did as I suggested, her eyes kept darting from the drawer to my face and back to the drawer. "All right, are you afraid you'll hurt my feelings? Are you disappointed it isn't something else?" I asked. "What would you have preferred?"

"Yes. No. I don't know," she stammered, and then she began to cry. I put my arms around her. Stretched out on the bed next to each other, we watched *Dynasty* on T.V. and forgot all about the watch.

My other children came to town for a wedding reception. Before Leslie and Dana departed, we had some good moments. Leslie spent some time with me. She reminisced about her father, spoke about her happy life with Michael, and shared her fears concerning her daughter growing up.

"How was the wedding reception?" I inquired.

"Morgan was there. He looked so handsome! He is handsome, but he's still a rascal. He referred to me as 'the princess' on our last river trip."

"Did it bother you?" I inquired with a smile.

"Yes, at first, but I got used to it," she said matter-of-factly.

Dana stayed somewhat longer, happy for the respite. Dana was preparing for the birth of her baby. She was also struggling with her marriage because Kevin was around too much of the time and emotions would build up. The air needed to clear.

I shared some of my own experiences on that topic with Dana by saying, "That situation is familiar to me. Because he could afford to do so, your father went through long periods of not working. I found those periods stifling for me. When he began to grow a beard, his mother said, 'If he had married anyone but you, Berta, that woman would have been long gone by now.'"

Dana explained how she and her husband were trying to work things out through communication. Then she said, "I like being here with you, Mom."

However, one morning I awoke covered with blood—my period had started—and I began to cry. When Dana brought me coffee, I told her how difficult it was for me not to be able to spring out of bed in the mornings and happily greet another day like I used to. "Oh really? You don't really want to have to make coffee, do you?" she said with a sly grin. In that moment, I burst into tears. Then, she said softly, "Oh dear, crying again?" She put her arms around me, which I found to be very comforting.

Before Christmas, Michael and Leslie invited the family to dinner at a small hotel in Westwood Village. As I ate my dinner, I thought about a street not far from where we were dining. On that street, Bill and I had lived next door to each other for a brief time. It was there that we met and fell in love. The church where we were married was also close by. I looked at each of my children who were seated around the table and marveled at what resulted from that meeting so long ago.

The dinner was our family holiday celebration. The children were planning to go to Hawaii and would be away over Christmas. I was happy to spend Christmas quietly at home. To create a festive mood, I got a small tree, which I decorated. The best part of Christmas was a visit from Sister Wilfrid. After she gave me Communion, she pointed at the crucifix hanging over the fireplace and said, "He is all you have right now."

"I know, Sister. I am aware that He has singled me out to walk this narrow path with Him. I also understand that I'm not a very steady companion."

~~~

When New Year's came, I had no resolutions, no plans, no thoughts or cares about walking again. In this way, my approach to life became more relaxed.

Daniel, my psychologist, was still concerned about my battle with depression.

"Your hormone imbalance is at the root of your depression," he declared.

"I'm trying to work with my doctors. As you know, I've had cancer. They've put me on estrogen to help with my depression, but the doctors think that estrogen contributes to cancer, so it's tricky." I offered.

"I understand."

"Would you like to hear about my recent dream?" I inquired.

"Is it important to you?"

"Yes. In the dream, I was drowning in my own urine. What does that mean?" I asked.

"You're afraid incontinence will ruin your life," he explained.

"Well, yes," I affirmed.

"You don't think your bladder will ever function normally again?" Daniel enquired.

"I'm fifty-five years old and the mother of five. Come May, those muscles will have been inactive for four years," I stated firmly.

"You've accepted the situation, then?"

"Yes."

"That's good for now. Live each day with acceptance."

We heard a car door slam. "Jennie and Bill are home!" I smiled.

"Well, I better leave you then," said Daniel, getting up from his chair.

Bill came to see me in my room and gave me a big warm hug. He looked tanned and healthy. "The trip was just what I needed," he said. "Leslie outdid herself with stockings and presents this year. However, she got out of control emotionally. She argued with Jennie and said things she shouldn't have said. You were the subject of the argument, Mom. The rest of us told her to shut up, even Kevin."

I asked Jennie if she had enjoyed her Christmas in Hawaii.

"We played tennis and swam at different beaches. Sometimes, we swam in the pool." That was all she had to say.

Bill and Jennie left Pasadena a day or two later. Jennie returned to school, and Bill went back to work.

I met with Sister Wilfrid to tell her about the argument between Leslie and Jennie.

"I don't know why I was drawn into the disagreement. No one offered to give me the details. So, I let it go," I said with some pride.

"I still feel there is some guilt there," commented Sister Wilfrid about Leslie.

After Sister's visit, I settled into my bed and reached for a book. The book fell open to the dying words of a Blackfoot Indian named Crowfoot:

What is life? It is that flash
of a firefly in the night.
It is the breath
of a buffalo in the wintertime.
It is the little shadow
which runs across the grass
and loses itself in the sunset.

In this manner, another day of my life would end, never to be repeated. I must strive to be happy in Christ during those hours that pass so swiftly.

Reality always interrupts that peace. I arose grudgingly at 7:00 A.M. when the roofers arrived. Irma took the day off to go to the doctor, which left me having to talk her replacement through my routine.

I settled in my favorite sunny corner of the living room expecting to write. My little corner of the house was becoming entirely too busy and too noisy with workmen pounding on the roof. Sister took me to my bed after Communion. And then Irma came home.

Irma told me the doctor had given her some good advice: no sugar, no salt, no fats. Although there was nothing serious at the moment, she was advised to carefully follow his instructions regarding her high blood pressure.

Unwisely, she started to clean the house, even though I told her that the roofers would return the next day.

How nice it will be not to worry about leaks when the rains come, I thought, as the men pounded away on the roof early the next morning. Debris fell everywhere, the lights blew out in my bedroom and bathroom, and it was freezing in the house because we could not turn on the heat while the roofers were working. The noise and the smells made my body a jangling, painful mass of nerves. Knowing the worst would be completed the following day when rain was expected, Irma said, "You are lucky that the weather's cooperating." And then, we went back to bed.

As both of us had been struck by the flu at the same time, we stayed in bed for days. Cindy and Imelda took over in caring for me. They cleaned me up after my bouts of diarrhea, which were unremitting, and put me on my stomach and off my bedsores.

While I was on my stomach—the pain in the nerve endings so severe I couldn't think straight—Jennie phoned to ask me to make an appointment with the DMV for her. I was not up to the task. Instead, I just stared out the window at the people walking by the house. A great deal of the past five years had been spent looking out my window, talking to Jesus and to my husband, and weeping. And now, I was mildly depressed again. Speaking to Jesus helped me get through it. I asked Him to help me carry my cross each day, and thanked Him for Cindy, Imelda, and Candy—a beautiful addition to our extended family who did my shopping and ended up becoming a dear friend to both my daughter and me.

As I recovered, I began spending time writing at my desk. One day, I wrote a letter to my daughter Dana:

> All is well, as far as my understanding goes, between Leslie and Jennie despite the friction in Hawaii.

And then I went on to say that I had been unable to reach Leslie.

> I wish Leslie would try to rid herself of whatever anger she still harbors towards me. She will end up damaging herself.

I explained that Bill had said, "We all stuck up for you, Mom." And then:

> I don't want anyone undermining the trust Jennie and I have placed in each other. I want Jennie to be her own person. She was born with her own eyes, mouth, nose, and ears. She is not a clone of you, Bill, or of Morgan. Sometimes, I think she feels she has to be like her brothers and sisters, and that is just not so. Her letters to me are very direct, and she has a clear understanding of her scholastic problems and how to approach them. I am very glad you phoned her at school this last week. You do try to help when necessary.

The letter continued on about everyday things and closed with:

You may read this letter to Leslie when you talk to her. I never know where she is, and I think she likes to keep her distance. She sends me bouquets, presents, and then disappears as rapidly as possible. On the other hand, forget all this. I'll tell her myself, if I can find her.

I'm not sure if I mailed this letter or if I just wrote it for myself.

Still struggling with the effects of the flu, Irma and I battled with the stove. The pilot light kept going out, and, after several attempts, I was unsuccessful in relighting it, so the house now reeked of gas.

Oh well, I thought, *so we blow up in the night.*

The following morning, the man from the gas company came to save us.

"The light goes out because your housekeeper lets the food boil over. Eventually, the line gets clogged. Please explain this to her," he emphasized.

"I *have* explained this to her, but she doesn't understand. I'll try again."

It took a great deal of dramatic arm waving, gesturing, and vocalizing "boom, boom," with many references to the word *"morir"* before I was able to get Irma to understand.

The drama of running a house never ends. I discovered that the automatic sprinklers at the rear of the house were no longer working and that the hose was too short to reach the azaleas.

Returning to the house with a soiled, wet nightgown, I phoned Charles, who was in town with his recovering mother, and asked him if he could come and help.

"No," he replied, and simply hung up.

I'm all right. Christ is with me—my only friend, I thought to myself.

Then I remembered how my husband used to patiently turn on, one by one, the many, many sprinkler heads that were necessary to cover the large pieces of property we had owned over the years. He would sit watching the water as evening approached.

When she lived at home, Jennie would water the garden without ever having to be asked to do so. Now I see that act as something special, something not to be taken for granted.

Morgan came by to visit. He had spent the previous day thinking about an essay I had written about his graduation from the twelfth grade and of the memories it revived concerning his father.

"I'd like to be able to talk to him now. I could use his support at this time," he said.

I replied, "I feel cheated myself, as I never had the kind of mother I could turn to for help. As you know, my father died when I was fourteen. The one thing I wanted for all of you was that you would have the kind of family I never had. Instead, life appears to be repeating itself, and I regret that your father and I aren't together to be there for each one of you. It seems so unfair, but I must trust that God has a plan for each of us."

~~~

Before January ended, I had some good news from Jennie! It knocked the fear right out of me.

Chapter 19

GOODBYE, HELLO

Like the tree I shall bow down.
Like a mountain I shall forgive
and keep my head high.
Like the mother I shall always remain awake
Like the heart I shall always worship.

—Sri Chinmoy

Chapter 19

Jennie was elected class representative! When I retired for the night, I said my rosary as a way of expressing my thanks. Excited as I was, the repetition of the prayers was calming, and I had a wonderful night's sleep. The following morning, I wrote to Jennie expressing my congratulations.

Later that day, Bill phoned to say, "I think it will take me about two years to complete my education." It pleased me to hear that he was returning to school to get back on the track from which he had been derailed after his father's death.

I replied, "That's okay. Jennie will be graduating from high school at the same time you graduate from university. Who knows? Maybe I'll be walking by then."

"That's right, Mom. We'll have a big party to celebrate," Bill suggested.

Morgan was proud of his wife Katy for the fine work she did on her end-of-the-quarter projects at the Art Center School of Design.

A conversation I had with my daughter Dana was about change. "I am not trying so hard anymore to direct my life. Life seems to open up more when I don't try to control it," she said. "I'm selling my house. There are 'For sale' signs springing up all over town."

"Why?" I asked.

"I bought it as an investment. The prices are high right now because of the oil market. The Texans and Oklahomans can afford to buy into the real estate market. When oil prices drop, we lose a big part of the seller's market here in New Mexico."

Then she talked to me about her volunteer work at the Folk Art Museum and Trading Post.

The ordinary, everyday things of my life were moving into first place. Aspects of my life mingled with aspects of my children's lives. I felt as if I were walking a clear, firm path laid with mosaic tile. And, I really needed a firm foundation now that my beloved Irma was leaving.

Irma's health had deteriorated to the extent that she was no longer able to provide me with the care I needed. We both accepted the situation. Irma would spend time recuperating and then find a job that would be easier on her.

"God cares about you. That's the way God wants things to be," Irma assured me.

Kevin showed up at my door unexpectedly.

"Oh, Kevin, thank God it's you. Irma is leaving today, and I'm not sure what course I should take. It is so expensive running this house with caregivers and nurses. The recent rains flooded the basement and knocked out the water heater. The new roof is leaking in several places, and the automatic sprinklers go on at three o'clock in the morning. I can't sleep at night, thinking of all that wasted money and water."

"This is a big house. Eventually you may want a smaller place," he suggested.

Changing the subject, he told me about the loud and lengthy arguments Leslie had with Jennie in Hawaii. He didn't reveal the subject of those arguments, but he did say, "None of us went near the room where they were arguing, but we could hear Jennie holding her own. She stood up for herself." Then he said that he noticed that Dana was paying increasingly more attention to her spiritual side, giving her an inner peace and a calmer attitude toward life.

I asked Kevin if I could read him a letter I had just written to Leslie addressing some of her recent concerns. The letter said:

> *Sometime in your life you will reach out and help others in need. You are great when it comes to the fun times—rafting trips, Hawaii trips, dinner parties, sending flowers, "goodies" (that is your term)—all very helpful to your family, but you sound annoyed when Michael gets the flu and your daughter insists that she is growing up. Well dear, that is what you are constantly referring to as real life, and you don't like it any better than anyone else.*

In the letter, I commented on the questions she raised about some physical problems she was experiencing.

*No, I never struck you as a child. Why you suffered from tinnitus,
the ringing in your ears, I don't know. As far as your neck problems,
one time, the front of your desk fell on your head, and perhaps the
incident was worse than we thought at the time.*

I explained to her I had smacked her brother Bill across the ear once
after I had repeatedly asked him to clean up his room and he did nothing
about it. I later found out that Bill had tonsillitis, and his adenoids were
swollen, so he was unable to hear my repeated requests.

*Lesson learned: never strike a child across the ear. I suffered more
than he did from my own guilt.*

Then I addressed her recent accusation that I had sent her to a "rotten
dentist":

*I have yet to meet a dentist who has a good word to say about
another dentist's work. Jennie's dentist in Pasadena was just as
critical of her Carlsbad dentist.*

Kevin's response to the letter was, "It's about time someone spoke up
to her. Everyone is afraid of Leslie. It's a great letter." He left quickly, but
not before giving me another reason to live: "I hope in the next two years
you'll be a grandmother again."

The letter to Leslie? I neither finished it nor mailed it. As usual, I wrote
it to myself as a way of releasing my anger.

Morgan and Katy came to say goodbye to Irma after I phoned to
inform them that she was leaving. Morgan felt sad, and Irma looked
downcast as they said goodbye to each other.

"You have wonderful children," said Irma, as she sat on my bed
waiting for her replacement to arrive. "Thank Leslie for the flowers. I'll
miss Jennie and Toto." Yes, how she loved our big cat, Toto, a large white
cat that had replaced dear Tom.

Irma's future was uncertain.

"First I'll rest, and then perhaps return to Nicaragua, but it
costs $600."

She said she wasn't eager to leave her room to share an apartment with her daughter, Anabel, and Anabel's husband.

"It is awful. I cause problems for them, and they play disco music all the time."

We hugged each other and said the Our Father together.

Imelda came over to help Irma pack. Since Imelda would be helping part time, Irma showed her how to make my bed in preparation for my therapy sessions with Larry.

Sandy, my new caregiver, did not come on time. She phoned to tell me that her car had been stolen.

"The thief used my car in an attempted burglary. He was caught, but the police have impounded my car," Sandy explained. She sounded upset.

"Oh dear, Irma, what am I going to do?" I sighed and shrugged my shoulders helplessly.

"I won't leave until she settles in," said Irma. Morgan later drove Irma home.

Working with a new caregiver was always a challenge. I phoned Sister Wilfrid for support.

"It is the feast of Our Lady of Lourdes," said Sister Wilfrid on the phone. "I've prayed all day that something good would happen for you."

With all honesty I replied, "It's been a terrible day."

"It's all good Berta. Your life is preparing you for the next phase. Irma said she would stay until you were walking, and she has done just that."

"Well, I am not really walking, as you know, dear Sister. My legs will not support me without braces and Larry's assistance." I replied. "Also, Sandy says she cannot live in as she thought."

Something good did happen that day, in answer to Sister's prayers. Mary, my friend and accountant, helped me work out a plan for my care. Sandy would work days and two nights. Nubia, the young Salvadorian who already knew my family, would work weekends plus Monday and Tuesday nights. A nurse recommended by Mary would fill in the gaps.

During our efforts to arrange a plan for care giving, I wondered aloud to Mary if I shouldn't be in a sanitarium.

"You wouldn't be able to afford the kind of place you should be in. You're not ready to be totally taken care of, and you definitely don't want to go into the convent. You'd go crazy surrounded by all those immature women. Believe me, it's the last place *I'd* want to be," said Mary, a cradle Catholic.

"So," I suggested, "if in two years I am not recovered, maybe it would be nice to sell this place and build a very small house at St. Lo: one room, with living, dining and kitchen all together, a bedroom and bath to suit my needs, and a small bedroom and bath for the children. I could at least watch the sunsets, the dolphins, the gulls. And, in the summer, the place is bustling with vacationers. My children would probably come and visit me because they like the beach. Help is easier to find there, and taxes are cheaper."

"I think that sounds like a fine idea," said Mary. "Pasadena is difficult. It is like rubbing salt into a wound. Too many invitations to evenings of dining and dancing and so forth."

"Yes," I agreed, "but many people say it would be a mistake to go back to St Lo. However, as a family we spent the best part of our lives at St Lo. The memories are mostly beautiful and far outweigh the tragedies that struck me down. I wouldn't mind dying there and being buried at sea with Bill."

Irma was gone, and life went on without her. We adjusted to the eighty-degree weather in February. It gave me the opportunity to write a note to Mary that said, in part:

> It takes patience to ride out these storms that blow over our lives
> from totally unexpected directions. And it takes good friends to
> keep putting us back on track.

I had good friends, like the woman who came by to read to me about the British Queen of Spain and those whose lives moved along the usual course. One friend in particular disliked having her retired husband around all the time. She said, "I wish I lived in Beverly Hills; I can't find any shoes around here."

I thought to myself that I would probably be uttering the same shallow words too if my life were so superficial. However, shoes were never a strong priority in my life. I always kicked them off as soon as I came into the house. Taking a moment to think about what my obsession would be, bibelots came to mind at once. My tabletops are covered with family pictures and bric-a-brac. Well, I grew up in a home where the Victorian age influenced the décor.

Before coming home for a long weekend, Jennie phoned to tell me that she was having headaches again. I suggested that she talk to the school nurse, but I'm not sure she heard me because, in the next breath, she said, "I've just read J.D. Salinger's *Catcher in the Rye*. Oh, Mom, what a terrific book—the best I've read. Would you like me to get a copy for you to read?"

"Yes. I've never read the book. Perhaps it's time."

The rains returned, and Sandy drove me along wet, slippery streets to pick up Jennie and a classmate of hers at the airport. I wanted to jump out of the car so badly to greet my daughter! When she and her friend Sally settled themselves in the car, I reached back and gave Jennie's hand a warm squeeze.

I expected Jennie to say something about Irma's absence. So I asked her how she felt now that Irma was gone.

"I don't like it. Her room will seem so empty. All her things will be gone," was her reply. But, when we got home, Nubia greeted us at the door. Jennie's face brightened at the site of Nubia. Nubia and Jennie were already friends. When Nubia and I had flown to Monterey one time to visit with Jennie, the two of them had spent a great deal of time giggling together.

Jennie proceeded to tell Nubia how difficult it was to return to her home without Irma in it. "But I'm happy you're here," Jennie reassured her.

The next morning, Jennie told me that she had gone to Nubia's room and talked till midnight. I was relieved at how much Nubia's presence had eased the impact that Irma's leaving had on Jennie. Jennie was all right!

Later that day, Jennie received her driver's license. *A step forward*, I thought. And then I made a silent prayer: *May God keep you safe through your years of driving.*

"I'll be so glad not to have to call people to take me places," Jennie declared before she drove away in my Volvo station wagon. Later, when she returned, she said excitedly, "I saw a friend and waved at her as I was coming home." It was easy to remember the excitement when one first begins to drive and a friend sees you behind the wheel.

Larry was helping me to walk, when suddenly Jennie flew into the living room all in tears because she had lost her airline ticket. But she had good news too: "I phoned United, and they said they would replace it if I brought a major credit card with me."

After placing me on my bed, Larry said, "She has really come into her own. She is a very lovely girl." When he saw Jennie in tears over the lost ticket, he wanted to console her. And also, knowing she had just received her driver's license, he wanted to do something to celebrate. So he went to his car and came back with a windup clown that played *It's a Small World.*

During Jennie's stay, Irma came by the house to pay her a visit, but Jennie wasn't home. Later, when Jennie pulled into the driveway, Irma excitedly dashed through the garage. They talked in a mixture of Spanish and English, and Jennie presented her with a Valentine's Day card.

Then Irma turned to me and said, "I know you don't believe me, but I prayed every night to get my strength back so I could finish the job I have here."

Yes, she returned to work for me, and I hired someone else to do the housekeeping. I was not about to burden Irma with that task. And now, she would have weekends with her family.

Sandy, the new caregiver—she would substitute for Irma on her days off—was a nice young woman married to a man who mistreated her. One day, she showed up with a black eye, and, when I asked her about it, she turned away without giving me an explanation. I had hired her husband from time to time to fix things around the house, but then he began hanging around every day. I told him that I did not want him around every day because it interfered with my routine. He flew into a rage, calling me later on the phone and threatening me with harm. I was terrified of him.

~~~

Alas, Jennie's return to school did not go smoothly. She phoned me from the airport to say United Airlines would not honor the credit card unless I was present.

"What shall I do, Mom? Come home and leave tomorrow?" Before I could answer, she said, "Oh, wait a minute, Mom." And then when she came back on the phone, she told me that a school friend had an extra ticket for her. "Besides, the storm in Northern California has caused the flight to be delayed. I won't phone when I get back to school because it will be too late. Bye, Mom."

I was very pleased by her thoughtfulness. "Thank you," I said to Our Lord after I put down the receiver.

In time, Irma moved back into my home. She had some pain in her left leg and needed to be careful, but she was happy to be there, and I was happy to have her back.

One day, when I was walking during a therapy session, I felt Irma's strong support. She was always there for me. She encouraged my efforts to restore my health through prayer and her positive attitude. When she changed my stockings, she immediately noticed how my leg stayed firm. Larry told Irma that it meant that my muscles were reacting and pushing against her. Also, the left knee was bending with some regularity when I walked. My right leg and my right side still showed a lot of weakness, but I was strong emotionally, which was more important as far as I was concerned.

While Jennie was home, the roof leaked and the basement flooded again. When Larry failed to show up the preceding Wednesday, my anger was beginning to build. I followed Daniel's advice and explained to Jennie the reasons why I was upset.

"What do you do with your feelings when you see me so upset? Do you feel angry?" I asked her.

"Well, I certainly feel anger, but I don't always know what to do about it," she replied.

"It is better that we acknowledge it, though, isn't it?"

"Yes," she agreed.

As Jennie was so young when it happened, the death of her father was something that would always stay with her and would influence everything she did. Her father would never be a part of all the special occasions, the celebrations, the milestones of her life—acquiring a driver's license, being appointed sophomore class representative, graduation, marriage, having children. She might do things with her father in mind, with a desire—whether conscious or unconscious—to please him. She might strive to accomplish more, driven by a desire to finish the unfinished, so to speak.

With the household humming along again after Irma's return, I decided to go to the convent and visit Sister Wilfrid, who was very busy going over candidates for admission to Mayfield. I received Communion from Sister without having to leave my car. We chatted for a few moments about Irma's return, recited a prayer of Thanksgiving, and then Sister returned to the duties waiting for her at school.

After leaving Sister Wilfrid, I went to the doctor's office. Irma went into the office and reappeared with the nurse. The nurse came over to me and gave me my estrogen shot. Curbside Communion and medical care were some of the advantages of paralysis!

It was a brilliantly sunny day. The San Gabriel Mountains rose up in unusual clarity and cradled the valley. I paid Aunt Alice a visit at a convalescent home, where she was recovering from hip surgery. I found her happy and accepting of what life had handed her. Charles, along with Alice's son-in-law and grandson, had visited earlier.

"Charles wasn't in good shape, and my son-in-law looked awful. You know, he was disheveled, and his hair stuck out in all directions." I noticed how she was having trouble moving her torso as she said, "I don't know why I can't stay here. I have everything I need: a television, my radio, and they bring me my meals."

I took a look around at the people and the surroundings. Having to be confined to a wheelchair myself—unable to walk, unable to perform my natural bodily functions on my own—I was very much in the same predicament as the people in the home, all of whom appeared to be very old. The only person close to my age was a woman bringing her mother back to the home after a day out. Well, maybe Alice enjoyed the atmosphere, but I didn't feel I belonged there.

Not wishing to demand too much of Irma—her sciatic nerve was inflamed—I phoned Sandy one morning to ask if she would like to take me out to breakfast.

Sitting in the cool morning air at a sidewalk café, Sandy said she had never eaten at such a place, but that she had worked as a waitress at Tiny Naylor's and Bob's Big Boy restaurants. Her remark made me aware that experiences I took for granted were not common to everyone.

"You look depressed," said Sandy.

It was not surprising to me that sitting outside this restaurant revived old memories of Bill and the children. We were sitting on the avenue where I shopped for the family and where, as a family, we ate together, usually in celebration of someone's graduation. The people at the other tables, like the people at Alice's convalescent home, were in their seventies. They looked drab and tired, like the oilcloths on the outdoor tables. The day was heating up as well, and with it came the smog.

When we got home, we found Irma sitting on the lawn, because she had forgotten her key. She appeared worn out from the stress of taking care of her family since their arrival from Nicaragua.

Was this reunion going to work out? Try as I might, it was difficult not to let my caregivers' insecurities play on my own. Unfortunately, I was rarely successful, as they came with their own set of problems that I would end up having to deal with. At times I wondered who was taking care of whom? Perhaps, it was all a part of God's plan.

The truth about middle age came from my friend Anne. When I told her about my visit to the convalescent home and my breakfast among the elderly, she said, "I always thought that when we reached this age we would just sit back and enjoy ourselves, you know, watching our children begin their adult lives. It is not like that at all. A certain amount of joy goes out of life. Children do not turn out the way you imagined—coming home for Sunday dinner and all that. Friends like yourself become widowed, ill, and gradually one realizes that the golden years aren't so golden after all."

After that conversation, I couldn't wait to get old. I figured that, if I managed to live that long, it would be smooth sailing, because not much is expected of you when you are seventy. Middle age, however, is much like the in-between age of the teen years. Just like teenagers are between childhood and adulthood, the middle-aged are between youth and old age.

~~~

I cheered up when Dana told me that I would be a grandmother in October. Dana, with her graceful gestures and gentle touch, would be a fine mother. This first became apparent when Jennie was an infant. On the evenings when Dana returned from boarding school, she would come to my room while I was nursing the baby and slip one of her fingers under the baby's tiny hand. The baby immediately grasped Dana's finger with her own tiny fingers. "I prayed you would have another baby," she said, on one such occasion.

It felt wonderful to see life continue. There had been too much death in the family: the death of the father, a sort of death in my relationships with my children as their lives changed, friendships that died along with our old life, and the slow death of the person I used to be.

Jennie's sense of well-being at school was much improved, according to the remarks made by her teachers on her school report card. For instance, her fellow students were eager to share a room with her.

Jennie phoned me after her report card had been sent.

"I know you want to talk about your grades. How do you feel about them?" I asked. She was discouraged, disheartened, and disappointed.

"I try so hard," she answered, her voice cracking from time to time.

"Go ahead and cry and then go talk to your teachers," I suggested.

Continuing, she said, "I get so discouraged, and then I think of you. I even said that to my psychologist last time we met." Oh, that remark was like the clouds opening up and seeing Christ descend. Courage and hope were overcoming despair.

Jennie had been on retreat and fasting. The day she talked to me, the retreat had just ended. She liked the priest in charge, and she and a friend had made plans to go and talk to him.

For Jennie, there would not be too much downtime. Her friend, Kate, would arrive at the school on Friday to spend the weekend. Together they would be busy on Spirit Day, when each class was to do its chosen activity, and all classes would participate in each other's programs. The Yale Glee Club was scheduled to sing for the students as well. It all sounded like fun to me.

At home, I was handling things better. Informed that termites were eating the house, I told the termite inspector, "The termites are welcome until Easter has passed. Then, I will vacate the house so that you can tent it."

~~~

A reunion between Leslie, her former husband, and their daughter Riley took place in Pasadena. Leslie was relieved to know that she and Paul could be friends. "After all, I initiated the divorce. I wanted the divorce," she admitted.

She then spoke to me about her physical and emotional problems. It was a sign of her renewed trust in me. She also was available to help me through a few difficult moments, and I thanked her for putting her loving heart in my hands. Shortly after spending time with Leslie, I decided to clean out my storage locker. It had taken me five years to get around to the remnants of my former life. When everything was gone, I felt lighter.

Jennie came home for the weekend with a friend whose name was Yuriko. Yuriko said "hello" through her mound of hair and not another word until they came home after a shopping excursion.

I joined them for dinner in the kitchen. Yuriko's pretty face peeked out from behind her hair. She was both sweet and talkative.

It was difficult for me to hold Jennie's attention when it became necessary to address practical matters of everyday life, such as dental appointments or cleaning her room and bathroom before leaving for school, so I rattled them off like a machine gun whenever I could get her to listen.

She looked extremely well, and I was grateful that she liked to bring her friends home from school. The night she left, I listened to a tape she had made of her school production, *Godspell*. Yes, she was drumming in the orchestra.

The grief group came to a close and I went through an entire week without talking to my psychologist. Was I becoming less dependent?

I made another list of things that I wanted to accomplish in my life:

1.To return to health

2.To find some new purpose to focus on as a way to fill the empty space my family once occupied

3.To find strength to develop my talent

4.To learn to love others and not be resentful of what they can do and what I cannot do

5.To see myself as a whole person and not as something broken and unworthy

6.To live a life of service to others

In reviewing my list, it was apparent to me that I had a change of attitude.

Dana came to visit, but, in spite of the fact that she was about to be a mother soon, she was not happy. While we were eating lunch at Alice's, I studied her heart-shaped face with those dainty features, that well-defined upper lip that was strikingly beautiful, and I wondered at the sadness there.

On our way home, she told me that Kevin was around the house too much, and they got on each other's nerves. As we drove through the streets of Pasadena, she commented on how wonderful the old houses were and exclaimed, "If I could find a place like that, I'd move back in a minute."

Daniel came to help me sort out my feelings concerning the children. I came to realize that when the children came home, I would revert back to the kind of mother I was at one time. When they were not home,

I established my own independent life, only to give it up again when they returned. I was better off being alone.

Jennie was well into her teenage rebellion. She was much too serious with her boyfriend, and that was worrisome. It was all right that she bought her clothes at secondhand stores. It was not all right that she told me, "I don't like Carmel or Pebble Beach. I'd rather be poor."

"Jennie," I reminded her, "we are not rich. It is only because your father left you some money that you are able to attend school in Monterey. If you don't like Carmel or Pebble Beach, you are not obligated to go there."

During Jennie's teenage years, I would feel a tremendous sense of relief when she left for school.

~~~

Why are we left with so little at the end of our lives? No matter how pleasant it is raising a family, all seems empty after all the effort. All the things accomplished—and all the things one will never accomplish—seem insignificant. Is it God's way of telling us to loosen our ties to earthly things?

I came to the realization that I had to face my spiritual struggles alone. I began to focus on handing over my life to Jesus. One morning, I looked at the crucifix and said, "This day belongs to you, dear Jesus." A few hours later, I took back my control again. Back and forth, back and forth went my trust in Him. It was like playing ping-pong with the Almighty. I wanted to slam that ball and know that I had won.

Chapter 20

"Sweet" Sixteen

Oh dear, what can the matter be?

—Children's nursery rhyme

Chapter 20

Something was very wrong. Jennie's silence was killing me. My calls to her at school went unanswered. Irma confirmed the lack of recent family interaction when she said, "Why doesn't Morgan visit anymore? We always had such a good time joking in the kitchen, and now Jennie doesn't come to my room anymore when she is home. We used to talk until late into the night." I was still unable to take Sister Wilfrid's advice about letting Jennie move on.

I couldn't wait to fall asleep at night, because I was hoping I might never wake up. "As far as I'm concerned, the milk of human kindness has dried up at the tits," I yelled at no one. I remembered that line from a movie.

During Jennie's last visit home, I noticed how she had matured. The beanpole look was gone—her body was filling out—and she was dating. Keeping her under lock and key was now neither desirable nor possible. Her natural progression in life made me sad, and I told her so.

"Kate's mom," Jennie commented, "isn't dealing with Kate growing up any better than you are." Kate was Jennie's best friend. It made me feel better to know my feelings were probably quite normal.

~~~

Well, I figured the time had come for me to meet "the enemy." Jennie invited him to dinner. Gerald was dark, attractive, serious, and sweet. Seeing him dressed in a dark suit, a porkpie hat, and a string tie brought out some undesirable prejudices in me until he handed me a bouquet of flowers. We had a relaxed and pleasant dinner together talking about art and engraving. Gerald was a printer as well as a student.

Widowed and crippled, I was in a distinctly different position now than when my older children were dating. I had lost confidence in myself. At the time, at least I had someone to talk to—my husband—and the children had a male role model. With Jennie so taken by this boy, I was concerned about the fact that her father was not around to serve as a role model, someone in whom she could confide. The idea of sex before marriage had definitely received society's stamp of approval, but not mine, so I decided it was time that Jennie and I had a talk.

She was already aware that I did not approve of sexual activity at such a young age, but I made it very clear that, if she chose to follow her heart instead of her head and ended up pregnant, she would have to keep the baby. That was about as modern as I could get.

The reason my letters and phone calls to Jennie went unanswered was because she was so wrapped up with Gerald. The silence left me wondering if I had offered her the wrong sort of advice. Our relationship was going to have to weather the temporary storms of adolescence.

Daniel pointed out the obvious: "Jennie is rebelling," he said. "When she comes home, just continue on as if nothing has happened, unless she wants to discuss your differences," he advised me.

A friend of mine offered the use of her lap pool, and my son Morgan said he would take me to her home. Once he had put me in the water, we would assume the position of two people about to dance. Morgan walked and floated the length of the pool backwards, and I floated along, trying to move my legs. The water held me up, giving me the illusion that I could walk just like anyone else. Once I was in the water, I felt like a whole person again.

"This is just like dancing at Holiday Assembly, except we were never allowed to dance so close together there," Morgan commented with a smile. After he lifted me out of the pool to place me in my chair, we sat in this garden of delight enjoying mint tea and cookies, courtesy of our hostess.

After returning from the burial of her mother in Nicaragua, Irma joined us in the Jacuzzi, as I swam and floated on my back staring at the beautiful trees that make Pasadena so special.

At long last, Jennie wrote me a letter. A few days after I received it, we agreed, as we talked on the phone, to forget all our differences that flared up when life pulled her away from me. Like my mother, I was terrified of being alone and ill in old age. How sweet Jennie's voice sounded to me. As we talked through our misunderstandings, Jennie's view of life surfaced when she declared, "I want to live a simple life like my brother Bill." *Nothing would make me happier,* I thought to myself.

~~~

I received a printed invitation along with a handwritten note encouraging me to come to a large dinner party in Pasadena. It was the first time I went on my own to a large gathering. I was scared. It was a formal affair, so I dressed appropriately.

Upon my arrival, I was seated between two gentlemen whom I had known for a long time and with whom I felt perfectly comfortable. I was relieved that music accompanied dinner. It gave me the perfect excuse to simply eat my meal quietly without the expectation of having to engage in conversation, which would have been very tiring for me. Everyone was captivated by the performance of a young cellist who played Bach and some works by Manuel de Falla. Then, madrigals were sung by a chorale directed by a gentleman who interspersed the performances with humor that solicited laughter from the assembled guests.

Looking around the room after supper, I noticed some people had nodded off. We were all in our fifties now, getting older. The passing years and dear old Bach were closing eyes all around me. One of the gentlemen sitting beside me stood up to offer his chair to my hostess. After I thanked her for encouraging me to come, we had a revealing conversation that I felt contributed to my education concerning the realities of life. Neither of her two children had married, much to their parents regret.

"So many parents are disappointed because they have no grandchildren," she said. Her husband was a recovered alcoholic. "I had to join Al-Anon myself just to get through my husband's recovery, and that is how I found God," she explained.

"Is *anybody* happy? It seems I have been totally unaware that friends and acquaintances were suffering so," I said.

"No, not anyone *I* know," she answered. "Think of all the married couples that are no longer sleeping together. They are just putting up a front." I was unaware of that sort of thing, so I kept quiet.

Then, we reminisced. "I remember you best from the Players," she said, reminding me of the plays we once took part in. "I always had this wispy hair, and you had that great long braid. I always wanted a braid like that. You were so sweet and gentle. Bill's sudden death must have been terrible for you."

The latter of course was true. "Sweet and gentle," however, could be translated to "shy and insecure." As for her reference to my hair, I always admired her pixie-like haircut and her always-cheerful personality, full of energy and verve. Then I asked her about a former member of our little group. Onstage and offstage, our group knew how to have a good time.

"How is Dorothy?" I asked. "I heard she was dead. The last time I saw her, she certainly looked like the walking dead. We ran into each other on the street many years ago."

"She survived alcoholism and is doing fine now," were the words I heard, to my relief.

"People no longer believe I will walk again," I said.

"Oh, I do, Berta. People recover from that sort of thing all the time. It just takes time and a lot of hard work," she said.

I squeezed her hand. Then, I left the gathering, where I felt my faith in others and in myself had been renewed—all to the accompaniment of Johann Sebastian Bach.

~~~

Summer was on its way, and it would take some time for me to adjust to living with the "new" Jennie and with Irma, who still couldn't decide whether she was coming or going. For me, this summer was no different than other summers since I became paralyzed—with therapy, unbearable physical pain, bedsores, bodily betrayals, an infected toe, plus the somewhat diminished fears and anxiety.

"Hail, hail to the summer," I said out loud to an empty room.

It was a delight to have Jennie home; it was difficult to have Jennie home. One evening, for example, when I was in the kitchen and Jennie was sitting at the kitchen table watching television, she suddenly turned off the T.V. and went to her room as soon as she realized I was going to hang around.

One afternoon, I looked at her school yearbook. The charming faces looking out at me were unmarked by life. Jennie was among them. Though she had been handed enormous trials in life—the death of her father and a mother with paralysis—her face looked as hopeful as the rest. The messages in the yearbook written by her friends were revealing. The word "unique" was applied to Jennie quite often—unique in her ability to help others, unique in her sweetness and sense of fun. "I hope you will find someone to help you when you get so stressed out," wrote a young girl who had become one of her closest friends and one who was familiar with the shadows in her life.

Later, Jennie brought me some photographs she and her friends had taken during her sophomore year. Seeing her with groups of friends, playing the drums, and jumping horses gave me an idea of what her life was like away from home.

When she approached me about going out with her boyfriend, I hemmed and hawed. "I just want to be able to do what I want to do," she said.

I came back with, "Yes, well, don't we all." Then, I thought of Sister Wilfrid's advice and changed my response to, "All right, all right."

For the second time, Sister Wilfrid had advised me to loosen the apron strings. "That is the decision God wants you to make."

"Yes, yes," I responded, testily. "She is trying very hard to do what is necessary to make things work around here. I know I can trust her, but I can't get myself to trust that God will handle the situation."

The summer would be up and down, but I would get through it, and Jennie would too. My fears came from lack of faith. I would only find peace when I trusted Jesus completely. So, on a Sunday when Irma, Jennie and I were at Mass, I prayed that God would remove the knot of fear in my stomach and replace it with a stronger faith.

One afternoon, Jennie drove me to Esther's home for lunch. When we arrived, Jennie reluctantly went inside at my hostess's request. Another woman close to my age was present. I looked at Jennie as she sipped some iced tea and answered questions about her life. She showed great self-assurance, and not once did she glance my way as young people do when their parent is present and they are being questioned by a mother's friend. Clearly she had matured, and it gave me a little more confidence to let go. After she finished her tea, she smiled at everyone, said thank you, and then said, "I'll return to pick you up, Mom."

Driving the car was a big plus for my daughter that summer. Although most parents worry about their sixteen-year-old driving, for me it was a relief that Jennie got her license. Now she could visit friends, see her brother Morgan, and run household errands.

Yes, I would speak up when she would kiss me and there was tobacco on her breath. "You stink," I said one day, but with a smile on my face. I also worried about drugs and when her boyfriend gave her a large pin with a peace sign. *Now who in the world with any taste would wear such an ugly thing,* I thought to myself.

Jennie phoned one evening to say she was going to be late.

"No, it's *already* late," I replied, and she came right home with her boyfriend.

"Hi," he said as I sat in the living room dressed in my nightgown.

"We'll be in my room," said Jennie, and they adjourned to her sitting room to listen to music or God knows what before Gerald said good night.

The two of them went to the beach together. When she returned, she looked so happy as she sat on the end of my bed. "Oh," she said, "It feels like summer again." We began to talk about other days at the beach and how alive we felt after a day of sun, sea, and finally a shower.

In the evening of that same day, the two of them went to her room to watch *Grease.* At 11:15 P.M., I climbed into my chair, went to Jennie's room, knocked on her door, and called, "Jennie," and again, "Jennie." Music was playing, the lights were out, but, after a few scuffling sounds, she opened the door. "I'm tired, dear, and I think it is time for Gerald to go home. After all, you've been together the whole day," I said, trying not to be too obvious about my concerns and, at the same time, knowing they knew what I meant. I returned to my room.

Then, Irma came by to say, "The garage door is open."

"I know, I know," I said, with some annoyance. "Jennie is saying good night to Gerald."

"She left the garage door open last night," said Irma, "and the door to the kitchen unlocked."

"Yes, yes, but she put the alarms on," I replied. Nevertheless, I once again maneuvered myself out of bed and went down the hall to secure the house. The garage and kitchen doors were open as the two young people were still saying their good nights.

I waited.

Then the cat sauntered though the garage and out into the night. *Aha,* I thought, *I'll close the garage door, and that will get their attention.* Ring, ring went the doorbell, and I headed for the button that released the gate in the garden wall. But the joke was on me when the alarms went off! Jennie had set them earlier that evening. Somehow it all struck me as rather sweet, funny. So, when Jennie walked into the house, I greeted her with a smile, and we kissed good night.

Jennie went to visit her grandmother in Los Angeles. She left at 11:30 A.M. And, at one o'clock, my mother phoned to find out where Jennie could be, but I had no idea.

An hour later, with still no sign of my daughter, I phoned the highway patrol to see if there had been any report on my car. No, there was no report on my car. I waited, and finally the phone rang.

Calling from her grandmother's, Jennie said, "I got totally lost. I was in a terrible part of town and afraid to get out of the car to phone." Well, thank God the lost had been found.

Leslie and Michael were helping me through this time in Jennie's life. Speaking to Michael, I told him she had become lost on her way to Los Angeles.

He said, "She's finding out it's a great big world out there."

During Jennie's little romance, I asked Leslie for her support. She told me she had already spoken to Jennie and that I should prepare for the inevitable. "Mom, you don't really expect her to go through high school *these* days without experimenting, do you?"

Well, yes, I believed it was possible and necessary.

The age of innocence was over. Daydreaming about the future no longer satisfied today's youth. Instead, they seemed more interested in instant gratification. What Leslie was saying was probably true, but I asked her to support me, regardless of how she felt.

During their stay on the west side of town, Jennie had dinner with Leslie and Michael. After dinner, Leslie phoned me to say, "Jennie is all right, Mom, but she has changed since December."

My mother had said earlier, "Uncle Phil and I think she is a truly mature girl."

That Sunday at Mass, I called upon Him, and He answered. The knot of fear was unraveling to be replaced by the love and peace of Jesus.

I felt centered, at least for the time being, so I concentrated on writing a poem for Aunt Alice's eighty-third birthday.

Alice's house looked bright and pretty. In the center of the patio table was a bouquet that Charles had arranged with daisies and bachelor's buttons from the garden. And, a beautiful bouquet from Leslie and Michael decorated the living room. Nine family members sat on the patio, which looked across the Rose Bowl in the arroyo below. While eating lunch, Charles told a joke. The rest of us were laughing when his mother said, "I don't get it, Charles."

"Ponder it, Mama," replied Charles. "Ponder it."

At one point, the conversation centered on a name for Dana's baby, who was due in October. Charles said he liked "O.P."

"Opie? You mean O-p-i-e?" someone asked.

"No," said Charles, "O.P., as in other people's children."

I tapped on my water glass to get everyone's attention. Then, I read my poem:

Alice at Eighty-Three

At eighty-three
Alice can see
the phone book
without
glasses.

At eighty-three
Alice's hip
has lost
its dip,
she cannot do
the tango.

At eighty-three
Alice says,
"I don't care"
and "No"
as firmly
as before!

At eighty-four
I think
there's more
of
ALICE.

Then, we all decided to call the baby "O.P.," and we raised our glasses of wine to toast new life.

"I believe I am handling Jennie's adolescence," I told Sister Wilfrid during her recovery from cataract surgery.

"Yes, you are." And then she repeated once again the position I should take. "Accept that the advice you gave her is what God wants. As your faith increases, your inner fear will dissolve."

Still, I continued to look for validation and support from my mother, my uncle, and my children. "You can do it, Mom," Leslie would tell me. And, I knew that I was capable of dealing with a young girl—a girl no different than any girl of her generation, albeit without the presence of her father.

Jennie drove me across the freeway to my neurologist. She *wanted* to take me, and I felt that was important for both of us. I discovered she was a good and competent driver.

The doctor told me, "You are a success. I know it has seemed endless for you, but, instead of getting worse, you are getting better. There are many, many changes. If you need assistance later on, don't worry; new technology will be available by then, due to the recent developments coming out of Wright College."

Physically healthier and emotionally stronger, perhaps, but by now I knew a sugarcoated pill when I was handed one. He said there was nothing more he could do and that I should go home and continue with my therapy.

On the way home, I felt alone.

As we passed a store devoted to items from the Art Nouveau period, Jennie remarked on her own future: "When I have my own place, that's how I want to decorate it." It brought to mind that my own future was uncertain. My decorating days were over. My first home was ranch style, of course: it was the '50s. (Whatever happened to those rooster lamps with the ruffled shades?)

Jennie's sixteenth summer moved along with more confrontations between Jennie and me concerning Gerald. Jennie asked me if she could take Gerald to the club. And, I said "yes"—but for all the wrong reasons. "He'll probably be uncomfortable," I added.

"I know that, but I'm no yuppie," she fired back, and I was admonished, and rightly so.

Jennie and I made a deal before she went with Gerald and his friends to Disneyland in my car. "When you go to Irvine for the concert next week, he has to pay for the gas," I demanded. Although Jennie was faithful to the rules we had set up at the beginning of the summer, it didn't keep me from thinking, *Oh, are you here again?* when Gerald showed up in the morning. He ended up staying the whole day until dinnertime, when I asked him to leave.

Occasionally, Jennie and I had a moment together when we would reminisce about St. Lo, especially after she had spent a few days there.

"It was quiet," she said, after returning from one excursion. "They are limiting the number of players," she said, referring to the tennis tournament. "The game got out of hand. And, everything, everybody has

changed, except for the Roses, who are still riding their Boogie Boards."
Yes, I thought, *right into their eighties.*

"Remember the night of your father's funeral when a friend held you in her arms and said, 'God never closes a door without opening a window'? Do you think He'll open a window for me?" I asked.

Tired of reminiscing, she said, "Maybe it's rusty."

My young friend Jane reaffirmed Jennie's comments about St. Lo. She went there looking for a house to live in year-round.

"Everybody's sick," she said, "or dying." The St. Lo I knew no longer existed.

Jane came often to pray with me during the hot summer months. Since her generation had been more experimental when it came to sex, I asked this mother of three—with a fourth on the way—to bring me up to speed on the courting rituals of the day. According to her understanding of things, it was no longer important to be a virgin before marriage. Jane suggested that I pray for Jennie always, and then added, "We both know Jesus wants you well, and you will probably counsel those women who still have their husbands and their health, but who will inevitably lose both. We looked up at your house on the hill, and soon we'll all be looking to you for advice. Jesus will look after Jennie."

~~~

Before the birth of her new baby, Dana came to town, and I gave her a baby shower.

"I haven't been the center of attention for a long time, and I'm nervous," she said.

It was fun to watch the different generations interacting and enjoying themselves. Only one of Dana's friends—at least among those present—had a baby. All were in their early thirties—married, working, or both. There were a few of my friends present, and one of them, Carla, was complaining about going to Perth, Australia for the America's Cup yachting race. "I'd rather go to Italy or London," she said.

Aunt Alice and my mother were the oldest ones present. Alice did not look well. My mother wore her dark glasses, which meant her eyes were still sensitive from her recent surgery, or that she was trying to draw attention to herself. Mother and Alice were old. Their train was coming into the station.

Surrounded by mostly youthful energy, I felt strong. When the gathering was over, I thought about those who were well—who still had their husbands and their health—yet complained about their lives. *When I am well, I will not be like them*, I thought.

After the party was over, the children made plans for dinner. Even though I was tired, and because I saw so little of them, I said, "May I join you?"

In an exasperated tone of voice, Leslie came back with, "Oh Mom," implying that I was not welcome. Not knowing what to say, I looked over at Dana in hopes of getting an explanation, but she looked embarrassed. So I decided to stay home.

As Irma prepared me for bed, she began to cry.

"It's over so fast," Irma said in reference to the gathering.

I thanked her for working so hard to make everything easy that day. She had gotten up at six in the morning and then came to my room to say, "I am ready for you." It was reassuring to me to know that she was available for me before the guests arrived.

On my way to the kitchen the following day, I glanced over at Jennie and Gerald, who were sitting in Jennie's room. My face must have had that "he's been here all day" look, because, soon after, she showed him to the door.

Then, Jennie came to talk to me.

"You just don't understand. I'll be going back to school soon, and he and I won't have as much time together. We want to spend time together because we enjoy each other's company. You should be glad he comes to the house and is willing to be here with the family around. He tries to do everything right. He doesn't know what to do."

Gerald was upset with me, and he was entitled to be, as all I could feel was my daughter slipping away from me, and that is where my anger sprang from. But I knew I couldn't stop the clock.

Jennie was growing tired of the summer—the heat was 100 to 107 degrees—and was looking forward to going back to school. The summer had brought many learning experiences for both of us, and I thought she had handled her own quite well.

Before the season came to a close, I received a postcard from Santa Fe. The picture on the card was that of a papoose. My daughter Dana wrote:

> *This is cute, but I think the baby carrier Jennie gave me is more convenient.*

At the end of August, Jennie came to my room to sleep on my sofa. (It was just for one night.) Seeing my sleeping daughter with her arm wrapped around her teddy bear made me think about being sixteen, when one is half in and half out of girlhood.

The last few days of vacation, Jennie said, "It has been a very special summer for me." And then, in the next breath, she said, "I think I have an ulcer." She told me that I was manipulative—I'd heard that one before— and "I've tried to help you on the difficult days, but all I hear is a repetition of the last six years." She was angry to the point of hysteria. I felt she was being overly dramatic, and I worried she would make herself sick. Then, I began to feel very, very calm, because what she said seemed to ring true. She had let go of the past, but I was still mired there.

That night, I had a terrible dream. In the dream, I was in an old-fashioned house with beautiful wooden interiors, all polished and gleaming. But, Jennie was missing. I searched the gardens, the house, and then I phoned the police. Jennie was found when the police removed the lid from a small wooden box—probably a coffin. "Oh, yes," I said, looking into the box, "That's Jennie." Standing in a row near the coffin were three suspects, all wearing hats, all dressed alike, all looking alike. *Gerald!*

The Jennie in the box was small and still; she looked about two years old. Her eyes gazed at me. I wasn't surprised that Jennie didn't look like a sixteen-year-old. Her face had a grayish pallor. And the police pointed to a small mark on her lip.

I interpreted the dream as follows: Jennie had grown up, had a boyfriend, and the dead baby in the box represented the baby part of herself that no longer existed. I could search the house, the garden, but I would never find the child again. Perhaps the mark on her lip was the love bite I had seen on her neck. Oddly, on the day of that dream, Gerald came to the house wearing his porkpie hat, and Jennie had dyed her hair and was wearing used clothing in the style of the '60s. Gone, the Jennie of the past was gone.

The day in September before she left for school, we had our final moments together.

"There are things I don't want to discuss with you, Mom. I'll talk to my shrink or my friends, but not with you," she said.

"We have only tonight, and we'll get through it. Don't think about tomorrow," I advised. We also talked about taking one moment at a time.

At 11:30 that night, the phone rang, and it was Gerald. I could hear Jennie crying on the phone. She had fallen in love at sixteen and was finding it hard to say goodbye. When everyone had settled in for the night, I heard Jennie screaming in her room, "Fuck this and fuck that," and she slammed her bedroom door so hard that Irma came out of her room to see what was the matter. I slid into my chair and wheeled over to Jennie's room for the same reason. So furious was my daughter after Gerald's phone call that I quickly gave up on the idea of trying to help.

Upset, I went to the living room to write, to calm down, and to turn on some music, hoping to drown out the voices in my head.

"For godssake, turn down the music. I'm trying to sleep," yelled Jennie. "You probably turned it up just so I would have to come and ask you to turn it down," she bellowed as she approached the doorway of the living room.

The next day, I asked her, "What are we going to do with all our anger?"

"Call me," Jennie said sweetly, and then she left for school.

Well, I lost the battle all mothers eventually lose. Your children don't need you after a while. Gerald and her friends are the ones Jennie turned to now, and, maybe, just maybe, that is what Bill saw coming, and he decided that it wasn't worth hanging around for the second act.

But, boy, they can sure fool you with their candy bars. 🐢

Chapter 21

THE NEW ARRIVAL

You will still feel the pain of the journey,
but now you will feel it easing.
It will have an end.

—Anon, "The Cloud of Unknowing"

Chapter 21

Whoa! I'm a grandmother again! Darling Dana had a baby boy the night of October 9. His parents named him Evan. Following the delivery, the baby was fine—but we almost lost Dana. There were a lot of complications. It was a difficult delivery, and we all worried that Dana and the baby might not make it through. Kevin said, "I never imagined I might lose my wife."

Days later, Leslie phoned to say, "I was out when the word came about the baby, but, when I returned, I found a note with a blue pin. I'm happy she has a boy, but I don't know what I would do without my Dana. Last night, I got my first night's sleep."

On Dana's thirty-first birthday, I phoned St. Vincent's Hospital in Santa Fe to wish her well. Kevin answered the phone and told me, "Dana is having a sitz bath. We are looking forward to going home today, and I'll have her phone you from there."

"How are you doing Kevin? How does it feel to have a son?" I asked.

"It feels wonderful," Kevin replied. "I'm sitting here, holding the baby." After a couple of questions, I found out that the baby's hair was reddish with blonde highlights, which made the hair look like a halo of curls around his head. The eyes were not revealing any particular color as yet.

So, at fifty-five, I was a grandmother for the second time and wishing I were well and that my husband were alive to be part of the experience. When I phoned my mother to share my joy, she barely responded and never even asked how her granddaughter was faring.

Gerald picked Jennie up at the airport and brought her home for the weekend. She looked very pretty, very happy, as the two of them left immediately for a party.

The following day, Jennie and I talked to Dana about the baby, who was now nursing.

"How are the cats?" Jennie asked Dana.

"Esme and Darwin don't seem to feel displaced, but they might not like it when Evan gets a little older and starts running around and pulling their tails," she said.

Jennie would fly into a tirade over things like her bank account and dental work. "I don't want a checking account anymore," she replied when I asked her why she could not make her allowance cover her expenses. "I just want cash to pay for taxis, stuff for school, school donations. I'm always overdrawn, and I try so hard to keep the balance up on my account. I just can't handle it anymore." Then, when I inquired about her dental problems, she went off again: "I've got this huge cavity, and it needs bonding, but I can't handle it right now," she complained.

The very next morning, she popped her head into my room with a big smile on her face and said, "Hi, Grandma."

Later on the same day, she brought me a chocolate bar. We talked about Christmas and the coming Parents' Weekend and about my future. "Well," she said, "Christmas is depressing. Everything has changed, so we have to accept it. Going to New Mexico would be nice," she suggested.

"Morgan and Katy are coming for Parents' Weekend, Jennie," I said.

"I don't care, just as long as somebody comes," she replied.

Then I told her it would probably take years to get my braces.

"Well, at least it's progress," she replied, somewhat indifferent.

She wasn't interested in my life anymore. Her own life was now more important to her. As for me, I was relieved that she was accepting things the way they were, instead of dwelling on how they could have been.

When I expressed to Larry my more relaxed attitude toward therapy, he informed me about what I could expect: another year of walking with assistance, followed by braces and crutches. "You'll tire easily. Once we get past this part, the big muscles should return very fast."

"I'll be sixty by then. Besides, the neurologist is telling me that I'll never walk again, so which is it? Maybe I should just stay in the chair and forget it. My children have adjusted, so perhaps I should do the same."

"You'll still have a lot of wonderful years if you keep trying. But, if it doesn't get better, you won't see your sixties, seventies, or eighties. The body will just give out very rapidly."

I felt I was getting mixed messages from Larry. Larry's words reinforced my feelings that I really didn't want to live my life just waiting to walk again. The ability to walk was no longer important to me. My whole life was being taken up by therapy; I was sick and tired of the whole process. There were a lot of things more satisfying to me that I wanted to do. I preferred now to focus my energy on painting, writing, and contemplation.

"I have turned a big corner," I told Sister Wilfrid when she brought me Communion. "If the miracle you've been praying for happens—the miracle of walking again—I'll know it happened through your intercession. My legs are still useless after five years of enormous effort, so I'm making plans for a different life. I'm so happy, Sister! I consider the change in my attitude a gift from God. A journey, a new place to live suddenly seems possible. Pray with me, and together we'll thank Jesus for all He has done to get me though this very difficult time."

Sister and I recited the Our Father and made a prayer of Thanksgiving.

"I know I haven't been the easiest person to pray for," I admitted.

"No, you haven't," she said with a laugh. "You have a very unusual relationship with God."

"You mean because I talk to Him rather casually as if He were my next-door neighbor?" I asked. "Surely, Sister, the people in your religious community all talk to God like that, don't they?"

"No, I don't really think so. Your connection with God and the closeness you share with Him is rare," Sister explained.

One October day, Jerry, the artist who had done our family portrait, came around with the painting of Bill and Jennie that he had completed long before Bill's death. It was an excellent likeness of Bill.

When Charles came by, he told me that someone had recently called him "Chaz." He looked at the painting and began to cry. "Nobody called me Chaz, except Bill," he said.

After Jerry and Charles departed, an insurance man dropped by. "Are you related to Bill Hees?" he asked.

"I'm Bill's widow," I replied.

"Didn't you and Bill live off of Orange Grove? I visited there once," he said.

"Of course, I remember you now," I answered.

"Bill and I went to Catalina Island School together, he was such a—" but his voice broke. He couldn't finish the sentence. After a moment, we got down to the business at hand.

As he was leaving, he said, "I think you are doing very well."

"Thank you."

"Are you an artist?" he asked, looking at a drawing on my easel.

"Yes, I thought I could continue with my art, but I don't paint anymore. It's too difficult because of the pain in my spine, and, aside from that, my desire to paint just left me.

"Well, it's excellent," he said about the drawing. Then he looked at me with great tenderness, bent over, kissed me on the cheek, and left.

That day ended, as they all do. When evening had come, I felt a sense of relief and peace. And, it hadn't been painful for me to think about Bill.

Jennie, now almost seventeen, surprised me with a late-night phone call. Jennie was back at school following her weekend at home. I listened—at 10:30 P.M.—to a crying and barely coherent girl who was trying to tell me that nothing in life was hopeful or good, including herself. The biggest blow came when she told me she had thought about suicide. "I don't think I could do it though," she explained. I made her promise to see her psychologist without delay and to talk to Sister Catherine. Jennie managed to calm down by half past midnight—when we said our goodnight.

My poor little girl. She had tried so hard to manage and to move on, but, like me, at times it was still all too much. Her best friend had come to Jennie's school for a visit. When her friend left, Jennie's mood plummeted. At this adolescent stage, every emotion was magnified. "I hate these mood swings. I'm so up one moment and down the next. I want to be somewhere in between," explained the darling of my heart.

When Morgan came to see me, I told him about my conversation with his little sister. His face turned gray. "I've just written her a letter. I always knew there was something going on underneath that cool exterior," he remarked.

"It isn't a cool exterior, she is only a very young girl having to deal with growing up and trying to find her way out of this mess," I corrected him.

Damian once told me that I enjoyed being unhappy. If that person ever existed, I was letting go of her now. During therapy, I felt like dancing. Whenever I heard music, I would remember the sensation in my legs and body as I used to move across the dance floor, either alone or in someone's embrace.

Once again, I entertained the idea of driving my own car. During rehab, I had learned how to drive a car with hand controls. I told Morgan I might give it some serious thought.

"I can't believe it!" he cried in excitement. "I was just imagining you doing that very thing."

I told him I was scared.

"Sure you are. It's like being sixteen and starting all over again."

"Why don't you do that?!" Irma encouraged me.

Morgan recalled a woman in Berkeley who drove a car that way. "At the time, I remember thinking what a great person she must be."

(Michael, while visiting Santa Fe, had watched a woman get out of a wheelchair and into her car. He suggested that it would be wonderful if I could do that too.)

Morgan and I talked about my fears. "All your children know that you are afraid to be out there, Mom, but the time has come to stop just looking out the window as a passenger." As he talked, I became more excited. "It might speed up your healing process and put some joy into your life. With a positive frame of mind, you'll get faster results. I can imagine you at the beach, driving to Palomar and all the places that you love, going out to do some sketching, or going to school. It would be so good for you."

I replied that I would need some time to think about it. "I might try for spring," I said.

"That's a good idea, because I'll have more time then. I can just see you coming over to visit Katy and me."

"Well, I can honk, but I can't manage the steps of your apartment."

"We won't always be in an apartment," he said firmly.

As November of 1986 came to a close, Morgan celebrated another birthday. He came to my house, and I gave him a present—a knife. He sat on my bed showing me how to open and close it. It was tricky; I couldn't master it. Odd that I should give him a knife when, only a few years ago, I had given him his father's bone-handled knife after I decided not to kill myself.

Irma came to my room after Morgan left. She was crying. "He massaged my back when he saw I was working. He is a beautiful person," she said.

"Irma I have a wonderful son," I commented as she continued to cry.

Jennie came home for Thanksgiving smiling and shining. When she walked into the living room with Gerald, the music was a mood setter, jazzy and upbeat. I hugged them both, and then they immediately left for yet another concert with some of Jennie's friends.

On her first morning home, Jennie woke up to a houseful of activity. Morgan and Katy, along with Katy's sister, were working on a photography project. Folk Art was the theme of Katy's Art Center assignment. Morgan popped into my room holding in one hand a carved wooden mask over his face and, in the other, a carved wooden snake. For several hours, I could hear laughter as they collaborated with each other, assembling different artistic arrangements of these artifacts that they would later photograph.

Later that morning, Jennie talked about how happy she was to have everyone at the house. "Sometimes I feel that we have all become so separated," she said.

My comment was, "I feel the same, but we are only separated geographically, not in our hearts." Then I told her, "I hope you still want to come to my room, snuggle beside me, and watch TV."

"Well, that would still be nice to do sometime," she agreed.

Maybe those days were behind us.

The baby was coming to visit, so I had to move some of my husband's possessions out of the way. Stored in the guestroom closet were the telescope that once stood on the terrace at St. Lo, the viewer he had used to sort his slides and photographs, and the movie projector he never could master. It was all too painful to see them in that setting.

Jennie and Gerald were out visiting friends. Sitting in the shower, I felt free to release some tears. Then, after attending to a bedsore and dressing, I sat on the patio to read Edward Weston's "Daybooks."

Remembering how once upon a time they had enchanted me—I felt I could have led a life like the author's—when Bill died, I entertained the idea of roaming from place to place painting and writing. However, I had a little girl to raise, and fate had placed its awful hand on me.

As the shadows fell, I went inside to write and to keep writing as a way to stem the tears that come with loss and regret. Then, I heard an absolutely beautiful track on the jazz station. Toto, our cat, jumped up on the desk to purr and listen with me. It was *Some Other Time*, sung by Tony Bennett, with Bill Evans on piano. "There's so much more to do" said the lyrics. The song addressed "words unspoken," "things to do," and "soon we'll part," but "Oh, we'll catch up some other time." *Of course, we never do*, I thought.

"Jesus, please look at your servant, Berta. I am alone on this earth," I prayed aloud.

The weather was clear, blue and sunny, but hot—too hot—as Morgan and I waited outside the patio door for Kevin, Dana, and baby Evan to arrive. We couldn't keep the smiles off our faces in anticipation of the visit. Finally, the car pulled up, and we could see baby Evan inside. Beautiful red-gold curls covered that little head, and clear blue eyes shone out from his alabaster white skin. He had his father's Irish genes, and he reminded me of those paintings of cherubs romping around in the clouds. He looked like he could have fallen off just such a cloud into our arms.

We sat on the patio soaking up the sun and watching Dana nurse her baby. She looked a little tired, and the luster that a woman has before a baby is born was gone from her face. I enjoyed watching Dana loving her baby, watching Morgan loving him, watching Kevin take the baby off his mother's hands when he began to fuss.

Bill arrived, and we all moved into the kitchen to prepare and eat hamburgers. We could all feel the circle of love Evan had created. Later, Sister Wilfrid would say to me, "Seeing the miracle of Evan and his power of persuading hearts to gentleness must be such a delight."

Morgan couldn't stay away. He drove across the freeway from Los Angeles on his lunch hour to sit with us on the patio. When Leslie and Michael showed up, we all moved to the front lawn to play with Evan while he lay on a blanket. I watched from my chair until they all set off for a walk in the arroyo with the baby. Gerald was among the group. When Leslie met him, she winked at me and said, "He's cute."

Thanksgiving dinner made it to the table, but not without a comment from Michael: "See Leslie, it doesn't have to be a big deal. Everyone's enjoying it because it's relaxed and informal. None of this having-to-make-everything-perfect, okay?" Uh-oh! I was sorry I had passed that one on to my daughter. Through therapy, I recognized what perfectionism could do, and I wished I had tossed that one out long, long, ago.

After eating Katy's exceptional apple pie, Bill got the old projector going. We laughed at the long forgotten images that flickered across the screen, accompanied by the occasional irreverent jest.

The morning that the family packed up to leave, Dana tucked the little baby in my bed, and, with his head on my shoulder, the two of us went to sleep.

Before Jennie returned to school, we had one last talk about her relationship with Gerald.

"We are apart so much of the time," Jennie explained. "Try to understand that is why we spend so much time together when I'm home."

"Are you having sex with him?" I asked.

"What do you mean?" she asked after a moment's hesitation.

"Are you having sexual intercourse with him?" I persisted.

"No."

"Please don't."

"I'll make up my mind about that; it is my decision."

I promised myself not to ask any more questions and to keep my sorrow close to my heart like Mother Mary.

~~~

The first week of December, I went on a spiritual retreat. Father Jack was in charge. He spoke about his own experience with physical suffering.

Pain, loneliness, fear, anxiety, the indignities endured during daily physical care—he had lived through all of it. His deepest sorrow had been the loss of independence. Mine had been the loss of privacy that comes with dependency; I understood all the other aspects of his suffering too, but, for me, that was at the forefront.

I was delighted by the fact that he took us through an exercise I had already done on my own for some time now: the inhalation and exhalation of the Holy Spirit.

"Be quiet, be aware, and think only of God as you inhale and exhale. This enables you to breathe out all the garbage that intrudes on your day," explained Father Jack. "God becomes more tangible to us as we inhale and exhale. He always dwells within us."

"I am with you coming in and going out," were the words that came to my mind—words that Jesus said to his Apostles.

Father Jack gave me some advice at the end of the retreat: "Stay out of His way instead of trying to impose your own will. When you are fearful, anxious, depressed, and crying, his peace cannot reach you. Let go and let God. Just be," were Father's instructions. His words were the sign I had been waiting for. I had been praying for a new direction, a clearer path, the road toward health and healing. So, I embarked on a new life that I hoped was closer to God by praying with patience for the courage I needed to welcome life in any form that was pleasing to Him.

~~~

I'm sure I woke up the dorm when I phoned Jennie on her seventeenth birthday. Pleasant and cheerful, she told me about her plans for the day.

"I have drum practice today, and tonight the school will entertain the students with something special for Christmas. Last year, we had mimes, but I don't know what we have this year."

After our short discussion about life at school, I said, "Happy birthday, darling. I love you."

"I love you too, Mom."

All that day, I remembered Jennie. I would have liked to share my reminiscences about Jennie with her father. Putting my thoughts in writing on the word processor relieved me of the frustration of not being able to directly communicate with Jennie's father.

Then came a phone call from Sister Wilfrid.

"I was in the chapel this morning, meditating on your unusual relationship with God, with Jesus. It really is something that few people have, Berta," said Sister.

How many times had she told me about a relationship that was still not clear to me? Again, I lost the opportunity to ask her what she meant.

After speaking with Sister, I phoned Leslie.

"Jennie is seventeen today. I just had to talk to a family member," I explained to Leslie. Leslie was so helpful. I shared with her all the memories I would have shared with Bill to honor Jennie's seventeenth birthday.

~~~

After Christmas, Irma, Jennie, and I flew to Santa Fe. Dana came to the hotel where I was staying and brought me homemade soups set on a tray with colorful placemats and napkins. They were like small works of art. Auntie Jennie was charmed by her new nephew, Evan. And Irma enjoyed walking around the plaza while Jennie and I went to a Georgia O'Keefe exhibit with Dana. The exhibit, consisting of O'Keefe's early work, was somewhat disappointing to us and to other museum-goers, as evidenced by their remarks.

One day, we visited the San Ildefonso Pueblo. The Buffalo Dancers came out and prayed for whatever they were in need of at that moment. Meanwhile, Jennie was crawling around with scruffy-looking dogs, kissing and hugging them all in turn.

On another day, we went to Pecos National Monument and to Puyo, where we ate sandwiches that Jennie had prepared. While the children hiked, I contemplated the Sangre de Cristo mountains in the distance and talked to God. He assured me I would be well as soon as I overcame my fear of the future. Watching Dana, the baby on her back, hiking down a trail with Jennie, brought a few tears, because I could not accompany them. We spent New Year's Eve quietly with my daughter's family in her home, the peace broken only by a frosty phone call from my mother and Irma's unexpected entrance. Irma was feeling lonely.

The day before we were supposed to leave Santa Fe, I ran out of the medication that helped my muscles to relax. When my blood sugar dropped, I had an anxiety attack. Irma and I had a terrible night. I discovered, as I lay awake, that Irma had sleep apnea. In those moments when she did drop off, she stopped breathing. Fear took over as I waited for her to start breathing again. Then, I had to wake her up over and over again because my emotional state was affecting my bladder.

Kevin and Dana rushed us to the airport the following day so that we could catch an earlier flight. Irma, Jennie, and I boarded a plane that was jammed with passengers and with flight attendants stressed out by too many flights. And I was wearing my last diaper, which was sodden. Irma leaned over and whispered in my ear, "You smell." *Oh dear*, I thought, reaching across the aisle to take Jennie's hand for comfort and reassurance. Her touch, her happy grin gave me courage.

When I got home, I felt regret over the disturbance I had caused a family with a new baby. If I traveled again, I would be better prepared. Nevertheless, the journey had made me stronger; ultimately, I met most of the challenges.

Back at school, Jennie phoned to say, "Mom, it was the best Christmas since—"

"Since your father died," I said, ending the sentence for her. That phone call alone made the trip worthwhile, in spite of all the discomfort I had to endure. Nevertheless, the change of scenery did me good and made me feel that I should consider traveling more often.

Before January ended, I was advised to sell my lot at St. Lo. But, my answer was an emphatic "No!" I still thought it might be a place to call home for Jennie and me once she graduated from school.

Just three weeks after my journey, Dana came with my grandson for a visit. Feeling confined and tired as a first-time mother, she wanted me to be near her son. I had the sweetest time talking to Dana in the morning while the baby—fed and content—rocked in his swing. I loved seeing all the baby paraphernalia around the house and hearing everyone getting up in the morning, Irma crooning to the baby, and the sounds Evan made now that he had found his voice.

We went to Aunt Alice's for lunch, where we got a chance to show off Evan. I noticed Charles's reaction to the O.P. As he took over attending to the baby, Alice whispered to me, "I know you miss Bill now that you have a grandson. I think of you all the time."

While we ate, we could hear the musicians rehearsing for the Super Bowl in the Rose Bowl below. The Goodyear blimp was flying overhead.

After the little family departed, I attended a Frida Kahlo exhibit at Plaza de Raza. The gallery was small, as was the exhibit. There was a film about her life that I viewed before looking at her work. I could relate to the artist's pain, suffering, and death. During my sleepless night in New Mexico, I had thought about my own eventual death. *Am I going to live much longer?* I wondered.

I discussed my preoccupation with death with Sister Wilfrid. "Maybe it means you have died to the old life, and the new one is beginning," she commented. "The change in attitude of your children is miraculous." A close friend, Mary, had said the very same thing about my children on the very same day.

It must have been "the beginning of the new beginning"—so reads the quote of Sir Winston Churchill. Cut from a magazine the day I became paralyzed, it had been tucked in my wallet all those years. I pulled the quote out of my wallet and reread it. Then, I said to God, "All right, where do I begin my new life? And how?"

Chapter 22

THE NEW BEGINNING

This is not the end.
It is not even the beginning
of the end. But it is, perhaps,
the end of the beginning.

—Sir Winston Churchill

Chapter 22

"This is your time, Berta," said Larry when I walked all by myself with my legs braced and supporting myself with crutches. My legs felt like they each weighed a ton. Graceful it was not! "We'll work on the grace later," he said when I complained about how difficult it was—so unwieldy, so unlike me.

God, help me to keep up my spirits, I thought.

When my visits with my children came to an end, I couldn't help but cry. However, now the children's attitudes had changed. Not one of them said, "Stop, Mom, I can't handle this," like they used to. My children were becoming more compassionate, more understanding, more selfless.

A simple drive with my friend Jean brought about even more changes. Community work, meetings, and chairing fundraisers no longer interested me. As we drove along, Jean talked about her involvement with community work, and it bored me to tears. I felt I had already done my duty for the community.

As we passed two houses, she waved at a nice-looking lady standing in her manicured garden and said to me, "I watched her turn an ordinary house into a charming one." The remark was almost the same when we drove by the second house.

"I'm sorry, but I just can't relate to that sort of life anymore—husbands, and gardens, and an existence that no longer has any meaning for me," I said.

When I got home, I thought, *Just what the hell is relevant to me anymore?*

I breathed in the Holy Spirit and then exhaled. Immediately after, I reached for the phone and called Marge—who had recently lost her husband and son in a plane crash. She wasn't home. One of her younger sons—a former classmate of one of my own sons—answered the phone. I offered my condolences to each member of the family.

Soon after, my phone rang. It was Leslie. "You've been through a lot too, Mom," Leslie sympathized when I mentioned Marge's losses. The topic of our conversation then turned to the property at St. Lo. "Well, I just never wanted to interfere with your decision about whether or not to sell the property at St. Lo. Michael and I have discussed the property along with the pros and cons of living closer to you," Leslie declared.

"Oh, please interfere! I need help with these decisions. For instance, I'm thinking of putting in a hot tub," I exclaimed.

"Go ahead," she replied. "While you're at it, put in an electric lift."

The hot tub was installed. In the evenings, I floated among the bubbles, feeling like a weightless astronaut in outer space. Since my muscles weren't functioning properly, I couldn't stay anchored. Floating in the Jacuzzi and enjoying a certain sense of freedom under the evening sky, I admired my magnificent wisteria vine. And my thoughts turned to Leslie. The loving person I knew Leslie to be had re-emerged. Her words—"Mom, you've been through a lot too"—etched themselves on my heart. I was grateful for the fact that she acknowledged my struggles over the past several years.

~~~

"You look so healthy. You didn't look very healthy for quite some time" were the encouraging words I now heard from my mother, but they didn't keep me out of the emergency room of the local hospital. I had a bladder infection, bedsores, and pain—all of which brought on an anxiety attack.

While I was being treated for my bedsores in the emergency room, I met a neurologist who would soon look after me. Dr. Howard was immediately interested in my case, so I promised to make an appointment with her.

The convenient location of the hospital was at once attractive to me.

At the doctor's recommendation, I had an MRI exam. I phoned Sister Wilfrid and asked her to pray for me. Then, I called my mother and uncle and asked them to look after my home during the test. With my predisposition to claustrophobia, it was difficult for me to imagine myself inside a tube. Once I was inside, I was told to keep my limbs away from the sides of the interior wall of the tube. I worried that my legs would spasm off the center support.

After being taken out of the machine, I felt as if I were leaving a place of perfect peace. The technician asked, as he was removing me from the scanner, "Have you been in an accident?"

"No," I replied. I had long since forgotten the accident on the ski lift in the winter of 1980.

Jennie, who had asked if she could come along, was sitting in the waiting room next to Emma, the friend who had brought us to the clinic.

"Well that didn't take long," I said, after the nurse brought me out to the waiting room.

"I'm late for a wedding," said Emma. Her remark surprised me because I thought I had been in the MRI scanner for only an hour. In fact, it had been four hours. "See, Jennie did my nails for me," she said as she extended her hands for me to admire.

"What time is it?" I asked.

"It's almost five o'clock."

I was embarrassed about making Emma wait. What I thought was going to be no more than an hour had turned into four hours. I must have lost all sense of time when I was in that machine.

As we pulled into my garage, the door to the kitchen opened, and there stood my mother.

"Uh-oh, are you ready for this?" said Emma when she saw my mother's face, whose mouth was tense and grim.

My mother pursued me down the hall asking to be taken out for dinner.

"Please, please leave me alone. Can't you see it's been an ordeal?" I cried. I went to bed, and she left with my uncle.

The ordeal was not the examination—I felt extremely peaceful during the MRI scan—it was coming home to an angry mother who demanded some sort of compensation for the daylong period of house-sitting. And, I regretted the delay I had imposed on my friend, who was gracious to the end. I was sad because I was beginning to think that my mother and I had finally reached a promising level in our relationship.

"Your mother suffers from an acute case of narcissism," Sigrid told me when we began therapy again together. "You'll never have a chance at a loving relationship with this woman." It took me a very long time to understand fully what that meant and how my life was affected by my mother's influence. Now the most difficult part of my relationship with her began for me—forgiveness.

When Dr. Howard received the results of my exam, she told me, "There is a narrowing of the spine at about T4 or T5, and that is why your legs don't work. There are some disc problems causing the pain. No tumors." Then she asked, "Have you ever been in an accident?"

"No," I answered. "Is it M.S.?"

"I don't think so," she replied firmly, emphasizing each word.

In a polite, tiny voice, I raised a question: "Does that mean an operation is possible?"

"I think so, but let me get a second opinion on that. In the meantime, I suggest you swim."

After returning home from Dr. Howard's office, I phoned a former therapist who was in charge of swimming at the local athletic club. He said he would be glad to help me, but, he said, "You'll have to become a member of the club. Get a prescription from Dr. Howard—that will speed things up." So I called the doctor's office to ask for a prescription.

"Dr. Howard doesn't give prescriptions for joining clubs," Dr. Howard's receptionist said. I asked her to repeat what she said.

Feeling embarrassed, I said, "But Dr. Howard said I must swim, and a therapist in charge of swimming works there. My request has nothing to do with joining a club. It is a matter of having access to a pool equipped for the disabled and with professional help at hand."

"Dr. Howard does not give prescriptions for joining clubs," the receptionist reiterated.

"Thank you," I said, and I hung up.

"Irma, Irma, come here," I hollered from the bedroom.

"I'm coming."

When she came to my room, I told her with some excitement that surgery was a possible option.

Irma told me that surgery was nothing to worry about. She had spinal surgery after her accident to correct the damage and explained how she was able to walk again. She showed me the scars on her body. There was the Caesarean scar, the one from a tumor removal, another from a pin in her hipbone, as well as quite an assortment of scars from bedsores and the spinal operation.

"The hospital is nothing," she tried to reassure me. Then came a full description of what I could expect: "Bedpans, catheters, more bedsores, lots of patience . . ."

Because of all the trials Irma had to endure over the years, she lunged at life like a lioness. That is how she left a husband, a good job, and even her children to come to the U.S.

On Holy Thursday, I visited Dr. Howard, who told me there would be no surgery—my spine had deteriorated to the point where nothing could be done. After his comment, I realized that I wouldn't be resurrected this Easter.

"I know from looking at your X-rays that the pain must be devastating." She suggested again that I swim, keep up my physical therapy, and drive a car.

Dr. Howard was the second neurologist to suggest that I drive a car. Her recommendation seemed absurd to me: my muscles went into spasm, my trunk muscles were not functioning, and the pain medication I was on made me drowsy. If I had to make a sudden stop, a seat belt would offer little or no protection. Neurologists always think that driving a car is a cure-all for something they cannot cure. They all seem to make that kind of suggestion when they run out of options.

Driving a car was actually something I did not miss. Certainly, physical therapy would continue to be part of my life, and I would swim when I could find someone who could lift me in and out of a pool. Hiring someone to do the job would be costly. I tried it once, but my overhead had already pushed my finances to the limit. So, I exercised in my Jacuzzi as much as I could.

Sister Wilfrid did not accept any part of the doctor's diagnosis. But, I knew what her motive was for holding on to her optimism. Mother Cornelia Connelly—the founder of Sister's Catholic order—was up for beatification. If Mother Connelly was to be moved on to sainthood, the church had to prove that she had performed a miracle. Sister had prayed that I would be that miracle. "You'll be standing in St. Peter's Square," Sister often said to me. Of course, if I were to accomplish such a thing, it would serve as living proof of Mother Connelly's saintliness.

I was tired of wavering back and forth emotionally for six years. I was ready to accept what had happened to me. Being a paraplegic was not my entire identity. Music, books, art, and travel were the things that sustained me. My spiritual life was continuing to blossom. And, I had a new grandchild!

The first thing I did when I got home was uncork a bottle of champagne, which I drank from the wooden cups Irma had brought me from Nicaragua. She shared in my celebration. "Free at last!" I declared. Together we became a trifle tipsy.

~~~

Sister Wilfrid was ill. She could not bring me Communion. Her voice was weak and she was having to look at the possibility of being hospitalized, so we talked on the phone.

"I want to walk with you, Sister, into that Mass of Thanksgiving we had planned so long ago. I know you are offering up your suffering for me and for all the people too numerous to mention that have asked for your prayers over time. Whatever happens to you, I will accept that Jesus sees the entire picture of your life and mine, and I trust that He knows best. If a true miracle happens in my life, it will be his gift to you."

Damian came to say goodbye before he left for the Far East. "You've cut your hair, but you haven't changed," commented Damian.

"You are losing your hair as well, but *you* haven't changed either," I pointed out. I began to sing the Beatles song, *When I'm Sixty-four*. When I got to the part about "losing your hair," Damian interrupted me.

"When you are sixty-five, you can build a house at St. Lo. I'll build mine next door," he grinned mischievously. But then, after a moment's pause, he reflected. "But seriously, Berta, I'd really like to settle down and get married someday."

He took my hand and kissed it, saying "I'll come and see you when I return." We embraced and said our goodbyes.

After Damian left, I prayed. "Please, Jesus, keep him from harm on the long and distant journey."

~~~

I turned my attention to writing a book. I wrote down "Clay Pot," or "The Clay Pot" as a possible title for my book. During the retreat I took just a short while ago, Father Jack's final sermon before he died was about spiritual treasures in clay pots. He had asked the group to pray for him "because I feel that there are many cracks in this clay pot."

I searched for a poem I wrote in 1980—the year Damian left St. Lo. It was a kind of prayer for spiritual direction:

Here I am, a small bit of clay only You can shape and mold.

Now, as I read it, it sounded more like a prayer, a prayer that was already answered. The shaping and molding began with Bill's death.

A few days later, in a state of contentment, I wrote to Leslie who was not feeling so content after a recent visit with her siblings:

Darling Leslie,

Just received your postcard. Jennie told me you were crying when you phoned her. I completely understand how difficult it is to part from your brothers and sister-in-law with your daughter leaving at the same time. We are a family with extremely strong ties and much love for each other. I know the best work I ever did with your father was to raise five sensitive and caring children.

Have I thanked you for all the gifts you bring and send with love? They are all cherished—or eaten, e.g., the popcorn and chocolates, with the love they bear. If I have not written a note for each gift, I thank you now for all your thoughtfulness.

Jennie showed me the pictures that were taken on her brief trip to Sun Valley. You all look so happy! I love the pictures of my granddaughter with her saxophone.

Jennie has just completed her U.S. history course. And, she really enjoyed summer school. She made new friends, and the teacher made the class very interesting. I think it was fun for her to study at a public high school. She got herself going each morning, studied hard at home and at the library. When I see her being so happy, I realize that she has escaped without permanent damage from the events of the last seven years. Looking back on the early days, months, years that have been so horrible, thinking about how young she was, and trying to put myself in her shoes, it is a miracle that she survived. She is very straightforward with me, and that makes me happy too. When we have a difference of opinion, I understand how necessary it is for us to discuss the situation right away until something is worked out.

Love, Mom

A month later, Leslie was filled with anxiety about the possibility of having cancer. She had undergone treatment for melanoma. She fretted about her husband, her daughter, but I was able to say with assurance, "Put your cares in God's hands," and she knew I meant it, because I had been there a thousand times.

She found some consolation in her faith. Soon after, she sent me a letter letting me know that the doctor had pronounced her cancer-free.

In reply, I wrote:

You may be baptized Catholic, but you can still personalize your faith. Be a maverick, open the doors — new doors — to discover what faith means to you. I've often felt myself to be an independent Catholic, and I believe that is why I find Thomas Merton so attractive. Many times I have told Sister Wilfrid that I have my own brand of Catholicism, that is to say, I don't want to be part of the "Catholic Mafia," because there is something numbing about someone else thinking they have a better understanding of life than I.

The family circle, though separated physically, began to grow closer again.

~~~

Irma and I took a brief and pleasant flight to the San Jose airport, where, under blue, blue skies, we were greeted by Bill.

Bill's home looked warm and inviting. I was touched by the fact that Bill had spent a great deal of time and effort fixing it up for our visit. A rented hospital bed awaited me, the windows were washed, the house vacuumed and dusted, flowers were in place. He had vacuumed and dusted the house, washed the windows, put flowers out, and had rented a hospital bed for me to sleep in.

After we went out for dinner, Bill and I talked as we settled in.

"I've invited Leslie, Dana, and Morgan to come up and stay," he said, "but they never come."

I was aware of that situation from what Leslie had told me: "Have you seen the house, Mom? He's never going to get it together." Certainly the three of them could have responded with more love and compassion. Yes, the house, the garden needed attention, but the neighborhood was very nice and reminded me of the first house my husband and I lived in—the house where Leslie and Dana were born—surrounded then, as their brother was now, by good neighbors.

Bill told me he was looking after the elderly lady next door. He drove her to her doctor's appointments, and he fixed things around her house. He rented the guesthouse on the property to a student at U.C.S.C., who was on his way to becoming a computer scientist.

We stopped talking for a moment as he introduced me to Chamita, the rabbit, Summer, the dog, and O.J., the orange cat.

"I'm terribly lonely without Serena, who, as you know, is visiting her family in Uruguay. She is the only woman who has said to me, 'Bill, you must not give so much of yourself to others. In the end, you will only be taken advantage of by everyone.' Mom, no one has ever said that to me before. I used to just give and give, and then, they would leave me, and I'd feel bewildered and empty."

He could have been describing his father. How often I had wanted to tell my husband that he was dealing with the wrong sort of people in some of his early business transactions, but then, wives of my generation were not inclined to interfere. My two sweet, humble, and naïve Bills reminded me of Melville's Billy Budd—the kind, handsome sailor who was misunderstood because of his stammer and was unjustly hung for killing his master-at-arms.

Bill would leave early for work or school, but not before he would bring me the paper. While I was checking out houses and condos for sale, Irma would bring me coffee, fruit, and toast, and then she'd start cleaning the house. When I told her not to, she would say, "I want everything to be nice for when Bill comes home."

One evening, Bill and I took Summer for a walk. I was holding Summer's leash when the dog suddenly took off, pulling me along in my wheelchair. Down the street we sped. Bill caught up with me and, grabbing the handles of my chair, said "just in case you go over the cliff, Mom." Since that creature was part husky, he must have thought he was pulling a sled.

Night had fallen, and it was dark when we reached the point overlooking the bay. The lights on the peninsula were winking across the bay. The tall smokestacks of Moss Landing were visible. With Summer romping around as he was, I thought that, with a few more tugs, I would end up in the bay. Dark thoughts on a dark, dark night. Bill took Summer's leash, and the frisky dog eventually calmed down.

Bill, Irma, and I strolled down to the village for a fish dinner. As we passed a place where Bill had once lived, he said, "That's where I was staying when I got the phone call informing me that Dad had died."

"Who called you? Was it Morgan?"

"No, it was Dana. I couldn't believe it. I still can't."

We were silent as we headed up the hill to his home.

Bill and I spent some days visiting various construction sights where he used to work: a spec house in Watsonville, a remodel in Aptos, a retaining wall he had built out of railroad ties.

On a Sunday, Irma took some time off to go exploring on her own, and Bill drove me to Nepenthe, in Big Sur, for lunch. Big Sur had not changed; Nepenthe had not changed. But I had changed. Returning to places I once visited with my husband wasn't important to me anymore.

As we ate our lunch, Bill said, "I recognize this music. We went to hear this guy play in Elkhorn, you know, Mom, when we were in Sun Valley the first Christmas after Dad died."

Neither of us could recall the musician's name, and it really didn't matter, because the present moment was enough. *Pay attention, pay attention, pay attention* (a Buddhist reminder to be in the moment).

When we got back to Santa Cruz, the traffic was heavy, and the beaches were alive with tourists and colorful umbrellas. As we eased our way into an intersection, Bill was given the finger and a loud "Fuck you!" from an elderly delinquent in a pickup truck. The back of his vehicle was plastered with bumper stickers that read "Save the Humans" (next to the picture of a whale), and "Please Don't Tell Me What Kind of Day to Have," and "If You Come Any Closer, You'll Have to Wear a Condom." Santa Cruz was full of rugged individualism.

I could love living there, so I said to my son, "Of all of my children, you would be the one I would live with—if life ever comes to that. But, I hope never to intrude—"

"Stop right there, Mom," Bill interrupted. "I don't want to hear you describe yourself as an intruder. You always have a home with me, or near me, or whatever. It would be my pleasure."

My first desire was to remain self-reliant. Nevertheless, it was nice to know I was welcome somewhere.

Irma had spent her day shopping in Capitola-by-the-Sea and stretching out on the beach. After she returned home, I asked, "How was your day?"

"There are not very many Latinos in Capitola," she murmured, not looking away from the television. "Please, Mrs. Hees," cried Irma, signaling me not to interrupt the program she was watching. "They are celebrating the Feast of the Immaculate Conception in San Francisco. There are all these Nicaraguans singing in a park." She fell to her knees and began to clap her hands and sing along. Tears fell down her cheeks. Knowing how lonely she must have felt, tears started to fall down my cheeks as well. Loneliness was a feeling we had in common.

It was time for a day of rest. I picked up the book I had brought with me—*Journal of a Solitude*, by May Sarton. In it, she writes about passionate love in middle age. Her view prompted me to include a story of my own experience in the outline of my book. Although May Sarton was a lesbian, the feelings she expressed were not in any way different from those of a heterosexual.

Getting down a few lines for my book, I began to relive the terrible despair I felt over my earliest trials. My feelings started to overwhelm me. I began to cry, but then held back my tears when a voice in my head said, "Stop!"

~~~

"I've been through some terrible girls," Bill announced one evening. "Terrible in the sense that they were so dependent that I would end up waiting on them hand and foot. Maybe one day, I'll find the right one." Bill was barbequing while we talked. I sat close by, enjoying the evening air. Bill continued: "I went to the Mayfield reunion to see my friends, but they still questioned me about how I could leave my mother when she was ill. I was furious. As we all know, not one member of the family was settled in life, and Dad's death and your illness was overwhelming for all of us. We all went crazy." I nodded in agreement.

"You know your father once told me that he had planned never to marry," I told him.

"I've thought about remaining single too. I enjoyed talking to Marion at the Mayfield reunion. You know, she gets prettier as she gets older. We liked each other when we were in school together, and we still like each other now, but she lives in Paris. I did ask her about the French men, and she said that they're too macho for her."

"Bill," I said, "if Serena doesn't work out, I'll buy you a ticket to Paris."

"Ha! C'mon, Mom," he laughed.

People in Santa Cruz were very fond of Bill—the couple that lived next door, for example. The woman was from Los Angeles—her father was a lawyer in that city—and her husband was a baker with a drinking problem. They were in the habit of talking with Bill about their marital problems. And then there was the Jewish lady at the market who kept trying to find a wife for Bill. She'd say, "Oh, Bill, listen, have I got a girl for you!"

Bill told me he was out in the community managing the local softball team and playing golf and horseshoes. "Oh, my God! My father—your grandfather—played horseshoes long ago," I cried in astonishment. "I didn't think anyone did that anymore. My Dad would have loved to share that with you," I told Bill.

"I'm glad to know that, Mom," he commented.

"What else do you do?" I asked Bill.

"I go sailing with a friend or fish for salmon in season," he replied. My son had recreated in this place something similar to the special years he spent at the Catalina Island School for Boys.

It was impossible for me not to wish with all my heart that Bill's father could have lived long enough to share the life his son had carved out for himself in this place. Imagining the two of them smiling and talking as they picked through debris on construction sites was not difficult for me to do. Somehow, Bill had created the kind of understated life his father would have loved. What came out of these last few years could have been the reward for all of the love my husband had for his son. It was a knife in my heart not to see the father and his adult son together.

Setting aside pen and paper on one of my resting days, I watched on TV a dramatized version of F. Scott Fitzgerald's *The Last of the Belles*. At the end of the film, the husband says to the wife, "That's the one thing about being a writer: I guess if you write the story often enough, one day it may have a happy ending."

As for me, I was no longer searching for happy endings. True, life is made up of endings: the end of childhood, the end of career or marriage, the end of youth, the end of health, and, finally, the end of life. So, is death the only beginning that has no end?

~~~

Now it was that time again—time to go home. While Irma packed our things, Bill and I took a drive together. I found the U.C.S.C. campus to be very pretty, but the brush was so dry. Along the way, we passed Dana's former dorm, but no sense of nostalgia surfaced in me.

Then, we headed up the Santa Cruz Mountains toward Bonny Doon. Bill knew the area well from his early years at the university and from the eleven years he lived in Santa Cruz. As he pointed out some of the job sites where he had worked, he shared some of the details about the men he had worked with and about the girls he knew back then. He concluded by saying, "I left behind all those men and women behind because I wanted to get on with my life."

I think he was referring to sowing his wild oats.

As we drove on, he pointed out the places where he liked to sit, trails he had hiked, and paths where he had ridden his bicycle. "I worked on that ranch," he said, pointing to a grove of apple trees. "They grow the apples that go into the juice you are drinking," he told me as he turned his head toward the bottle in my hand.

On the way down the mountain, I said, "It's strange how little I knew about your life, Bill. Except for the time your father and I came to visit you when you were starting out at the university, we only saw you on those occasions when you came to St. Lo. I realize we were moving to the beach and Jennie was starting first grade and all, but, still, I wish we would have taken the time to come and visit you."

"Well, you're here now, Mom," he pointed out.

On the way home, we drove past the Santa Cruz boardwalk. All that summer activity—kids with surfboards, young families hustling children off the beach as the afternoon comes to an end, the usual stores with T-shirts, second-rate and third-rate motels, garish signs painted on store-front windows, the roller coaster in the distance—no longer appealed to me.

Another time, another place, another life—not suited to me now; no regrets about losing the sense of excitement I felt when I watched my children leave for boarding school and, eventually, college. Well, Jennie still had to finish her education. However, when the time came, it was more like: "Thank God, Jennie, we made it!"

Chapter 23

LAUDATE SUNDAY

Faith lifts the suffering save
on one side,
Hope supports it on the other.

—St. Elizabeth Seton

Chapter 23

After a wonderful visit with Bill in Santa Cruz, it was time for me to go back to Pasadena. I phoned Jennie from Santa Cruz to tell her that Irma and I were on our way home. She sounded a little forlorn. After I returned home, I suggested we go to St. Lo for a couple of days to lift her spirits. It was a very pleasant trip, and I came to the realization that I wouldn't build a home there again on the land I still owned. Was it possible that my new home would be in Santa Cruz?

During our brief visit to St. Lo, I noticed a change in Jennie. Her compassionate nature was refined by the losses that she had to endure in her youth. Jennie had finally found her footing: she made First Honors. And, she was following her compassionate nature by going to Gateway, a center for retarded adults, on Tuesday afternoons to help them read and to read to them. She was also looking forward to spending two weeks this spring in Mazatlán, where she would work with children in an orphanage.

Jennie left for Monterey. She phoned me after settling in for her senior year.

"I've been assigned to the junior dorm until November. I was really upset about it, Mom," Jennie admitted. "But, I went to Mass to vent my anger on God, and I'm okay now. Besides, the campus gardens are beautiful—so many flowers! Balloons are everywhere too. The freshmen arrive tomorrow." I prayed that her senior year would be successful and fulfilling for her. She deserved it.

Irma took off for her vacation after we came home from Santa Cruz. A succession of caregivers took her place. One by one, they came to tell me, "Mrs. Hees, there is the most beautiful cross in the sky outside my bathroom window. It is this huge," they said, stretching their arms out wide to indicate the size of the apparition. Their faces expressed disbelief and excitement at the same time. Some seemed hesitant to tell me and apologized for interrupting me in the night. Finally, after several reports of such sightings, I maneuvered into my wheelchair to go and see "the miracle." It was gone.

"But it was there, Mrs. Hees, I saw it," one caregiver exclaimed.

"I believe you, but perhaps it was the moon reflecting off the glass," I suggested.

"Maybe," she replied.

When another caregiver—a pragmatic Pole named Josephine—came to work for me, she casually said while opening my shutters in the morning, "There was an enormous cross in the sky last night. Big, big, really big. It frightened me. I thought it might be a sign, you know, with all the disasters we've had lately." It was true—earthquakes, riots, fires, had plagued Southern California recently.

Josephine would continue to work for me on and off while Irma rested and helped her family to settle in.

While Irma was away, I had my chimneys repaired after an earth-quake. The police came to search the house because the alarm went off, and the plumber came to fix the pump in the basement that flooded when it rained. I took care of all of this calmly and with great aplomb.

~~~

"Berta, you do a lot," said Larry during therapy. "So many people in your condition spend about two hours out of bed, take pills, and drink. You write, read a lot, go out when you can, socialize, and travel. You do a lot."

My morale went up several notches when I heard him say that.

From the very beginning, writing had kept me sane. *A Death at the Wedding* seemed to be a good title for an essay that was based on an unusual occurrence. Sadly, one week earlier—when the actual wedding took place—the bride's aunt dropped dead during the reception.

"She probably had some champagne," I said to Sister Wilfrid, who had attended the affair.

"Several glasses," Sister clarified, "and she was dancing at the time."

"What a great way to go," I proclaimed.

A super scenario, I thought, as ideas flowed faster than my pen. *Does the orchestra continue playing? Do the guests leave, saying, "What a lovely reception but . . . "? Does that mean the aunt must be taken to the mortuary before the honeymoon begins? As the deceased was from England, would she have to be shipped home? Were the newlyweds planning a European honeymoon? Could the wedding flowers be used at the funeral? Should the ushers keep their rented tuxedos and act as pallbearers?*

On a walk with Lawrence, I told him about the newlyweds' misfortune.

"If I were the groom, I'd wonder if this wasn't some ominous sign," he commented. Curiously, after a few years of wedded bliss, the groom died.

Lawrence left me one day to help Aunt Alice for the first time. As he was leaving, he said, "I phoned to ask her if 3:30 P.M. would be all right.

She replied, 'Four would be just fine,' and then hung up.

"Have fun Larry," I said. I thought, *Good old Alice.*

I took another big step forward with regards to how I dealt with people criticizing me about my way of life. I listened more and explained less. This approach was less disturbing to my nervous system. I found that it sapped my energy to explain my life to people; they wouldn't be able to understand it anyway. So, I ended up telling them "I'm just fine" no matter what they asked about my situation.

~~~

Bill drove down to Pasadena from Santa Cruz in the pouring rain—his pickup loaded with lumber. He set aside two weeks to build a deck for Morgan and Katy's new home. We usually dined at Morgan's house or mine, and, on occasion, we ate out. In the evenings, Bill spent time with his friends.

"Everywhere I go, I run into people I know. I'll be coming down more often," he said, while looking much less lonely than when he arrived. "See you very soon, Mom," he promised when we said goodbye.

Indeed, it was almost immediately after that visit that we saw each other again. He, along with Serena and Jennie, met me at the Monterey

Airport. They all greeted me with big grins when I arrived for my final Parents' Weekend. After we exchanged hugs all around, Bill drove us all to the hotel, where we prepared for a reception at Jennie's school.

The rain stopped during the reception, so the four of us stepped outside into a crisp, dark, starry night. The chapel was open, and the interior light streamed out through the stained glass windows of the chapel carving colorful images into the black night. At my request, we went inside to say hello to Him. Just sitting and gazing at that dear presence brought a smile to my face and joy to my heart. *Thank you*, I whispered.

We left the chapel and went out to dinner. After Bill and his girlfriend Serena went back to Santa Cruz, Jennie and I returned to the hotel. Jennie stretched out beside me on my bed. I put my head on Jennie's shoulder for comfort, saying, "I'll be the daughter for a moment and you be the mommy."

"I understand," replied Jennie. "I miss Dad too."

We didn't speak after that, but it was a silence filled with contentment. Then, it came time for me to sleep and for Jennie to return to her room to read.

The following day, we attended the senior luncheon where I met the girls with whom Jennie planned to go to Europe after graduation. With parents in tow, this small group went out for dinner.

As we ate, the conversation centered on mutual interests. When a question arose, one of the fathers said, "Let's ask Berta." I felt a renewed confidence and a stronger sense of self as I interacted with everyone. Grief and sorrow had transformed me into a new, totally self-confident person—the person He intended me to be.

Back on campus, we went to the performing arts center to watch a production of *The Madwoman of Chaillot*. I left early with Jennie and her pretty friend Sheila. Sheila kept looking at me throughout dinner that evening with sadness in her eyes.

As Jennie later explained, the sadness was not about me. Then, she asked me if I had noticed that Sheila's father looked sad as well.

"Yes, and he seemed to have a need to explain himself. He spoke to me of his life in Germany when his father was helping the Allies divide that country into East and West. He was only six at the time. It was interesting, and he seemed to be a very gentle man," I told Jennie, "but I'm sorry I didn't get to meet his wife, your friend's mother."

"She is very occupied socially, and my friend rarely gets to spend any time with her mother," said Jennie, which explained the sadness of father and daughter. You don't have to lose a parent through death or illness to feel separated from them.

When Dana was attending this same school, Bill and I never missed a Parents' Weekend. We never imagined being anywhere else.

The evening ended on a happy note when Jennie and Sheila joined me in my hotel room to eat chocolate cake and watch *Dirty Dancing*. The title of the film is somewhat provocative, but the story is sweet and charming. On Sunday morning, we went to the chapel for Mass.

This was to be Irma's last trip to Monterey with me. She was not well. As I sat in the kitchen at home, I tried to sort out my feelings as Irma packed up her belongings. On the positive side, I hoped her departure would bring renewal into both of our lives. The time was right. I was stronger, as evidenced by how I handled the nights I spent alone since our return home. Irma, on the advice of her doctor, was now coming to work in the morning and leaving in the evening.

"Oh, Mrs. Hees, all this black blood poured out," she said, pointing to the incisions in her arm. "The doctor told me I must calm down. My cholesterol level is too high, and so is my blood pressure."

When Irma walked into my home at St Lo in July of 1981, her goal was to eventually reunite her family in the USA. Her husband was not included at that time, but he was back in the picture again. Now her wish was coming true, one relative at a time. Her other objective was to get me up on my feet before she left my employ. I was not walking, but I was better at dealing with life, and that was an enormous gift. Just before she left, she asked, "May I come to Jennie's graduation in June?"

The usual household routine did not run smoothly after Irma's departure. A succession of young Filipino women came and went. They were kind, hard-working, and professional. However, all new caregivers are presented with challenges as they adapt to a new job, new routines, and new homes. Some needed to be trained in the particulars of my daily care. And of course, they couldn't be expected to know where things were in a different home. The training period was always tiring for me. When I left to celebrate the holidays with family and friends, I would always be concerned about whether they felt left out and lonely.

"Were you lonely while I was away?" I remember asking one of my new caregivers.

"Oh, no," she replied. "I have my Bible." Her remark resonated with me and made me feel better about the situation.

In spite of the adjustments the new caregivers and I had to make, I did have the pleasure of enjoying a varied cuisine and learning a new language. Pansit was a delicious rice dish prepared by the Filipinos. I often served it when I had company. Tagalog, the Philippine language, was a real hurdle for me. The word for "cat" is pusa, "daughter" or "girl" is babae, "son" is lalake, and "grandson," "granddaughter," or "grand-children" is apo.

During this period of time, my mother fell and broke her hip. She phoned to tell me she was on the floor next to her bed.

"I can't straighten out my leg," she said calmly. Her neighbor was with her.

After she was taken to the hospital, I spoke to her doctor on the phone. He confirmed that she indeed had a broken hip and would require surgery. Then, he warned, "The anesthesia will affect her thinking processes."

Meanwhile, the children were gathering to celebrate their grand-mother's ninetieth birthday. All of us, even Leslie, were saddened by Mom's misfortune. Leslie said earlier, "Mimi was not particularly friendly towards me. She has not changed in the least with me. No wonder we do not want to be around her when something goes wrong."

Dana and little Evan kept me busy while I tried to decide what to do about my mother's birthday, as all the arrangements had already been taken care of.

Evan was an explorer. In the mornings, he would toddle into my room and yank on the lace curtains, or play with the shutters, open the sweater closet to pull out the contents, or take a girdle out of a drawer or the tassel off the knob of my armoire. He ate the toast that came with my tea and then headed for the kitchen to munch on Auntie Jennie's toast while sitting on her lap.

Bill and Dana accompanied their grandmother to the hospital. (They planned on staying there until her surgery was completed.) When they got to the hospital, they found out that the operation had been postponed until 7:30 P.M. Already regaled with flowers, cards, and hugs from her friends, my mother continued to celebrate her ninetieth birthday with Dana and Bill before she went in for surgery.

We had arranged months in advance to have a dinner celebration at the club, and now it was too late to cancel on such short notice. So, Leslie came up with an idea of how to turn the situation to our advantage. "Why don't we make it into a birthday party for Jennie?" Why not? She had been allowed to come home for her grandmother's party, and she was about to turn eighteen in another couple of days.

Jennie had no idea what was in store for her when she showed up at the club. Seating herself on a flowered sofa, she was wide-eyed as little brightly wrapped gifts were placed on the coffee table before her.

When everyone was present, I said, "We are celebrating your birthday. Why don't you open your gifts?"

Surprised and happy, my adorable Jennie was overcome with joy when she read the words on a piece of paper that said, "Michael and Leslie will give you a trip to Europe after your June graduation, with much love, from M. & L." Tears of happiness ran down everyone's cheeks.

After lunch, we all remained at our tables when Leslie arose to pay homage to her little sister. She read aloud a poem she had composed filled with memories of Jennie's life, from birth to her eighteenth year. The poem began by describing how thrilled the family—especially her sisters—was about Jennie's birth:

> *The two big girls called Leslie and Dana*
> *Relieved to have a little sister*
> *The younger boys—Bill and Morgan—*
> *Someone new for them to pester!*

The poem went on to say how much we all enjoyed watching Jennie grow up and how everyone loved her even more when "Dad left us to go to early open heaven's gate."

So with your family gathered here
Please stand with us
These words to hear:
Happy 18, O Birthday Queen
We hope that life don't treat you mean.
We hope that it stays free from strife
As you enter adult life.
Happy Birthday Jennie!

Interwoven in these words rang the pride we all felt for Jennie as she struggled through the years after her father's death, after my paralysis. She became an example of strength to her entire family. Jennie ran to her sister and embraced her.

As we all wept, I softly uttered a prayer: "Thank you Jesus for healing us all."

I suddenly felt lighter and more energized as the weight of caring for Jennie was lifted from my shoulders. She was now 18, an adult. Soon she'd be in college and then off on her own. I had already accepted the fact that I would live the rest of my life without the use of my legs and in great pain. I would persevere only through the grace of Our Lord. Though Jennie was grown, Mother was recovering from surgery, so I still felt some responsibility to look after her.

"Berta, I have been beaten and injured," she cried over the phone.

"No, Mom, you fell and broke your hip."

"Oh, is that so?" she groused. "Is Uncle Phil dead?"

"No, Mom, he is sitting near your bed with Ida, the nurse who will look after you. I can't come to see you as often as I would like because I am paralyzed."

"Oh, you are? That's too bad."

She would talk to all the newsmen on the television. She arranged—or thought she was arranging—press conferences with the reporters she had known during her career as public relations director for the Ambassador Hotel.

I spoke to Ida. "Please, Ida, don't let my mother phone me when she is in this condition. I feel helpless and unable to do anything," I said firmly. It was raining very hard the day I had this conversation.

After thinking about how impossible it would be for mother to live in her home, I began to sing a refrain from a song I liked:

> *Once you warned me that if you scorned me*
> *I would be playing solitaire*
> *Uneasy in my easy chair*
> *It never entered my mind.*

I suppose those words could apply to the situation. I phoned Irma to ask her to pray for my mother.

Well, I was on my own. My sister absolutely refused to come out from Virginia. She was angry when I suggested she come to see Mother.

"I flew out there the last time she was operated on, and it was all for nothing," Jeannette protested. (It was indeed true that my mother never did acknowledge my sister's invitation to live with her family in Virginia.) "You know I'm still taking care of my mother-in-law, and I can't leave my husband and family at Christmas. I'm terrified of flying; you know that. Besides, the weather is terrible, and the flights are crowded. I'd be on standby, be left waiting on the tarmac for hours," she ranted, painting a picture of the worst-case scenario.

"But you promised me you would help when the time came," I reminded her, knowing in my heart she would let me down. Her personal issues were greater than mine as far as Mother was concerned.

However, I continued, saying, "Please don't dump your anger on me; it is misdirected. And she is as much your mother as she is mine. Please don't try to make me feel guilty."

"Oh, I'm sorry, I'm sorry. Please, let's be friends."

"We are friends." Then I suggested that one of her boys could come instead.

"No, they can't, and my husband can't come either. Too busy."

On one thing we agreed: we were both sick of having Mimi's friends call us to ask why we couldn't help our ailing mother.

Only recently, I heard one of them say, "I hear you are going to Hawaii."

"Not today, Polly, not tomorrow, not ever." I responded. "Those days are over. It's impossible with a spine full of crushed discs. I would probably urinate in my seat, or worse, as I am incontinent."

"Oh, I did not know," she said with some embarrassment. Of course, Polly didn't know.

The next three days were spent acquiring as much information as I could about my mother's financial status. Not surprisingly, she never told me what, if any, arrangements had been made for her care as she grew older. We had spoken only briefly about where she would like to be buried. "Not near my father or my brother," she spouted, "because they don't keep the place up." End of discussion.

In the middle of the night, I dealt with thoughts of my aging mother, her doctor, and her hospitalization. I also thought about Mother's lawyer and about my sister.

Pasadena was struck by a severe rainstorm. Sixty-mile-per-hour winds howled, windows rattled, and branches crashed down on the roof of my home. I covered my eyes with the palms of my hands and tried to listen to the voice of Spirit within.

My mind's eye traversed the interior of a church during the quiet of night. The votive candles burned brightly in their red and blue glass containers. A side door swung open, and a priest in a black cassock entered. He moved quickly past a side altar, and he approached the main altar. The priest then genuflected and moved on toward a door on the opposite side of the church.

I folded my hands across my chest and contemplated what I had just experienced. It was not possible to enter a church at any time of day or night—at least not anymore. After the last Mass was said, the priests locked the doors. I didn't quite understand why the priests—who live by faith—seemed determined to protect themselves from the outside world. (Lately, there had been a lot of criminal activity: drug addicts who stole valuable chalices, the money from the poor box, candelabras—anything they could grab to feed their habit.)

On a recent visit, Sister Wilfrid said, "I have to hurry back to the convent; they lock the gates before dark." She then told me how disturbing it was to be alone at night in the echoing halls of the convent. Like the priests, she was frightened by the possibility of intruders disturbing the sanctuary. What ever happened to "Be not afraid"? (A phrase the late Pope Paul used to use.)

With the winds still howling outside, I thought, *Why am I left alone here with my faltering courage? Why am I trying to replace fear with love? Those supposedly living with faith in God close their doors in fear and retreat to their convents and churches.* It seemed to me that they weren't practicing what they preached about faith and courage.

Unable to sleep, I struggled into my chair and headed for the kitchen. I found my bottle of Scotch on the counter and poured a small amount into a glass. I drank it down and angrily returned to my bed and then fell into a dead sleep.

~~~

Each time I thought that I was gaining ground, something would happen to knock me down. After a satisfying summer for Jennie and the best Parents' Weekend for both of us, I came home to face the loss of dear Irma and the task of finding someone to a replace her. There was also the problem of an "aged-p," or aging parent. (My sister and I adopted this Dickensian description for Mother.)

Baffled by life, I said to my son Morgan, "I'm just muddling through."

He came back with, "We're all just muddling through."

I laid out all my problems before Sister Wilfrid and read my midnight piece about courage, on which she made no comment.

"Advent ended today. It is Joyful Sunday—Laudate Sunday," Sister Wilfrid pointed out, trying to calm me down. It was a cold day. The winds had made a mess of the garden, and it was too chilly to go to Mass.

"Where is the joy, Sister?" I asked.

"Perhaps Monday will be better," she replied.

Before "Joyful" Sunday was over, I spoke with Mother, who was much more lucid than usual that particular day. I made the decision to have her moved to her home before Christmas. A hospital bed would be placed downstairs, where she would have twenty-four hour care.

"Please put my bed under the painting of the Blessed Virgin Mary," was my mother's only request. Her request surprised me. Although she was thoroughly Anglican, she was not a follower of the High Episcopal Church that venerates the Virgin Mary.

That same day, my sister called to tell me she would come out to California in January. And my sons said they would help to move Mother to a convalescent home. Soon after these plans were firmed up, I said a prayer of thanks.

Then, I thought about Mother and me. My mother was afraid of death; she refused to discuss any of the necessary steps that would have to be taken by her loved ones when her life would come to an end.

I, on the other hand, was quite willing to die whenever God called me. But for now, I felt great anticipation and joy at the prospect of celebrating another birthday.

Chapter 24

A CLEAN SLATE

Why are you afraid?
Have you no faith?

—Mark 4:35–41

Chapter 24

Alice and Charles prepared a lovely surprise for me on my fifty-seventh birthday: lunch on the patio with a few of my close friends, including Sister Wilfrid, on that mild December afternoon.

A day or so later, Larry came by to help me through a therapy session. I told him about the party.

"Charles asked me to say grace. I was so surprised," I commented. "Charles has never been a practicing Catholic."

"Well," laughed Larry. "I was giving Alice physical therapy the day after the party, and Charles said to me: 'We were surrounded by Catholics.'"

I chuckled at that. I could just hear Charles uttering those words as if he were making some grand announcement.

When I came home from the celebration, I found a note from Damian on my front gate. He was back from his travels to India, Tibet, and Afghanistan. I couldn't wait to see him and hear of his adventures.

"You look like someone I used to know," I said when he arrived two days later, sporting a beard.

"You mean Bill? It's the beard."

He presented me with an embroidered stole from Kashmir. Recovering from jet lag and the flu he had acquired in India, he looked peaked and exhausted.

We talked about having dinner together. "You haven't seen my house yet," he said.

"No, I haven't," I replied.

"You'll have to come over to dinner. I'll call you after the holidays."

I told him that I would really enjoy having dinner with him and thanked him for the visit.

~~~

Christmas was spent with Jennie, Kevin, Dana, and baby Evan. Jennie, home for the holidays, bought and trimmed the tree. Together we celebrated Charles's sixtieth birthday, had dinner with Morgan and Katy, and brought dinner to my mother and uncle. Despite Mother's infirmities, Christmas brought out the spirit of celebration. Towards the end of January, when everyone was gone, I had dinner with Damian in his new home. When he came over to pick me up, I noticed how handsome he looked dressed in a dark suit and tie. I thought, *How sweet. This is going to be quite the occasion.* I immediately regretted deciding against the beautiful dress I was planning to wear in favor of my more casual attire consisting of slacks and a sweater.

As we left in my car, he reached over to hold my hand. Once again, I felt like an awkward teenager. Still, it was very nice to feel the warmth of his hand on mine.

On the way to the front door, there was a steep grassy hill that he would have to maneuver. Once out of the car and into my chair, I realized that it was impossible to move the chair over the soggy grass, so Damian carried me up to the house. It was not the grand entrance I had imagined, nor one that Damian was prepared for. Perspiring, he paused to remove his jacket and tie after we entered the house.

The first room I noticed was the living room to the right of me. It was a scene of exotic chaos, but with an artistic flair. Paintings and memorabilia from the Far East filled almost every space. The lighting illuminated the gem-like colors. It was like looking through a kaleidoscope. Oh, how I wished I had worn that beautiful dress, as the colors would have complemented those that met my eyes.

"Our picture is at the end of this hall," said Damian, pointing to the area to my left. Yes, there it was: the painting of the man wearing white robes, his wings encircling the woman who stood before him.

In 1982, I bought the painting to hang in my bedroom, where I could contemplate the light-filled canvas until a peaceful sleep came over me. The painting was part of my healing process. When I felt stronger, I returned the painting to Damian.

"Are you sure you want me to have it?" he asked.

"Yes, and I don't want my money back. I want you to remember me."

The painting was next to his bedroom door. On that chilly night, the view from the bedroom window was stunning. The San Gabriel Mountains and Mount Wilson were sparkling with brilliant lights. I looked at the clothes hanging in the cedar closet.

"I didn't know you were so interested in clothes, Damian," I remarked.

"Yes, I am. I have some of my father's things."

But I remembered a very casual Damian at the beach, where you don't put on your best clothes to paint. Looking at his bed, I longed to share another special moment with him.

The Christmas decorations were still up in the dining room. A green cloth covered the table, and placemats, adorned with tiny mirrors and embroidery, were arranged on the tablecloth. He removed several of the mirrored place mats from India, saying, "They might be soiled."

After seating me at the table, he brought me a Scotch and water. He sipped a glass of wine as we ate Thai food and resumed a conversation begun in the car. We had both received invitations to the showing of a local art group who favored the contemporary work of the Diebenkorn variety. Damian's work was from the plein air style of early California.

"Here I've just returned from Afghanistan, the first American artist to do any recent work in that country, and they ignore me," he said angrily.

Speaking of his adventures, he mentioned he had dressed as a Moujahadeen in order to move around for a week with that group in Afghanistan. He had nothing to report about the deplorable way in which they treat the women there. "I never saw any women there," he remarked.

The Islam religion was a mystery to him. While visiting Tibet, he spoke with some Tibetans about Buddhism as a way of life. The Chinese had intermarried with the Tibetans, but he found even the young Tibetans faithful to the Dalai Lama.

Damian did not find India so surprising or enchanting, as he had traveled there before, and there were still lots of Westerners who had been in that part of the world for some twelve to fifteen years. "I think they come from unhappy homes," he said.

For a segment of his China trip, he traveled with an American girl, but, "I didn't sleep with her," he said with a smile on his face.

Before he left on his journey, he was involved with a married woman down the street. "You met her at St. Lo over a year ago," he said.

"Yes, that's true," I laughed.

"Why are you laughing?" he asked.

"I'm imagining the woman of many new parts"—(Damian had told me about her numerous plastic surgeries)—"who usually wore a bikini with a push-up bra—hardly in keeping with the general tone of St. Lo." I paused. "Though, I'm sure many of the male residents took pleasure in the way she looked dressed in such attire."

"She picked me up at the airport when I returned from my trip," he told me. "December 14 was the date I chose to return because that is my parents' anniversary, and the next day is your birthday."

Deeply moved, I reached out for his hand. We looked at each other for a moment. "One of the reasons I began to work with you years ago was because of our twenty-year age difference. I felt safe," I smiled.

We touched upon the question of whether we would make love again.

"If I were twenty years younger and not paralyzed," I assured him.

"How about twenty years older *and* paralyzed?" he asked.

"Yes," I answered firmly but with reservation because I still wasn't yet at peace with my physical handicap. And then, as I threw up a protective barrier around myself, we dropped the subject. "Do you realize how much you helped me to value myself? 'You can be anything you want to be' was a phrase I remember from our conversations back then. And laughter! I love to laugh. But Bill and I rarely laughed together. If I was being playful with Bill, he would immediately turn away from me. He didn't like anyone making fun of him either. Once, I put the kind of candles that don't blow out on his birthday cake. Bill huffed and puffed until I told him it was a joke. Anger spread across his face. Since the children thought it was all great fun, I made light of the situation. I don't think he was particularly fond of practical jokes. Well, I guess we all drag something from our past into marriage."

I read Damian some quotes from Thomas Merton that I intended to use in the chapter about him. I also read him the poem Leslie had written for Jennie's eighteenth birthday. "Leslie looked so beautiful as she recited it," I added.

"She is always beautiful. Damn that other fellow," he said, referring to her first husband, but he said it with a smile, implying he was just feigning jealousy.

I would have gone to bed with Damian that evening, but I was embarrassed by my body now that I was paralyzed. Damian could have dealt with any obstacle, but my fears got in the way.

We postponed the slide show of his trip he had prepared for my visit. "I'd better go home, I might wet my pants," I said.

"Oh, do you still have that problem?" he asked with sadness in his voice. My forthrightness managed to kill any desires of the flesh.

After I left the house on that decidedly unromantic note, the evening just got worse.

Pushing my chair over the soggy ground toward the car, Damian pulled a muscle in his back. He looked angry as he drove me home, and he swerved the car as we crossed the railroad tracks.

"Whoops, we almost got wiped out by Amtrak," he yelled. There was no train in sight. It was Damian's way of trying to break the silence.

"Well, that wouldn't have been such a bad thing after all, as far as I'm concerned, I mean, getting killed by a train," I responded.

We were both disappointed by the way the evening had turned out: I was looking forward to just being with him; he was hoping for a more intimate reunion.

Damian complained about his back, and then he added, "Well, I suppose you have that problem *all* the time."

"Twenty-four hours a day."

When we pulled into my garage, I asked him to kiss me goodnight. He reluctantly obliged.

Somehow, I felt responsible for ruining the evening, so I wrote him a letter:

Dearest Damian,

You looked so very handsome when you arrived last night. I immediately wished I had worn the dress I was originally planning to wear, but I chose comfort and warmth because of the chilly night. No, truthfully, I was frightened and nervous about being with you again. Well, you know, will you still like me, etc.? I felt as though I were going out on my first date! It taught me one thing—I still have to love myself more. So, I should have worn the beautiful dress, and if Damian thinks I am trying to be more than just an old friend, well, so what?

Oh God, if I could just let "the dress drop to the floor"—a quote from Thomas Merton. But I guess I don't have the courage. I don't feel that I have anything left to give any man anymore. That is why I am working on my spiritual life, the inner life. I know that He will always be there. With Him, there is no "till death do us part."

I was overjoyed when you said, "How about twenty years older and paralyzed?" I answered, "Yes," and I meant yes, because any other answer would have been a lie. If I had lied to you, I would have lied to God as well. He knows me very well. He also knows how dear you are to me, and He is happy when I am happy. He brought you into my life for a reason, just as He took Bill away as part of his plan for me. This all sounds very serious, but I am trying to work out the confusion about you that confronts me. The best thing for me is not to try. I have found that letting go and being happy in the moment is best. It is true I miss having someone to share my love with, both physically and emotionally. I felt that very vividly last night. It frightens me.

Your house is so beautiful. It is the best gallery in the world in which to hang your work. Seeing how much painting you did on your trip amazes me. Will you ever have that kind of energy again?

I did not hear enough about your journey and should have given the evening to you instead of spending so much time reading Leslie's poem and the quotations that I will probably use in my book.

Damian, perhaps I did pray you safely through your journey. I will continue to pray that, soon, you get the recognition you deserve. It will happen, but maybe not with the resources now available to you. I will also ask God to send someone to share your life. It will not be the neighbor down the street. Yes, I remember seeing her a year or so ago at St. Lo—She's not you at all.

Well, well, well, the evening certainly turned me upside down. But it was fun, charming, romantic, and funny too. Thank you.

God bless, you are never far away from my heart. I take you with me wherever I go.

Love, Berta

~~~

It was settled: my mother and Uncle Phil had decided to move into the nearby Episcopal Home. Mother, Uncle Phil, Morgan, and I met with the representative of the Senior Care Network. I was impressed with the way Morgan spoke on behalf of his family in a very calm and poised manner.

Immensely relieved as I was for everyone concerned, Morgan and I drove home to find Bill sitting on my doorstep. Morgan phoned Katy to say, "Bill is here. Mom wants you to join us for dinner."

At dinner, Bill talked about his forthcoming trip to Rio de Janeiro. Serena, who was back in his life again, would meet him there. He was nervous about his first trip outside the U.S. To encourage him, Morgan, Katy, and I made a toast to Bill, wishing him well on his journey.

"At last, the Hees family is finding some happiness," Bill added.

My new full-time caregiver Thelma had lovingly prepared our delicious meal. Thelma was married. Her two children were still in the Philippines with their grandparents. Her husband Steve was with Thelma. Without my knowing, Steve would come to spend the night with his wife, which would have been perfectly fine had they arranged it with me ahead of time. They were an attractive couple. His presence in the evening gave me an added sense of security.

~~~

Shortly after my mother was settled into her very nice room at the Episcopal Home, I went to see her. Surrounded by pieces of furniture, including her four-poster bed and many bibelots—my mother's word for her collection of knickknacks, all chosen by her—she looked very much at home. Uncle Phil's room was directly across the hall, and they both kept their doors open so they could wander back and forth.

Mother made me a cup of tea on a small stove. As I expected, she was feeling agitated after such a big move.

It really began to become clear to me that she was in need of care when I saw letters hanging out from underneath her mattress. I retrieved her unpaid bills and mailed them to her accountant. I now felt greatly relieved and ready to get on with my life knowing she was safe and in good hands.

Everybody I loved would soon be gone except for my children, perhaps. Soon, no one who was a part of my youth would remain.

Now, my concern turned to Charles. I shared my concerns with Larry about Charles's health.

"Charles phoned me yesterday, and he was very depressed. He said he was worried about finances," I told Larry. "His mother has left her considerable estate to her grandson. Charles has also stopped drinking, and his legs are shaky. I asked him to come to see me before he went to Charlottesville to see Caroll, his companion, but he said he couldn't. His voice sounded dull and flat. Larry, I think he's dying."

"Does his mother know?" Larry asked.

"No. Larry, I think Charles has AIDS: he has brown spots on his body," I said, half-guessing about his condition.

"No, people with AIDS have *red* spots; brown spots indicate a *liver* problem." Larry said, correcting me.

I began to cry: "I love him so much!"

Charles and I had lunch at his mother's house after his visit with Caroll.

"Charles, you don't look well," I commented. His stomach was horribly bloated.

"I guess I'll have to buy some new clothes," he said, tugging at the zipper on his Bermuda shorts.

Just as I came back from lunch, I heard my phone ring, so I raced over to pick it up.

"This is Rosa, Mrs. Hees. Charles is dead. Alice and I are at the hospital. Alice wants you to come."

Charles was buried in the family plot. At his mother's request, Rosa, Thelma, and I stayed on after the burial for a picnic lunch in the cemetery. It was not a sad occasion, contrary to what one might think. We enjoyed reminiscing about the eccentricities of various family members we loved, all of whom were resting in peace only a few feet away. Alice and I were sitting in our wheelchairs sipping on wine and nibbling on sandwiches while our caregivers were nearby, talking about the cross in the window that they had seen and about Charles's ghost.

"I saw it too," said Rosa, referring to the cross. Rosa had seen the cross when she worked for me. "The moon was always full whenever the cross appeared, and I saw it through a pane of glass." It could have been a distortion of the moon's rays, but I preferred to think of the cross as a sign of His presence. Most of my caregivers had commented on the sighting.

Alice and Rosa talked about Charles's ghost.

"I heard him flushing his toilet and slamming down the lid," Rosa claimed quite nonchalantly. "I also heard the clinking of glasses," she added. And then she turned to me and whispered, "He's waiting for his mother."

To dispel the sadness I felt at the loss of Charles, I accepted an invitation to speak at a convention for wound care at the Long Beach Hyatt.

Speaking extemporaneously, I began: "I experienced my first bedsore when I was in the hospital before starting rehab. When you first become paralyzed, you're not aware of all of the complications that will arise because of your condition such as bedsores, bladder infections, and the like."

The audience of doctors, nurses, and company representatives nodded in agreement. "Stop them before they start by having caregivers check the skin day and night. Oh, by the way, I have a pressure sore on my derriere right now, so perhaps I should moon the audience?" I concluded amidst laughter from the assembled group.

As I was about to leave the Hyatt, someone handed me a check for fifty dollars! I actually received compensation for my speech! Going home with the first money I had earned in forty years, I felt triumphant.

~~~

The mail brought an invitation to the showing of Damian's paintings from his recent trip to China, Afghanistan, India, and Tibet. After attempting to write several letters in reply, I gave up on letter writing and picked up the phone instead.

Damian was painting when I called. I assured him that I had forwarded the extra invitations to Leslie and Dana, as he had requested. Then, I encouraged him to go to Sun Valley, Idaho to stay with Michael and Leslie: "The summer would be a good time to paint, and they have an extra cabin you could stay in." He did not respond to my suggestion. Instead, he spoke about the agreement just signed regarding the Afghanis and their future.

"Is it good or bad?" I asked.

Damian felt it was not a positive move. Our local representative in Washington, D.C. felt the same way about it.

"The U.S. government should continue to support the Moujahadeen. The Moujahadeen were not supported at the recent meeting in Genoa."

"I've been watching the reports on our local PBS station," I said. "Last night there was a photo of the Afghanis marching through the snow. It was just like your painting. With so much news about Afghanistan, your show should be a success."

"Come to the gallery the day before the opening," he suggested.

~~~

Jennie came home on her last open weekend. During that time, she decided, with the help of her brother Morgan, to attend St. Mary's College in Moraga, California. After she returned to school, Jennie wrote me a letter:

> The times we spent together during my high school years were so meaningful. I treasure those moments. I want to make an effort to spend time with you when I go away to college.

We both knew she wouldn't be coming home as often.

Leslie, Riley and Dana, would spend a long weekend with Jennie before her graduation. Bill would join them one night for dinner. I would not see Jennie again until her graduation.

~~~

Sister Wilfrid—who was ailing—brought me Communion. "God, in your mercy, will you soon take me home?" was my prayer. Sister phoned me that evening, but I couldn't speak because my physical and emotional pain was too severe.

The next morning when I awoke, my rosary was in pieces. I had torn it apart in my sleep while I dreamt of Jennie. Her graduation from high school plus her impending move to college had impacted me emotionally. I gathered the pieces of the rosary into my hand and, looking at them, thought, *Well, at least she'll remain in California.* Leaning over the side of my bed, I dropped the pieces one by one into the wastebasket.

~~~

After giving some thought to attending Damian's showing, I set aside my fears and phoned Tristan to ask if he would take me to the showing. Tristan was a young artist I had met through my massage therapist. His mother Nancy had invited me to her home on one or two occasions, and from there our friendship blossomed.

When I phoned Tristan, he said, "I'd be delighted to take you. I was just talking with another artist about Damian and his wonderful adventures. I told him I'd really like to see that show, and then you phoned." He had met Damian at one of his own exhibits. "I thought it was kind of him to take the time to be there," he remarked.

When I informed my massage therapist that I had phoned her friend and that he had accepted, she said, "Wait 'til you see him. He's terribly handsome."

That particular Saturday evening was very sweet, just like the dashing gentleman who escorted me. When we got to the gallery, it was early and not too crowded, so we had a good chance of seeing Damian's work before proceeding to a larger room to enjoy some champagne. We agreed he had done some remarkable work under very difficult conditions.

Loud enough for the entire gallery to hear, Damian said over and over again, "Berta Hees is here, Berta Hees is here." I felt embarrassed, not only because I was in a wheelchair, but also, as Damian approached us, I felt that every eye was upon me.

As I introduced the two artists, my escort reminded Damian that they had met once before. Then Damian told us he had sold several of his works and would donate the money to the Afghanistan War Relief.

The following morning Damian telephoned. "I was surprised to see you at the gallery. Thank you for coming," he said.

"Why wouldn't I come?"

"Because it is so hard for you. I know how much energy and preparation it takes for you to go anywhere. Getting into your car isn't easy. For that matter, getting out isn't easy either."

"Oh yes! By the way, how is your back?" I grinned, and we both laughed.

A week or so after Damian's showing, I went to Mayfield High School to meet a group of teenage girls born with various neurological disorders.

The day began with Mass in the auditorium. When Mass was over, each girl was given a plastic box with a figure inside.

"Please come forward and explain how you relate to your symbol," asked Edith, the occupational therapist who had accompanied the girls to Mayfield.

I was also given a box. "My symbol is a giraffe," I began, when it was my turn. "The giraffe has a long neck. He can see what is going on around him. I am an observer of life. I watch people, and what I see comes out in my writing and painting."

Before I left the school, I approached the occupational therapist.

"Edith, this girls' school: is it located near Wellington Road? That's the neighborhood where I grew up.

"I drove down Wellington Road recently in a hailstorm," she said. "It is beautiful. I really love that area, and I envision a big old house where the girls could learn to live independently."

Wishing her and her girls the best, I rolled over to talk to several of Jennie's former grade school classmates.

"Where is Jennie going to college?" they wanted to know.

"She's going to St. Mary's in Northern California. Are any of you going there?" I asked them. They all shook their heads no.

I marveled at how grown up they were. Like Jennie, they had outgrown childhood and blossomed into young women.

To keep my strength up for the upcoming graduation, I began swimming again. The Glendale Adventist Hospital had an indoor pool—comfortably heated—and a lift that lowered me into and lifted me out of the water.

One day, a new swimmer floated over to me in her inner tube.

"Welcome to the group!" I said with a smile.

"What's wrong with you? Why are you here?" she inquired in a friendly manner.

My story came out of me as if it had been on tape. Honest to God, she started to sob, her tears falling into the water.

I returned the question, "And what happened to *you*, if I may ask?"

"The surgeon cut my sciatic nerve during hip surgery," she explained.

"There is little I can say except that the medical profession has changed since my father practiced medicine. It seems like it's out of the doctors' hands now. The insurance industry has taken over healthcare. You don't get the individual care you used to get when my father was a doctor," I responded sympathetically.

We became more than passing acquaintances after we discovered that we had something in common: both of us had British mothers. "I was in my fifties," she remembered, "before I could finally figure my mother out."

"Amen," I responded, and so we became an intimate club of two.

~~~

Many of my responsibilities were coming to an end. With the help of her school counselor, Jennie decided where she would go to college, and the gentleman handling Jennie's trust said she could use the principal from her paternal grandmother's trust to pay for her college education. Jennie was now able to take care of her financial affairs, and I could sign off as executor. At last, I was only responsible for myself. Well yes, there still was Mother to look after, but at least she was in a good place.

Jennie phoned to tell me that her final Parents' Weekend was "fun." After I hung up the phone, I realized how close Jennie was to her high school graduation. Had I gone on with my life as she was about to move on with hers? What exactly would the future be like without my little Jennie around? I had to face the fact that she was not so little anymore.

Chapter 25

RECEIVING OUR WINGS

*If we view freedom as an
opportunity for further growth
we automatically surrender to its
influence, allowing ourselves to
become caught up in a timeless
current of spiritual nourishment.*

—Anon

Chapter 25

"Oh," sighed Sister Wilfrid, "thank you for telling me about your depression. Shall we say the Gloria?" So we recited the prayer together at the end of our conversation about a recurrence of depression.

My internist, Dr. Holmes—a young woman who recently became the mother of two children—asked me, "Do you think you should be hospitalized?"

"No, not yet. I'll think about it after Jennie's graduation," I answered.

"When is that?"

"June the fourth," I replied. "My life is too hard, Doctor."

"I know," she acknowledged. "For a woman your age, it is a tragedy. Do you have a psychologist?"

"Yes, he is coming next week."

"Do you just think about suicide, or do you plan how you are going to do it?"

"I just think about it but, no, that is a half-truth."

"There are a lot of people who love you."

"How do you know?" I asked.

"Your mother loves you," she replied. (The kind doctor took care of mother at the Episcopal Home.) "I'll be on call all weekend, Berta," she reminded me as I left her office.

Sister Gemma, whose support group I was still attending, provided the answer to my severe depression. "I think right now you are dealing with two things: Jennie's graduation and the fact that you are not walking. I know how much you wanted to walk into her graduation."

"A few days ago, Sister, I felt like running out the door of my home," I said with regret at the return of my depression.

My "loving" mother phoned me at home to say, "You are a wicked, wicked girl for putting me in such a place."

Then the phone rang again, and it was Sister Wilfrid saying, "I had a message from your mother to phone immediately. Is it urgent?"

"No," I answered firmly. *Where did my mother find Sister's phone number?*

For Sister's sake, I pulled myself together to attend a large fundraiser for Mayfield School. As I was leaving the party, I slipped on the floor of my car while transferring from my wheelchair. A crowd gathered, but no one volunteered to help, and the gentleman who had walked me to my car had serious back problems, so he wasn't able to pick me up. Two young men, who were parking valets, lifted me up from under the dashboard and onto my seat.

"I've had lots of experience. My cousin is a quadriplegic," one of them said. His easy remark swept away the embarrassment I felt under the eyes of curious onlookers.

~~~

As the weeks moved towards Jennie's graduation, I dragged fear along with me. I was dealing with a bedsore. It worried me that I would be sitting for many hours at a time.

The week before graduation, Nubia—who came round to help me pack my things—said, "You look so much better. A few days ago, I thought, *Uh-oh, Berta's not going to be up to making the trip,* because you looked so tired."

But the flight to Monterey was easy. The flight attendants were cheerful and, above all, helpful. The pilot said we would land in drizzle and mist. Instead, I was carried off the plane by two laughing men, under the clear sky of Monterey. A cool breeze swept across my face. It was a pleasant surprise—a welcome relief from the heat and humidity of Pasadena.

"Hi, Michael," I cried, relieved when I spotted my son-in-law at the rent-a-car- counter. Moments later, Leslie showed up as Michael helped Nubia with our luggage and then went to pick up the rental car.

Michael returned and said, "Nubia's okay, Berta, but the car feels a little strange to her. So tell her to take it easy." Michael loaded our luggage into the trunk of the car.

Nubia, still learning to drive, drove off the road only once the entire weekend. She knocked down a No Parking sign as we turned into the hotel where we were staying. There was no damage to the car or its occupants, so we drove on. The sign was back up the following day as we drove by the same location; it didn't have a scratch.

Our first evening in Monterey was Prize Night. Those members of the family who had gathered at the school went out for dinner at a French restaurant without the graduate.

"We brought Jennie here not long ago and got her drunk on champagne," laughed Leslie. Did I really need that piece of news? *Well, better with family than with strangers*, I thought.

The Baccalaureate Mass was held Saturday morning in the chapel on the school grounds. I sat to one side of the altar. Jennie was only allowed two guests. She chose her godparents, Judith and Harry. They sat behind me, lending their support with an occasional tap on the shoulder.

At the sound of Purcell's *Trumpet Tune in D Major*, the graduates entered the chapel singing:

> *All creatures of our God and King*
> *Lift up your voices and with us sing Alleluia, Alleluia!*
> *Thou burning sun with golden beam,*
> *Thou silver moon with softer gleams,*
> *Oh, praise Him, oh praise Him*
> *Alleluia, Alleluia!*

With the graduates now sitting in the front pews facing the altar, I looked for my daughter. Since she was sitting on the other side of the center aisle, I could not see her from where I was sitting.

The priest offered the greeting, "Kyrie eleison, Christe eleison," and the congregation replied. We sang: ". . . let children's happy hearts, in this worship bear their parts." The graduates were encouraged to follow God's commandments: "I have set before you life and death, the blessing and the curse. Choose life!"

I will, I thought.

"Do not conform yourselves to this age but be your own mind, so that you may judge what is God's will," said the priest, quoting St. Paul.

Finally, the Beatitudes: "Blessed are the poor . . ." and then, "You are the salt of the earth."

The Mass ended, and one of the graduates sobbed loudly as the girls sang *A Prayer for Tomorrow*. As Purcell's *Trumpet Voluntary* sounded, the graduates arose and left the chapel, and the girl was still sobbing.

~~~

Not far away in Santa Cruz, Bill was playing host to his siblings while I attended Mass and then had breakfast with Jennie and her godparents. It occurred to me that Bill must have been overjoyed to finally have his brothers and sisters gathered together in his home to celebrate Jennie's graduation.

After a short rest, I returned to campus under brilliant blue skies and a very warm sun. The Monterey breezes cooled the rows of chairs facing the front of the library. Passing the study hall, I caught a glimpse of the bouquets of long-stemmed roses tied with wide satin ribbon that were lined up on the edge of the stage waiting for eager hands to collect them.

Jennie's dear godparents sat beside me waiting for the ceremony to begin. They filled the empty space Bill would have occupied. My other children sat several seats to my left.

Looking at Dana, I wondered whether she might be remembering her own graduation day in this place. I wondered what her thoughts were for the future then. Had any of her hopes and dreams come true?

I opened Jennie's yearbook, which I was holding in my lap. Her feelings about her graduation were expressed in a quote from Jim Morrison: "This is the end my friend, this is the end, the end of all our elaborate plans." After forming close bonds in boarding school, time had finally run out. Is that why the girl sobbed so wrenchingly during Mass?

The Thirty-sixth Annual Commencement Exercises began at Sullivan Court precisely at 2:00 P.M. A trio of piano, violin, and cello played the Processional. Words of blessing were spoken along with an Irish saying: "May the wind be always at your back." I breathed the clear, true voices of the school choir into my soul before they disappeared into the air. "No applause please" was printed in the program, and the audience politely complied.

The speaker—a well-known writer —looked so frail I thought the Monterey breezes might blow her away. Was she even five feet tall? Her bobbed, straight hair fell forward and covered her face. She never made eye contact with the audience. The graduates in their long white dresses— the bouquets of red roses now settled on their laps—were sitting in a semi-circle on each side of the speaker.

In her message to the graduates, she urged them to go out and join the fray. Her voice broke as she spoke about her daughter—her only child— who was photographing her way through Guatemala at the time. Then she told the girls that, as women, they lived in fortunate times, because they could seek opportunities that were never available to their mothers when they were younger. That was the gist of her address. When she returned to her seat, her eyes remained focused on the ground.

I was left with the impression that Jennie's class, if they supported the speaker, would all be out carrying placards for one cause or another in order to clean up the mess in the world. True, these young women were entering a life filled with many more opportunities, many more choices, and a great deal more freedom. But, with freedom comes responsibility. Choices must be made with care. I thought over what the priest had said about not following the crowd or the fashion of the day—how critical it is to be an independent thinker, not a sheep.

The speaker choked up when she spoke of her daughter, but there was no mention of parenting as a life of service. If these girls are bearing placards or the burdens of high paying jobs, who will bear the babies? As an older mother, I saw parenting as a life of service quite unlike any other: a lesson in selflessness—demanding and occasionally heartbreaking. But, in the end, rewarding—a joy!

There will always be causes to fight for, such as the poverty amongst some of our sisters and brothers. While raising our families, we need not neglect those in our own communities. Helping seniors, speaking up for immigrant families, providing an environment where youngsters could safely go to spend after school hours while learning a skill, raising money for arts and education—all of these were part of my life. Was I a liberated female? I don't know. But, in all fairness, I felt the speaker could have mentioned parenting as a choice. After all, she *was* addressing a Catholic audience, among whom were families even larger than mine. Was I feeling resentful? Yes.

Suddenly, I was jerked back into the present when Jennie Jane Hees, five-feet-ten-inches tall, strode toward the trustees and the head of the school to smilingly receive her diploma. Then turning toward parents and friends, she bowed and nodded in thanks.

The "No applause, please" rule was now disregarded as I yelled, "Yay, Jennie!" along with her brothers and sisters. I felt the grief, anger, and depression that had weighted me down for so many years suddenly lift. The rite of passage brought celebration and the joy of a new beginning to this mother, this daughter. Sister Catherine gave me a thumbs-up sign.

After Benediction and the Recessional, my children stumbled over my chair, saying one after the other, "Jennie looks just like you," as if they had recognized the resemblance for the first time.

We all moved under a nearby arbor, where Jennie and I embraced for a long time. When we parted, I saw Gerald, opened my arms to give him a hug, and thanked him for driving back and forth from Southern California to Monterey, where he had attended various dances and now the graduation. Tomorrow, he would pack up Jennie's belongings and drive her home.

Leaving the school, I passed the lawn where parents, students, faculty, and graduates stood in groups, smiling and laughing. For a moment, I envisioned three people that I knew very well—Bill, Dana, and me—back to the time when Dana graduated. He, with curly brown hair, a beautiful smile, cameras slung around his neck, was crouched with his lens aimed at a young girl with long blond hair. She was wearing a white dress and holding a bouquet of roses. And, there I was standing next to her—a tall, slender woman, her hair pulled back in a chignon. She was removing a speck of lint from a navy knit suit. I kept them in view until they vanished somewhere into the past where they came from eighteen years before.

After a brief rest, we all met again for a reception at the Pebble Beach Lodge. The lodge was noisy and crowded, and I found it difficult to find my children. Then I spotted them outside on the terrace. They looked very happy, and they were laughing when I joined them, but I felt quite alone without Jennie's dad. Looking out toward the bay, I saw several boats bobbing at anchor. They looked lonely too.

Eager to leave the crowded reception, we went out to dinner at a small French restaurant in nearby Pacific Grove—arranged by Jennie and her friend, Sheila, and Sheila's parents.

After getting settled in a private dining room at La Provence at about 7:00 P.M., we ordered our meal. Michael and Leslie were already flying home to Sun Valley, Idaho, to attend my granddaughter's graduation from eighth grade while we waited, waited, and waited for our food to arrive.

After a good deal of bread and butter, washed down by champagne, my son-in-law Kevin said sarcastically, "I feel like someone in an internment camp. Pretty soon I'm going to reach over and stab whatever is on that man's plate." He pointed out one of the men sitting at the table who had been fortunate enough to order something the chef didn't have to make from scratch. "I don't care what it is, I'm going to eat it," Kevin declared. Finally, at nine o'clock, the food was served just as we were running out of conversation and feeling sleepy from the champagne. As we ate, my children smiled at me from time to time or reached toward me to pat my head. It was as if they were saying, "Mom, it's okay even if he's not here."

After I left the restaurant, I saw Gerald sitting on a bench all by himself. He looked very lonely. Had he slipped out quietly? I smiled at him and pointed up at the stars. We looked up at the exquisite night sky, where every star in the universe shone brightly. And then we gazed across the bay at the lights of Seaside. It seemed as though thousands of stars had fallen to earth there.

The following morning, Jennie came to the hotel to say goodbye. Nubia was packing as I shared breakfast with Jennie, who looked tired and sad. Everyone was gone now, and so she wept for a while. "See you soon," I said as we left the room. She would be driving down the coast with Gerald. I left for the airport.

On the way to the airport, Nubia turned the car onto Garden Drive. I looked to my right and saw the red tile roofs of Jennie's school that rose above the pines and the cypress trees. Overcome by emotion, I shouted out, "Goodbye, school. Goodbye, Jennie's dorm. Goodbye, classroom and graduation day, June 4, 1988." Graduation day was already a day and a half into my memory bank. I waved farewell to the past, then turned my head to the future.

The joy of the last two days was almost overshadowed by the driver I had hired to meet me at LAX. He came bearing down on me, his face unshaven and with fury in his bloodshot eyes. "You don't take care of your car," he yelled at me. "I had a flat on the freeway. I'm not driving you again." Before I could reply, he grabbed my luggage and tore off toward the parked car. Nubia pushed my chair as fast as she could to keep up with him.

As he dumped the luggage in the car, Nubia positioned my chair next to the passenger seat, and, as I was about to sit on my sliding board, the driver picked me up and dumped me into the car. Nubia straightened out my tangled legs and realigned my torso. As we sped off, I said to the driver, "You owe me an apology, Mr. O'Brien. You had no right to yell at me like that. I have just returned from a happy occasion. "Besides," I went on unnecessarily, "the car was thoroughly gone over before I left."

Silence.

Then he said, "You people are all alike. You are used to telling others to do this, do that, demanding to be waited on." His rage surprised me until I realized he was hung over; his breath gave him away.

"You have no right to assume anything about me. But think what you like, you are not going to spoil my day." I turned my head to look out the window.

"Let go of it, Berta," said Sister Wilfrid's voice in my head. But, for a moment during his tirade, I wished that my husband—always a gentleman through and through—were driving me home.

Revenge came quickly when the arm of my chair flew off the roof of my car. Mr. O'Brien had to circle around and dash into oncoming traffic to retrieve the arm he had left on top of my car when he stowed my folded chair into the rear of the station wagon. Nubia and I looked at each other and grinned with satisfaction.

The day ended when Jennie came home with Gerald. She walked quietly into my room to say, "Goodnight and thank you." After kissing her dear face, I fell peacefully asleep.

The next morning—Monday—didn't start out well. Some of the freshmen at Jennie's college had to find temporary housing off campus. She had agreed to share an apartment with one of the other graduates until her friend's father phoned me and said, "I want my daughter to live on campus, so, after speaking with the administrator, they have found a place for her." I could not argue with him because I had woken up with a sore throat and a voice that was barely a whisper. Upset, I told him politely that he was leaving Jennie no choice but to live alone and to pay more than she could afford, neither of which pleased my daughter or me.

I received a letter in the mail from the father saying he and his daughter had a bitter fight over their abandonment of Jennie, and he was running around looking for possible places for Jennie to stay off campus.

While that was being dealt with, I addressed the suggestion my financial advisor had proposed to me before leaving for Monterey. "Summer is a good time to put the property at St. Lo on the market. Now that you are certain about the permanence of your physical condition, you will need the money to work for you. Your overhead will be high."

My decision to sell the lot came easily even though it was the last tie with my old life. The years had changed St. Lo, and all desire to return had died in me.

The children reacted in different ways. Bill was fine with it. Dana and Morgan asked me, if they put up fifty thousand dollars each, would I build a spec house? No, I wouldn't. Morgan told me I worried too much about money.

I began to write my book at the encouragement of my friends. With less weight on my shoulders now, I was able to concentrate better.

While lunching with Aunt Alice, I spoke with Alice's friend, Harriet, who had written a successful book late in life. I told her I was writing a book about loss—the theme she had used in her lovely story.

"I'm leaving for Mexico," she said.

Thinking she was returning to the setting of her story, I said, "You're not going back to—"

"Oh, no," she interrupted. "I'm going to Cuernavaca."

"A beautiful place," I said, remembering the time Bill and I shared lunch there as peacocks roamed the surrounding gardens.

"I'm selling my property at St. Lo," I told Harriet, who once owned a house there.

"Good thing," she began. "St. Lo is too much like Beverly Hills with all those enormous houses. They should have kept it small and cottage-like."

The conversation reinforced my decision to sell the property.

Jennie's report card came in the mail two weeks after her graduation. The realization that Jennie's high school years were over became apparent to me after reading her teachers' and classmates' comments.

A picture of her maturing character could be drawn from the words of her teachers: "Jennie loves to read, write, act, play the drums, likes science, but math eludes her in spite of the effort she puts into it; physical education is met with some disinterest, but she is a good equestrian, and she loves animals—all animals; sensitive, creative, compassionate; she has a wonderful ability to juxtapose themes in literature to contemporary events and issues; critical of many aspects of the current world; trying to find answers to her questions and to apply possible reforms; her ideas are worth expressing; Jennie's independent study in Mexico resulted in daily participation in class, and her independent project on Ana Maria Matute was brilliant in style and content."

Jennie had taken an interest in acting since sixth grade, so remarks on "Rehearsal and Performance"—regarding her drama class—were supportive: "Jennie has natural talent as well as an understanding that talent is not enough, that a deep commitment to learning the craft is required." I was so proud of her when she won an award for her performance in *Joseph and the Amazing Technicolor Dreamcoat*.

"Jennie has taken risks and sees the results," the report continued. What a change from her freshman and sophomore years when it was difficult for her to participate in class, rarely putting her hand up—still so traumatized from the losses in her life.

Her music teacher summed it up when he wrote, "She plays the drums with a fine sense of musicianship. To her, the best!"

The report concluded with expressions of hope for Jennie's future and well-being, the joy of knowing her for four years. Each year signified her growth.

The notes penned by her classmates in her yearbook echoed the sentiments of her teachers—that she was caring and able to help others when life was bearing down.

When she walked into my room back then, I saw a new confidence in her and genuine contentment. It was a true rebirth. My prayer had been to be reborn with Jennie, to walk again when she graduated. God said, "No." It was time to pass the torch to my children and to discover what direction my own rebirth would take. 🐢

Chapter 26

GOD IN CONTROL

It is time for you to look ahead
and forget what is behind you,
time to pay attention to what you still need . . .
God is a jealous lover . . .
He wants your simple, undistracted gaze.

—Unknown, "Cloud Of Unknowing"

Chapter 26

While Jennie was up north signing up for her college classes, my mother came to visit. After I greeted her with "It's good to see you," there was an icy silence. "Can't you say 'It's good to see you, too'?" I inquired as gently as possible. However, she went into how poorly things were handled when she was moved out of her home.

"Mother, don't you see how Morgan and Katy were wonderful? Try to appreciate the time and care Morgan took to make a very difficult task as easy as possible." Openly expressing my own feelings in a natural, relaxed way was a huge step for me.

My mother's face softened, and the glacial look melted. I expected my mother to say that indeed she did appreciate what had been done for her. Her thoughts, however, moved away from the subject at hand. She began to talk about her childhood in England: "As children, my brother John and sister Margaret joined me in sticking pins in the corners of the graves to try to disturb the dead, or so we imagined. Then we would run like mad. The graveyard was near Peterborough Cathedral where we attended services. John sang in the cathedral choir. After the services, Mr. Hagen, the organist, would pump up the organ, and, with other children, we would stand outside and wait for the big whoosh of steam to erupt from the steam-powered organ. Twilight in the cathedral was eerie," she added.

Clearly, my mother was somewhere far, far away. I let her continue because she seldom spoke about her years in England when she enjoyed horse and buggy rides with her mother, Nellie. "I remember visiting Dr. Kirkwood with my mother. Dr. Kirkwood picked me up and put me on his knee. 'Just think, Nellie, this child could have been ours,' said the doctor. I think they were in love," said Mother. "I remember the incident clearly," and she smiled.

"Mother, were you happy as a child?" I asked her.

"Yes, we all got along," she answered. "My father spoiled my brother. He wouldn't give his daughters sixpence, but Jock," she said, referring to the name his family called him, "could have anything he wanted."

"Was your mother happy?" I asked.

"No, I don't think so, but in those days you bore your sorrows in silence. I don't like to hear about the world today. When I was a child, life was quiet, calm and beautiful. We had good friends, good neighbors." Then she added, "When there is little left to do in life, that is when you want to go. Where are you going to be buried?" she asked me.

"I want to be cremated and have my ashes scattered at sea. That's where Bill is."

My mother left that day with a sweetness in her face. Smiling, she said, "I'll come whenever you want me. It is nice being here."

"I've enjoyed having you here," I emphasized.

After I told Sister Wilfrid about mother's visit, her comment was, "Now she can be at peace, and so can you. What a wonderful gift. You are living very close to God." Together we offered prayers of thanks.

Jennie came home after registering for classes and visiting her brother Bill and friends in the Bay Area.

She would come to my room at night after she had been out and if my light was still on. We talked about everyday things, and, when I repeated myself, she would laugh and say, "I already told you that, Mom."

Secretly, I detested what medication, stress, pain, and now aging were doing to my memory. Nevertheless, there were small signs of progress, indicating to me that I was mending. For instance, my thirty-eighth wedding anniversary—or what would have been my thirty-eighth—had slipped by without me noticing. Usually, the day of our anniversary brought with it a bittersweet feeling. Now, it was just another day.

Instead of going to Europe her first summer out of high school, Jennie was volunteering at Children's Hospital and arranging her college expenses with an advisor who was helping her take over the management of her affairs.

"I will be working with children from four months to four years of age," Jennie said about her volunteer work.

While Jennie was busy working, I had time to think about how to move forward with my own life. Time was on my side as I lay facedown healing a pressure sore I had acquired from the long days of Jennie's graduation.

First, I focused on a plan to sell the lot at St. Lo. The children had moved on with their lives and had accepted the fact that the lot had to be sold. There was some opposition to the idea of selling the lot, most of which came from Morgan. Perhaps it was because he and his wife, Katy, still lived nearby, and they saw St. Lo as an extension of their lives.

Mother and I were getting along well, even after Uncle Phil died in July. "He didn't survive the move," the Senior Care Network official had said.

"I'm so sorry," I said to the official. "Only a few weeks ago, Phil had asked my mother to marry him. He phoned and asked me to come see the two of them. They were sitting side by side when I arrived. Holding hands, their eyes twinkling, he said to me, 'We're off to Shangri-La.' I kissed them both."

My mother said little about his death, except, "Oh, everybody around here is being so nice to me." Only when I told her that I had phoned my sister, Jeannette, with the news did she begin to cry. Each one of her grandchildren had phoned her—as did my sister—and Mother was happy because the entire family provided her with support.

We did not go to his funeral in Redlands—where he had lived as a boy. He still had nephews in the area, and they made the arrangements. When we were young, my sister and I always enjoyed going to Redlands to visit his parents' ranch. I remember fondly how we used to smell the orange trees, pick blackberries, wade in a stream, and run barefoot. And, as we grew, we made friends with the boys on the neighboring ranch. I wanted to keep those memories as they were—these were the kind of innocent, carefree days that we so enjoyed under the smog-free, blue California skies of the '30s and early '40s.

My mother had another surprise for me. "I'm eighty-seven years old," she informed me, handing me her British birth certificate.

"But we were going to celebrate your ninetieth last year until you fell and were hospitalized," I said.

"I never was very good with figures," she replied, the implication being that she was never good at mathematics.

Summer no longer bothered me. I became used to the fact that friends had left town and that the phone was not ringing. I saw myself as a Victorian woman, wearing a long-sleeved, high-necked blouse, a broach at my neck, a lace handkerchief peeking out of a sleeve, shut-in, disabled, and waiting for God to take me away.

When the Fourth of July arrived, Jennie stood in the doorway of my bedroom waving a sparkler at me. And my granddaughter Riley paid me a visit before leaving for Africa. Riley sat in my electric cart in all her teenage glory. Bangle bracelets jingled on her arm, drop earrings swung from her ears as she said, "I don't want to go to Africa. My friends in Sun Valley have just returned from their vacations, and I am leaving for Africa, so I won't be able to enjoy them. Oh, I guess I'll be all right once I get there."

"She wept into her baked potato when I told Riley we were going to Africa," Leslie informed me.

"Well, there's no shortage of spuds in Idaho," I remarked jokingly.

Death had touched Riley's life as well. One of her best friends—a fourteen-year-old driving legally in Idaho—turned her car over four times on her way home from a Bob Dylan concert. She was seriously injured. One girl died, another ended up brain damaged and yet another became paraplegic. Riley was probably safer in Africa.

I began to make some changes in my life. I told Larry to come only once or twice a month, and I gave my massage therapist the same message. I said "no more" to my neurologist on my final visit.

Kevin, Dana, and my grandson Evan were visiting St. Lo. It was important for me to see Evan in that particular "sandbox by the sea"—as we use to call the beach—so I drove down to St. Lo from Pasadena for the day. There were lots of babies for Evan to play with, but the place seemed crowded and smaller. Except for a handful of old-timers, I no longer recognized everyone. Some very large homes had been built. They were out of character with the St. Lo I remembered. They detracted from the charm of the small village-like setting that I loved so much.

Before Jennie left for college, she broke up with Gerald, and, because I had become so fond of him, I felt genuinely sad. It wasn't pleasant for me to hear my daughter arguing with him on the phone and then slamming down the receiver.

"I'm ready to end it," she told me, but unfortunately Gerald didn't feel the same.

Jennie phoned me when she first arrived at St. Mary's College. Instead of living on campus, she was forced to rent an apartment nearby. "Nothing but men in my building," she said. "There's one guy, about forty, living downstairs along with two male students from Santa Clara. And, living on my floor, there are a few men in their early twenties. Erin, my roommate, is easy to get along with. And we have a beautiful view from our deck."

Eventually, she moved into a dorm on campus where she felt much more a part of campus life.

My daughters phoned me to see how I was holding up.

"I'm going to Mexico," I said.

I arrived at LAX with Nubia and my friend, Mary Jane—whose daughter owned the condo where we would be staying. We boarded the plane and were served breakfast after takeoff. I nodded off for several hours.

The next thing I knew, I was being carried down a steep flight of stairs to the tarmac. Below me, I saw one nervous flight attendant, the pilot, and Mary Jane. Mary Jane was crying as she tried to explain to anyone who would listen how I was stricken with paralysis overnight.

The manager from Terra Sol greeted us and showed us to our cars. After giving Nubia instructions on how to get to our destination, he left to take our luggage to the condo.

God, it was hot! The air conditioner in the car didn't work, and we got lost. Nubia stopped the car several times to ask in Spanish for directions to our condo. No one had heard of it.

As we drove along, I noticed how similar Cabo was to other parts of Baja that were familiar to me. In the shallows, the water along the coastline was aquamarine. Still, there were the shacks, highway litter, underfed children and animals—so typical of that part of Mexico.

Just months before Bill died, he and I had planned on making the drive down to Cabo. Because of the unusually heavy rains that year, we decided not to go. The wonderful sense of adventure that I remembered from our frequent forays across the border was now gone. Only the memory of our final New Year's together at Las Gaviotas could rekindle anything similar to those feelings of adventure. The memories were bittersweet.

Finally, we found the condo. However, the manager who was bringing my wheelchair and our luggage had not made an appearance yet. Hot, tired, and wet, I lost my sense of humor. "Nubia, please find someone who can open this door," I barked.

Then, just as Nubia showed up with two strong men, Mary Jane announced, "I have a key."

After the door was unlocked, I was carried into the condo and placed on a bed. The wheelchair and the luggage showed up soon after. "Gracias a Dios," I mumbled.

Nubia tidied me up, and then left for the market while I rested. We were in the first condo in a string of sandy-colored condos on the beach. My room afforded me a magnificent view of the sea.

In the evening, the three of us settled in the tile-floored living room to devour quesadillas made with warm, fresh tortillas. We quenched our thirst with margaritas provided by room service and laughed about our recent adventures.

Falling asleep to the sound of the surf revived a memory of St Lo for me. Oh, how I missed the thunderous sound of waves crashing on the beach there.

In the morning, I opened my eyes to a lovely scene of a cruise ship rounding a giant cliff and a flock of pelicans dipping low over the ocean. Nubia bathed me and washed my hair before helping me stretch out on my tummy to air my fragile skin.

I thought about Damian and remembered one particularly bright and sunny afternoon when Damian and I were sitting on my terrace at St. Lo. At that time, he asked me to go to Mexico with him. I said, "no," but meant, "yes." Ten years had passed since that moment, and now I was in Mexico, alone.

With plenty of help to get me in and out of the pool, I swam each day. As I swam the length of the pool, it was necessary to overcome the pull of the stronger muscles on my left side. They tried to pull me over on my back. By the time I reached a stool at the swim-up bar, my muscles were stretched out enough so that I could sit comfortably without floating away from my perch. Sipping a margarita, I looked past the bar toward the beach, the ocean, and listened to Julio Iglesias singing.

I sat there thinking about the night before when we dined out on the terrace of a hotel that looked out across the harbor: below us, small tables for two were set out on the sand. They were covered with white cloths—a lighted candle in the center of each table. A bonfire crackled nearby, throwing sparks into the night sky. The setting rekindled memories of my honeymoon in Mexico—it was June, 1950, so very long ago.

Two ladies swam up to the bar, interrupting my reverie. With a smile, I acknowledged their presence, and then they introduced themselves.

Eager to talk, they told me they were from Atlantic City. One of them designed condos, and the other was married to a man who operated a casino. When I saw an opening in their conversation, I quickly asked, "Like Donald Trump?"

"He is a very nice man," they said in unison, as if to discourage anything negative I might say about the "nice" Mr. Trump.

Curvaceous, pretty Nubia attracted all the men. They kept coming to our condo to fix things. "I don't like them if they have bad teeth," said Nubia. So far, Arturo evidently had outdistanced Ricardo, Felix and the others. He was indeed cute, polite, and I suppose his teeth were okay.

We chose a swinging-singles disco for our next night out. Young adults in their twenties and thirties crowded the place. The club was noisy, but the atmosphere was cheerful. And, lo and behold, I was actually having fun again! High on the pure delight of being alive, I could almost feel my body shifting gears as it took me to a place I had all but forgotten.

When I returned to the condo, Nubia helped me to settle in happily for the night. Then she left to walk in the moonlight. She had taken her tape player "por la música." *Is somebody out there? Arturo perhaps,* I wondered.

Swimming again—so good for my body, which was twisted by the heat—I struck up a conversation with a young and attractive twenty-five-year-old graphic artist named Anna.

She told me that she was in love with an American who lived in the States but that, at the moment, she was having an affair with the manager of the place where we were staying. She had lived in Puerto Vallarta, but, ". . . it is too transient—a wonderful place, but as soon as you make a friend, they leave."

She told me her father didn't like his daughters-in-law "because they work." I hadn't spoken a word beyond our introductions and Anna was telling me her life story. I closed the confessional by saying, "I'm happy to have met you, but I need to stretch my muscles." I then swam away.

Arturo—the one with the good teeth—was now part of our group. He took us sightseeing among the vacation homes of the rich and the rock stars on La Piedragava. We visited the distant town of Cabo San Juan, which was reminiscent of colonial Mexico but not as pretty. The splendid sunset we saw as we drove to a restaurant Arturo had selected for dinner more than compensated for the extremely hot day.

That particular night, the seas were heavy. The eight- to ten-foot waves rattled the windows of the restaurant, but it was the music that made me put my fork down. I hummed the long forgotten melody *Saberme* (To Know Me).

Oh, the moonlight, the sea, the food, the music, Mexico. I'm alive!

Returning to the condo, I explained to the housekeeper, "Nubia was putting my shoe on when this great hairy, spidery leg appeared on my toes. Since I feel no sensation in my legs, I didn't realize that something was in my shoe as I lifted my leg with both hands and my shoe fell off. Nubia grabbed the spider's leg, ran to the bathroom and flushed it down the toilet."

The housekeeper left, but soon returned with a dead spider in a plastic bag.

"Yes, that's it, but that is a baby, mine was tarantula size," I explained.

"We'll have to spray again," the housekeeper calmly said.

The spider, called a "deer killer," was of the deadly variety—one bite and it's all over. *Death by spider couldn't be any worse than what I've already been through*, I thought.

But, in spite of the spider, I went to look at condos with the idea of buying one. A gorgeous man—he could have been Harry Belafonte's double—came to show me around. "My name is Stonewall, but people call me Stoney," he said, introducing himself.

The first condo I checked out didn't have a view of the sea; the second one had three bedrooms, a better view, and was architecturally more inter-esting—oddly, it was the cheaper of the two.

Upon returning to our vacation condo, I was introduced to Cathy, who talked dollars and cents before she told me her life story. I went into my mother-confessor mode again as I listened to this forty-one-year-old tell me how she had lost her husband to a heart attack, leaving her with a nineteen-year-old son. After working for an insurance company, she came to Cabo to sell real estate and then decided to stay. She loved the commu-nity. "I needed a fresh start away from men who wouldn't leave me alone after I became a widow, away from couples who knew my husband and me. The wives don't want you around when you're widowed and alone," she explained.

"Ah yes, I remember," I acknowledged, recalling that first year after Bill's death.

After concluding business, we offered Cathy and Stoney a drink. Nubia fixed Stoney her Ishmael special, a drink concocted for her by Ish, the bartender at the pool. Poor Stoney! He wasn't prepared for Nubia's concoction. "My God, what's in this?!" he asked as he slumped down in a chair, his head buzzing. Cathy carried on with business while Stoney sat in a stupor—the result of Nubia's drink. When Stoney was able to get up on his feet, Cathy and Nubia helped an embarrassed Stoney out the door.

When they were leaving, I said to Cathy, "I have to talk to God about purchasing a condo."

~~~

Mary Jane and I ate leftovers from the night before and then went to bed while Nubia left for a sightseeing cruise with Anna and another woman named Josefina.

Full of excitement when she returned from her excursion, she said, "Now you just rest, and I'll tell you a story about Love's Beach—a place we went to see. There was an old lady who lived in Cabo long ago. Her name was Nacha. One night, she was discovered making love to a young man on the beach, and, for many, many nights thereafter, people would spy on her and her young man. That's why it's called 'Love's Beach,'" she concluded.

"Well, maybe I should buy the condo after all," I said under my breath.

"Did you say something, Mrs. Hees?" asked Nubia. I didn't answer.

Overcome with fatigue, I rested the following day. Nubia went to a disco with Arturo. She had wavered at first, but, with some slight encouragement from me, she left.

"I didn't get home until three-thirty this morning," she said, as she helped me get ready for the day.

"Did you have a good time?" I asked.

"Yes, it was great. You know something, Mrs. Hees, an American boy asked me to dance with him. I asked Arturo if it would be okay with him. He said 'fine,' and that was that. Remember? You told me to live in the moment. And I did."

Nubia, a wonderful mix of the realist and the innocent, always giggled when she shared something of a personal nature with me.

Our final day, a Sunday, was hotter than hot. Without air conditioning in the car, we drove to a beautiful old hotel for brunch. Three men carried me up the stairs to a terrace overlooking the pool and the sea. Mary Jane's daughter had been married in the chapel on the grounds of the hotel. And a good friend had encouraged me to come to this place after Bill's death. But I thought I would have disliked being there without Bill.

That night, resting peacefully in our air-conditioned condo, I thought about Nubia at the disco. "I danced with an American," she had said, as if a dream had come true for her. Then, I wondered if I possessed the courage to actually live there. No, probably not. But, I prayed that Pasadena would not be my final home and that Nubia, in time, would find her American. Both prayers were eventually answered.

The following day, we boarded the plane for the trip home. I soon became aware that Nubia and I had forgotten to change my soggy diaper. I didn't care.

Once home, the best news was from Bill: he had found his true love. "She even cooks for me, Mom," he said with some astonishment. *Of course she does; she loves you,* I thought. I couldn't wait to meet his Kathy.

Before saying our goodbyes, Bill informed me that his boss had told him he had great natural ability in construction. He had inherited his father's engineering skills and the love of working with his hands.

Marge, the nurse, came to check my skin to see if it had survived the trip. "You'll be famous one day," she said as she left my room. Famous for what? Writing a book? Helping others? I wanted to be well, not famous.

My sister visited from Virginia. She spent the better part of her time with our mother. What a momentary relief for me! It was one more weekly trip I didn't have to make for a short while. Mother was probably seeing her oldest daughter for the last time. I new Jeannette would never come again; the trip was too emotional for her. Besides, she hated to fly. When my sister was leaving, I promised her I would come to visit her in Virginia. (I kept that promise.)

I told Sister Wilfrid about the happy reunion with my sister, and how much it had meant to me.

"It is only a foretaste of the reunion you will have in Heaven," she said.

Heaven came to earth for a moment. The property at St. Lo was sold; this was no small miracle. And, my faith in Nancy—my girlhood friend— was rewarded: she sold the lot for seven times the amount it had been appraised for at the time of Bill's death.

Immediately I began to think about where I would really enjoy living. Perhaps another trip should come first. Why wouldn't it be possible to travel and, at the same time, find the place where I would settle down?

Change was in the air. For the first time in thirty-eight years, I spent Thanksgiving alone in perfect peace. Solitude is a beautiful state of being, as it invokes for me a deepening of faith and a devotion entirely to God.

With December came my fifty-eighth birthday and a quiet celebration. Jennie was home, so together we faced the cold and rain to have lunch with Aunt Alice. It was not exactly the pleasant moment I had imagined it would be because Charles was dead.

Alice wanted to hear about Mexico. When I told her about the spider story, Alice said as she closed her eyes, "That would do it right there!" enunciating each word with great clarity. Baja and its spiders were not for her.

Flowers were awaiting me when I came home. The children phoned me. But one very important thing did not occur: for the first time in her life, my mother forgot about the day, and, yes, I found that rather sad.

I felt very emotionally independent by Christmas. That was my greatest gift. My son Bill felt the shift in me. His life began to blossom in the company of a very special woman who would soon be his wife. Just as the '80s were coming to an end, he phoned to say, "Won't you be glad when it is 1990? This last decade has been terrible for all of us."

For Jennie, for me, life began anew as she embarked on her college years. Out of high school, she was flourishing as she made new friends, visited new places, and found a new boyfriend. It didn't bother us at all that we no longer kept in constant touch, because, as she put it, "We both love books and love to discuss what we have read."

There was one more ritual to be observed. We—the family—all gathered together during the Christmas season to watch our dear baby Jennie make her appearance as a debutante at the ball. As outdated as a debutant ball was for that day and age, Jennie and her friends nonetheless decided "it would be a blast."

The house looked remarkably lovely before the ball. The children, full of love and so supportive, looked very grand in their formal attire. The tree, decorated in large pink bows, strands of pearls and small white lights, suggested innocence.

After dinner, we went to the club to watch Jennie enter the ballroom on the arms of her brothers, greet the guests, and finally—standing directly in front of me as I sat in my wheelchair—she dropped into a deep curtsy. As she stood up, we looked into each other's eyes for a moment. She turned away to take her place among the other debs. The ball—as old-fashioned as it was—nevertheless brought some civility into a world that was losing its manners.

On New Years Eve, I attended a costume party hosted by Damian. By the time I got there, the temperature had taken a sudden drop. It was bitter cold outside. The cold hurt my spine. The people I knew had already come and gone; it was mostly a young crowd. Amongst the revelers were many of Damian's ex-girlfriends, as Christopher—Damian's artist friend—pointed out. Handing Damian a balloon as I greeted him, I felt a familiar caress on my finger and detected a searching look in his blue eyes for one brief moment. Then he walked over to a microphone and sang *Happy Birthday* to his housekeeper, Theresa.

The following day, when I called Damian to thank him for inviting me, he said, "I ramped the entrance for you and covered it with balloons so you could make a grand entrance through them when you arrived, but they kept popping."

What magic or mysterious connection can keep two souls in love, especially when they are separated by an age difference of twenty years? Ten years had passed since that mysterious, always unexplainable thing called "falling in love" had happened.

Recently, his sister told me, "He talks about you all the time." At an earlier Christmas gathering, Damian sat next to me, kissed me, stroked my hand and said, "You look adorable." But, I want my heart free, so only the fullness of God's love can enter it.

After seven years, the butterfly was about to emerge from her cocoon. It made me think of the biblical seven—for example, God resting on the seventh day of creation. (The things that occur in my life, I equate with Biblical symbolism.) I had rediscovered the joy of life, and I was responsible to no one but God. On his time, St. Lo would be erased from my memory; on his time, as I ventured forth into a new life, I would discover the plans He had for me.

Chapter 27

BELLS OF LIBERATION AND HOPE

From everywhere, filling the air,
Oh how they pound, raising the sound,
O'er hill and dale, telling their tale.

—*Carol of the Bells*

Chapter 27

I realized that there was no way to buy back the years I spent on my rehabilitation. Nor did I wish to waste any more time in the company of frustration, anger, despair, and loneliness. I felt I was getting a better sense of what true happiness was all about, and it certainly didn't include wallowing in negativity.

It was impossible to remember any Christmas when it was as difficult to take the tree down as the Christmas of 1988. Such a sassy tree. With its decorated pink bows, a string of pearls and white lights, it represented for me the celebration of youth and new life. In the coming New Year, I became a grandmother again. Morgan and Katy told me the good news on New Year's night. In case it was a girl, the pink bows would be on the tree once again the following Christmas, so I folded them carefully and stored them away.

Dealing with the sale of the lot at St. Lo stirred up some resentment that was still lingering among the children, and, to my surprise, even a few of my friends had their opinions about my decision.

My son-in-law, Kevin, speaking on behalf of himself and Dana, said, "We don't have a lot of money, so it would be great for us to have the beach at St. Lo to go to for a vacation." Knowing it would cost me a great deal for caregivers and housekeepers during the years to come, I was not about to take on the responsibility of maintaining a second residence, one that I had no desire to return to.

Morgan said, "My wife cried about the sale of the lot." Why was *she* crying, I wondered, it was *my* past that was disappearing?

"It isn't the '50s, the '60s or even the '70s, Morgan. You and Katy will have to manage your own lives," I said.

"It's always been 'me, me, me' with you, Mom. Go ahead, spend your money anyway you wish." Did I ask for his opinion? There was no stopping him. "Suffering does not make you a saint, and you only had five children because you are Catholic and didn't practice birth control," he ranted. I looked at my son at that moment and wished I *had* practiced birth control.

"They got a bargain," was one outsider's opinion—a woman who knew nothing about the transaction and less about dealing with the sale of the property at St. Lo. It was part of her nature to find the downside of everything; it made her feel better about her own life.

"No they didn't," I replied. "I was very pleased with the offer and felt that my home was sold for a fair price."

I went to an exhibit at the Pacific Asia Museum hoping to get away from all the opinions regarding the sale of my property at St. Lo. It was nobody's business but my own. Suddenly, I found myself face to face with a part-time inhabitant of St. Lo. She bent over me as she spoke. "Is it true that you sold your lot?" she asked.

"Yes," I replied.

"May I ask how much money you received for the lot? I heard that it was a great deal of money."

"Yes, it was more than I expected. And, no, I will not tell you how much I was paid," I responded, hoping to end the conversation.

The woman looked thoughtful for a second. Then, "God, I own a lot at St. Lo. I wonder how much it's worth?"

"I've no idea," I said, when, thankfully, we were interrupted, and the conversation ended.

Sympathetic words came from a woman named Maggie. She and her husband were selling the home they lived in for thirty-eight years. "We are scaling down, Berta. It is just too much. I'm no longer interested in keeping the place up. It is time to let go. The children hate the idea, because they will miss the country club with the pool and tennis courts. In circumstances such as yours, and with an overhead I can't imagine, you are doing the right thing."

There was more. I needed a quitclaim from the St. Lo association to clear the title. Bill and I had allowed the members to blacktop a small portion of the property to allow more space for parking near the tennis courts. Mike, who had sold my house for me in 1981, had somehow maneuvered himself into the deal. "I'm coming right over because you were stupid to sign a subordination agreement with that man," he said rudely, referring to the gentleman who was purchasing the property.

I was about to say, "No, thanks," but he hung up on me, and seconds later the doorbell rang.

My caregiver Thelma answered the door, and in walked Mike, my uninvited guest.

"Why are you here, Mike?" I inquired.

Mike immediately began to explain what he thought I should have done.

I interrupted him, saying, "I've had very good advice. I don't need any more advice, especially when it's not wanted."

He talked over me, saying the situation was not to my advantage. "It is risky, but it could be okay," he concluded.

"Mike, are the owners of my former home trying to torpedo this deal or are you sniffing the money trail?"

"Well uh, well uh, we don't like this deal for you. You are taking all the risks."

"They're *my* risks, and I'll happily accept them."

As he was leaving, he said, "I'll have Daniel phone you."

Daniel had been practically a neighbor at St. Lo. He was quiet, reserved, and a lawyer as well. I was disappointed that he had agreed to get in line with Mike. When Daniel phoned, he said, "Listen to Mike," and hung up.

A few days later, Mike was back on my doorstep, unannounced. "Do you want me to call your real estate agent or not?" he asked.

My patience was thin indeed, but, just to be mean, I smiled my "show me" smile and strung him along. "I don't remember suggesting that you call my agent. If I say okay, how much is it going to cost me?" There was no reply, so I threw out a figure. "Well? $20,000? What, fifteen, ten?" I went on.

"No, I won't charge you anything if I can't do anything. I charge $315 per hour," I heard him say.

I replied, "That's a big 'if,' Mike."

Before he left, he tried for the sympathy vote: "You know she has a problem with the new owner already," he said, referring to the woman who had bought my house in 1981. "I've been playing golf with her husband, and it's true," he concluded. At last he showed his hand, and I was not surprised but still saddened by this particular effort to derail my plans.

I should have sent each of the people involved in this effort a bill for damage to my already frayed nervous system and for the resulting visits to my psychiatrist. However, I privately thanked them for making it easier for me to let go of the last string tying me to my past.

The escrow closed. The lot was gone. My dear friend Nancy brought me the check and a basket of goodies. Thanking her for what she had accomplished, I then told her about the meddling from various parties.

"I don't give a damn how they feel," she commented. Nancy was a lady through and through. Her comment surprised me.

"Nancy, I didn't know you had it in you." I declared. "Now I know why you're such a great real estate agent." Nancy smiled.

"Well, it's a tough business." We hugged each other, and I thanked her for her help and support. "Berta, I'd do anything to help you. I'm sorry that other people have upset you with their unwanted and unsolicited advice," Nancy sighed.

The mail arrived with a letter from Mike. Would he never give up?! In the letter he wrote:

> *Nancy and the brokerage firm were negligent in their handling of the sale of your property, but my intervention put the buyer on guard.*

He pointed out to me that he had spent nine hours working on my behalf, but he would not charge me anything. Since he was so specific as to the number of hours he had spent working on my behalf, I understood that he probably was expecting to be compensated for his time. I never asked for his help, I didn't trust him, and I certainly wasn't about to pay him for unsolicited aid.

This final ordeal left me temporarily disillusioned with family and friends. As parents get older, they have fewer concerns about the future, unlike their children who are living in the present and are fashioning their lives. Some friends are, as the saying goes, only with you in fair weather.

The vultures in the mix were few, and I accepted it all as the natural order of things.

Much had been accomplished as far as family was concerned. Leslie was coping with her teenage daughter; Dana was caring for her husband and young son and continuing her education; my sister was staying in touch with me and our mother; Bill was working on his house while he prepared for married life; Morgan was studying for his Masters Degree in Economics while waiting for his first child to be born; Jennie was enjoying college life.

And my mother was becoming more open with her feelings as she played out the end of her life. "You are such a lovely girl," my mother told me recently. "I tell everyone that," she added.

"Thank you, Mother, and now you have finally told me," I whispered, trying not to cry.

One Sunday in May, I had a dinner party for Leslie, Michael, Dana and little Evan, Aunt Alice, and my mother. Nubia helped me set the table, my daughters arranged the flowers, Michael brought the wine, and the caterers saw to the food. When mother arrived, her eyes filled with tears of joy to see nearly everyone together again.

For the first time in eight years, I felt comfortable with myself and with my family. No longer the onlooker, I was connected to life again. My body was totally calm, my spine remained strong, and I never felt stressed. The old fears, the anxieties were gone. At long last, I was comfortable with myself, so much so that I calmly announced my plans to go to Italy. Everyone applauded my decision.

"To Mom and Italy!" someone shouted, and then everyone raised their glasses of wine in a toast. Thanks to my inheritance from Uncle Phil, it was possible to spend two grand weeks away from everything, away from everybody.

Damian's mother introduced me to a travel agent who was her friend and was confined to a wheelchair. She carefully mapped out my itinerary. My traveling companion would be my caregiver's brother-in-law. Tony—or Nonoy, as his family called him—was a doctor. He was nice-looking, intelligent, a traveler like me, and he enjoyed my sense of humor. At that time, he was in research, studying the metamorphosis of tadpoles and how that might translate into a cure for muscular dystrophy.

When we were first introduced, I asked him about his research.

"I want to be remembered for something when I die," he stated.

"Tadpoles?" I inquired humorously. "Oh, a cure for muscular dystrophy! That's wonderful, Nonoy. How do tadpoles come into the picture?"

"They lose their tails, yet something prevents them from further loss of bodily material," he answered.

"That's a plus. You'll probably need a sense of humor yourself, because we will be sharing the same hotel room. I'm not paying for an extra room," I explained.

He replied, "I'm a professional, and I'll be there if you need any help." (Nonoy would not only be my companion but my personal physician as well.)

I intuited that my children and Sister Wilfrid were concerned about the trip and my traveling companion, though they said little about it. I, on the other hand, had no worries whatsoever. I felt completely confident about my journey to Italy.

Sister Wilfrid called me one day to say that she had been in the chapel praying for me.

"I know. It was at lunchtime. I felt His magnificent peace," I told her. Sister Wilfrid was ailing. However, she came to my home, gave me Communion, a medal that had been touched by Cornelia Connelly—who founded Sister Wilfrid's order—and a rosary that belonged to her cousin, a Dominican nun.

As departure time grew closer, Dana phoned with goodbyes from Leslie and Morgan. They all wished me *bon voyage*, but they were nervous about my journey. My daughter's voice sounded rather flat.

Jennie drove down from college to say goodbye. She would be in Europe before the summer began, but we would not connect while we were both in Europe. However, the morning I left, she hugged me several times. "Maybe you won't come home," she said, implying that I might prefer to live in Italy.

"Yes, I will. This is my home, but I need some distance from the past. Surely you understand that," I replied.

"Maybe I'm the one who won't come home," she said with an impish smile. Jennie and I enjoyed travel and different cultures. Her comment didn't surprise me. My doctors prepared me for the trip so that I would be as comfortable as possible—that included implanting an indwelling catheter. The indwelling catheter would change my life—no more diapers or self-catheterization every four hours. I would continue to wear one successfully from then on. I was ready for my big test: I would soon literally take flight from my past life and plunge into an unknown future.

Nonoy went over the map of our itinerary, and we discussed how to handle my care while en route. With the new catheter, it would be easy. He could empty my urine bag into a portable urinal when necessary and take it to the nearest bathroom or, as it turned out, to the nearest field as we drove from place to place.

While going about the business of tucking my passport, travelers' checks, and foreign currency into the pockets of my purse, I thought about Bill. I recalled some of his travel rituals. I listed all the numbers of my traveler's checks on a separate piece of paper, just like Bill used to do.

On May 21, 1989, I was sitting—for the very first time—in the VIP lounge at LAX and sipping a Scotch while Nonoy ate peanuts and drank Coke. Thelma and her husband, Steve, had calmed my last minute jitters before Nonoy and I went through security. I was excited, feeling confident as I confronted any remaining fears that might block my ability to lead a full life. It was a journey of faith. I had to trust God completely, with my whole heart, my whole soul.

~~~

Boarding Alitalia for the flight to Milan wasn't easy. The Port Authority had closed the door near the nose of the plane and refused to open it, so I couldn't get to my very expensive seat—the one my travel agent had insisted on because of the legroom.

The plane was practically empty, so I would spend the night in coach on a bed made up of a row of empty seats. Nonoy sat nearby and took care of my immediate needs. We were served first-class meals, waited on constantly, so much so that I was happy when the cabin quieted down for the night. The only other person I saw in the wide-bodied jet was a gentleman sitting directly behind me.

For me, flying is at its best at nighttime. The lights are dim, and you hear the soothing sound of rushing air. I fell asleep immediately, and I didn't wake up until one hour before landing in Milan.

Nonoy emptied my urine bag, helped me into a sitting position, straightened my clothes, and put a pillow on my legs and my train case on top of the pillow so I could comb my hair and fix my face. The train case was a comfort to me. The only piece of luggage to survive the years since my honeymoon in 1950, it looked better than me. If it is possible to cherish an inanimate object, that was how I felt about the dark blue case, with white leather-bound edges and my initials on the front.

The gentleman behind me tapped me on the shoulder to say good morning. Turning my head as best I could, I was greeted by the most beautiful smile I've ever seen on a man or woman. I felt I could look into the man's soul. His eyes were so warm, I could feel the warmth on my skin.

After breakfast was served, the gentleman began to whistle. It was no ordinary sound that emerged from his lips. Sweet, melodious notes poured forth. It was like having a bird on my shoulder.

When we landed, Nonoy and I struggled a bit trying to transfer me into my chair until the man with the smile hopped up and immediately lifted me into my chair.

"Grazie," I whispered, hoping I had pronounced correctly the only Italian word I knew, but, apparently, the gentleman had vanished.

There was no direct access to the terminal from the plane, so I was lifted aboard an old vehicle used solely for transporting passengers across the tarmac.

The Malpensa airport was pristine, small, uncrowded, and quiet, but the luggage moved slowly, very slowly, from the plane. When the luggage finally showed up, we strolled past the drug- and bomb-sniffing dog held by one of the well-armed guards.

I was upset with Nonoy for neglecting to bring his visa, especially since I had told him earlier he would need one. He said, "It's all right, I'll take care of it." Then I saw him talking amiably with the authorities, who stamped his passport after sizing up the situation. They reminded him he would have to have it stamped again in eight days.

In no time at all, we were in our rented four-door Ford. The passenger seat reclined, and I took advantage of the unexpected comfort as we headed for Cernobbio and Lake Como. Lake Como was a sentimental stop on my Italian excursion. My husband's parents—William Rathbun Hees Jr. and Anne Dana Ayer—had met and fallen in love at the Villa d'Este while on the Grand Tour with their parents. It was in the '20s after World War I and after my father-in-law had left Princeton to serve in the French Ambulance Corps.

For years, each time I saw Hortense—a friend of my mother-in-law—she would tell me the same story: "I was staying with my family at the Villa d'Este at the same time as Anne's family. One afternoon, I watched Anne as she was being rowed away from the villa out on Lake Como. She looked so beautiful in her large picture hat. She turned her head to smile and wave. I can still see the picture in my mind, even after all these years." I suppose, by coming to Lake Como, I also wished to recapture the essence of that long-ago time and place. Nonoy and I were laughing about how the scenery looked so much like the scenery along the freeways at home. The look of old Europe did not become apparent until we drove through South Como. It was then that stucco houses with shuttered windows, small balconies, low walls accented with wrought iron and lots of flowers began to appear.

As we drove along the bumpy cobblestone streets, I looked up at the people who were leaning out of windows and watching the evening traffic go by. The owners of the lovely, quaint shops were leaning up against the colorful doors and enjoying the day. Ahead were green hills wearing church steeples like children's party hats and, finally, the lake.

It was 7:00 P.M. when we arrived at Villa d'Este, and the church bells were ringing. The woman at the desk was abrupt, rude even, as I handed her my letter from the travel agent. She threw it back at me saying, "You are on a waiting list for your return visit."

"But the letter confirms it," I said. Without a word, she handed me some mail.

Moving toward the lobby and the grand staircase, I paused to open my mail. There was a note card with a painting of a view of Tangier by Henri Matisse in the first envelope. The card read:

Dear Berta,

Welcome to Italy!!! I trust you're getting fresh air, not too tired, and eager with anticipation. Keep all in your head, or better, in a brief journal. Am so anxious to hear all about it in July.

Love, Alice

Before I left for my trip, Alice had said, "Probably your life wouldn't have been so different if you had the use of your legs."

The other note was from Sister Wilfrid:

Dearest Berta,

This is truly a RED LETTER DAY. Your pilgrimage was made in JOY, FAITH and TOTAL TRUST of the Blessed Lord who is healing you every moment of your VERY DEAR life. With more love and prayers than can be measured,

Faithfully, Sister Mary Wilfrid, SHC.

The man who showed us to the elevator was very polite, but he bristled—probably annoyed by a foreigner's comment—when Nonoy said, "They should make these things bigger," as the man struggled to squeeze me into the elevator.

I quickly said, "The elevators were probably made for genteel times," and the man smiled and nodded in agreement. Later, a smaller chair was brought to my room. We used it to go down to the lobby and kept mine in the car to be used when we went out.

I suddenly realized how tired I was from traveling as I rested on the empire bed covered with linen sheets. Catching a glimpse of myself in the mirror before retiring, I noticed how pale I looked and that my eyes were rimmed with dark circles. For a moment, I felt that I had come here too late in life, that I had almost missed the train of life and was barely hanging onto the caboose. On the other hand, the fact that I was here pleased me, because to me it underscored my courage and strong will to venture forth in spite of my paralysis. Bill, I thought, with his courtly old-world image, would have blended right in with the setting. Oh, how I hoped he could see me.

Some distant church bells were ringing as I gazed at the evening light on the gold brocade bedspread; the matching swag drapes were tied back from the shuttered French windows now open to the evening air. My bed faced the gardens. Birdsong and the sound of a nearby bell ringing out its solitary tone filled the room.

My thoughts turned to a conversation I had with Aunt Alice before I left for Italy. She spoke about her time spent there with her family. The family consisted of Alice's parents, her twin sister Anne (my mother-in-law). A nurse traveled with them because Anne's mother had tuberculosis. "It was a long time ago. I don't remember much. Annie and I took picnic lunches out on the lake," said Alice.

I asked about her mother.

"No one talked about her health. I remember rubbing my father's head," she said, pointing to her temple. "He had terrible headaches."

"Migraines, just like Bill?" I asked.

"Yes," she replied. "He had high blood pressure too."

"Just like Bill?" I repeated. But then I remembered: *Oh, come to think of it, his mother had died of a heart attack one Christmas Day!* I had so truly believed that Bill's ailments had come from his father's side of the family—I was shocked. I wondered why my husband's mother never mentioned her father's blood pressure and migraines to her son, who also suffered from the same things.

Alice continued, "My father died two years after that trip. On the boat home from Europe, he went down several decks to see the engine room. That's what did him in," Alice said. "It was climbing up all those stairs."

"Oh, I thought your mother died first."

"No, Annie and I were seventeen. My mother died when we were twenty-five."

As I ate a light supper, my eyes took in the room. On the gray walls hung a gold-framed mirror and old prints framed in mahogany. An enormous armoire, also made of mahogany and in Empire style, had a full-length mirror in the center and now held my clothes carefully hung there by Nonoy. A small dressing table with yet another large mirror suggested that, long ago, occupants of this room put a great deal of attention into dressing for dinner or for an afternoon stroll on the large veranda and through the gardens. A brass lamp with a curved silk shade sat atop the dresser, and from the ceiling hung a crystal and bronze chandelier. The floor was carpeted in green-gold—the color of the leaves outside the windows. White lawn curtains—that matched my white ruffled cotton gown edged in lace—billowed into the room. The yellow glow of evening poured like honey across the room as the maid removed my tray. "Buona notte, Signora," she said, closing the door on her way out. It was 8:30 P.M. I was jet-lagged, so sleep came swiftly.

I was still tired when the waiter arrived at 9:30 A.M. with breakfast. "Buon giorno," he said as he placed a tray with cafe latte, croissants, toast, jams, jellies and white butter.

"Oh, I ordered orange juice not tomato juice, Nonoy." After one sip it became obvious to me that it *was* orange juice after all—red oranges! I chose something from the basket of fruit and stole a daisy from the bouquet on the tray to put in my hair.

It was easy for me to move around, because the room was large, as was the white marble bathroom, which was absolutely made for my chair.

One morning, I was driving with Nonoy to Lugano, Switzerland. Dana had gone to school there, and I wanted to see where she had spent her year abroad. But disappointment would be mine when the border guards did not let us pass—Nonoy's visa again.

The disappointment didn't last however, because I so enjoyed the winding narrow streets, huge pristine lakes, exquisite villas, pretty apartments, hotels, old people walking hand in hand. It was such a pleasure to simply sit and watch the world go by and to take in the lush greenery and the small sparrows darting around church steeples, or hearing a tired mother telling her children "non molestarme" ("don't bother me"). While Nonoy went into a supermarket, I watched from the car as other young mothers were loading up on Pampers. They were dressed in jeans and T-shirts with logos just like their counterparts in the United States. Middle-aged women were smartly dressed in tailored suits or in skirts with silk blouses buttoned up the neck. And their leather shoes with short, square heels afforded them comfortable walking.

After returning to the Villa, I sat in the sun on the veranda to look out at Lake Como. The railings on the dock were covered with climbing roses as big as cabbages. Wheeling myself to the edge of the veranda, I leaned forward to see the colorful fish swimming in the clear, clear waters.

My inability to communicate in Italian didn't detract from the enjoyment I experienced from hearing the language. The afternoon hours, when the stores were closed, reminded me of siesta time in Mexico. I wished I could look in every direction simultaneously, as I knew that each and every sight would be beautiful to behold. Distracted as I was by all the sights and sounds of my adventures, I forgot all about my pain and physical limitations.

My three-day stay at Villa d'Este was so relaxing that I fell asleep early the night before we were to leave for Asolo. I was reading a bit of history about Villa d'Este, but I got no further than the first line: "Caroline of Brunswick was a busty piece of *sachertorte mit der schlag.*" Caroline was just going to have to wait for my return.

The drive to Asolo was autostrada all the way. It could have been the United States, with all the trucks and terrible drivers. Fortunately, Nonoy entertained me with his songs—he had a very nice singing voice—and, occasionally, I sang along.

My travel agent had recommended Asolo because it was quiet and throughout its history has been the home to some well-known expatriates such as Robert Browning and Eleanora Duse.

Once we were beyond the wall at the entrance of this medieval town, I saw a castle on a hill, a boy filling a water jug at the fountain in the square, and a priest wearing a black beret flying down the cobblestone street on a Vespa. *Is this for real, or am I on a movie set?* I wondered.

The streets were very narrow, and the villa where we were staying had an entrance on a blind curve, so the manager suggested we park in the parking garage across the street and then come in through the kitchen—where there were no steps.

The chef was preparing the evening meal for the guests of this villa-hotel. I greeted him with a friendly "buona sera."

He swept off his hat, and, returning my smile, bowed and said, "Sera, signora."

On the way back to my room—via an elevator just big enough for Nonoy, my chair, and me—I was overcome by exhaustion. So, Nonoy prepared me for bed, and a member of the gracious staff brought me supper on a tray.

While eating my supper, I looked at a large painting of Asolo when it was a Roman municipium in the first century B.C. The town had survived the barbaric hordes of the Middle Ages. However, the picture that really captured my attention was the one that hung over my bed. It was a print of an elegant gentleman on horseback, entitled *Lord William*. William III, Bill, Billy: I thought of all the variations of my late husband's name. "How nice of you to find me here," was my vocal acknowledgement to Lord William.

The following morning, Nonoy pointed out that the bathroom door had been removed for my convenience. Still, it was an effort for me—even with competent help—to get in and out of the tub. Anxiety struck, along with some tears, until Nonoy said, "Okay, try to relax; I have you. You won't fall. Don't worry."

The time I spent at Asolo was quiet, tranquil, almost monastic, as the churches on the distant hills rang out the Angelus. When I was resting, I would look out the casement window of my corner room to watch the men tilling the vineyards below. The hills—covered with churches—went on and on until they disappeared into the haze. It was so romantic until a jet plane would scream by overhead.

While resting in my room, I decided to sketch the view. My skills were a little rusty, but soon I rediscovered the joy of creativity. Time and place ceased to exist as I worked. I continued the practice as I moved from hotel to hotel.

The days were interrupted by delicious meals of veal piccante, fish served in shells—all accompanied by tomatoes, eggplants, and asparagus with fresh parmesan and garlic butter. The vegetables were grown in the garden of the villa, as was the fruit in the large bowl on the coffee table.

Then there was the delightfully humorous incident when Nonoy's request from the concierge for some cornstarch—"you know, like flour"—was met with the delivery of an enormous bouquet of fresh flowers to replace the still very fresh flowers already in our room.

The weather was warm, and, after the "flour" misunderstanding, we decided I needed to do something to protect my perspiring skin. So, off Nonoy went to the drugstore. "It's only three kilometers away," he explained.

Nonoy was gone so long that my old fears rose up inside of me. My mind reeled with questions: What to do if he was picked up by the carabinieri? Whom should I call? Should I hire an Italian nurse? How to get home?

I thought about my children, especially Jennie, who would arrive in Europe in a few days. Occasionally, I had experienced some melancholia at Lake Como, but, without too much difficulty, I was able to brush it off and return to the moment. Now, once again, I found myself repeating that exercise, at least until Nonoy returned.

"Sorry," said Nonoy as he walked into our room clutching a large container of Johnson's baby powder. The druggist had to run two blocks for a translator, and the drugstore was ten kilometers away instead of three.

One morning, as the maids were changing the beds, they talked about the famous people—mostly from England—who had settled in Asolo. "It is so beautiful. I wish you could see it," said one of the women about the former home of Eleanora Duse. "A lady from Texas owns it now," she added.

"Who owns the empty villa on the hill outside my window?" I asked.

"A young man lived there with his family. He was studying medicine. An explosion in his basement lab killed him. The family left, and no one has lived in it since. It was a very long time ago."

The Villa Armani looked solitary and sad as it stood on its hill watching over the well-tended vineyards. As I sketched it, I wondered if it was for sale.

"Oh, Signora," sighed the housekeeper when she was leaving the room, "you should go down in the garden to sit. It is so beautiful."

Soon after, I was in the garden, sipping a glass of wine and sketching. At times, I glanced at two lovers resting side by side on a large chaise. The girl was beautiful, the man handsome, and they had eyes only for each other on this quiet, sunlit, drowsy day. *Honeymooners,* I thought, when she moved to nibble on his toes.

Some laughter came across the lawn from the terrace. I turned my head to look at the people having lunch there and noticed the wishing well lavishly adorned with white climbing roses.

Suddenly, I felt as though the entire world and the wonderful people in it were truly one family. "We are all brothers and sisters," the priest often intoned at Mass. I usually understood he was referring to those present at church. But, as my heart opened to welcome all humanity in that moment, my entire being was flooded with love.

"I was so happy to see you in the garden today. Are you a painter?" asked our waiter. Nonoy and I were having dinner in the dining room, enjoying the geraniums clustered on the sill, the soft evening air flowing into the room from the spacious window next to our table. We heard conversations in German and French, but most of the diners, who were British, spoke softly. So, the simple but charming room seemed very intimate. The eyes of the guests were sparkling as they chatted, drank wine and ate fresh fish, vegetables, salads, and pasta with herbs.

After dinner, I went out onto the veranda and was struck by the luminosity of the white roses outlining the wishing well. A wedding and reception had taken place there earlier in the day.

The Sunday we left Asolo, I turned on the television set for the first time to hear President Bush speak about "the fragile peace in Europe," as the camera panned over the soldiers, sailors, and marines standing at attention. He had been greeted by the Presidente d'Italia, Pinochet, and together they stood in front of the World War II Memorial in Rome. The names of the American dead were inscribed there: boys from California,

Maine, Nebraska, the Third Artillery, First Bombardiers—all the soldiers who had given their lives for the liberation.

In a burst of patriotism, Nonoy began to sing *The Star Spangled Banner*, and I soon joined in singing with him.

Chapter 28

OUR LADY OF THE VILLA D'ESTE

But on you will go
though the weather be foul
On you will go
though your enemies prowl
On you will go
though the Hakken-Kraaks howl
Once and up many
a frightening creek,
though your arms may get sore
and your sneakers may leak.

—Dr. Seuss, *Oh the Places You'll Go*

Chapter 28

The choice was there for me to make if I felt well enough to continue my journey. After a five-day rest, I was ready to go to Venice.

Three tall, dark, handsome men, attendants from the hotel where I would be staying, approached Nonoy and me when we reached the point of embarkation for Venice. Looking elegant and efficient in their starched white trousers, short-sleeved white shirts with shoulder epaulets and brass buttons, they pushed me in my chair toward the waiting launch. I felt light as a feather as they lowered me onto the deck of the polished and gleaming craft provided by the hotel we would be staying at for several days.

As we sped across the water towards Venice, I closed my eyes and tried to remember what it was like when Bill and I visited there in the '60s. A symphony orchestra playing under a starry sky while an enormous moon hung over San Marcos Square immediately came to mind. When I opened my eyes, I saw in the distance the campanile and the dome of the cathedral San Marcos rising above the square.

It was a holy day of obligation, and it was my desire to attend Mass, to give thanks for a safe journey to Venice. When we arrived at the hotel, I asked the concierge if Mass was being said at San Marcos.

"Si, signora," he replied with a smile.

I had to cross one bridge to get to the cathedral. Three small steps leading up to the bridge confronted me. However, shopkeepers ran out of their stores to help me. An American couple, living in Venice, also offered to lend a hand.

"We have a friend in a wheelchair. Venice is not made for wheelchairs," the man commented.

"Then what am I doing here?" I quipped.

The carabinieri were holding back a large group of people at the entrance to San Marco. Apparently, I was too late for Mass, but benediction was about to begin. Someone pushed me to the front of the crowd of people as the procession emerged from the church. Children lead the procession, followed by monks, priests, and nuns. I smiled at them; they smiled at me. The priest, holding the monstrance, went by under a canopy as the bells of the campanile resounded throughout the square.

After receiving the blessing from the priest, I sat at a table sipping a cup of coffee. Lifting my face to the evening breeze, I closed my eyes. My vision settled inward. The face of one of the monks in the procession appeared. He was young, gaunt, with hair black as coal curled around his head like a feathery cap. Black, heavy brows did not hide the deep-set blue, blue eyes with long black lashes. His eyes had shot me a laser-like glance. He was a painter's dream, a perfect model for a mystic or an idealized saint. He didn't smile at me as the others had done; the piercing glance was enough. This image remained in my memory for years.

Opening my eyes, I looked around the square. There was no one else in a wheelchair. Three nuns who had been in the procession and a couple who had come over with me on the vaporetto walked by me and waved.

Doves flew around looking for crumbs of bread among the tables. The bells continued to ring for a short time, lovers kissed, teenagers giggled, old people strolled by as I observed and was observed in turn.

Nearby, the small orchestra began to play *Perfidia*, one of my husband's favorite songs.

One morning, I was blow-drying my hair and preparing for the day. Suddenly, my right leg extended straight out in front of me. As there was no sensation in that part of my body, I was amazed to see it stretched out in space—I could have hung my towel over it! I saw it as a good omen. Something was out there waiting for me.

All too soon, I was saying goodbye to Venice. I had taken the elevator to the top of the campinile to stare out across the beautiful city. I found a charming out-of-the way restaurant a shopkeeper had suggested. I returned to tell the shopkeeper what a lovely dinner I had enjoyed. Looking around his shop, I purchased a small glass pyramid and a round leather box in which I later kept my wedding ring at night.

My final goodbye went to all the cats that would gather in a square outside the window of my room. When I was resting, I would look for my favorites to show up, and took delight in watching them as they played or dozed and stretched in the sun, or guarded their territory from unwanted intruders. Plump and happy, they seemed to have the perfect cat life. I was envious.

The drive to Florence via Ravenna was long but scenic. Ravenna had been taken over by urban sprawl, and those enormous hourglass-shaped towers, like the ones on Three Mile Island, came into view immediately. I didn't like them. They reminded me of the threat of the nuclear reactors I had to drive by on the way to St.Lo.

The final part of the journey was through the Alpennes Mountains. I wondered how anyone could get up to the old farmhouses situated near the top of those mountains, but the smoke curling from the chimneys indicated that the quaint dwellings were indeed occupied.

The villages we passed through were, for the most part, populated by elderly folk—mostly women wearing simple black dresses with aprons tied around their waists. They would pass the time watching the cars go by or working in their gardens and tending their roses. The young people probably moved away to seek their fortunes in the city. I imagined myself sitting among these women in my one black dress. The simplicity appealed to me.

Florence was one big traffic jam. And, it was wet, cold, and rainy. But I didn't really mind, as I had visited this remarkable city before to experience all the magnificent art and antiquities.

While Nonoy went to visit the statue of David, I rested on my bed and watched the scullers on the river Arno as they rhythmically rowed in sync to the calls of their coxswains.

Like Ferdinand the Bull—one of my favorite storybook characters as a child—sitting under the cork tree, smelling the flowers, I was content to observe life passing by my window and to smell the roses brought to my room each day.

Rain or shine, the scullers would be out there on the Arno. One sunny day, I was moved to capture the images of fair-skinned Florentinos, their bodies sparsely clothed, stretched out on the cement embankment of the river. As I sketched, I thought how easy it would be to continue moving from place to place, to have no roots. Home, after all, was not really home for me anymore: no husband, no children were waiting for Mommy to return.

Yes, I thought, I will keep traveling. When summer comes, I will visit Bill in Santa Cruz; in the fall, a visit with my sister in Virginia. We'll sit on her terrace and look across the pond. My brother-in-law, a retired Marine Corps colonel, will try to teach me how to shoot a pistol, and then Jeannette and I will travel down the road to Washington D.C. for a visit to the National Gallery to see the sights we had enjoyed as children for an entire summer long ago.

Nonoy and I ate dinner at the restaurant on top of the hotel. It was famous for its view of Florence.

"Oh, isn't it nice to have an orchestra playing while we dine, Nonoy?"

"Turn around," he said. There was a man playing an electric keyboard.

"How sad," I said resignedly. From the moment I landed on Italian soil, the realities of a changing world had replaced fantasies that were realized on an earlier visit to Europe.

Before going to sleep that night, I thought about Jennie, who by now was in London—a very cold London of 15 degrees. Although we were far apart physically, I felt close to her spiritually. God had answered my prayers: our lives were taking on new directions now that Jennie was grown.

Next day, the sun came out, providing us with clear skies and warm weather for our drive to Sienna. When we got there, we went to an outdoor cafe to enjoy sandwiches and cappuccinos. St. Catherine of Sienna was in my thoughts. I wondered how she knew at such a young age that her life belonged to God.

I decided not to go to Rome as I didn't want to disturb the memory of celebrating my husband's 36th birthday in that city. I said, "How about Pisa? I've only seen the leaning tower from the train."

Sun still shining, we motored past Pisa about ten kilometers. The sloping banks of the Arno were dotted with small cottage-like houses. Their porches stood on stilts over the water. Seeing the residents fishing from their porches made Nonoy homesick for the Philippines.

A little farther down the road, the breakwater came into view, where the river emptied into the Gulf of Genoa. There, we came upon a small beach town, the Marina de Pisa. The beach was deserted. The main street was lined with shops, and there was not a pedestrian in sight. Still, the street appeared alive because brightly colored plastic beach toys hung from every storefront. The beach balls, the rubber rafts, pails, and shovels danced around in a strong breeze.

"Nonoy, stop!" I hollered. I had spotted a large, green, plastic dinosaur. "I'd like to get that for my grandson Evan."

I watched Nonoy enter the store. To my surprise the door was open. When Nonoy returned to the car he said, "It's the last one the owner has, and he won't deflate it."

I looked at the dinosaur with longing. *I'd have to buy an extra seat on the plane*, I thought. My grandson would have to live without. I returned to Pisa.

The leaning tower of Pisa is slowly sinking, but tourists were still allowed to climb it if they so desired. When my legs were functioning, I would not have attempted the climb. I was afraid of heights. So, while Nonoy climbed up the winding steps inside the tower to reach the top, I sat at a small cafe eating pizza and reading a small paperback book on the histories of Florence, Pisa, and Sienna. As I bit into a slice of pizza, *Chuck E.'s In Love* blared out of the sound system. I almost choked on my piece of pizza. I started to laugh at the sound of the music. It did not blend with the atmosphere. I took a gulp of wine from my glass. Then, I grabbed my camera and took a shot of Nonoy coming down the outside of the tower. The sight of people clutching the walls as they spiraled down the exterior amused me. One man froze near the top until two teenaged girls peeled him off the wall.

After a good night's sleep at the hotel in Florence, I packed my clothes and wheeled myself into the nearby cathedral to attend Mass before returning to Como. Three very young girls assisted the priest—one of them was wearing a T-shirt with Mickey Mouse on the front. And I thought, I am so far away from the world of Disney, but here is Mickey Mouse assisting at Mass. I figured it was time to go home, but not before offering thanks to all the people who had lifted me up the stairs, into vaporettos, over bridges, and up and down curbs.

The room with the view was mine when I returned to the Villa d'Este. The concierge said she was pleased to see me as she showed me to my room. I was so excited after she opened the door to my corner room overlooking the lake that it caused the woman burst into tears. She quickly excused herself and left, and I immediately rolled myself over to one of the casement windows.

"I could simply drop a line and fish," said Nonoy, peering over my shoulder.

Something was different. The lake had changed. And then I realized that the mountains reflected in the lake were covered with snow. The scene was exquisite. I raised my eyes toward the opposite shore and saw the green trees poking through their white blanket. The Sunday sailors didn't seem to mind the weather; the lake was dotted with sailboats.

There were many beautiful moments during my brief journey. But just before returning home, the real reason for me being here in Italy was about to present itself, as I would soon discover.

As I dressed for dinner on our last night at the Villa, I reflected on the days I had particularly enjoyed in this place: the drive around the lake, a little shopping, and talking to the proprietor of one of the stores—she had lived in Santa Monica but "I had to come back to my home. I was born here" was how she put it.

Then there was the quiet time I spent at a café near the lake. A boat that ferried people across the lake was anchored there. I watched a small flow of people get on board as I sipped some wine.

At breakfast on the veranda of the Villa, I saw a little girl play Old Maid with her father. *Bill and Jennie*, I thought, as I smiled at the man, and he smiled back at me.

"I'll be seeing you," sang Nonoy as we dressed for dinner. The familiar and nostalgic song brought tears to my eyes as we headed for the elevator to go down to dinner.

Our last dinner in Italy was enhanced by a dazzling display of lightening over the lake. When we had finished eating, I wheeled myself to the front desk. Along the way, two grand paintings hanging in the lobby caught my attention: "The Sacking of Rome" and a painting of Jesus just down from the cross. His mother Mary was holding Him in her arms. I felt the latter painting was saying goodbye to me.

With arms waving and eyes flashing in excitement, a young French woman planted herself in front of me. "Parlez-vous français?" she asked.

"Un peu," I replied, but I was soon over my head as she asked me what was wrong with me and if I was getting better. The gentleman she was dining with came to my rescue at her request. He spoke English and acted as translator.

"Are you an artist, a writer?" she inquired.

"I've dabbled in both," I replied.

"You will write a book and then this," she gestured at my legs, "will all be over. Does the number five mean anything to you?" she continued.

"I have five children."

"The fifth child, is she in the story?"

"Yes."

"Does she have something on her arm?" was her next question.

"No, but . . . "then I told her she once had melanoma on her arm.

"Do you paint in an abstract style?"

"No."

"You will someday when you are well," she said. Another coincidence? I did plan to do an abstract painting from a sketch I had done of my paralyzed self. "This is like a desert for you. You will walk again," she concluded.

I offered to pay her, but she just laughed. And then said with a big smile on her face,"Non, non, non! I am psychic." She was jumping around excitedly. I took her hand and apologized for offering her money.

"When will I walk again?" I asked.

"One year. Non, non, non, two, maybe," she said, and returned to the dining room.

Nonoy, who was a witness to this, said," She was watching you all through dinner."

Hope, it was a message of hope that I had come all this way to hear, to this place where my husband's parents had fallen in love. The end of one journey and the beginning of another that was different, but just as interesting.

As he readied me for bed that night, Nonoy was singing *Saberme.* "That's the second time I've heard that song in less than a year," I said.

Sleep was impossible for me that night. My mind replayed the incident in the lobby over and over again until I thought of Caroline—"A busty piece of sachertorte mit der schlag." I turned on the light, reached into the nightstand and finished her story:

> *Her marriage to the Prince of Wales wasn't working out, as they say. So she came to Northern Italy and bought the Villa d'Este on the shores of Lake Como. It's a grand hotel now. But much of Caroline is preserved. The gardens have been tended since 1568 when it was built by an Italian cardinal. Some cardinal! He built villas from Rome to Como, so that in traveling he could sleep every night under his own roof . . . She spent her generous allowance improving the Villa d'Este. In the gardens, stone Greek gods nod in their niches. An avenue of cypresses goes up the mountainside where Hercules has put a half nelson on Lyca . . .*
>
> *After five years, she returned to England, where George was crowned king. He pushed her out the door of Westminster Abbey and divorced her.*

The following is an excerpt from a letter Caroline wrote to Lady Charlotte Campbell in 1817 from Villa d'Este:

> *I should be happy to see you in my little nutshell, which is pretty and comfortable and my gardens are charmante.*
>
> *I lead quite a rural life, and where I work the garden myself, which do my mind and body good.*

"Thank you Caroline, I whispered. "Your little nutshell has done my mind and body good as well."

At last I felt rooted, like the plants in Caroline's garden. From my new position of strength and trust—no longer the victim of fear—the roots found nourishment from which came courage, hope, and the energy to fight for life.

I began to put my hands together in an attitude of prayer. Instead, my palms turned upward in an attitude of praise.

"Totus, tuus ego sum, amen." The Latin words sprang involuntarily from my lips. "I am all yours!"

Epilogue

Remember the nurse who told me about her dream? In her dream, she saw me hitchhiking up to Northern California. Well, after Jennie's graduation from college, I sold my house in Pasadena and moved up to Santa Cruz. There were many reasons behind my decision to move. All the children were married with the exception of Jennie. They had left the town where they grew up and were living elsewhere.

Mother, Uncle Phil, and Aunt Alice died in their nineties. Mother, God bless her, didn't want to be buried in the same cemetery as her father and brother, because, as she put it, "The groundskeepers don't keep the place up." And so, she was buried where I will also one day be at rest as the bagpiper plays all her favorite tunes, such as *Loch Lomond, Onward Christian Soldiers*, and, of course, *God Save the Queen*. My dear sister, whom I had the good fortune to visit in Virginia, has passed on as well.

My final visit with Sister Mary Wilfrid was at Huntington Hospital in Pasadena. She was not well enough to continue with her duties at Mayfield School. I brought her a dress to wear on the airplane that would take her to the motherhouse of her order in Pennsylvania. The sisters greeted her warmly when she arrived and threw her a party. Following the celebration, she went to bed and died peacefully in her sleep during the night.

Many of my friends had died. So, I felt it was time to leave dear Pasadena. And, I didn't want to spend my remaining years going to funerals.

After visiting young Bill in Santa Cruz throughout the years of my illness, I felt, as did Bill, that I should live near him. So, in time, I found myself near the sea once again. A prayer was answered!

"El Retiro" is the name of my new home. It sits on a hill over-looking Monterey Bay. The Forest of Nisene Marks stretches out beyond my deck and the terraced garden at the rear of the house.

Bill remodeled an existing structure into a Southwestern-style home. With its connecting round towers and many windows, it stretches across the property. There are beautiful views from every terrace. Every part of it is wheelchair-accessible.

I was amazed by the friendliness of my neighbors when I moved in. One of my neighbors, Wayne, decorated my house; others called on me to welcome me to the hill. I've made many new friends: the people who help me deal with everyday necessities, like the women at my bank; Del, who runs the nearby art gallery; and John, the son of friends from Pasadena, who owns a beautiful store just down the hill.

Santa Cruz County is a piece of heaven on earth for people who are handicapped like me. Thanks to the local city councils, the area has been made handicap-accessible. If I run into any difficulty, strangers—young and old—help me.

While my son Bill was busy remodeling my house, Cathleen, a friend of my daughter Dana, introduced me to the area. Cathleen suggested I attend classes at the Stroke Center as I waited for Bill to finish the job. At the Stroke Center in beautiful De Laveaga Park, I met some brave and interesting people and a caring staff. I was able to engage my creative side by making ceramics, learning Japanese brush painting, and sketching with pastels.

People at the Bible study class at St. Joseph's Catholic Church in Capitola were also very welcoming. Sister Marie was an excellent teacher who acquainted Catholics of all ages with the Bible. At the time I converted to Catholicism, reading and interpreting the Bible wasn't particularly encouraged. After morning class, we often went out to lunch together.

With Jehan McCloskey, my massage therapist, I became acquainted with downtown Santa Cruz. We ate at some of the fine local establishments, shopped downtown, went to the Museum, and enjoyed the street musicians who added to the colorful atmosphere. Together, we went to the artists' Open Studios on weekends. And visiting the wineries in the Santa Cruz Mountains was always a giggle.

Shakespeare in the Glen is a delight. I shared picnic dinners and wine with Bill and his wife Kathy there on a few occasions. In November, I went with them to hear the Mt. Madonna Choir at Holy Cross Church. The church, with its tall, white steeple, sits on Mission Hill above the town of Santa Cruz and reminds me of an earlier era. The Art and Wine Festival, held in Capitola Village, is colorful, cheerful, and friendly. It takes place just below Bill's home, so I can easily go down to the village in my motorized wheelchair. On the way, I have the added pleasure of taking in the sweeping view of Monterey Bay.

After settling in my home, I decided to give something back to the community. Each year, during the Cabrillo Music Festival, I invite a performer to stay in my home. The singers, dancers, and musicians I have hosted have brought me great joy. Two dancers performed the tango on my deck. Jeannette Blakeney, a soprano singer, sang *Amazing Grace* in my bedroom.

When my grandchildren came to town, they would accompany me to the concerts. Every year, there is a special concert for children. The street outside the auditorium is alive with entertainers and with vendors of exotic foods and wares, all of which we enjoy.

In addition to attending Mass at my parish church, I was able to help in a small way with the rebuilding of a new and strikingly beautiful church. The Renew groups that I hosted in my home were educational. Renew began as one more attempt to make Catholics more familiar with the Bible. Now that my spine has worsened with age, the parishioners bring Communion to my home.

With a friend, caregiver, or with family, I have eaten in some great restaurants, attended the theater, and the cinema. San Francisco is a magnet for me because Jennie lives there. Leslie and her husband

Michael often visit the city, and I join them at showings at the Museum of Modern Art.

After living in Santa Cruz for a few years, I had an operation for colon cancer. I took it in stride. While recovering, I settled down and wrote this book.

The happiest moment, among many happy moments, was seeing Jennie married to John Gregory Sanchez. They got married one April in my garden. It was a magical setting: the forest was alive with spring, and the trees on my lower terrace were abloom with large, fluffy, and white "puff balls," as I call them. All of Jennie's siblings attended. Friends came from Pasadena, and some of Jennie's former classmates from Santa Catalina School in Monterey and St. Mary's College in Moraga took part in the wedding. Leslie and Michael hosted a buffet the following morning at Seascape Resort for all the guests.

A few years later, Jennie and John had a baby girl named Violet. I was present for her birth and later at her baptism at St. John of God Church in San Francisco.

Riley was married in Sun Valley, Idaho, and now she has two sons, making me a great grandmother twice over. They visit me from time to time.

Life—normal, everyday life—has returned! I am still paralyzed. The pain in my body has not diminished, but the anguish of waking up each day is gone. I offer up the physical pain for those who are in need, and there are many. I've come a long way in the healing process, just as the woman in Italy said I would.

At this time of my life, I take a great deal of pleasure in sitting by my windows and watching the storms as they blow in from the north. The fog rolls in, just like it used to at St. Lo. In good weather, I can see sailboats gliding out from Santa Cruz Harbor and around Pleasure Point. On windy days, I gaze at the whitecaps that crash on the beach.

Because of the forest behind my property, I have birdsong all day long. Hummingbirds feed from the flowers, and woodpeckers fly down from their redwood condos to splash in the birdbath, along with the doves, finches, robins, and star jays. Migrating monarchs fly overhead. Deer come by to visit me. Quail skitter around the garden in single file. If I am up at night, I watch the family of raccoons sneaking down the driveway.

I live on "turtle time."

Remember the story of the hare and the tortoise? Well, we all know who won the race! The tortoise of course, and that's me.

Printed in the United States
45655LVS00004BA/73-108